savoring the day

OTHER BOOKS BY JUDITH BENN HURLEY

The Good Herb

Garden-Fresh Cooking

Healthy Microwave Cooking

The Healing Foods
(Patti Hausman, coauthor)

The Healthy Gourmet
(Patti Hausman, coauthor)

The Surgeon General's Report on Nutrition and Health
(Patti Hausman, coauthor)

savoring the day

recipes and remedies to enhance your natural rhythms

Judith Benn Hurley

WILLIAM MORROW AND COMPANY, INC.
NEW YORK

Library of Congress Cataloging-in-Publication Data

Hurley, Judith Benn.
    Savoring the day : recipes and remedies to enhance your natural rhythms / Judith Benn Hurley.
        p.   cm.
    Includes bibliographical references and index.
    ISBN 0-688-14292-3
    1. Clinical chronobiology   2. Alternative medicine.   3. Naturopathy.   I. Title.
RZ999.H87   1996
615.5—dc20   96-18954
                                                                                         CIP

Printed in the United States of America

First Edition

1 2 3 4 5 6 7 8 9 10

BOOK DESIGN BY VERTIGO DESIGN

For Patrick, of course

And in loving memory of
Cy and Vanessa,
the two best friends
a writer ever had

acknowledgments

I am so lucky always to have the best people helping me. Some of them are

For editorial wisdom, Toni Sciarra, Katharine Cluverius, Ginny Croft, Vertigo Design, Kim Yorio, Helen Pratt, all the hard-working people at William Morrow, Dr. Bob and the Buddha Girls; and The Chinaman.

For research, Nancy Zelko and Stan Benn.

For testing recipes, and providing resources and techniques, JoAnn Brader, Gail Concannon, Linda Cucher, Karl Erdlitz, Alexandra Rose Grace, Sharon Grace, Diane Grandstrom, Judy Lieberman, Antoinette Retter, Jane Runyeon, Andrea Smith, Ashley Smith, Susan Stanton, and Karen Wenrich.

contents

before you begin this book

When Japanese engineers first computerized a train to run itself, they discovered that humans made better drivers. Whereas the computerized train jerked and twitched as it reacted to curves and hills, human conductors kept the ride smooth by anticipating and accommodating natural deviations in the route. Similarly, by foreseeing your body's natural rhythms, you can gently drive it to operate optimally whenever you wish. Employing such knowledge is the essence of *Savoring the Day*.

The simple wisdom in this book can enrich your life in many ways. For instance, a headache, stiff neck, moodiness, or lack of concentration can dampen your enjoyment of the day. But by using specific herbs, aromas, foods, or activities such as yoga or self-massage to complement your body's natural cycles, you can counteract or emphasize how you're feeling.

modern rhythms

Scientists first became intrigued with chronobiology, or the study of natural rhythms, in 1931, when the first case of jet lag was documented. On July 23 of that year, pilot Wiley Post took off in his Lockheed Vega monoplane for a record-breaking eight-day flight around the world. Post finished the trip, but the jet lag almost did him in. At one point, when landing to refuel, he took off without remembering to put a drop of gas in the tank. Later in the journey he fell asleep while being interviewed by a reporter.

In the early 1950s John F. Dulles, secretary of state under Eisenhower and an expert in international relations, flew to Egypt to negotiate the building of the Aswan High Dam. He arrived and went right to work, but his abilities to reason and communicate were dulled by jet lag, and the United States lost the billion-dollar job to the Soviets.

Since then, chronobiologists have branched out from jet lag to study dozens of natural rhythms. For example, recent research reveals that the threshold for tooth pain is highest between one and three in the afternoon. In fact, it's 30 percent higher than in the early morning, making mid-afternoon the ideal time to schedule a dental appointment. Skin can be 100 percent more sensitive at midnight than it is at noon; taste and smell are at their sharpest between five and seven in the evening. Even more remarkable, if you had two identical physical exams, one mid-morning and one mid-afternoon, your blood pressure, urine, and body temperature would vary vastly.

ancient rhythms

Three thousand years ago, before blood pressure monitors and jet lag, the Vedic sages of India chronicled the relationship of people to such external influences as time of day, as well as work, sleep, diet, and seasonal changes. These teachings, called Ayurveda, or the knowledge of life, have been a major influence on this book. A simple example of an Ayurvedic observation is that morning is the clearest thinking time for many people. Amazingly enough, modern science agrees, especially since the identification of cortisol, the human hormonal wake-up call that brightens our thoughts after a night of sleep. Moreover, the Vedics recognized mid-afternoon as a time of possible fatigue and irritability, a theory we moderns have all experienced firsthand at one time or another.

At about the same time that the Vedics were developing their philosophy, early Chinese physicians were working on a complex system called the Five Elements Theory, another big influence on this book. One part of the Five Elements Theory describes how people's senses and emotions change depending on the time of day. For example, the Chinese believed (and still do) that noon is the time of joy and laughter. Interestingly, this timing corresponds with the natural surge from our brains through our bodies of what twentieth-century researchers call serotonin, the good-time hormone. Chinese doctors of long ago could never have known of serotonin, but they nonetheless made the same connection. Despite the sophisticated world we have created, it seems our natural rhythms have changed little in thousands of years.

using natural rhythms

This book contains two main sections. Part One divides the day into six sections: Early Morning, Mid-Morning, Noon, Mid-Afternoon, Evening, Night. Each time of day contains suggestions on how best to tend your body and mind by using a self-massage point, a yoga pose or stretch, herbal teas to drink, aromas to inhale, and best foods to eat. In addition, each section contains culinary recipes suited for that specific time of day, including fat and calorie counts. Each recipe also suggests seasonal variations, intended to help balance your body and your mood to the pulse of your environment. I believe you are more intuitive on this subject than you may have realized. For example, you may instinctively eat a cucumber on a hot day to refresh yourself. However, you probably would avoid the cooling vegetable in freezing weather, reaching instead for such warming foods as cinnamon-scented oatmeal or a spicy gingersnap cookie. The same rationale, based on ancient Chinese theory and Indian Ayurveda, was used to create the seasonal suggestions in each of the 250 recipes.

As an example of how you can make the information in *Savoring the Day* work for you, let's say you're groggy throughout the morning. Simply turn to the "Early Morning" section (page 3) and discover that eating such complex carbohydrates as whole grains will give you the sustainable energy you need. For breakfast you can enjoy pear and buckwheat pancakes, cherry-vanilla granola, or a creamy barley cereal with warm berry sauce. You can also perform a three-minute rev-up yoga exercise. Or take one minute and massage an area at the base of your spine that will help you become alert and think clearly. Other choices include sipping thyme and fresh lemon tea or inhaling the uplifting aroma of rosemary. You can choose to explore all of the suggestions or just one or two. *Savoring the Day* works with whatever suits your personal style.

For quick reference, Part Two of *Savoring the Day* features nearly forty entries on such specific conditions as asthma, insomnia, reviving romance, depression, anxiety, hot flashes, neck and shoulder tension, sinus pressure, jet lag, and fatigue. Each entry advises when symptoms are likely to occur and offers ideas for abating them, including self-massage, a yoga posture, herbal tea, aromatherapy, and foods that help prevent and cure the specific ailment. Entries also list such helpful resources as support groups, sources of hard-to-find products, and hot lines.

As a final but important point, I realize that it is sometimes difficult to develop an awareness of your own natural rhythms and the ability to become their conductor, so to speak. I initiated my own journey some twenty years ago with an exam by a Chinese doctor in Hong Kong. After asking many questions, checking each of my twelve pulses, and performing face and tongue analysis, he told me that although I was generally healthy, I tended to have a cold, damp spleen that could not be corrected with warming foods because the corresponding stomach organ might become aggravated as a result of unmanaged stress. Not only did I have deficient spleen *chi* but my fire and wood elements fluctuated during hot weather, causing fatigue, surface heat, nutritional deficiencies, and possible stagnation in my lung meridian.

"Do you understand?" he asked.

"I don't understand a thing," I replied.

And without blinking an eye, he said, "And so we begin."

beneath every ruin
lies a treasure.
—Rumi

recipes for savoring the day

PART ONE

early morning

A FACE TO THE SUN

best time of day for:

Romance. since testosterone levels are at their peak

Eating to lose weight. because activity throughout the day helps burn off what you consumed

Exercising to increase energy and raise metabolism for the day

a Bushman spotted me as I shambled from my hut near Hwange, Zimbabwe, where it was not yet eight in the morning and already nearly 100 degrees. Accurately observing that I was less than alert, the Bushman advised me to "put my face to the sun," eyes half open, while breathing deeply for five minutes. He explained that this ancient morning ritual creates *juba*, or energy, in the body. And happily it did in mine.

Thousands of miles away I met a Pennsylvania Lenape Indian woman who early each morning also goes outside to face the sun. There she "addresses the day's issues." Then, breathing deeply, she turns south clockwise back to the east while chanting "Ho!" 11 times—11 because the Lenape believe there are 11 layers of consciousness between earth and heaven.

Since the first spark of civilization, people have performed early-morning rituals, making obeisance to a magical sun. Early Egyptians told of the Phoenix, a mythical bird that burst into flames every 500 years, a new Phoenix rising from the ashes. The Phoenix, of course, symbolized the sun that dies at night, born anew in the morning. Early Christians, enchanted by the idea, adopted the Phoenix as a symbol of immortality and resurrection.

The Aztecs, perhaps also imagining the sun in flight around the earth, worshipped Huitzilopochtli, a sun god in the form of a hummingbird that was born afresh each morning. Huitzilopochtli was also a memorial of sorts to Aztec warriors, since the Aztecs believed that soldiers returned from the dead as hummingbirds.

Literature, too, is brightened by symbols of the sun and dawn. For instance, ever since P. G. Wodehouse scribed it, "Came the dawn" has become a chiché for the end of "troubled times." The dawning of civilization has become synonymous with the beginning of a new era, and *dawning* alone is often a metaphor for a new political scene. Figuratively, *dawn* means the rise, beginning, or first glint of anything. And when used as a verb, *to dawn*, it paints a picture of expansion, development, visibility, and brightness—all positive notes on which to start a day.

To shed a more scientific light on morning as it relates to our daily lives, modern research concurs with both the Bushman and the Lenape Indian: sunlight is a wake-up aid, and those who bathe in it upon rising may be more alert than their counterparts who remain in the dark. Sunlight appears to stimulate the brain's production of the hormone cortisol, which literally helps to wake us up. That's why the Bushman's tip works and why Lenape Indians continue their traditional morning ritual. It is also the reason why it's harder to rise on a dark and dreary morning.

But light alone is often not enough to rouse us from slumber. A late or fatty meal eaten the night before may sap morning energy, as can too much alcohol, seasonal changes, travel, stress, and some medications. To make your morning easier, try one or more of these energizing tips and recipes.

relief at your fingertips

.THE ONE-MINUTE VITALIZER

This rousing rub is based on a Chinese accupressure point called Sea of Vitality, used to fight morning fatigue and strengthen the immune system. To try it, rub your hands together until they're warm, about 10 seconds. Then fold your hands behind your back at waist level with your thumbs parallel with your spine, each about one finger's width away from the spine. Rub vigorously up and down, pressing your thumb knuckles onto the skin, for about one minute. The area will feel warm. Relax for a few seconds, breathing deeply, noticing the energizing warmth radiate from the area. You can perform the rub on bare skin or over light clothing, but don't use a massage oil because the friction caused by the brisk rubbing could irritate the skin.

Stimulating facial circulation can help to create a more lustrous and youthful complexion, as well as aid in clearing morning sinus congestion. This technique is loosely based on *marma*, an ancient Ayurvedic face massage, with the addition of several Chinese accupressure points. You'll be using both index fingers to press firmly on specific facial points (if you have long fingernails, use your index finger knuckles). Press each point for one full breath, inhaling and exhaling deeply through your nose.

Rub your hands together briskly until they feel warm, for about 10 seconds, then press these areas for one full breath—an inhalation and exhalation:

1. The middle of the chin

2. The outside corners of the mouth

3. The bottom of the cheekbones (feel the bones)

4. The outside corners of the nostrils

5. The middle of the bone under the eye

6. The inside corners of the eye socket (feel the bones)

7. The outside corners of the eye socket (feel the bones)

8. Under the eyebrow at the inside corners (feel the bone)

9. Where the bridge of the nose meets the forehead

10. The middle of the forehead

11. The crown (top) of the head

12. The area behind and slightly below the ear lobe (feel the jawbone)

Repeat the marma twice, for a total of three times. You can do it daily after washing and moisturizing your face, or twice a week in conjunction with Smoothing Morning Massage-Cleanser.

smoothing morning massage-cleanser

The ground almonds and oats in this cleanser provide a gentle, nourishing exfoliation, while the lavender soothes inflammation and tones the skin.

$^1/_2$ cup rolled oats $^1/_2$ cup almonds
$^1/_4$ cup dried lavender flowers

COMBINE THE OATS and lavender in a blender, food processor, or spice grinder and process until smooth. Scoop the mixture into a small jar.

ADD THE ALMONDS to the blender, process until smooth, then stir into the jar. You'll have about ⅔ cup of cleanser.

TO USE, MIX 1 tablespoon of the cleanser with 2 tablespoons of warm water and massage onto warm, damp skin before performing marma. For dry skin, add 1 teaspoon of skin-softening rosewater to the water before mixing or substitute soothing brewed chamomile tea for the water. To balance and constrict the texture of oily skin, use freshly squeezed lemon juice instead of water, and in the case of inflamed skin, use healing aloe jelly instead of water.

AFTER PERFORMING MARMA, rinse 15 times to remove the cleanser, and moisturize your skin while it's still damp, since it is then most receptive to the smoothing properties of nourishing creams.

PREVENTING PAIN

To help prevent and cure common headaches, which some scientists say are more likely to occur in the morning, make this easy scalp rub: Combine ½ teaspoon of untoasted (light) sesame oil and 1 drop of essential oil of rosemary (available at natural food stores and herb shops). If you don't have sesame oil, use a good-quality cooking oil such as olive or canola. Don't substitute anything for the rosemary, however, because essential oil of rosemary contains over a dozen volatile oils that ease a headache while stimulating the central nervous system.

Lightly dip all 10 fingertips into the mixture. Burrow them under your hair and onto the scalp, massaging in firm little circular motions while breathing deeply for about 3 minutes. Notice how rosemary's bracing, piney scent is clearing and strengthening to your entire head area, gently promoting alertness. Then style or wash your hair.

Rosemary's penetrating action also soothes aches and pains in other parts of the body. This may be especially important to those suffering from rheumatoid arthritis, since some researchers say that the pain from this condition is worse in the morning. Combine 1 ounce of your favorite body lotion, 10 drops of essential oil of rosemary, and 5 drops of essential oil of lavender (available at natural food stores and herb shops), rubbing into such sore areas as hands, neck, arms, and joints.

morning meditation

Medical research has verified what monks and Indian yogis have known for thousands of years—regular meditation can help you manage stress, a condition that may exacerbate depression, digestive problems, headaches, heart palpitations, high blood pressure, insomnia, immune disorders, eating disorders, skin problems, muscle pain, behavioral disorders, heart disease, and even cancer.

Meditation works by affecting your autonomic nervous system, one job of which is to pump you up to flee or fight when you're threatened. Regular meditation has a balancing effect that keeps you relaxed, though alert, whether you are threatened or not.

Meditation is simple. Its foundation is breathing in and out slowly. As they breathe, some meditators visualize a light or glow an inch or two below the navel, in an area the Japanese call the *hara*, or "seat of the soul."

Some people also repeat a *mantra*, or sound, such as OHMMMM or NNNNNN, either softly aloud or to themselves. Some behavioral therapists advise repeating HUM on inhaling and SHAA on exhaling—sounds that actually mimic the breath.

As for body position, sit up straight rather than reclining, so you will be less likely to fall asleep. Some people find that resting their hands on their legs, palms up, is conducive to a meditative state, and most people prefer to close their eyes.

Meditation experts advise beginning with a 5-minute meditation in the morning, adding 1 minute each week until you are meditating for 15 or 20 minutes. To time yourself, sit in front of a clock or use a wristwatch, checking the time by opening one eye. If thoughts enter your mind while meditating (Buddhists call this "monkey mind"), acknowledge them, then go back to your mantra. When you're finished meditating, keep your eyes closed, stretch your body, and remain seated for a minute or two before resuming activity.

You can meditate anywhere—on a bus, on the beach, on an airplane, or at home with a quiet pet on your lap. Meditate alone or with another meditator. Most experts advise meditating twice a day, once in the morning and again in the evening. (For more meditation tips, see the "Evening" section, page 135.) To achieve the best results, it's important that you meditate daily.

As well as being a tool for managing stress, regular meditation provides a spiritual construct of "mindfulness" that enriches our daily lives. In old Buddhist texts mindfulness is depicted as a bell. It is often referred to as "the bell of mindfulness," the bell being an internally heard reminder to respond to stimuli, regardless of how stressful, in a balanced and thoughtful manner. Indeed, the mindfulness and self-reflection that come with regular meditation help us to be more sensitive to our own and to other people's feelings, thus leaving our hearts open to better communication with friends, co-workers, lovers, and family members.

potent pose

Many years ago in London, a yoga instructor taught me to do a series of five morning *asanas*, or postures, that he claimed would energize the body, boost the immune system for the day, and oxygenate the tissues to help prevent premature aging. Tibetan yogi masters, who call this the Five Rites, say the ritual "unclogs" the seven *chakra*, or energy centers, in our bodies, making us more vitalized and balanced. Practitioners of the Five Rites report improved energy, healthy digestion, decreased headaches, and a more youthful attitude and appearance.

chakras at a glance

Chakras are seven invisible energy whirls located in a line from the tailbone to the crown of the head. Associated with seven endocrine areas in the body, well-tuned chakras help harmonize body chemistry by energizing glandular and hormonal systems. A brief rundown of each chakra (which means "wheel" in Sanskrit) follows.

CHAKRA	ASSOCIATED GLAND OR ORGAN	WHEN WELL TUNED YOU FEEL	ASSOCIATED COLOR
7 CROWN	Pineal gland at the top of the head	Limitless	Purple
6 THIRD EYE	Pituitary gland between the eyes	Insightful	Blue
5 THROAT	Thyroid at the throat	Expressive	Blue-green
4 HEART	Heart	Caring	Green
3 SOLAR PLEXUS	Digestive system	Courageous	Yellow
2 SEX ORGANS	Reproductive organs	Energetic	Orange
1 ROOT	Sacrum	Secure	Red

On a scientific level, apart from the chakra influence on the endocrine system, the Five Rites may be verified by their stretching actions, which dissipate lactic acid buildup in stressed, unworked, or overworked muscles. Lactic acid buildup can cause soreness and pain, and Ayurvedic and Chinese healers believe it causes toxins to accumulate in the "clogged" tissues. The stretching movements involved in regular practice of the Five Rites may help prevent and cure aches and pains, headaches, constipation, complexion problems, and stress-related disorders.

For the most potent benefits, perform the rites each morning, at least six times a week. In the first week, do 3 repetitions of each rite a day, doing the first rite 3 times, the second rite 3 times, and so on. In the second week, increase that number to 5 reps; in the third week, increase it to 7 reps, and so on until you're doing 21 reps of each rite a day. Continue doing 21 reps each day, which should take you only 12 to 15 minutes to complete. Between each rite, pause briefly, paying attention to how the areas you've just worked feel. When applicable, be sure to inhale upon exertion and exhale on release. The rites are as follows:

1. With your arms held horizontally away from your sides, whirl, at whatever speed is comfortable, in a clockwise direction. If you feel at all unsteady while whirling, spreading your toes apart will make you feel more sure-footed.

2. Lie on your back, hands palms down under your rear. Inhaling, lift your head and legs (knees slightly bent) as high as you can, then exhale as you lower your head and legs. Try to engage or tighten your abdominal muscles as you lift your legs.

3. Kneel, with your rear resting on your feet, hands on hips, knees 6 to 8 inches apart. Upon inhaling, raise your body up, head back, arching your back comfortably. As you arch your back, try to stretch and lengthen your abdominal muscles. Exhale as you resume the original position.

4. Sit on the floor with your arms at your sides, palms pressed on the floor, knees bent and feet about 6 inches apart in front of you. Inhaling, let your head fall back and lift your torso up to form your body into a table shape. While you're in this position, try to stretch and release your chest muscles and upper-arm muscles. Exhale as you resume the original position.

5. Lie on your stomach, legs straight and about 6 inches apart, arms bent and hands just above your shoulders. Inhaling, straighten your arms, gently pressing your head back and stretching your abdomen as you go. Then raise your rear, heels up and toes gripping the floor, shaping your body into an inverted V, looking between your legs. While in this position, try to stretch out the muscles in your lower back. Exhale as you resume the original position.

try a tea

PEPPERMINT TEA

Once when I was in Egypt, an herbalist taught me to make a refreshing, stimulating, caffeine-free morning tea by steeping 2 handfuls of fresh peppermint leaves in 1 quart of room-temperature water, covered, overnight. In the morning, discard the peppermint and enjoy the energizing infusion. Peppermint is effective as a morning refresher because it is swiftly absorbed by the stomach membrane, where it acts as a mild stimulant.

THYME TEA

French herbalists recommend thyme tea as a mild morning stimulant and to treat sluggish metabolism. Steep 1 teaspoon of dried thyme leaves or 2 teaspoons of fresh leaves in 1 cup of boiling water, covered, for 4 minutes. Then strain and sip. For cases of morning constipation, add 1 teaspoon of lemon juice and a pinch of cayenne pepper, both of which are gentle digestive stimulants.

GINSENG TEA

Some Chinese doctors hold that the body becomes more energized when adrenal-supporting herbs are introduced. To that end, they recommend a morning dose of Siberian (Eleuthero) ginseng, taken in tea or capsule form (available at natural food stores or herb shops). The herb acts as a long-term tonic, taken over a period of months to help restore vitality to an otherwise fatigued body. People with high blood pressure should check with a health professional before taking Siberian (or any) ginseng, since it may interfere with blood pressure medications.

CIDER TEA

To boost immunity to colds and flu, some New England herbalists recommend a morning brew of cider vinegar and honey, combining 1 tablespoon of each in 1 cup of room-temperature water. For a similar taste, try 1/2 cup of kombucha tea, available brewed, bottled, and chilled at natural food stores.

ECHINACEA TEA

For further immune support, English and German herbalists advise a morning dose of echinacea tincture (available at natural food stores and herb shops). It's generally taken each morning for two weeks at the onset of the cold and flu season, working at a cellular level to help prevent viruses from invading the body. Follow the dosage instructions on the bottle, which can be anywhere from 8 to 28 drops in a small cup of warm tea or water.

HEALTHFUL COFFEE

Since coffee is the morning stimulant of choice for many people, it pays to know how to drink it in its least harmful incarnation, and these tips will help.

- *For the best flavor and least toxicity, buy organically grown beans and grind them yourself.*

- *If coffee gives your stomach acidity, prevent it by adding one crushed cardamom pod to the pot for each cup of coffee you're brewing. Additionally, choose a low-acid coffee variety, such as Sumatra.*

- *Don't drink coffee that's been sitting on a burner—it's too acidic. Store brewed coffee in a thermos instead.*

- *Don't buy or drink coffee with artificial flavors. If you enjoy flavored coffee, buy a naturally flavored brand, available at natural food stores, herb shops, and some supermarkets. To flavor your own, add one slit vanilla bean or one 2-inch cinnamon stick to the pot for each 4 to 6 cups being brewed.*

- *To help prevent insomnia, try to drink your daily dose of coffee before noon, giving the caffeine's effects time to wear off.*

- *Try to limit coffee consumption to 2 cups or less a day, for a total of no more than 500 mg of caffeine. If you imbibe tea, soda, or hot chocolate, be reminded that they also contain caffeine. Excessive caffeine, or more than the 2-cup daily allotment, may aggravate such health conditions as high blood pressure, irritability, and other nervous disorders. Additionally, immoderate amounts of caffeine can increase the risk of osteoporosis, or porous bones, since it actually robs the bones of calcium.*

making scents

Stimulating aromas such as rosemary, peppermint, and lemon can lift a sluggish morning mood. For a simple approach, place 2 drops of essential oil (available at natural food stores and herb shops) of any of the aforementioned aromas on a tissue and inhale. Or place 2 or 3 drops on a cotton ball, tucking it into a shirt pocket or bra. In addition, you can make a bracing spray by combining $1/2$ cup of distilled water in a spray bottle with 10 to 15 drops of your essence of choice. Piney rosemary is welcome in the winter; cooling peppermint is a summer refresher. Alternatively, use brewed, cooled rosemary or peppermint tea by steeping 1 tablespoon of dried or 2 tablespoons of fresh herb in $1/2$ cup of boiled water, covered, until cool, at least 20 minutes. Either way, spray the area around your head and face, even over makeup. This can be especially refreshing during airplane travel or in stuffy offices.

TEA TREE OIL

For an essential oil that provides immune support (it's antiviral, antibacterial, and anti-infective) as well as an energizing camphor-like aroma, try tea tree oil. Mix 10 drops of essential oil of tea tree (available at natural food stores and herb shops) with $1/4$ cup of your favorite body lotion and rub all over your body while your skin is still damp from bathing or showering. (The mixture may be too astringent for most complexions, so keep it off your face.) Massage therapists report good results from a daily tea tree treatment for such conditions as fatigue and morning depression.

best foods

To sustain energy levels as well as blood sugar levels throughout the morning, eat foods that are low in fat and high in energy-building complex carbohydrates, such as cereals and baked goods made from whole wheat, buckwheat, barley, and brown rice. In addition, these whole foods offer B vitamins and folate, which promote mental alertness.

Such stimulating spices as cinnamon, ginger, and fennel can be invigorating to a sluggish mind and sluggish digestion as well.

The recipes that follow contain all of the aforementioned, plus natural, food-based sources of nutrients such as vitamin C and beta carotene to help protect the body from viruses, pollution, and the ravages of stress throughout the day.

Special recipes, such as Rice Cereal, Chinese Style, may help soothe morning aches and pains when eaten over a period of time. Rice Cream cereal is immediately helpful in cases of morning queasiness and morning sickness. No-Cook Whole Wheat Cereal can ease morning constipation. Date and Raisin Granola contains a dose of high blood pressure–regulating potassium, and PMS irritability may be soothed for the day by the phytohormones in Apricot and Raspberry Jam. Hydrating Pineapple Wake-up Shake may help a hangover, and anyone can gain immuno-enhancing benefits from Morning Immune-Boost Spread or Miso-Vegetable Soup.

pear and buckwheat pancakes

MAKES 8 PANCAKES, OR 4 SERVINGS
245 calories per serving; 1.25 grams fat; 6% calories from fat

Buckwheat appears frequently in old Russian and Japanese healing recipes for warming the body, making these pancakes a good breakfast choice for a chilly autumn morning when pears are in season.

3/4 cup unbleached all-purpose flour

1/4 cup buckwheat flour

1/4 teaspoon ground cinnamon

1 1/2 teaspoons baking powder

3 tablespoons barley malt

3/4 cup low-fat vanilla soy milk or skim milk

1/4 cup egg substitute (see Note), 2 egg whites, or 1 egg

1/2 cup (packed) cooked buckwheat

1 pear, grated (including juice)

1 teaspoon canola oil

IN A MEDIUM bowl, combine the all-purpose flour, buckwheat flour, cinnamon, baking powder, and barley malt. In a second bowl, combine the soy milk, egg substitute, cooked buckwheat, and pear, whisking well.

POUR THE LIQUID ingredients into the dry and use a large rubber spatula to combine. For the lightest texture, don't overmix. About 15 strokes should do.

PREHEAT A WELL-SEASONED cast-iron skillet on medium-high. Add the oil, spreading it evenly over the surface. Drop the pancake batter into the skillet, using about 2 well-rounded tablespoons for each pancake. Let the pancakes sizzle until cooked through, 2 to 2 1/2 minutes on each side.

SERVE WARM.

Note: To make an egg substitute, boil 1 tablespoon of flax seeds in 1 cup of water until reduced to 3/4 cup, about 3 minutes. Chill before using 1/4 cup for each egg.

IF THE WEATHER IS HOT AND/OR DRY:
Serve with sliced fresh pears.

IF THE WEATHER IS COLD AND/OR DAMP:
Double the cinnamon and serve with Peach and Blueberry Jam with Fresh Ginger (page 29).

giant pancake with berry sauce

MAKES 4 SERVINGS
104 calories per serving (using egg substitute): trace of fat

The blueberries and raspberries in this sauce contain vitamin C, which may help lessen the respiratory congestion that can occur at this time of the day.

$^1/_4$ cup egg substitute (see Note, page 13), 2 egg whites, or 1 egg

$^1/_2$ cup low-fat vanilla soy milk or skim milk

$^1/_4$ cup whole wheat pastry flour

$^1/_4$ cup unbleached all-purpose flour

$^1/_2$ teaspoon canola oil

$^2/_3$ cup fresh blueberries

$^2/_3$ cup fresh raspberries

2 tablespoons apple juice

2 teaspoons lemon juice

pinch of cinnamon

2 teaspoons honey, if the fruit is excessively tart

PREHEAT THE OVEN to 450°F.

IN A PROCESSOR or blender, combine the egg substitute, milk, whole wheat flour, and all-purpose flour, until the batter is smooth.

PREHEAT A 10-INCH cast-iron skillet or round glass baking dish in the oven for 5 minutes, then brush with the oil. Pour in the batter and bake in the middle of the oven until the pancake is puffed and cooked through, about 18 minutes.

MEANWHILE, IN A clean processor or blender, combine the blueberries, raspberries, apple juice, lemon juice, cinnamon, and honey (if needed), whizzing until the ingredients are well combined but the fruit is still slightly chunky.

WHEN THE PANCAKE is done, remove it from the skillet or dish and slice it into 4 wedges with kitchen shears. Serve warm, drizzled with the fruit sauce.

IF THE WEATHER IS HOT AND/OR DRY:
Garnish each serving with mint sprigs and extra berries.

IF THE WEATHER IS COLD AND/OR DAMP:
Add $^1/_2$ teaspoon of finely minced fresh ginger to the berry sauce before serving.

mochi pancakes

MAKES 12 PANCAKES, OR 6 SERVINGS
230 calories per serving: no added fat

A favorite breakfast of Sumo wrestlers, mochi is also recommended in Japan to those who are lethargic or anemic. The little pancakes, which are crisp on the outside and creamy within, contain only brown rice and can therefore be enjoyed by those who must refrain from eating wheat.

2 cups short-grain brown rice   pinch of sea salt

2 1/2 cups water

COMBINE ALL OF the ingredients in a pressure cooker and cook according to manufacturer's instructions until tender, about 30 minutes. Let the pressure cooker release the pressure naturally. If you don't have a pressure cooker, combine all of the ingredients in a soup pot and bring to a boil; reduce the heat, cover loosely, and cook until tender, about 50 minutes. Either way, let the rice sit until it's cool enough to handle.

PREHEAT THE OVEN to 400°F.

IN BATCHES OF thirds, puree the rice in a processor until it's smooth. If you don't have a processor, pound the rice in a mortar. Then, to form each pancake, wet your hands and grab a golf-ball-size lump of dough, shaping it into a smooth ball. Set each ball on a parchment-lined cookie sheet, flattening each slightly. Bake in the middle of the oven until lightly browned, fragrant, and puffed, about 20 minutes. Serve at once. Or to store uncooked mochi pancakes, set them in a refrigerator container between sheets of waxed paper. Cover and refrigerate for up to a week.

IF THE WEATHER IS HOT AND/OR DRY:
When forming each mochi pancake, work in 1 tablespoon of fresh blueberries, finely chopped fresh fruit, or raisins. Then drizzle the baked mochi with barley malt or Cherry Jam with Walnuts (page 28) before serving.

IF THE WEATHER IS COLD AND/OR DAMP:
When forming each mochi pancake, work in 1 tablespoon of aduki beans (or other cooked beans) and drizzle the baked mochi with reduced-sodium soy sauce before serving.

cinnamon-oat refrigerator muffins

MAKES ENOUGH BATTER FOR 12 MUFFINS
100 calories per muffin; 2 grams fat; 18% calories from fat

To save time—and stress—in the morning, make this muffin batter ahead and store it, tightly covered, in the fridge for up to 2 weeks. Then bake as needed.

½ cup whole wheat pastry flour

½ cup unbleached all-purpose flour

1½ cups rolled oats

2 teaspoons baking powder

½ teaspoon baking soda

1 teaspoon ground cinnamon

¼ cup egg substitute (see Note, page 13), 2 egg whites, or 1 egg

1 cup low-fat vanilla soy milk, skim milk, or buttermilk

1 tablespoon canola oil

3 tablespoons barley malt or pure maple syrup

PREHEAT THE OVEN to 375°F.

IN A MEDIUM bowl, combine the whole wheat flour, all-purpose flour, oats, baking powder, baking soda, and cinnamon, stirring well. In a second bowl, combine the egg substitute, milk, oil, and barley malt, using a hand mixer to combine well. Pour the liquid ingredients into the flour mixture and use a large rubber spatula to mix well. For the best texture, don't overmix; about 15 strokes should do.

STORE THE BATTER, covered, in the refrigerator for up to 2 weeks. To bake, spray as many muffin cups as you need with nonstick spray. Fill each cup three-quarters full and bake until cooked through, about 18 minutes.

IF THE WEATHER IS HOT AND/OR DRY:
Spread a muffin with Cherry Jam with Walnuts (page 28).

IF THE WEATHER IS COLD AND/OR DAMP:
Serve with hot spiced apple cider.

ginger-carrot breakfast cookies

MAKES 12 COOKIES

105 calories per cookie (using egg substitute); 2 grams fat; 16% calories from fat

Ginger contains compounds that stimulate digestion and circulation, making it a celebrated morning herb.

1 cup whole wheat pastry flour

1 1/2 cups rolled oats

1 cup grated carrot

2 teaspoons baking powder

1/2 teaspoon baking soda

pinch of sea salt

2 teaspoons grated fresh ginger (including juice)

1/4 cup egg substitute (see Note, page 13), 2 egg whites, or 1 egg

2/3 cup low-fat vanilla soy milk or skim milk

1 tablespoon canola oil

3 tablespoons barley malt or pure maple syrup

PREHEAT THE OVEN to 375°F.

IN A MEDIUM bowl, combine the flour, oats, carrot, baking powder, baking soda, and sea salt. In a second bowl, combine the ginger, egg substitute, soy milk, oil, and barley malt, using a hand mixer to combine well. Pour the liquid ingredients into the dry, using a large rubber spatula to combine well. For the best texture, don't overmix; about 15 strokes should do.

LINE A COOKIE sheet with parchment paper, then drop on the batter, using about 2 rounded tablespoons for each cookie. Bake in the middle of the oven until cooked through, about 25 minutes.

IF THE WEATHER IS HOT AND/OR DRY:
Serve the cookies with fresh peach slices.

IF THE WEATHER IS COLD AND/OR DAMP:
Increase the ginger to 1 tablespoon.

three-grain scones

MAKES 6 SCONES
110 calories per scone; 1.5 grams fat; 12% calories from fat

Thanks to brown rice, these low-fat breakfast snacks are a good source of magnesium, a mineral that can help maintain a smoothly functioning nervous system throughout the day.

¹/₄ cup whole wheat pastry flour	2 teaspoons canola oil
¹/₄ cup unbleached all-purpose flour	pinch of sea salt
¹/₄ cup yellow cornmeal	¹/₄ cup low-fat vanilla soy milk or skim milk
1 teaspoon baking powder	
1 cup cooked brown rice, cooled	

IN A MEDIUM bowl, combine the whole wheat flour, all-purpose flour, cornmeal, and baking powder. Add the rice, oil, salt, and milk and mix well.

PREHEAT A WELL-SEASONED cast-iron skillet on medium-high. Alternatively, use a nonstick sauté pan but don't preheat. To shape each scone, grab a golf-ball-size piece of batter, using your hands to round and then slightly flatten it. Set each scone in the skillet and bake until cooked through, about 5 minutes on each side. Let cool on a wire rack before serving.

IF THE WEATHER IS HOT AND/OR DRY:	IF THE WEATHER IS COLD AND/OR DAMP:
Spread the scones with all-fruit apple butter or orange marmalade.	*Add ¹/₄ teaspoon freshly grated nutmeg to the batter before baking.*

millet breakfast cereal

MAKES 4 SERVINGS
185 calories per serving: no added fat

Since millet is the most alkaline of all grains, it can act as a morning tonic for those who awaken with cranky, acidic stomachs.

1 cup yellow millet, rinsed well	2 1/4 cups vegetable stock
1 1/2 cups cubed butternut squash	pinch of sea salt
1 bay leaf	

COMBINE ALL OF the ingredients in a pressure cooker and cook according to manufacturer's instructions until soft, about 20 minutes. If you don't have a pressure cooker, simmer the ingredients in a soup pot, loosely covered, until soft, about 40 minutes. Serve warm.

IF THE WEATHER IS HOT AND/OR DRY:
Reduce the amount of squash to 3/4 cup and add 3/4 cup fresh corn kernels.

IF THE WEATHER IS COLD AND/OR DAMP:
Reduce the amount of squash to 3/4 cup and add 2 cubed carrots. Or add a pinch of ground cinnamon to each serving.

barley for breakfast

MAKES 4 LARGE SERVINGS
120 calories per serving: no added fat

Those who have trouble maintaining their energy level throughout the morning may find that barley, thanks to the soluble fiber it contains, helps to stabilize fluctuations. Soluble fiber acts as a sort of slow and steady time-released energy source, as opposed to the jolting, short-lived zap that comes from sugar-based pastry.

$1/2$ cup pearled barley	pinch of sea salt
$1^1/2$ cups apple juice	2 tablespoons barley malt or pure maple syrup
$1^1/2$ cups water	$1/2$ teaspoon ground cinnamon
1 bay leaf	

COMBINE ALL OF the ingredients in a large soup pot and bring to a boil. Reduce the heat to a simmer, cover loosely, and simmer until the barley is tender, about $1^1/2$ hours. Serve warm.

IF THE WEATHER IS HOT AND/OR DRY:
Add $1/2$ teaspoon ground cardamom before cooking or serve with chilled peppermint tea.

IF THE WEATHER IS COLD AND/OR DAMP:
Increase the amount of cinnamon to 1 teaspoon or serve with hot cinnamon tea.

rice cereal, chinese style

MAKES 6 CUPS, OR 6 SERVINGS
230 calories per serving: no added fat

The Chinese call this energizing breakfast cereal *congee*. In China it's sold on the street, steaming hot, often topped with shredded scallions. More Western palates might like a swirl of maple syrup or barley malt instead. Some Vietnamese healers believe that a steady diet of brown rice, rather than white, will eventually ease the pain of osteoarthritis.

1 cup short-grain brown rice

5 cups water

pinch of sea salt

COMBINE ALL OF the ingredients in a pressure cooker and cook according to manufacturer's instructions until tender, about 35 minutes. If you don't have a pressure cooker, bring the ingredients to a boil in a soup pot; reduce the heat, cover loosely, and cook until tender, about 50 minutes. Stir well and serve warm. Or make the cereal ahead and keep it, covered and refrigerated, for up to a week.

TO REHEAT ONE serving in the microwave, scoop the cereal into a bowl, cover, and microwave on full power for about 2 minutes. Let the cereal stand for about 1½ minutes before removing the cover and eating.

IF THE WEATHER IS HOT AND/OR DRY:
Top the cereal with sliced bananas.

IF THE WEATHER IS COLD AND/OR DAMP:
Use half rice and half yellow millet.

rice cream

MAKES 3 SERVINGS
170 calories per serving: no added fat

This creamy cereal is easy to digest and is recommended in Japan as a nourishing nostrum for upset stomach, flu, or morning sickness.

¹/₂ cup brown rice	pinch of sea salt
3 cups water	

POUR THE RICE in a blender and whiz until it has been ground into a flour. Then, in a medium saucepan, combine the ground rice, water, and salt and bring to a boil, stirring constantly, until slightly thickened, about 5 minutes. Serve warm.

IF THE WEATHER IS HOT AND/OR DRY:
Use half apple juice (or other unsweetened fruit juice) and half water to cook the ground rice.

IF THE WEATHER IS COLD AND/OR DAMP:
Add a minced scallion or ¹/₄ teaspoon grated fresh ginger to each cooked serving.

no-cook oats and raisins

MAKES 2 SERVINGS
285 calories per serving: no added fat

Medical research confirms that oats contain a type of fiber that can help regulate blood sugar levels, thereby regulating energy levels. One unconfirmed report holds that Attila the Hun fed his soldiers a morning porridge made of oats, which helped them sustain energy during battles.

$^1/_3$ cup rolled oats	2 tablespoons raisins
$^1/_3$ cup boiling water	pinch of sea salt
$^1/_3$ cup hot apple juice	

THE NIGHT BEFORE, combine all of the ingredients in a small thermos bottle and cover. In the morning you can enjoy a hot cereal at home or work. To reheat the cereal, put it in a bowl, cover, and microwave on full power for about 30 seconds.

IF THE WEATHER IS HOT AND/OR DRY:
Omit the raisins and use 2 tablespoons fresh raspberries or blueberries.

IF THE WEATHER IS COLD AND/OR DAMP:
Add $^1/_2$ teaspoon apple pie spice or cinnamon to the thermos.

no-cook whole wheat cereal

MAKES 2 SERVINGS
260 calories per serving: no added fat

Whole wheat is a high-energy food that is low in fat and sodium. Not only that, but since whole wheat is a good source of dietary fiber, regular morning consumption can help alleviate constipation.

⅓ cup bulgur	2 pitted prunes, chopped
⅔ cup boiling water	pinch of sea salt

THE NIGHT BEFORE, combine all of the ingredients in a small thermos and cover. In the morning you can enjoy a hot cereal at home or work. To reheat the cereal, put it in a bowl, cover, and microwave on full power for about 30 seconds.

IF THE WEATHER IS HOT AND/OR DRY:
Omit the prunes and add 2 chopped pitted plums to the thermos.

IF THE WEATHER IS COLD AND/OR DAMP:
Use brewed cinnamon or other spicy tea (available at supermarkets and natural food stores) instead of water.

cherry-vanilla granola

MAKES 4 SERVINGS
225 calories per serving: 7 grams fat: 28% calories from fat

This cereal is free from saturated fat and refined sugar, so it will help you feel bright and even-tempered throughout the morning.

$^1/_4$ cup barley malt or pure maple syrup	2 cups rolled oats
1 teaspoon vanilla extract	$^1/_2$ cup sunflower seeds
1 tablespoon canola oil	$^1/_2$ cup whole dried cherries

COMBINE THE BARLEY malt, vanilla, and oil in a small bowl and set aside.

TIP THE OATS and seeds in a large nonstick sauté pan and heat on medium-high, stirring frequently, until lightly browned and toasted, $2^1/_2$ to 3 minutes. Immediately pour on the syrup, reduce the heat to low, and continue to heat, stirring constantly, until fragrant and dry to the touch, 4 to 5 minutes. Stir in the cherries and serve warm, or place in a jar and keep, refrigerated, for up to 2 weeks.

IF THE WEATHER IS HOT AND/OR DRY:
Serve the granola with nonfat yogurt or soy yogurt. topped with chunks of fresh. juicy fruits such as nectarines and mangos.

IF THE WEATHER IS COLD AND/OR DAMP:
Add $^1/_2$ teaspoon cinnamon to the syrup before mixing it with the oats.

date and raisin granola

MAKES 4 SERVINGS
262 calories per serving: 4 grams fat: 14% calories from fat

Consider this cereal to be a morning nerve tonic, since the dates and raisins both contain potassium, which aids normal nerve function. Additionally, the fennel seed can help relax a digestive system that's gone haywire from last night's meal.

$^1/_4$ cup pure maple syrup or barley malt	2 $^1/_2$ cups rolled oats
1 teaspoon vanilla extract	2 tablespoons fennel seeds
1 tablespoon canola oil	$^1/_2$ cup finely chopped pitted dates
$^1/_2$ teaspoon ground cinnamon	$^1/_2$ cup raisins

COMBINE THE MAPLE syrup, vanilla, oil, and cinnamon in a small dish and set aside.

TIP THE OATS and fennel seeds in a large nonstick sauté pan and heat on medium-high, stirring frequently, until fragrant and lightly toasted, about 2$^1/_2$ minutes. Pour on the syrup, reduce the heat, and stir constantly until the granola is dry to the touch, 4 to 5 minutes. Mix in the dates and raisins and serve warm, or place in a jar and keep, refrigerated, for up to 2 weeks.

IF THE WEATHER IS HOT AND/OR DRY:	IF THE WEATHER IS COLD AND/OR DAMP:
Use the granola as a topping for a fresh fruit salad.	*Increase the cinnamon to $^3/_4$ teaspoon and add a pinch of ground ginger.*

apricot-almond granola with coconut

MAKES 4 SERVINGS
309 calories per serving: 8.5 grams fat: 24% calories from fat

A steady diet of foods containing mucus-eliminating beta carotene, such as these apricots, can help clear a stuffy morning nose.

$^1/_4$ cup all-fruit apricot jam

1 tablespoon canola oil

$^1/_4$ teaspoon ground cinnamon

$2^1/_2$ cups rolled oats

$^1/_4$ cup chopped almonds

$^1/_2$ cup finely chopped dried apricots

$^1/_4$ cup grated dried unsweetened coconut

IN A SMALL bowl, combine the jam, oil, and cinnamon and set aside.

TIP THE OATS and almonds in a large nonstick sauté pan and heat on medium-high, stirring frequently until lightly toasted, $2^1/_2$ to 3 minutes. Pour on the syrup, reduce the heat, and stir constantly until the granola is dry to the touch, 4 to 5 minutes. Stir in the apricots and coconut and serve warm, or place in a jar and keep, refrigerated, for up to 2 weeks.

IF THE WEATHER IS HOT AND/OR DRY:
Serve with low-fat vanilla yogurt or soy yogurt and sliced fresh apricots.

IF THE WEATHER IS COLD AND/OR DAMP:
Omit the coconut and serve the granola with hot orange-spiced tea.

cherry jam with walnuts

MAKES ABOUT 1 CUP, OR 16 (1-TABLESPOON) SERVINGS
55 calories per tablespoon: 2 grams fat; 30% calories from fat

Anecdotal evidence holds that the consumption of cherries, when paired with a low-fat diet, can ease the pain of gout and rheumatoid arthritis. Scientific research has yet to confirm this theory; however, it does document that the pain from these diseases is generally the most debilitating in the morning, making this tasty jam worth a try for sufferers.

$^1/_2$ cup chopped walnuts

1 lemon, seeded and chopped (including peel)

$^1/_3$ to $^1/_2$ cup orange juice

2 cups pitted fresh whole sweet cherries

$^1/_4$ to $^1/_3$ cup barley malt or pure maple syrup

$^1/_2$ teaspoon ground cinnamon

$^1/_4$ teaspoon ground cloves

TIP THE WALNUTS in a large nonstick sauté pan and heat on medium-high, stirring frequently, until lightly browned and toasted, about 2 minutes. Remove the pan from the heat and add the lemon, $^1/_3$ cup of the orange juice, the cherries, barley malt (if the cherries are sour, use the larger amount), cinnamon, and cloves.

RETURN THE PAN to the heat and cook on high, stirring frequently, until the jam is slightly thick and the fruit is soft, 15 to 20 minutes. If the jam begins to get dry, add the remaining orange juice. Let the jam cool before serving, or place in a jar and keep, refrigerated, for up to 2 weeks.

IF THE WEATHER IS HOT AND/OR DRY:
Eliminate the cinnamon and cloves and add $^1/_2$ teaspoon grated fresh orange zest.

IF THE WEATHER IS COLD AND/OR DAMP:
Add $^1/_4$ teaspoon ground ginger.

A TOAST TO FIBER

Toasting bread can increase its dietary fiber content. This happens during the browning process when a chemical reaction occurs between carbohydrates and amino acids. The process triggers color and texture changes, the results of which are similar to lignin, a component of dietary fiber.

peach and blueberry jam with fresh ginger

MAKES ABOUT 1 CUP, OR 16 (1-TABLESPOON) SERVINGS
15 calories per serving: no added fat

Those who don't like to eat in the morning may benefit from this aromatic jam, since peaches are tasty and easy to digest.

½ pound ripe peaches (about 2), peeled, pitted, and chopped

½ pound blueberries (about 1 cup)

1 tablespoon lemon juice

1 teaspoon fresh ginger juice (see Note)

2 tablespoons barley malt or pure maple syrup, or to taste

½ cup apple juice

COMBINE ALL OF the ingredients in a large sauté pan and heat on high, stirring constantly, until the mixture boils. Reduce the heat to medium and cook, continuing to stir constantly, until the jam has thickened and the fruit has softened, 15 to 20 minutes. Let the jam cool, then serve, or place in a jar and keep, refrigerated, for up to 2 weeks.

Note: To make 1 teaspoon ginger juice, grate about 1 tablespoon of fresh ginger, then squeeze.

IF THE WEATHER IS HOT AND/OR DRY:
Use the jam to flavor plain nonfat yogurt or soy yogurt by spooning 1 tablespoon of jam into ½ cup of yogurt.

IF THE WEATHER IS COLD AND/OR DAMP:
Double the ginger and spread the jam on Three-Grain Scones (page 18).

apricot and raspberry jam

MAKES ABOUT 1 CUP, OR 16 (1-TABLESPOON) SERVINGS
16 calories per serving: no added fat

Women who waken with a tinge of irritability from PMS or menopause may benefit from regular raspberry consumption. The fruit contains plant-based hormones that can help balance and soothe a jagged female disposition.

$^{3}/_{4}$ pound ripe apricots, pitted and chopped

$^{1}/_{4}$ pound fresh raspberries

1 tablespoon lemon juice

1 vanilla bean, slit vertically

2 tablespoons barley malt or pure maple syrup

$^{1}/_{2}$ cup apple juice

COMBINE ALL OF the ingredients in a large sauté pan and bring to a boil, stirring frequently. Reduce the heat and cook, stirring frequently, until the fruit is soft and the jam has thickened, about 15 minutes. Let the jam cool, then serve, or place in a jar and keep, refrigerated, for up to 2 weeks.

IF THE WEATHER IS HOT AND/OR DRY:
Use the jam as a spread for such dry-textured breads as corn muffins and English muffins.

IF THE WEATHER IS COLD AND/OR DAMP:
Add $^{1}/_{2}$ teaspoon ground cinnamon before cooking.

orange-scented strawberry syrup

MAKES 1 CUP, OR 4 (¼-CUP) SERVINGS
20 calories per serving: no added fat

If you enjoy bacon for breakfast, you may want to find a place in your meal for strawberries. Most bacon contains nitrates, which are compounds that, once in the body, transform into nitrosamines—strong cancer-causing substances. But strawberries, such as those in this fragrant syrup, contain compounds that block the transformation process.

1 cup ripe fresh strawberries

¼ cup apple juice

1 teaspoon finely grated fresh orange zest

COMBINE ALL OF the ingredients in a blender or processor and whiz until smooth. Then pour into a saucepan and cook on medium-high until fragrant and slightly thickened, 2½ to 3 minutes. Serve warm or chilled on pancakes, waffles, scones, muffins, or fruit salad.

IF THE WEATHER IS HOT AND/OR DRY: *Instead of heating the syrup, let the flavors marinate in the fridge overnight before serving.*

IF THE WEATHER IS COLD AND/OR DAMP: *Serve the syrup warm with ½ teaspoon ground cinnamon swirled in.*

morning immune-boost spread

MAKES 2 SERVINGS
95 calories per serving: 4 grams fat: 37% calories from fat

The secret ingredient in this spicy-sweet spread is *chavanprash,* an Ayurvedic herb paste based on the Indian gooseberry, called *amla.* Each tiny fruit contains 3,000 mg of vitamin C, along with friendly tannins that prevent heat and storage from dissipating the nutrient's potency. Vitamin C can help your body fight infection and disease and can be taken in the morning as a hedge against viruses and other stresses you may encounter throughout the day. Chavanprash is available at Indian markets, herb shops, and health food stores. For the best quality, be sure that amla, not sugar, is the first ingredient.

1 tablespoon chavanprash

1 to 2 tablespoons water

1 tablespoon tahini (sesame paste)

IN A SMALL bowl, combine the chavanprash, tahini, and 1 tablespoon of water and use a small whisk to combine well. If the mixture is too thick, whisk in more water. Spread on muffins, scones, or toast.

Note: If this recipe contains too much fat to suit you, substitute an all-fruit jam, such as Apricot and Raspberry Jam (page 30), for the tahini.

IF THE WEATHER IS HOT AND/OR DRY: *Substitute lemon juice for the water.*

IF THE WEATHER IS COLD AND/OR DAMP: *Add a pinch of ground ginger to the mixture before combining.*

pineapple wake-up shake

MAKES 1 SERVING
190 calories per serving: no added fat

Pineapple contains an enzyme, papain, that aids digestion and cleanses the system, making this easy breakfast a handy restorative if you overindulged the night before.

1/2 cup chopped fresh pineapple

1 small banana, quartered

1 cup cold peppermint tea

2 ice cubes

COMBINE ALL OF the ingredients in a blender and whiz until thick and smooth. Serve chilled and don't store.

IF THE WEATHER IS HOT AND/OR DRY:
Add 1 tablespoon lemon juice before blending.

IF THE WEATHER IS COLD AND/OR DAMP:
Substitute unsweetened grapefruit juice for the peppermint tea.

miso-vegetable soup

MAKES 1 SERVING
80 calories: trace of fat

To Western minds this may sound like a peculiar breakfast, but in China and Japan miso soup is a common and healthful way to start the day. In one Japanese study people who drank miso soup daily had a 33 percent lower cancer mortality than those who did not partake. What's more, Japanese nutritionists recommend miso to neutralize acidity in the body, the effect of which enhances immunity and resistance to disease.

Miso is a savory, slightly salty bean paste that is available at health food stores, Asian markets, and some supermarkets.

1 ¼ cups water

1 carrot, sliced into thin half moons

1 small onion, thinly sliced

2 teaspoons minced fresh parsley

1 teaspoon miso (see The Savory Pantry, page 424)

1 scallion, minced

IN A SMALL saucepan, combine the water, carrot, and onion and bring to a boil. Reduce the heat to medium, cover loosely, and let the soup cook until the vegetables are tender, about 20 minutes.

REMOVE THE SOUP from the heat and stir in the parsley. Set the miso in a small strainer, then submerge the strainer in the soup and use the back of a spoon to push the miso through the strainer into the soup. Garnish with the scallions and serve warm.

Note: If you are on a sodium-restricted diet, reduce the amount of miso to ½ teaspoon.

IF THE WEATHER IS HOT AND/OR DRY: *Substitute ⅓ cup corn kernels for the carrot.*

IF THE WEATHER IS COLD AND/OR DAMP: *Substitute ⅓ cup (not packed) chopped kale or mustard greens for the carrot.*

mid-morning

mid morning

FINDING FOCUS

best time of day for:

| Getting work done, since people are at their most energetic | A photo, because skin is at its most radiant |

*a*n Ayurvedic healer from India gave me a small vial of rose essence to inhale while he deciphered why I sometimes felt scattered in the middle of the morning. Rose, he said, contains eight different volatile oils that combine to produce a profound psychological effect that both coolingly refreshes and focuses the mood. Three of those volatile oils, citronellol, geranium, and nerol, merge to make what Ayurvedics call a nervine, or in the case of rose, an aromatic nerve tonic.

He continued by explaining that in Ayurveda, which means "science of life" in Sanskrit, people fall into one or more *doshas,* or mind-body categories—*vata, pitta,* and *kapha.* Although Ayurveda is quite a complex system, on a basic level the vata dosha corresponds with air; pitta with fire; and kapha with water and earth. Vata, pitta, and kapha also influence various times of the day. Mid-morning, as the day is warming up, is ruled by fiery pitta.

Pitta, he went on, also controls the process of thinking, from the conception of ideas, through discrimination, to conclusion. Consequently, if pitta is too predominant —which can happen mid-morning, especially to people who naturally possess some pitta dosha, or if the weather is hot, even to those who don't—the thinking process can become too intense. In that case, people attempt to do five or six things at once, diminishing their powers of comprehension and thus becoming scattered. This is what sometimes happens to me.

To help me focus, the Ayurvedic healer recommended that I try to relax by closing my eyes for a minute or two and breathing deeply from the vial of rose essence while concentrating on one important project. He also advised that I sip room-temperature basil tea throughout the mid-morning period. Basil, he said, is a mild nervine with a cooling, anti-pitta effect. Additionally, basil is said to give *sattva*, or enlightenment and harmony, to the thinking process.

As instructed, I made my tea by steeping 2 handfuls of fresh basil in 1 quart of room-temperature water overnight. In the morning I discarded the basil and sipped several room-temperature glasses of the refreshing and rejuvenating brew while inhaling the occasional whiff of essence of rose. I was delighted to discover that I was able to focus on this very chapter all morning.

Although the healing science of Ayurveda is thousands of years old, current research concurs with Ayurvedic practitioners' mid-morning theories. It seems that during this period of the day, people are at their most alert and energetic. This is because of profoundly low levels in the body of a naturally occurring sleep-inducing hormone called melatonin. Normally melatonin originates in the brain to course through our systems at night, acting as a natural sedative, then diminishes with daylight to become barely detectable by mid-morning. That's why, ideally, people are most awake and clear-witted mid-morning. Even those who have slept poorly the night before are at their brightest at this time of day. But influences such as a fatty breakfast, stress, dreary weather, some medications, and sugary snacks can sabotage your energy and scatter your thoughts, making you less than sharp. To heighten your mid-morning concentration, try one or more of these focusing tips and recipes.

relief at your fingertips

SOOTHE A HEADACHE

To ease an inconvenient mid-morning headache, a Greek massage therapist taught me to employ a Chinese pressure point called Gateway to 1000 Lives. Since this mini massage takes less than 5 minutes, perform it during a quick break at work. First, rub your hands together briskly for about 10 seconds. Then find the whorl of hair at the crown (top) of your head, using your middle finger to press firmly into the area for 15 seconds. Then relax for 15 seconds. Continue to press and relax for 1 to 2 minutes. While you're pressing and relaxing, close your eyes, breathe deeply, and visualize a soft glow on the area on which you are pressing.

Interestingly, Ayurvedics call the same point *agnishikha*, or Crest of Fire. They say that for the best focus and concentration, energy must flow unimpeded through the area, and they often press on it to converge their thoughts. This connects them, they say, to *rtam*, or the rhythm of the universe. In honor of this important point, ancient Vedic sages grew a little ponytail tuft right on the area, massaging it daily.

CLEAR YOUR MIND

To focus your thoughts and improve concentration before an important meeting, press a point the Chinese call The Third Eye. Rub your hands together briskly for about 10 seconds. Then, using a fingertip (or the side of your finger if you have long nails), firmly press the area where the bridge of your nose meets your forehead. Continue to press, eyes closed and breathing deeply, visualizing a glow just below your navel, for 1 to 2 minutes. Some people say that, while pressing, they can feel a "heartbeat" at the point. Some also attest that regular touching of The Third Eye increases intuition and spiritual awareness. On a more corporeal note, pressing The Third Eye point can help to temporarily eliminate mid-morning eyestrain.

CLEAR YOUR SINUSES

Since mid-morning can be the worst time of day for hay fever and sinus congestion, engaging two sets of points, one after the other, may provide relief. The first set, called Welcoming Perfume, is located in the groove beside each nostril. Rub your hands together briskly for about 10 seconds. Then, using both of your index fingers (or knuckles if you have long nails), press firmly on the points, eyes closed, breathing deeply, for 1 to 2 minutes. While you're pressing, envision fresh air flowing unimpeded in and out of your nose. When you're finished, keep your eyes closed, relaxing for a minute. Then proceed with the next set of points, called Drilling Bamboo, located at the little ledges at the inside end of the eyebrows, above the corners of the eyes. Use your thumbs to firmly press on the points, eyes closed and breathing deeply, for 1 to 2 minutes. If the area feels sensitive, breathing more fully and picturing a warm glow just beneath your navel will help. (Drilling Bamboo is also used to eliminate eyestrain.) You may repeat these decongesting points as necessary.

potent pose

One hot July in Arizona, to help bring my attention into focus, a Hopi woman taught me to employ a body stretch called the Tree. To try it, stand barefoot, left foot pointing out, so your feet form an L. Bending your left knee as high as it will go, tuck your left heel into your right thigh just below your crotch. To keep your balance, you can bend your right knee slightly. If that doesn't help, lean against a wall until you get your balance, but note that yoga instructors say that balance is all mental. Continue the pose by placing the palms of your hands together, pointing up, atop your head. Then, breathing deeply, find a visual point to focus on, such as a flower or a mark on the wall. Hold the pose for 5 to 10 full, deep breaths, visualizing a glow just beneath your navel. Release the Tree and repeat with your right leg. While doing the Tree, attempt to stretch every muscle in your body. And if your thoughts later become uncentered, breathe deeply, recalling what it felt like to visualize the mark on the wall while performing the Tree.

try a tea

Based on recent dehydration studies, scientists have discovered that the more hydrated you are, the more conscious and alert you are. Drinking coffee, black tea, and sodas and eating such salty morning foods as bacon and ham can dehydrate the body, so for that reason alone, it's beneficial to sip an herbal tea or two mid-morning. Add to that the fact that these particular tea suggestions can help increase focus and concentration, and quaffing the brews becomes a very smart mid-morning activity. Additionally, since mid-morning headaches and hay fever can impair mental focus, specific teas are offered here to ease those discomforts. For an instant remedy if you're headache prone, fill a thermos with your tea of choice and take it to work with you.

THREE TEAS TO SOOTHE MID-MORNING HEADACHES

1. *FRONT-OF-THE-HEAD HEADACHE:* Japanese healers hold that this type of headache is often caused by excessive sugar and alcohol consumption and can be soothed by introducing the opposite, salty flavor. To make such a brew, grate 2 tablespoons of fresh ginger and squeeze the juice from the gratings into a mug. You'll have at least 1 teaspoon of ginger juice. Pour in 1 cup of hot water and add 3 drops of tamari soy sauce. Sip the tea while it's warm.

2. *ORIGINATING-FROM-THE-BACK-OF-THE-NECK HEADACHE:* This is a classic stress headache. It can be mitigated during the mid-morning period with such soothing/focusing herb combos as chamomile-peppermint. To make the tea, combine 1 teaspoon of each dried herb with 1 cup of just-boiled water and steep, covered, for 4 minutes. Then sip warm or chilled, depending on the weather. The chamomile contains compounds that can help soothe stress, and the zippy aromatic oils in peppermint help heighten mid-morning concentration. For extra aromatics, steep the herbs in heated orange juice instead of water. *Note:* Peppermint may block the absorption of homeopathic medications, so those who take such medications should omit the herb.

3. *THROBBING-TEMPLE HEADACHE:* Massage therapists call this a "gallbladder" headache, saying it is exacerbated by eating fatty foods for breakfast or for dinner the previous evening. Since the problem probably originates somewhere in the digestive system, a mild digestive "cleanser" is recommended, such as the juice of half a lemon squeezed into a cup of hot water. Those who don't mind the flavor can add a pinch of digestion-stimulating ground cayenne pepper before sipping. As a morning bonus, the volatile oils in lemon combine to create an aroma that promotes alertness.

If a headache lasts more than a day or so, or if it causes blurred vision or dizziness, it may be a symptom of a serious illness and should be evaluated by a health professional.

TEAS TO RELIEVE HAY FEVER AND CONGESTION

To help prevent nasal congestion due to allergies, hay fever, and sinusitis, strengthen your immune system with a daily mid-morning dose of an Ayurvedic herb blend called chavanprash. The sweet and spicy jamlike compound contains a big dose of vitamin C, plus a variety of immuno-supporting herbs in combinations that change slightly depending on the manufacturer. Buy chavanprash at herb shops, natural food stores, and Indian markets, choosing a brand that lists amla as the first ingredient, not refined sugar. The amla, or Indian gooseberry, is the source of vitamin C and the most important ingredient in the blend.

For a mid-morning beverage to help ward off congestion, swirl ½ to 1 teaspoon of chavanprash into 1 cup of warm thyme or sage tea. To make the tea, steep 1 teaspoon of dried herb in 1 cup of just-boiled water, covered, for 4 minutes. Thyme contains anti-infective volatile oils that help prevent and soothe respiratory problems. Sage has compounds that help soothe and heal mucus membranes, but since it may cause uterine contractions, pregnant woman should avoid sage and use the thyme.

TEAS TO FOCUS YOUR POWERS OF CONCENTRATION

Agrypnotics, or substances that promote focus and wakefulness, come in two categories. The first and most famous are the caffeine-containing stimulants, such as coffee, black tea, some colas, and chocolate. While occasional use of these stimulants is quite effective for sharpening the mind, Chinese herbalists hold that daily use eventually robs the body (via the adrenals) of vitality, thus actually backfiring in the long run.

Consequently, Chinese herbalists recommend the more nutrient-containing, foodlike, herbal stimulants that make up the second category of agrypnotics. These include such aromatics as ginger, cinnamon, and fennel, which revive the mind and increase circulation. For a quick and simple tea, combine a slice of fresh ginger, a 2-inch piece of cinnamon stick, and ½ teaspoon of fennel seeds in a large mug. Add 1 cup of just-boiled water, cover, and let the tea steep for 10 minutes before straining and sipping. This tea travels well, so pour it into a thermos to refresh yourself later, before that late-morning meeting or during a long car trip. It is also what herbalists call a carminative, or digestive tonic, making it a good pre-lunch tea choice.

A popular choice on some Caribbean islands, as well as among Jamu herbalists in Indonesia, ginger can also be successfully paired with peppermint for a stimulating mid-morning repast. Prepare it by grating about 2 tablespoons of fresh ginger, then squeezing the gratings with your hand to release about 1 teaspoon of ginger juice into a cup. Add 1 teaspoon of dried peppermint and pour in 1 cup of just-boiled water. Cover and steep for 4 minutes, then strain and sip warm. In warmer seasons, enjoy this zesty beverage slightly chilled. *Note:* Those taking homeopathic medications should avoid peppermint, as it may prevent these medications from working properly.

As an alternative, Jamu herbalists recommend lemongrass to stimulate mental concentration. A good combination is 1 teaspoon of dried lemongrass curls and 1 teaspoon of green tea leaves. Steep in 1 cup of just-boiled water, covered, for 2 minutes. Note that green tea contains a small amount of caffeine, about 25 mg per cup of brewed beverage.

The most simple of all agrypnotics can be made by dropping a fresh sprig of basil or rosemary into a glass of water before sipping. Both herbs contain aromatic compounds that act as mild nerve and circulatory stimulants, thus lifting a muddled mid-morning mood.

Similarly, some herbalists recommend a liquid homeopathic compound of the herb clematis, available at natural food stores, herb shops, and some supermarkets. Clematis is said to promote clarity and focus and is usually taken by dropping 4 drops into a glass of water before sipping. Stash a small bottle in a desk drawer at work to have on hand if you need it.

making scents

In a recent study mistakes were reduced by 54 percent when Japanese factory workers were exposed to essential oil of lemon on the job. Interested in experimenting with herb and plant essences to promote mental clarity in their workers, some U.S. companies tried distributing various essences through workplace ventilation systems. Obtaining positive results, more and more companies are allowing employees, by vote, to choose if they want an essence infused in their workplace. If they say "yea," employees then vote on the essence to be used. Employees who have elected essences report more pleasant workdays, and employers are pleased with productivity.

In a union of modern science and ancient practice, everyone wins, thanks to aromatherapy, the alluring art and science of using plant essences to, in this case, create a mood of clarity. Like the rose essence that helped me focus (see page 116), the essences, called essential oils, are the steam-distilled aromas of plants, available in small, opaque bottles at herb shops, natural food shops, and some supermarkets. In addition to rose and lemon, there exists a virtual plant pharmacopoeia to awaken concentration.

Pine, for instance, helps clear the mind and create focus. The simplest way to employ it is to place 2 drops of essential oil of pine on a tissue and inhale. For a fortifying combination, use 1 drop each of pine and lemon.

Peppermint, rosemary, cardamom, or basil can increase clarity when administered using the tissue inhalation method. In addition, try making a room spray by combining 12 drops of any one of the aforementioned essences with $1/2$ cup of distilled water in a small spray bottle. Spray the area, as needed, in your office or whatever space you're in. Apart from boosting alertness, peppermint, lemon, and cardamom are refreshingly cooling and are best used in warmer climates. Rosemary and pine have a mild warming action, and basil can be used in all weather.

Aromatherapists advise using essential oils in specially designed room diffusers that release drifts of fragrance into the air. Some diffusers use candles or light bulbs to gently heat essences that have been diluted in water. More sophisticated diffusers use minute vibrations to emit the pure fragrance. Either way, aromatherapy diffusers, available at herb shops and natural food stores, are an efficient way to distribute clarity-promoting plant essences into your mid-morning air.

To illuminate your concentration topically, create your own Invigorating Peppermint Neck Gel.

invigorating peppermint neck gel

This easy-to-make aromatherapy potion helps promote well-defined thought and clarity in the midst of mid-morning muddle.

15 drops essential oil of peppermint	1 ounce aloe vera jelly

COMBINE THE PEPPERMINT and aloe in a small glass jar, mixing well. Apply a pea-sized portion to the back of your neck and rub gently while breathing deeply for about 5 full breaths; repeat as needed. Wash your hands before touching your face, since the gel is too concentrated to use on facial skin. Pop a jar into your purse, briefcase, or car glove box to revive yourself as needed. Store the gel, tightly covered, at room temperature for up to 3 months.

ESSENCES FOR ALLERGIES

Those who suffer from mid-morning stuffiness due to hay fever, allergies, or sinusitis may find relief from inhaling two drops of essential oil of eucalyptus or tea tree from a tissue. Both essences are stimulating to the respiratory system and can help temporarily to clear the head and nasal passages.

best foods

Once in London a rather dashing Irishman was taking some ribbing from three Englishmen about the lack of sophisticated cuisine in his native country.

"In Ireland all they eat is oats," laughed one Englishman, "while in England we feed oats to the horses!"

"And that is why," replied the Irishman, "England has the best horses and Ireland has the best men!"

It's an amusing tale to be sure, but also a droll reminder of how poignantly diet affects mental clarity. The English diet was, for many years, famous for its fat. Happily, that has changed, since saturated fats can inhibit circulation to the brain, resulting in a languid disposition and lack of concentration.

On the other hand, oats, which contain both protein and complex carbohydrates, can increase alertness by stimulating neurotransmitters in the brain. Consequently, many of these mid-morning recipes, such as Oatmeal Scones with Rose Water, Blueberry-Cinnamon Muffins, Spicy Apple Bread, and Sweet Potato Bread with Orange and Rosemary, contain oats. These whole grain baked goods are similar to some of the "early morning" recipes, but they differ in their flavorings, which are brighter and more aromatic to focus the mind and enliven the senses. Fresh lemon and orange zest, nutmeg, cinnamon, peppermint, cardamom, lemongrass, and ginger all contain aromatic compounds that aid clarity at this time of day.

Moreover, since Ayurvedics believe that dates abate a foggy mood, a 2,000-year-old fruit spread recipe has been modernized into low-fat Banana-Date Butter for use on muffins, scones, or toast. Similarly, a reformulated ancient Chinese pumpkin potion, to quiet a queasy mid-morning stomach, emerges as Pumpkin-Cranberry Butter. And those who spend their mornings working at computers will find an eye-protecting shot of beta carotene available in Carrot-Raisin Muffins, which can be taken to work and warmed in the microwave on full power for 10 to 15 seconds.

oatmeal scones with rose water

MAKES 9 SCONES
115 calories per scone; 1.7 grams fat; 13% calories from fat

Eating oats may help create a feeling of clarity because of a compound they contain called avenine, which has a strengthening effect on the nerves. These scones also contain aromatic rose water, which can assist in refreshing the mood.

$^3/_4$ cup plus 1 tablespoon whole wheat pastry flour

$^3/_4$ cup plus 1 tablespoon unbleached all-purpose flour

$^3/_4$ cup rolled oats

2 teaspoons baking soda

$^1/_2$ teaspoon ground cinnamon

$^1/_4$ cup barley malt or pure maple syrup

1 small banana, quartered

$^1/_4$ cup low-fat vanilla soy milk or skim milk

1 teaspoon rose water

1 tablespoon canola oil

$^1/_4$ cup egg substitute (see Note, page 13) or 2 egg whites

PREHEAT THE OVEN to 375°F.

IN A MEDIUM bowl, combine the whole wheat flour, unbleached flour, oats, baking soda, and cinnamon. In a second bowl, combine the barley malt, banana, milk, rose water, oil, and egg substitute. Use a hand mixer to blend until the banana is nearly smooth. Then pour into the dry ingredients and use a large rubber spatula to combine well. For the best texture don't overmix; about 15 strokes should do.

LINE A COOKIE sheet with parchment paper and drop well-rounded 2-tablespoon mounds of the batter onto the parchment. Bake in the middle of the oven until fragrant and cooked through, 20 to 25 minutes.

IF THE WEATHER IS HOT AND/OR DRY:
Increase the rose water to 2 teaspoons and serve with an all-fruit jam, such as Cherry Jam with Walnuts (page 28).

IF THE WEATHER IS COLD AND/OR DAMP:
Increase the cinnamon to 1 teaspoon and serve with spiced all-fruit apple butter.

blueberry-cinnamon muffins

MAKES 12 MUFFINS
120 calories per muffin: 2.5 grams fat; 19% calories from fat

Cinnamon contains volatile oils that can act as a mild stimulant on a sluggish mid-morning nervous system. In addition, the cardamom is recommended by Ayurvedic herbalists for good concentration.

1 cup whole wheat pastry flour

1 cup unbleached all-purpose flour

$1/2$ cup rolled oats

2 teaspoons baking powder

1 teaspoon ground cinnamon

$1/4$ teaspoon freshly ground nutmeg

$1/4$ teaspoon freshly ground cardamom seeds

$1/2$ cup fresh blueberries

$1/4$ cup egg substitute (see Note, page 13) or 2 egg whites

2 tablespoons canola oil

1 cup low-fat vanilla soy milk or skim milk

$1/4$ cup barley malt or pure maple syrup

1 teaspoon lemon juice

1 tablespoon orange juice

PREHEAT THE OVEN to 400°F.

FOR THE BEST texture, preheat the flours by combining them in a 4-cup measure and microwaving on full power until warm, about 2 minutes. Alternatively, combine the flours in a large nonstick sauté pan and heat on low (but don't toast), stirring constantly, until warm, about 3 minutes.

ADD THE OATS, baking powder, cinnamon, nutmeg, cardamom, and blueberries to the warm flour and combine well. In a medium bowl, whisk together the egg substitute, oil, milk, barley malt, lemon juice, and orange juice. Pour into the dry ingredients and use a large rubber spatula to combine. Don't overmix; about 15 strokes should do.

SPRAY 12 MUFFIN cups with nonstick spray and evenly distribute the batter among them. Bake in the middle of the oven until cooked through, about 18 minutes.

IF THE WEATHER IS HOT AND/OR DRY:
Serve with chilled hawthorn berry or peppermint tea.

IF THE WEATHER IS COLD AND/OR DAMP:
Substitute raisins or currants for the blueberries.

carrot-raisin muffins

MAKES 12 MUFFINS
135 calories per muffin; 2.5 grams fat; 17% calories from fat

By mid-morning some people have worked at a computer for hours. If that's your scenario, regular consumption of these muffins may serve as eye-disease prevention, since the carotene that carrots contain may help prevent damage to the lens of the eye.

1 1/4 cups whole wheat pastry flour

1 cup unbleached all-purpose flour

2 teaspoons baking powder

1/2 teaspoon ground cinnamon

1/4 teaspoon freshly ground nutmeg

1/2 cup raisins

1/4 cup egg substitute (see Note, page 13) or 2 egg whites

2 tablespoons canola oil

1 cup low-fat vanilla soy milk or skim milk

1/4 cup barley malt or pure maple syrup

1 teaspoon vanilla extract

1 cup coarsely grated carrots

PREHEAT THE OVEN to 400°F.

FOR THE BEST texture, preheat the flours by combining them in a 4-cup measure and microwaving on full power until warm, about 2 minutes. Alternatively, combine the flours in a large nonstick sauté pan and heat on low (but don't toast), stirring constantly, until warm, about 3 minutes.

ADD THE BAKING powder, cinnamon, nutmeg, and raisins to the warmed flour. In a medium bowl, whisk together the egg substitute, oil, milk, barley malt, vanilla, and carrots. Pour into the dry ingredients and use a large rubber spatula to combine. Don't overmix; about 15 strokes should do.

SPRAY 12 MUFFIN cups with nonstick spray and evenly distribute the batter among them. Bake in the middle of the oven until cooked through, 20 to 22 minutes.

IF THE WEATHER IS HOT AND/OR DRY: *Omit the raisins and use 1 1/2 cups grated carrot. Or serve the muffins with a fresh fruit salad that includes cherries, grapes, or juicy plums.*

IF THE WEATHER IS COLD AND/OR DAMP: *Increase the cinnamon to 1 teaspoon and enjoy the muffins with hot rosemary or basil tea (steep 1 teaspoon dried herb in 1 cup of boiling water, covered, for 4 minutes).*

bran and date muffins with lemongrass

MAKES 12 MUFFINS
135 calories per muffin; 2.5 grams fat; 17% calories from fat

Aromatherapists recommend refreshing lemongrass to heighten concentration and banish a sullen morning mood.

$3/4$ cup bran nugget cereal (no sugar added)	1 teaspoon baking soda
$1/2$ cup rolled oats	2 tablespoons canola oil
1 cup brewed lemongrass tea	$1/2$ teaspoon ginger juice (see Note, page 29)
$1/2$ cup low-fat vanilla soy milk or skim milk	$1/4$ cup barley malt or pure maple syrup
1 cup whole wheat pastry flour	$1/2$ cup chopped pitted dates
1 teaspoon baking powder	$1/2$ cup grated carrot
	1 teaspoon finely minced fresh lemongrass

PREHEAT THE OVEN to 400°F.

COMBINE THE BRAN cereal, oats, tea, and milk in a bowl. Sift in the flour, baking powder, and baking soda.

IN A SECOND bowl, combine the oil, ginger juice, and barley malt, using a hand mixer to blend well. Pour over the bran mixture, add the dates, carrot, and minced lemongrass, and fold all together using a large rubber spatula. Don't overmix; about 15 strokes should do.

SPRAY 12 MUFFIN cups with nonstick spray and distribute the batter evenly among them. Bake in the middle of the oven until cooked through, about 20 minutes.

IF THE WEATHER IS HOT AND/OR DRY:
Serve with chilled hibiscus-lemongrass tea. Many ready-made blends are available (read labels) at herb shops, health food stores, and supermarkets.

IF THE WEATHER IS COLD AND/OR DAMP:
Increase the ginger juice to 1 teaspoon and serve the muffins with hot spiced tea.

spicy apple bread

MAKES 10 SLICES

120 calories per slice; 3 grams fat; 22% calories from fat

Nutmeg, a prominent spice in this snack bread, contains aromatic oils that act as a mild stimulant. This has prompted herbalists to recommend the spice to temporarily heighten mental and intellectual abilities. This bread makes great French toast.

1 cup unbleached all-purpose flour

$^1/_2$ cup whole wheat pastry flour

$^1/_2$ cup rolled oats

2 teaspoons baking soda

1 apple, grated (including juice)

1 cup low-fat vanilla soy milk or skim milk

3 tablespoons barley malt or pure maple syrup

$^1/_4$ cup egg substitute (see Note, page 13) or 2 egg whites

2 tablespoons canola oil

1 teaspoon vanilla extract

$^1/_2$ teaspoon ground cinnamon

$^1/_4$ teaspoon allspice

$^1/_2$ teaspoon freshly ground nutmeg

PREHEAT THE OVEN to 375°F.

FOR THE BEST texture, preheat the flours by combining them in a 4-cup measure and microwaving on full power until warm, about 2 minutes. Alternatively, combine the flours in a large nonstick sauté pan and heat on low (but don't toast), stirring constantly, until warm, about 3 minutes.

ADD THE OATS and baking soda to the warm flour and combine well. In a medium bowl, combine the apple, milk, barley malt, egg substitute, oil, vanilla, cinnamon, allspice, and nutmeg, using a hand mixer to combine well. Pour into the flour mixture and use a large rubber spatula to combine. Don't overmix; about 15 strokes should do.

SPRAY AN $8^1/_2 \times 4^1/_2 \times 2^1/_2$-INCH loaf pan with nonstick spray, then scoop in the batter, smoothing the top. Bake in the middle of the oven until cooked through, 45 to 50 minutes. Let cool completely before slicing.

IF THE WEATHER IS HOT AND/OR DRY: *Substitute a grated medium-ripe peach for the apple.*

IF THE WEATHER IS COLD AND/OR DAMP: *Increase the nutmeg to $^3/_4$ teaspoon.*

sweet potato bread with orange and rosemary

MAKES 16 SQUARES
85 calories per square: 2 grams fat: 21% calories from fat

Rosemary contains over a dozen fragrant volatile oils that combine to uplift the mood and relieve mental strain.

$^3/_4$ cup whole wheat pastry flour

1 cup unbleached all-purpose flour

1 teaspoon baking soda

$1^1/_2$ teaspoons baking powder

$^2/_3$ cup rolled oats

$^1/_2$ cup egg substitute (see Note. page 13) or 4 egg whites

$^1/_3$ cup barley malt or pure maple syrup

1 cup mashed cooked sweet potatoes

2 tablespoons canola oil

$^1/_4$ cup orange juice

$^1/_2$ teaspoon finely grated fresh orange zest

2 teaspoons minced fresh rosemary or 1 teaspoon dried

PREHEAT THE OVEN to 375°F.

IN A MEDIUM bowl, combine the whole wheat flour, all-purpose flour, baking soda, baking powder, and oats.

IN A SECOND bowl, combine the egg substitute, barley malt, mashed sweet potatoes, oil, juice, zest, and rosemary, using a hand mixer to combine well. Pour into the dry ingredients and use a large rubber spatula to combine. Don't overmix; about 15 strokes should do.

SPRAY AN 8-INCH square cake pan with nonstick spray and scoop in the batter, smoothing the top. Bake in the middle of the oven until cooked through, 45 to 50 minutes. Cool completely before cutting into squares.

IF THE WEATHER IS HOT AND/OR DRY:
Serve with chilled fresh orange sections.

IF THE WEATHER IS COLD AND/OR DAMP:
Add $^1/_4$ teaspoon ground ginger to the dry ingredients before combining.

banana-date butter

MAKES ABOUT ²⁄₃ CUP, OR ABOUT 10 (1-TABLESPOON) SERVINGS
51 calories per serving: 1.4 grams fat: 26% calories from fat

Ayurvedic healers prescribe dates to relieve grogginess and create clarity of the mind.

8 pitted dried dates, chopped

¼ cup orange juice

1 large banana, sliced

1 tablespoon unsalted butter or canola oil

1 tablespoon lemon juice

IN A SMALL saucepan, combine the dates and orange juice and heat on high until the dates have softened slightly, about 2 minutes.

COMBINE THE DATE mixture (including the juice), banana, butter, and lemon juice in a processor or blender and whiz until the mixture is smooth but flecks of dates still remain. Serve warm or place in a jar and store, refrigerated, for up to a week. Great on waffles, toast, whole wheat English muffins, and rice cakes.

IF THE WEATHER IS HOT AND/OR DRY:
Serve with a fruit-filled muffin, such as Blueberry-Cinnamon Muffins (page 44).

IF THE WEATHER IS COLD AND/OR DAMP:
Serve atop a spicy treat, such as Ginger-Carrot Breakfast Cookies (page 17).

pumpkin-cranberry butter

MAKES 1½ CUPS, OR 12 (2-TABLESPOON) SERVINGS
47 calories per serving: trace of fat

Some Chinese healers recommend cooked pumpkin to soothe the kind of jittery stomach that interferes with concentration.

1 pound sweet potatoes, peeled and cut into 1-inch chunks

1 pound butternut squash, peeled and cut into 1-inch chunks

¼ to ⅓ cup apple juice

1 tablespoon lemon juice

¼ cup dried cranberries or raisins

1 tablespoon tahini (sesame paste)

pinch of sea salt

STEAM THE SWEET potatoes and squash over boiling water until very soft, about 8 minutes. When the vegetables are cool enough to handle, tip them into a processor or blender along with ¼ cup apple juice, the lemon juice, cranberries, tahini, and salt and whiz until pureed. If the mixture is too thick, add more apple juice during processing. Spread on whole wheat raisin toast or bran muffins, or place in a jar and store, refrigerated, for up to a week.

IF THE WEATHER IS HOT AND/OR DRY:
Omit the dried cranberries and, after pureeing, fold in ⅓ cup finely chopped fresh pineapple.

IF THE WEATHER IS COLD AND/OR DAMP:
Before blending, add ½ teaspoon each of ground cinnamon and ground ginger.

apple butter with blueberries

MAKES 1 1/2 CUPS, OR 12 (2-TABLESPOON) SERVINGS
45 calories per serving; 1 gram fat; 20% calories from fat

Enjoying this spread at your morning tea break can leave you feeling gently energized. The reason is that it contains natural fruit sugars, which have a more subtle effect on the body than the dramatic energy surge created by snacks containing refined white sugar.

1 pound cooking apples (about 6 medium), peeled, cored, and thinly sliced

1/2 cup fresh blueberries

2 tablespoons apple juice

1/4 teaspoon ground cinnamon

1 tablespoon unsalted butter or canola oil

1 tablespoon lemon juice

TOSS THE APPLES, blueberries, and apple juice in a large sauté pan and cook over high heat, stirring occasionally, until the fruit is very soft, 12 to 15 minutes.

WHEN THE FRUIT is cool enough to handle, tip it into a processor or blender and whiz until smooth but not watery (about 5 seconds), adding the butter and lemon juice halfway through. Serve on sourdough toast, pancakes, scones, or muffins, or place in a jar and store, refrigerated, for up to a week.

IF THE WEATHER IS HOT AND/OR DRY:
Use as a dip for sliced fresh fruit such as papayas, peaches, and nectarines.

IF THE WEATHER IS COLD AND/OR DAMP:
Increase the cinnamon to 1/2 teaspoon.

cranberry cider

MAKES 4 CUPS, OR 4 SERVINGS
135 calories per serving; no added fat

Those who study fragrance psychology hold that the volatile oils in lemon, such as those offered in the halves that flavor this zesty beverage, may help to increase alertness.

For convenience in making this recipe, dry the lemon ahead of time.

2 tablespoons plus 2 teaspoons granulated barley malt sugar or maple sugar

1 teaspoon ground cinnamon

$^1/_4$ teaspoon freshly grated nutmeg

$^1/_4$ teaspoon ground cloves

1 lemon, halved

2 cups unsweetened cranberry juice

2 cups apple cider

MIX TOGETHER THE sugar, cinnamon, nutmeg, and cloves. Use a grapefruit spoon to remove and discard the lemon pulp, leaving two shells. (Most of the lemon's volatile oils are in the peel.) Pack the spice mixture into each shell, tamping it down tightly. Then set the shells on a wire rack and let them dry in a cool place for about a week.

TO MAKE THE cider, combine the dried shells, cranberry juice, and cider in a medium saucepan and simmer on low for about an hour.

IF THE WEATHER IS HOT AND/OR DRY:
Simmer the cider as recommended, then chill before serving, garnishing with juicy orange slices.

IF THE WEATHER IS COLD AND/OR DAMP:
Increase the nutmeg to $^1/_2$ teaspoon, and add $^1/_4$ teaspoon ground ginger.

peppermint punch

MAKES 2 SERVINGS
65 calories per serving; no added fat

Peppermint's uplifting aroma can be an antidote to focus-robbing fatigue. If you have a refrigerator at your workplace, keep the ingredients on hand to make a quick restorative.

1 cup brewed peppermint tea, chilled   ¹/₂ cup sparkling mineral water, chilled
¹/₂ cup fresh pink grapefruit juice, chilled

COMBINE ALL OF the ingredients and pour into chilled glasses.

Note: Peppermint can block the absorption of homeopathic medications. Those who are taking such preparations can substitute brewed lemongrass tea for the peppermint.

IF THE WEATHER IS HOT AND/OR DRY:
Garnish with lime wedges.

IF THE WEATHER IS COLD AND/OR DAMP:
Substitute brewed spearmint or basil tea for the peppermint and garnish with a cinnamon stick in each glass.

noon

THE JOYOUS HOUR

best time of day for:

Finishing important	Socializing. because
projects. since alertness	people are generally in
levels peak around now	the best mood of the day

One hot noon in Hong Kong, I lined up at an open-air tea bar with my teacher/doctor and dozens of Chinese people, awaiting my bowl of thick, black, herbal tonic. Although this occurred almost 20 years ago, I still vividly remember the sweet and bitter brew, as this was my first lesson in holistic healing.

While I was sipping, my teacher pointed to a nearby hill, explaining that good health relies on the union of two opposite forces, yin and yang. These two labels are exemplified by two sides of a hill, the sun shining upon the yang side, the yin side shaded. To the Chinese, all things in the universe are composed of both yin and yang characteristics. To distinguish yin from yang, he advised, just think of the hill—sunny-sided yang attributes are warm, bright, active, dry, hard, while yin attributes are cool, shaded, gentle, moist, soft. Noon, my teacher

*"An inevitable dualism
bisects nature, so that
each thing is a half; and
suggests another thing to
make it whole; as spirit,
matter; man, woman;
subjective, objective; in,
out; upper, under;
motion, rest; yea, nay."*

*—Ralph Waldo Emerson,
from his essay on "Com-
pensation"*

continued, being a warm time of day, is yang. And that is why Chinese tea bars serve cooling yin blends during the hot Hong Kong mid-day—to help balance the body and mind, creating good health.

Chinese healers associate times of day with particular organs, noon being the time for the heart. They hold that if a person's yin and yang are balanced and healthy, the heart will be joyous, especially at noon. If not, anxiety or depression may ensue.

Current Western research runs along similar lines, revealing that a substance released in the brain, called serotonin, ideally should peak about noon. Serotonin, the "good-time hormone," helps make us calm and joyous. Lack of it, due to conditions such as dreary weather, no exercise, loss of sleep, poor stress management, and poor diet, can, like the imbalance of yin and yang, cause anxiety or depression.

Although everyone becomes anxious or depressed from time to time, being stressed or sad day after day may indicate a serious problem and should receive professional attention. For the occasional irritable or low mood, however, and to guarantee that noon remains the intended "high point of the day," adopt one or more of these mood-balancing suggestions or recipes.

relief at your fingertips

MID-DAY MOOD ENHANCER

When noon finds you feeling less than cheerful, try to collect yourself long enough to observe your breathing. Chances are, it's shallow and tight. Simple as it seems, consciously deepening and slowing your breathing may improve your mood in merely a minute or two. Try it in combination with a Chinese accupressure point called, aptly, Gates of Consciousness. First, grab two pennies. Place them in the indentations at the base of the skull, located between the top of the spine and the two neck muscles. Holding the pennies firmly, lean your head back to rest on your hands, breathing fully and deeply, eyes closed, for 1 to 2 minutes. As you breathe, picture a glow of light just below your navel, which can help you breathe more abundantly.

Slowly open your eyes, lifting your head to its normal position. At first your head may feel pleasantly energized. Then notice the gentle, balancing wave of energy slowly move down through your body, all the way to your toes. Apart from staving off depression, working the Gates of Consciousness may also soothe mild headaches.

KEEP BREATHING

At daybreak one Sunday morning in the upper Sonoran Desert, I met a chiropractor from San Diego who encourages his patients to meditate, exercise, and eat well to augment their healing treatments. Before departing, he gave me his business card, on the back of which was printed, "Keep Breathing." At first the advice just seems obvious, but when you begin to notice your own breathing—that it's shallow when you're stressed, for instance—the message, much like the breathing itself, becomes much fuller.

SOOTHING MID-DAY STRESS

If you feel tense and irritable, try a noontime mood-balancing point called Heart-7. Rub your hands together briskly for about 10 seconds, then, running either middle finger down the outside of the opposite hand, stop when you come to the indentation on the wrist, just south of the round bone. Closing your eyes, breathe deeply for 10 complete breaths, taking care to relax and untense your shoulders as you do so. As you breathe, visualize a glow just below your navel, a practice that will help you breathe extra deeply. Repeat with the other hand.

Open your eyes, let your hands relax, and sit calmly for a minute before resuming activity. Heart-7, which is used to soothe a stressed, or yang, condition, is a yin-producing point. For that reason, along with peacefulness, you may experience some extra yin characteristics, such as a moist mouth and a slight chill after performing Heart-7. These effects are temporary and will balance out momentarily.

potent pose

At a roadside Buddhist shrine near Kuala Lumpur, Malaysia, I learned about a centuries-old self-massage/exercise method called Do-in, which is said to rejuvenate and refresh the body and mood. Practitioners of Do-in maintain that their simple stretches, each of which corresponds with an internal organ, can balance you from the inside out. They believe, as do Chinese acupuncturists, that the meridian, or channel, that carries energy to and from the heart runs along the arm. To perform a Do-in stretch to "lighten a heavy heart," I began by kneeling on the ground, rear on heels, with my hands laced behind my back and arms perfectly straight. (Alternatively, you can kneel on the floor or sit in a chair. At first it may be difficult to keep your arms straight, but just do the best you can and your stretch will eventually improve.) Inhaling, I bent forward at the waist as far as I could go, extending my arms up as far as they would go. Breathing deeply, I visualized a glow of light just below my navel. I held the position while breathing for three full, deep breaths. Eyes still closed, I slowly sat up as I gently dropped my arms to my sides. I noticed how the tension moved out of my shoulders, down through my arms, and out my fingertips.

When you try this Do-in stretch, do so at about noon every day, increasing the number of breaths you take while holding the stretch and working on straightening your arms. Although the connection between the stretch and creating a joyful, light-

To turn an otherwise ordinary glass of iced tea into a tension tamer, simply add two crushed cardamom pods to the brewed tea before sipping. Cardamom, which has a soft, flowery flavor, is used by herbalists to promote a joyful, calm mood.

hearted mood is not scientifically documented, many people do report a surging release of stress upon performing this stretch, a result that may indeed be beneficial to heart health, especially when repeated on a daily basis.

try a tea

In one Russian study, participants with mild, occasional depression experienced considerable benefits from ingesting fresh ginger. Rich in the volatile oils zingiberene and zingiberol, ginger can mildly stimulate the mind and body from a sullen state. Again, it's a case of balancing yin and yang; mild noontime depression, which is an inactive, glum, overly yin state, is stimulated into activity by the yang properties of warm, zesty ginger.

Make a ginger tea by grating 1 teaspoon of fresh ginger right into 1 cup of hot water or a glass of regular iced tea. For an even bigger boost, add the ginger gratings to a cup of refreshing (warm or cool) peppermint tea. Also a mild stimulant, peppermint helps to stimulate circulation and strengthen the nerves, because of the menthol it contains. Alternatively, combine ½ cup of warm or cool peppermint tea and ½ cup of warm or cool chamomile tea with the ginger. The chamomile, aromatherapists say, is a mild nervine (see page 408) whose presence helps soothe stress. *Note:* Those taking homeopathic medications should avoid the peppermint and use the chamomile alone, since the peppermint may prevent the medications from being absorbed by the body.

Lemon balm (*Melissa*) has been used for centuries by German and English herbalists to treat depression. The herb contains aromatic oils that soothe digestive spasms and thus is recommended to treat intestinal problems associated with depression. In addition, although it is not a substitute for high blood pressure medication, lemon balm is a mild vaso-dilator, which lowers high blood pressure and acts as a heart tonic.

You can use lemon balm to make a tea to treat noontime depression. Combine 2 teaspoons of the dried herb with 1 teaspoon of dried linden flower (tilia) and steep in 1 cup of just-boiled water, covered, for 10 minutes. Strain and sip warm or slightly chilled.

STEEPED IN SERENITY

For a soothing, rejuvenating repast, try steeping one slice of Chinese licorice root in your hot tea, right along with the tea bag or leaves. Research shows that licorice can help stabilize blood sugar and energy levels, and its naturally sweet taste eliminates the need for added sugar or other sweeteners. Note: Since licorice can raise energy levels, it can act as a hypertensive, and so people with high blood pressure should avoid it.

making scents

A massage therapist mixed 3 drops of essential oil of clary sage with 1 tablespoon of canola oil and went to work on my sore right knee. As I inhaled the warm, musky, sagelike aroma, my mood lightened considerably within minutes and I actually became rather giggly.

She explained my giddy condition by saying that clary is what aromatherapists call a euphoric, a substance that, upon inhalation, creates a cheerful mood. Although this phenomenon is not scientifically documented, many aromatherapists and massage therapists report "mild intoxication" and "contentment" from using clary, praising its ability to lift depression. In my case, the massage therapist used clary's yang properties to improve my temporarily dreary, excessively yin mood brought about by fretting over my sore knee. I have employed the herb in various forms ever since.

Apart from massage, for tinges of wistfulness due to PMS and menopause, I place a drop each of essential oil of clary sage and rose geranium (available at herb shops and natural food stores) onto a tissue and inhale. Or I dot the drops on a cotton ball and tuck it into my bra, where body heat sends cheering whiffs up to my nose, like a therapeutic perfume.

The cotton ball can also be stashed in a shirt or blouse pocket or tucked into a trouser pocket and produced for a noseful as needed. The technique, aromatherapists say, is also useful for helping to lift postnatal depression.

Another way to apply clary to create a cheerful noontime mood is by simply rubbing and smelling a fresh leaf. Clary leaves, much like the leaves of their cousin, common sage, are large, green, and pebbly and will last a full day in a pocket without shriveling. You can also try the same with a fresh rose geranium leaf for a mildly stimulating rosy scent with a natural lemon twist.

Since an aromatherapy full-body bath may not be convenient at noon, here's a quick way to abbreviate the procedure to improve a mid-day mood. Rinse out a bathroom sink with mouthwash or with very hot water. Fill the sink with warm water, adding 3 drops of essential oil of clary sage, rose geranium, or lavender. If you don't have the essential oil, swirl in about 1 tablespoon of fresh or dried clary, rose geranium leaves, or lavender flowers. Roll up your sleeves and bathe your arms, hands, and neck in the scented water, breathing deeply and inhaling the illuminating fragrance. If you're not wearing makeup, splash your face with the water too. If you have time, remove your makeup and reapply after the bath. Continue rinsing yourself and breathing deeply for about 5 minutes, or until the water becomes cool. To finish, apply a refreshing lotion to your skin while it's still damp. Try scenting your own by adding 3 to 5 drops of essential oil to $1/4$ cup of unscented lotion. For dry skin, use hydrating clary and/or lavender, and for oily skin, use balancing geranium and/or lavender. For normal skin, use straight lavender.

best foods

For you to gain the best results from what you eat for lunch, you must pay attention to how you feel and prescribe your own food accordingly. You may feel happy and well balanced, in which case you may eat either foods high in complex carbohydrates or foods high in protein. But if you feel less than perfect, there are two options from which to choose.

When you're stressed, eating foods high in complex carbohydrates can calm you down. A Chinese doctor might explain this by saying that stress makes the body and mind tight and contracted. So eating such soft, moist, yin-inducing complex carbohydrates as brown rice and barley can help to balance the overly yang tension. A Western doctor might explain it by saying that these complex carbohydrates contribute a calming effect because they increase levels of serotonin in the brain, which induces a calm and happy mood. Either way, your stress may be soothed.

But perhaps you are feeling sluggish or depressed, both overly yin conditions. In that case, eating high-protein foods such as lean fish or poultry will help to energize you. A Chinese-style explanation would be that the warm, tight-fleshed, yang fish will balance your dreary excess yin. Western theory holds that eating lean protein encourages the flow of energizing norepinephrine and dopamine from the brain through the body, making you feel refreshed and alert.

For your convenience, the recipes in this chapter are highlighted either *energizing* or *calming* so that you can quickly choose what you need to help alleviate how you feel. Energizing examples include low-fat, high-protein dishes such as Herbed Salmon Spread, Grilled Chicken Sandwiches with Sesame and Chives, and Salmon Soup with Garlic and Ginger. Combined bean and grain dishes, such as Pinto-Buckwheat Burgers and Ayurvedic Strengthening Stew, also fall under the energizing umbrella. Fresh Salsa, though not a protein dish, is recommended for sluggish moods because it contains the mild stimulants garlic, shallot, citrus, and jalapeño peppers. If you're lunching out, simply use the information as a guide, ordering from the menu accordingly.

sesame squash soup

calming

MAKES 4 SERVINGS

85 calories per serving; 1 gram fat; 11% calories from fat

soups

High in immuno-boosting beta carotene, this easily prepared soup is a smart lunch choice for those who work in polluted areas.

- 8 ounces peeled butternut squash, cut into 1-inch chunks
- 1 10-ounce rutabaga, peeled and cut into 1-inch chunks
- 1 carrot, cut into 1-inch chunks
- 1 onion, peeled and cut into 1-inch chunks
- 1 clove garlic, very finely minced
- 1 thin slice fresh ginger, finely chopped
- $1\frac{1}{2}$ cups vegetable stock
- 1 teaspoon toasted (dark) sesame oil
- pinch of sea salt
- freshly ground black pepper
- 2 tablespoons minced fresh chives

IN A LARGE soup pot, combine the squash, rutabaga, carrot, onion, garlic, ginger, and stock and bring the mixture to a boil. Reduce the heat to low and simmer until the vegetables are fragrant and tender, about 20 minutes.

LET THE SOUP cool slightly, then remove and discard the ginger. Puree the soup in batches in a processor or blender until smooth, adding the sesame oil, salt, and pepper halfway through. Garnish with chives and serve warm or chilled.

IF THE WEATHER IS HOT AND/OR DRY:
Omit the ginger, increase the sesame oil to 2 teaspoons, and serve chilled.

IF THE WEATHER IS COLD AND/OR DAMP:
Add 1 teaspoon (or to taste) hot pepper sauce and serve warm.

NATURAL NOONTIME STRESS RELIEF

A "Jamu man" (Indonesian herbalist) I met maintains that the best antidote for a tight, stressed, yang condition is to eat a piece of moist, juicy yin fruit such as mango, pear, or ripe peach.

SWEET RELIEF?

If you crave rich, gooey desserts when you are stressed, what you are intuitively trying to achieve is a yin balance to your yang tension. The sweets, being soft, moist, and yin-producing, may well relieve a hard, stressed, overly yang state of mind and body. Since many desserts are lacking in nutrients and are full of fat, choose wisely with low-fat, fruit-sweetened puddings or sorbets.

carrot soup with light miso and ginger

calming

A mid-day general body tonic, this fragrant soup contains nettle, a good source of botanically based iron and calcium. The burdock root helps to clarify the skin and aids liver function, as do the dandelion greens and ginger. In addition, the miso contains live organisms that are beneficial to intestinal health, thus aiding immunity.

1½ cups vegetable stock

2 teaspoons dried nettle (see The Savory Pantry, page 424)

1 12-inch fresh burdock root, thinly sliced (see The Savory Pantry, page 422)

1 large carrot, thinly sliced

1 clove garlic, minced

¾ teaspoon finely grated fresh ginger

2 tablespoons rolled oats

1 cup minced dandelion greens

1 teaspoon light miso (see The Savory Pantry, page 424)

IN A MEDIUM pot, combine the stock, nettle, burdock root, carrot, garlic, ginger, and oats and bring to a boil. Reduce the heat to medium-low, cover loosely, and simmer until the vegetables are fragrant and tender, about 20 minutes. Toss in the dandelion greens and simmer for about 2 minutes more, then remove the pot from the heat.

SCOOP THE MISO into a small strainer and submerge it in the soup. Use the back of a spoon to push the miso into the soup, then stir well. Let the soup sit for about 2 minutes, but for the most healthful benefits from the miso, don't boil again or the "friendly" bacteria will be destroyed. Serve warm.

IF THE WEATHER IS HOT AND/OR DRY:
Garnish with minced fresh cilantro.

IF THE WEATHER IS COLD AND/OR DAMP:
Increase the ginger to 1 teaspoon and garnish with minced fresh scallion.

mochi soup with green beans and corn

Mochi, which is often made from brown rice, is a good source of the mood-enhancing B vitamins, making this an ideal lunch choice for those who are depressed as well as stressed. Make your own mochi (page 15) or buy prepared mochi at natural food stores.

4 cups vegetable stock

1/2 cup corn kernels

1/2 cup chopped green beans

2 shallots, minced

3 cakes mochi

1/2 teaspoon minced fresh dill

2 tablespoons minced fresh chives

pinch of sea salt

freshly ground black pepper

IN A LARGE pot combine the stock, corn, beans, and shallots and bring to a boil. Reduce the heat to medium, covering loosely, and simmer until the vegetables are fragrant and tender, about 15 minutes. Grate in the mochi and continue to simmer until the mochi has slightly thickened the soup and it has become creamy, about 5 minutes. Add the dill, chives, salt and pepper and serve warm.

IF THE WEATHER IS HOT AND/OR DRY:
Add 1/4 cup finely chopped fennel bulb to the soup before cooking.

IF THE WEATHER IS COLD AND/OR DAMP:
Substitute mustard greens for the dandelion.

red bean stew

Aduki beans and brown rice combine to make an energizing protein dish. For an extra boost, the jalapeños serve as a mild stimulant by helping to regulate blood flow throughout the body.

1 cup short-grain brown rice

1/4 cup dried aduki beans (see Note)

5 cups vegetable stock

2 leeks, rinsed and minced

1 to 2 fresh jalapeño peppers, cored, seeded, and minced

2 cloves garlic, finely minced

1 bay leaf

1/2 cup Fresh Salsa (see page 73) or good-quality bottled salsa

3 scallions, minced

1/4 cup grated soy Parmesan or regular Parmesan cheese

COMBINE THE RICE, beans, stock, leeks, peppers, garlic, and bay leaf in a large pot and bring to a boil. Reduce the heat to medium, cover loosely, and simmer until the rice and beans are tender, about 1 1/4 hours, stirring occasionally. Serve warm, garnished with the salsa, scallions, and cheese.

Note: To improve the digestibility of the beans, soak them, along with the rice, for at least 30 minutes before cooking. Be sure to change the water before proceeding.

IF THE WEATHER IS HOT AND/OR DRY:
Substitute a mango or other fruit-based salsa (see page 124) for the tomato salsa.

IF THE WEATHER IS COLD AND/OR DAMP:
Before garnishing, swirl in hot pepper sauce to taste.

ayurvedic strengthening stew

This is a variation on an ancient Indian healing recipe, still used today to "balance energies in the body."

1/2 teaspoon olive oil or ghee	1/2 cup cooked split mung beans
3/4 teaspoon whole cumin seed	2 cups brewed nettle tea (available at herb shops and natural food stores)
3/4 teaspoon ground coriander	2 cups water
1/2 teaspoon ground turmeric	
1/2 cup cooked short-grain brown rice	

PREHEAT A LARGE soup pot on medium-high, then add the olive oil. When the oil is warm, add the cumin seed, coriander, and turmeric and sauté, stirring constantly, until lightly browned and fragrant, about 5 minutes.

ADD THE RICE, beans, tea, and water and bring to a boil. Reduce the heat, cover loosely, and simmer until thick, about 25 minutes. Serve warm.

Note: Since nettle may increase blood pressure levels, those with the condition should substitute vegetable stock.

IF THE WEATHER IS HOT AND/OR DRY:
Add 1/2 teaspoon ground cardamom when sautéing the other spices.

IF THE WEATHER IS COLD AND/OR DAMP:
Substitute cooked white rice (basmati is nice) for the brown rice.

white bean and eggplant stew

calming

125 calories per serving (with soy Parmesan); 4 grams fat; 28% calories from fat

Chinese healers often recommend eggplant to soothe a stressed stomach.

2 teaspoons olive oil

1 medium onion, minced

2 cloves garlic, minced

$1/4$ cup minced fresh celery leaves

2 cups cubed eggplant

6 plum tomatoes, seeded and chopped (including juice)

2 cups vegetable stock

1 teaspoon minced fresh thyme or $1/2$ teaspoon dried

1 teaspoon minced fresh rosemary or $1/2$ teaspoon dried

1 cup cooked white beans, such as cannellini

2 tablespoons grated soy Parmesan or regular Parmesan cheese

PREHEAT A LARGE soup pot on medium-high, then add the oil. When the oil is warm, add the onion, garlic, and celery leaves and sauté until the onion is just wilted, about 3 minutes. Add the eggplant and tomatoes, cover loosely, and simmer for about 7 minutes. Stir in the stock, thyme, rosemary, and beans and continue to simmer until the eggplant is very tender, about 20 minutes. Serve warm, sprinkled with the cheese.

IF THE WEATHER IS HOT AND/OR DRY:
Serve with a fresh tomato and basil salad.

IF THE WEATHER IS COLD AND/OR DAMP:
Stir in a pinch of cayenne pepper just before serving.

salmon soup with garlic and ginger

energizing

140 calories per serving; 3 grams fat; 20% calories from fat

In addition to containing protein, salmon also offers tryptophan, an amino acid recommended by nutritionists to treat depression.

3 cups vegetable or fish stock	1 pound boned and skinned salmon fillet, cut into 1-inch chunks
1/4 cup mirin or dry sherry	1/3 cup sliced fresh mushrooms
4 slices fresh ginger	3 scallions, minced
3 cloves garlic, peeled and halved	

COMBINE THE STOCK, sherry, ginger, and garlic in a medium saucepan and bring to a boil. Reduce the heat to a simmer, cover loosely, and simmer for about 5 minutes.

USE A SLOTTED spoon to remove and discard the ginger and garlic, then add the salmon and mushrooms. Continue simmering, loosely covered, until the salmon is cooked through, about 5 minutes. Serve warm, sprinkled with the scallions.

Note: For the best flavor and the least amount of fat, ask for a salmon fillet from the tail end.

IF THE WEATHER IS HOT AND/OR DRY:
Serve with a mixed green salad dressed with lemon vinaigrette.

IF THE WEATHER IS COLD AND/OR DAMP:
Sprinkle with freshly ground black pepper before serving.

shiitake stock

MAKES 1 QUART STOCK, OR 4 (1-CUP) SERVINGS
30 calories per serving: no added fat

calming
energizing

This tasty and quick vegetable stock can serve as the base for any of the soups in this chapter. Japanese healers purport shiitake to be strengthening to the body as well as relaxing, and they sometimes prescribe it to help lower high blood pressure.

4½ cups water

1 bay leaf

1 clove garlic, peeled

1 medium onion, quartered (including skin)

8 dried whole shiitake mushrooms, rinsed

1 small carrot, quartered

COMBINE ALL OF the ingredients in a soup pot and bring to a boil. Reduce the heat, cover loosely, and simmer until fragrant, about 20 minutes. Strain and use in soups, stews, or sauces. To make your own soup recipe, just add your choice of 2 cups of cooked vegetables.

IF THE WEATHER IS HOT AND/OR DRY:
Use as a base for chilled soups, such as cucumber.

IF THE WEATHER IS COLD AND/OR DAMP:
Add 1 dried hot pepper to the mixture before cooking.

grilled chicken sandwiches
with sesame and chives

MAKES 4 SERVINGS
325 calories per serving: 3.5 grams fat: 9% calories from fat

In addition to being a good source of energizing protein, chicken contains B vitamins, which can perk up a sullen noon mood.

1 tablespoon fruit chutney or all-fruit apricot preserves

1 tablespoon prepared coarse-style mustard

$^1/_4$ cup fresh lemon juice

1 pound boneless, skinless chicken breast, cut into 4 pieces and pounded flat

4 large red leaf lettuce leaves

8 slices whole wheat toast

2 tablespoons toasted sesame seeds (see Note)

2 tablespoons minced fresh chives

PREPARE THE GRILL or preheat the broiler.

IN A SMALL dish, combine the chutney, mustard, and lemon juice, then spread it evenly over the chicken. Grill or broil about 5 inches away from the heat source until cooked through, about 7 minutes on each side. To test if the chicken is done, cut into it—the meat should be firm and white, with no pink meat or juices.

SET A LETTUCE leaf on each of 4 pieces of toast and place a piece of chicken on each. Sprinkle with sesame seeds and chives, cover with the remaining bread, and serve.

Note: To toast sesame seeds, place them in a dry nonstick sauté pan and heat on high, stirring constantly, until just lightly browned. Once they get hot, they'll pop, but that's okay.

IF THE WEATHER IS HOT AND/OR DRY:
Serve with an avocado and pink grapefruit salad.

IF THE WEATHER IS COLD AND/OR DAMP:
Spread the bread with mustard before building the sandwiches.

herbed tostadas with zucchini, carrot, and red onion

calming

MAKES 4 SERVINGS
175 calories per serving (with soy mozzarella): 4 grams fat: 21% calories from fat

To help combat stress, experts often advise eliminating nutrient-void junk food from the diet. These tasty tostadas are a healthful, low-fat alternative.

1 medium zucchini, grated

1 medium carrot, grated

1 medium red onion, finely minced

$^1/_2$ teaspoon freshly ground cumin seed

1 teaspoon minced fresh oregano or $^1/_2$ teaspoon dried

1 tablespoon minced fresh cilantro or parsley

1 clove garlic, mashed through a press

1 to 2 fresh jalapeño peppers, seeded, cored, and minced

6 small corn tortillas

$^1/_2$ cup grated soy mozzarella or low-fat regular mozzarella cheese

PREHEAT THE OVEN to 400 °F.

IN A MEDIUM bowl, combine the zucchini, carrot, onion, cumin, oregano, cilantro, garlic, and jalapeños. Spread the tortillas out on a large cookie sheet and divide the vegetable mixture evenly among them. Top with the mozzarella and bake in the middle of the oven until the cheese has melted, about 4 minutes. Serve warm.

IF THE WEATHER IS HOT AND/OR DRY:
Serve with chilled catnip-chamomile tea. (Per serving, steep $^1/_2$ teaspoon of each dried herb in 1 cup of boiling water, covered, for 4 minutes. Then chill and serve.)

IF THE WEATHER IS COLD AND/OR DAMP:
Serve with a spicy salsa (see page 73).

herbed salmon spread

energizing

MAKES 1 1/4 CUPS, OR 5 SERVINGS
65 calories per serving: trace of fat

The mustard in this dish makes it a source of magnesium, a mineral needed for healthy functioning of the nervous system throughout the day.

1/2 pound salmon fillet, boned and skinned	2 teaspoons minced fresh dill or 1/2 teaspoon dried
1/3 cup Faux Ricotta (page 127) or low-fat cottage cheese	2 teaspoons minced fresh chives
1 tablespoon prepared mild mustard	1 teaspoon minced fresh parsley

STEAM THE SALMON over boiling water until cooked through, about 8 minutes. When it's cool enough to handle, put the salmon in a processor or blender with the ricotta, mustard, dill, chives, and parsley, whizzing until smooth. Serve on toasted black bread or whole wheat English muffins.

IF THE WEATHER IS HOT AND/OR DRY:
Spread on cucumber and zucchini slices.

IF THE WEATHER IS COLD AND/OR DAMP:
Increase the mustard to 2 tablespoons.

pinto-buckwheat burgers

calming

Buckwheat is a good source of vitamin E, a nutrient that can help alleviate PMS stress.

1/2 cup buckwheat	2 scallions, finely chopped
1 cup vegetable stock	1 slice whole grain bread, torn into pieces
1 bay leaf	2 teaspoons reduced-sodium soy sauce
1/2 cup cooked pinto beans	1 teaspoon olive oil
1 carrot, grated	1 teaspoon minced fresh sage or
2 tablespoons minced fresh parsley	1/2 teaspoon dried

COMBINE THE BUCKWHEAT, stock, and bay leaf in a small saucepan and bring to a boil. Reduce the heat, cover loosely, and simmer until the buckwheat is tender, about 15 minutes. Discard the bay leaf.

IN A PROCESSOR or blender, combine the cooked buckwheat, beans, carrot, parsley, scallions, bread, soy sauce, olive oil, and sage whizzing until smooth, about 20 seconds.

TO SHAPE THE burgers, wet your hands and divide the mixture into 4 parts, forming each into a tight ball. Then flatten each ball into a 3 1/2-inch burger. Store, covered and refrigerated, for up to 5 days, or sizzle in a nonstick sauté pan until warmed through. Great served in pitas and topped with alfalfa sprouts.

IF THE WEATHER IS HOT AND/OR DRY:
Serve with thick slices of juicy tomato.

IF THE WEATHER IS COLD AND/OR DAMP:
Serve with Fresh Salsa (page 73).

fresh salsa

MAKES 1 CUP, OR 4 ($^1/_2$-CUP) SERVINGS

53 calories per serving; 1 gram fat; 17% calories from fat

This zesty condiment is a strengthening tonic to the nervous system.

4 plum tomatoes, seeded and chopped (including juice)

2 cloves garlic, minced

1 shallot, minced

juice of 2 limes

juice of 1 lemon

3 tablespoons minced fresh cilantro

1 teaspoon olive oil

2 jalapeño peppers, seeded, cored, and minced

pinch of sea salt

COMBINE ALL OF the ingredients in a processor or blender, whizzing until mixed well but not completely smooth. Use to spice up sandwiches such as Pinto-Buckwheat Burgers (page 72) or with baked corn chips.

IF THE WEATHER IS HOT AND/OR DRY: *Serve the salsa with a poached fish sandwich.*

IF THE WEATHER IS COLD AND/OR DAMP: *Stir in freshly ground black pepper before serving.*

garbanzo burgers

MAKES 4 BURGERS

255 calories per burger; 1 gram fat; 3% calories from fat

Chickpeas, or garbanzo beans, contain folate and iron, making this dish a mid-day immune system stimulant.

2 cups chickpeas	1 tablespoon minced fresh thyme or 1 teaspoon dried
2 cups cooked brown rice	
3 scallions, minced	1 tablespoon reduced-sodium soy sauce
2 tablespoons minced fresh parsley	$1/4$ cup egg substitute (see Note, page 13) or 2 egg whites

COMBINE ALL OF the ingredients in a processor or blender and whiz until the mixture is the consistency of hamburger meat. Using wet hands, form the mixture into 4 patties.

SPRAY A LARGE nonstick sauté pan with nonstick spray and heat on medium-high. Add the burgers and sizzle until heated through, about 4 minutes on each side. Serve on toasted whole wheat buns with mustard and red lettuce.

IF THE WEATHER IS HOT AND/OR DRY:
Serve with juicy tomato slices and chilled lemon-mint tea.

IF THE WEATHER IS COLD AND/OR DAMP:
Serve with Fresh Salsa (page 73).

black bean-veggie burgers

MAKES 8 BURGERS, OR 4 SERVINGS
176 calories per serving; 1 gram fat; 5% calories from fat

To ensure a sociable afternoon, the bay, thyme, and ginger help the beans become more digestible.

1 cup dried black beans	1 tablespoon minced fresh thyme or 1 teaspoon dried
1 bay leaf	splash of hot pepper sauce
1 slice fresh ginger	2 teaspoons balsamic vinegar
4 cups vegetable stock or water	2 teaspoons soy sauce
2 teaspoons olive oil	1/2 cup grated carrot
4 scallions, minced	
1 clove garlic, very finely minced	

COMBINE THE BEANS, bay leaf, and ginger in water to cover and soak overnight.

DRAIN THE BEANS, discarding the bay leaf and ginger. Combine the soaked beans with the stock in a large soup pot and bring to a boil. Reduce the heat, cover loosely, and simmer until the beans are tender, 40 to 45 minutes. Alternatively, you can pressure-cook the beans for 10 minutes. Either way, you'll have 2 1/2 cups of cooked beans.

PLACE THE COOKED beans in a processor or blender and puree, adding the olive oil, scallions, garlic, thyme, hot pepper sauce, vinegar, soy sauce, and carrot halfway through.

SHAPE THE MIXTURE into eight 2 1/2- to 3-inch burgers, place in a dry nonstick sauté pan, and heat on medium-high until warmed through, 2 to 3 minutes on each side. Serve warm in pitas or on whole wheat English muffins.

IF THE WEATHER IS HOT AND/OR DRY:
Pack alfalfa sprouts and thinly sliced cucumbers into the sandwich.

IF THE WEATHER IS COLD AND/OR DAMP:
Increase the garlic to 2 cloves and serve with a spicy salsa, such as Fresh Salsa (page 73).

chinese tofu salad with honey-ginger dressing

energizing

250 calories per serving; 6 grams fat; 22% calories from fat

Soybean-based tofu is a light source of protein that is easier to digest than poultry or beef, thus contributing to a more energetic afternoon.

1 cup julienned carrots

1 cup julienned bok choy

12 ounces extra-firm reduced-fat tofu, cut into 1-inch chunks

1 red bell pepper, cored, seeded, and julienned

¼ cup toasted sliced almonds

2 tablespoons rice vinegar

2 tablespoons lemon juice

1 teaspoon reduced-sodium soy sauce

2 teaspoons toasted (dark) sesame oil

1 teaspoon honey

2 teaspoons grated fresh ginger

1 teaspoon hot pepper sauce, or to taste

STEAM THE CARROTS, bok choy, and tofu over boiling water until the vegetables are just tender, about 2 minutes. This also helps the tofu become more digestible. Then toss in a large bowl with the bell pepper and almonds.

IN A SMALL bowl, whisk together the vinegar, lemon juice, soy sauce, sesame oil, honey, ginger, and hot pepper sauce. Pour over the tofu mixture and toss well to combine.

LET THE SALAD marinate for at least 30 minutes or overnight. Serve in toasted whole wheat pitas or open-faced on whole grain toast or lettuce petals.

IF THE WEATHER IS HOT AND/OR DRY:
Core and seed a large ripe tomato and spoon the salad inside.

IF THE WEATHER IS COLD AND/OR DAMP:
Instead of steaming the tofu, grill or lightly brown it in a dry nonstick sauté pan (still steam the vegetables).

tofu-basil club on a baguette

energizing

MAKES 4 SERVINGS
190 calories per serving: 3 grams fat: 14% calories from fat

The garlic and basil in the marinade can help circumvent a drowsy afternoon.

3 tablespoons lemon juice

2 teaspoons reduced-sodium soy sauce

1 clove garlic, very finely minced

1 tablespoon minced fresh basil or
  1 teaspoon dried

1 tablespoon tomato paste

12 ounces extra-firm reduced-fat tofu,
  sliced into 4 steaks

1 whole wheat baguette

1 tablespoon prepared Dijon-style mustard

red leaf lettuce or arugula for serving

IN A GLASS pie dish, combine the lemon juice, soy sauce, garlic, basil, and tomato paste, then set in the tofu steaks. Let them marinate for about 15 minutes on each side.

SIZZLE THE MARINATED tofu steaks in a dry nonstick sauté pan over medium-high heat until heated through and lightly browned, 4 to 5 minutes on each side.

MEANWHILE, SLICE THE baguette into 4 lengths, then slice each length in half. Spread with the mustard, then top with the lettuce and tofu.

IF THE WEATHER IS HOT AND/OR DRY:
Add a slice of fresh tomato to the sandwich and spread the bread with Tofu Mayo (page 82) instead of mustard.

IF THE WEATHER IS COLD AND/OR DAMP:
Add 1 teaspoon of grated ginger to the marinade and toast the bread.

dilled potato pie

calming

97 calories per slice (with soy milk, egg substitute, and Parmesan): 2 grams fat; 18% calories from fat

The dill in this mild and wholesome pie is a potent digestive restorative that can soothe even the most nervous of mid-day stomachs.

2 pounds new potatoes, cut into $1/2$-inch cubes

1 small onion, finely chopped

1 clove garlic, minced

$1^1/2$ cups chopped watercress leaves

$1/4$ cup chopped fresh parsley

1 tablespoon minced fresh dill or $1^1/2$ teaspoons dried

$1/4$ cup low-fat soy milk or regular skim milk

$3/4$ cup egg substitute (see Note, page 13) or 3 eggs

2 teaspoons olive oil

pinch of sea salt

3 tablespoons grated soy Parmesan or regular Parmesan cheese

STEAM THE POTATOES, onion, and garlic over boiling water until the potatoes are very tender, about 13 to 14 minutes. Then tip into a bowl and mash. Fold in the watercress, parsley, dill, milk, egg substitute, olive oil, and salt.

SPRAY A GLASS pie dish with nonstick spray, then spoon in the potato mixture, smoothing the top. Bake in the middle of the oven until puffed and golden, about 30 minutes. Let the pie rest for about 5 minutes, then sprinkle with Parmesan and serve.

IF THE WEATHER IS HOT AND/OR DRY:
Serve chilled with a salad of mixed greens.

IF THE WEATHER IS COLD AND/OR DAMP:
Serve warm, drizzled with Fresh Salsa (page 73).

pizza with fresh basil

calming

MAKES 8 SLICES

110 calories per slice (with soy mozzarella); 2 grams fat; 16% calories from fat

In Ayurveda, general herbalism, and aromatherapy, basil is considered a supreme nervine (see page 36) and is often recommended to alleviate mental strain during daily activity.

1 teaspoon quick-rise dry yeast (about 1/2 package)

1/2 cup warm water (about 115°F)

1 tablespoon olive oil

1/2 cup plus 2 tablespoons whole wheat pastry flour

1/2 cup plus 2 tablespoons unbleached all-purpose flour

1/2 teaspoon sea salt

1 cup chopped fresh tomato, drained

1/3 cup loosely packed fresh basil leaves

1 cup nonfat soy mozzarella or part-skim regular mozzarella cheese

PREHEAT THE OVEN to 500°F.

IN A MEDIUM bowl, combine the yeast, water, and oil and mix well. Stir in the flours and salt and mix until a cohesive dough has formed. Let the dough rest for about 5 minutes.

SPRAY A PERFORATED pizza pan or cookie sheet with nonstick spray (you can also use a pizza stone, but don't spray it). Set the dough on the pan and shape into an 11-inch round. Sprinkle with the tomato and basil, then the cheese. Bake in the middle of the oven until the crust has cooked through, about 12 minutes. Slice with kitchen shears before serving.

IF THE WEATHER IS HOT AND/OR DRY:
Serve with a beverage made of half brewed peppermint tea and half sparkling water.

IF THE WEATHER IS COLD AND/OR DAMP:
Double the garlic and add crushed dried hot pepper to taste.

energizing sandwich spread

MAKES 2 CUPS, OR 8 (¼-CUP) SERVINGS
58 calories per serving; 1.4 grams fat; 20% calories from fat

In addition to the invigorating high-protein tofu, this mid-day bracer contains garlic, onion, mustard, lemon, nettle, and hot pepper sauce—all considered to be mildly stimulating.

2 medium carrots, sliced

1 small onion, sliced

2 cloves garlic, peeled and coarsely chopped

10½ ounces silky-textured low-fat tofu

1 teaspoon white miso

1 teaspoon prepared Dijon-style mustard

2 teaspoons tahini or sesame paste

2 tablespoons fresh lemon juice

1 tablespoon minced fresh oregano or 1 teaspoon dried

1 teaspoon dried nettle

½ teaspoon hot pepper sauce, or to taste

½ teaspoon reduced-sodium soy sauce, or to taste

STEAM THE CARROTS, onion, garlic, and tofu over boiling water until just tender, about 6 minutes.

TRANSFER THE STEAMED foods to a processor or blender and whiz until smooth, adding the miso, mustard, tahini, lemon juice, oregano, nettle, hot pepper sauce, and soy sauce halfway through. Cover and refrigerate the spread for at least 2 hours to give the flavors time to become acquainted.

IF THE WEATHER IS HOT AND/OR DRY:
Serve as a dip with a platter of fresh vegetables.

IF THE WEATHER IS COLD AND/OR DAMP:
Increase the hot pepper sauce to taste and use as a sandwich spread for toasted whole grain flatbreads.

white bean hummus with tuomato and fresh basil

Lemon, a predominant flavor in this spread, is often recommended as a pacifier for acute anxiety.

2 to 3 cloves garlic	1 slice whole wheat bread, crumbled
¹/₂ cup vegetable stock	2 ripe medium tomatoes, chopped (including juice)
1 slice fresh ginger	
1 bay leaf	1 tablespoon minced fresh basil or 1 teaspoon dried
3 cups cooked white beans	pinch of sea salt
Juice of 1 lemon	freshly ground black pepper

IN A SMALL saucepan, combine the garlic, stock, ginger, and bay leaf and bring to a boil. Reduce the heat and simmer until the garlic is tender, about 8 minutes. Discard the ginger and bay leaf and place the stock and garlic in a processor or blender along with the beans, lemon juice, bread, tomatoes, basil, salt, and pepper; process until smooth.

IF THE WEATHER IS HOT AND/OR DRY:
Use the lesser amount of garlic and serve the hummus as a filling for hollowed-out fresh tomatoes.

IF THE WEATHER IS COLD AND/OR DAMP:
Use the greater amount of garlic and serve on toasted pitas or spread on cornbread as an open-faced sandwich.

tofu mayo

MAKES ABOUT ⅔ CUP, OR 4 (2½-TABLESPOON) SERVINGS
65 calories per serving: 1.5 grams fat; 21% calories from fat

Most mayonnaise is predominantly composed of saturated fats that can inhibit the brain's neurotransmitters, resulting in a sluggish afternoon for those who partake. This mayo is made from energizing low-fat tofu and has the opposite effect.

6 ounces soft-textured low-fat tofu	1 tablespoon lemon juice
1 tablespoon cider vinegar	2 teaspoons prepared Dijon-style mustard

COMBINE ALL OF the ingredients in a processor or blender and whiz until smooth. Spoon into a jar and store, refrigerated, for up to a week.

IF THE WEATHER IS HOT AND/OR DRY:
Add a tablespoon each of minced fresh dill and chives or 1 teaspoon toasted (dark) sesame oil to the recipe.

IF THE WEATHER IS COLD AND/OR DAMP:
Add 2 teaspoons (or to taste) hot pepper sauce or 2 teaspoons (or to taste) good-quality curry powder to the recipe.

one-hour whole wheat sage and garlic bread

calming

MAKES 1 LOAF, OR 8 SERVINGS
244 calories per serving; 2.75 grams fat; 11% calories from fat

Sage is often recommended by German and English herbalists as an antidote to daytime mental strain.

2 cups whole wheat bread flour

2 cups unbleached all-purpose flour

$^1/_2$ teaspoon sea salt

1 tablespoon baking powder

$^1/_2$ teaspoon baking soda

1 tablespoon barley malt

2 cups (approximately) plain low-fat soy milk or buttermilk

1 tablespoon olive oil

2 tablespoons minced fresh sage

1 to 2 cloves garlic, finely minced

PREHEAT THE OVEN to 425°F.

COMBINE THE FLOURS in a large bowl and stir in the salt, baking powder, and baking soda.

IN A MEDIUM bowl, whisk together the barley malt, soy milk, olive oil, sage, and garlic, then pour into the flour mixture and mix well. When the dough becomes too sticky to stir, use your hands to continue mixing, kneading just until the dough is smooth and the ingredients are well combined.

SET THE DOUGH on a parchment-lined cookie sheet and shape it into a round loaf about 8 inches in diameter. Use a large knife to slash an "X" in the top to prevent the loaf from cracking as it bakes. Bake in the middle of the oven until cooked through, 40 to 45 minutes. Let the bread cool on a wire rack before slicing.

IF THE WEATHER IS HOT AND/OR DRY:
Add a pinch of saffron to the liquid ingredients before whisking.

IF THE WEATHER IS COLD AND/OR DAMP:
Use the greater amount of garlic and add freshly ground black pepper to taste before mixing.

fresh daikon pickle, korean style

energizing

MAKES 6 SERVINGS
32 calories per serving: 1 gram fat; 28% calories from fat

This is a variation of *kimchi*, which is served in Korea to accompany any meal, even rice porridge at breakfast. Try it as a bracing accompaniment to a sandwich or salad. The garlic, ginger, and hot chilies act as mild stimulants, both to the mind and to the digestive system. In addition, Chinese doctors advise eating daikon radish to help the body process energy-robbing fats. If you don't have daikon radish, any type of radish, including red garden radishes, will have the same taste and effect.

2 scallions, finely minced	1 teaspoon *nam pla* (Thai fish sauce)
4 cloves garlic, finely minced	1 tablespoon fresh lime juice
1 tablespoon minced fresh ginger	1 teaspoon toasted (dark) sesame oil
2 teaspoons hot pepper sauce, or to taste	1 10-inch fresh daikon radish, shredded (see The Savory Pantry, page 423)
1 teaspoon barley malt	
2 tablespoons rice vinegar or cider vinegar	

IN A MEDIUM bowl, combine the scallions, garlic, ginger, hot pepper sauce, barley malt, rice vinegar, fish sauce, lime juice, and sesame oil, stirring well to combine. Add the shredded daikon radish and toss to combine, making sure that all the shreds have been bathed in the mixture.

IF THE WEATHER IS HOT AND/OR DRY:
Serve as an accompaniment to a mixed green salad.

IF THE WEATHER IS COLD AND/OR DAMP:
Eliminate the lime juice.

potato salad with watercress and smoked trout

energizing

MAKES 4 SERVINGS

190 calories per serving; 3 grams fat; 14% calories from fats

Watercress has been used as a mild stimulant since ancient Greek and Roman times, and its consumption is still advised in France, England, and Germany as an appetite and digestive stimulant.

1 pound new potatoes, quartered

1 bay leaf

1 cup chopped fresh asparagus

2 cups fresh watercress leaves

juice of $^1/_2$ lemon

2 teaspoons olive oil

4 ounces smoked trout, finely chopped

2 scallions, finely minced

STEAM THE POTATOES over bay-scented water (drop the leaf in the water before boiling) until not quite tender, about 8 minutes. At that point, add the asparagus to the steamer and continue to steam until the potatoes and asparagus are tender, about 2 minutes more. Pat dry and toss with the watercress.

WHISK TOGETHER THE lemon juice and olive oil, then stir in the trout, scallions, and potato mixture. Serve warm or chilled.

IF THE WEATHER IS HOT AND/OR DRY:
Serve chilled with iced mint tea.

IF THE WEATHER IS COLD AND/OR DAMP:
Serve warm with a sprinkle of freshly ground black pepper.

calming

wild rice salad with lavender

MAKES 4 LARGE SERVINGS
255 calories per serving: 4 grams fat: 16% calories from fat

Those who suffer from lunchtime stress headaches may find relief from the lavender and rosemary in this aromatic dish.

³/₄ cup brown rice

¹/₂ cup wild rice

1¹/₂ cups vegetable stock

pinch of sea salt

1 bay leaf

4 scallions, minced

1 carrot, coarsely grated

2 tablespoons minced fresh lavender flowers (available at specialty food stores) or 2 tablespoons minced fresh rosemary (see Note)

¹/₂ teaspoon minced fresh rosemary leaves

1 tablespoon olive oil

1¹/₂ teaspoons balsamic vinegar

1¹/₂ teaspoons lemon juice

1 teaspoon prepared Dijon-style mustard

IN A LARGE pot, combine the brown rice, wild rice, stock, salt, and bay leaf and bring to a boil. Reduce the heat, cover loosely, and simmer until the rices are tender, about 50 minutes. Alternatively, you can pressure-cook the rices according to manufacturer's instructions for about 30 minutes. Let the rice cool to room temperature, then stir in the scallions and carrot.

MEANWHILE, WHISK TOGETHER the lavender flowers, rosemary, olive oil, vinegar, lemon juice, and mustard. Pour over the rice mixture and toss well to combine.

Note: If fresh lavender flowers are unavailable, substitute 2 tablespoons of minced fresh rosemary leaves (for a total of 2 tablespoons plus ¹/₂ teaspoon).

IF THE WEATHER IS HOT AND/OR DRY:
Serve slightly chilled on a bed of crisp mixed greens.

IF THE WEATHER IS COLD AND/OR DAMP:
Add 1 clove of minced fresh garlic to the dressing and serve warm.

mixed greens with orange, radish, and whole wheat croutons

calming

MAKES 4 SERVINGS
138 calories per serving: 3 grams fat. 20% calories from fat

Normal morning stress can play a negative role in your body's ability to combat diseases such as colds and flu. This lunch salad, however, may help dilute those effects by offering ample immune protection in the form of beta carotene and vitamin C.

6 cups mixed greens, such as red oak, romaine, radicchio, and dandelion

1/4 cup fresh cilantro leaves or parsley leaves

5 red radishes, thinly sliced

1 orange, peeled, seeded, sectioned, and chopped

4 slices whole wheat bread, cut into irregular 2-inch pieces

3 tablespoons prepared Dijon-style mustard

2 teaspoons olive oil

1 tablespoon balsamic vinegar

freshly ground black pepper

IN A LARGE salad bowl, combine the greens, cilantro, radishes, and orange.

TOSS THE BREAD in a second bowl, add the mustard, and toss well to combine. Transfer the coated bread to a large nonstick sauté pan and heat on medium-high, stirring constantly, until lightly browned, 2 to 3 minutes.

IN A SMALL bowl, whisk together the olive oil, vinegar, and pepper. Pour over the greens and toss well to combine, about 30 times, then add the croutons and toss. Don't store.

IF THE WEATHER IS HOT AND/OR DRY:
Use two oranges instead of one.

IF THE WEATHER IS COLD AND/OR DAMP:
Use parsley instead of cilantro and add a clove of finely minced garlic to the dressing.

chopped vegetable salad with oregano and lemon

calming

50 calories per serving: 1 gram fat; 18% calories from fat

Mild, aromatic oregano is an old folk remedy for soothing daytime headaches and stomachaches that are caused by stress.

2 green bell peppers, cored, seeded, and finely chopped

1 large cucumber, peeled, seeded, and finely chopped

2 ripe medium tomatoes, cored and finely chopped

4 large green olives, pitted and minced

2 scallions, minced

1 tablespoon minced fresh oregano or 1 1/2 teaspoons dried

2 tablespoons fresh lemon juice

freshly ground black pepper to taste

red leaf lettuce leaves for serving

IN A MEDIUM bowl, combine the peppers, cucumber, tomatoes, olives, scallions, oregano, lemon juice, and pepper and toss well. Place on nests of lettuce leaves and serve as a side dish to spicy soups, stews, or couscous dishes.

IF THE WEATHER IS HOT AND/OR DRY:
Garnish with fresh cilantro leaves.

IF THE WEATHER IS COLD AND/OR DAMP:
Add 1 teaspoon (or to taste) hot pepper sauce.

spicy potato salad

calming

When scallions are eaten regularly, the mild sulfur compounds they contain serve as a potent heart tonic and may help regulate stress-induced high blood pressure.

2 pounds waxy-type potatoes, cut into 1-inch chunks

2 teaspoons olive oil

1 shallot, finely chopped

2 cloves garlic, minced

1/2 teaspoon finely grated fresh ginger

1 teaspoon ground turmeric

1 teaspoon ground coriander

1 roasted red bell pepper, finely chopped (see Note)

1/4 cup lemon juice

8 scallions, minced

cayenne pepper to taste

sea salt to taste

freshly ground black pepper to taste

STEAM THE POTATOES over boiling water until tender, 12 to 14 minutes, then pat dry.

POUR THE OLIVE oil into a nonstick sauté pan and heat on medium-high. Add the shallot, garlic, ginger, turmeric, and coriander and sauté, stirring constantly, until the mixture is warm and fragrant, 3 to 4 minutes. Scoop it over the potatoes, add the roasted pepper, lemon juice, scallions, cayenne, salt, and black pepper, and combine well. Serve warm or chilled.

Note: To roast peppers, core and seed them, then set them on a cookie sheet under the broiler, roasting until all sides are charred. Put the peppers in a covered bowl and let them cool. Remove the skins with your fingers or a sharp paring knife and discard.

IF THE WEATHER IS HOT AND/OR DRY:
Reduce the garlic to 1 clove and use 2 roasted peppers.

IF THE WEATHER IS COLD AND/OR DAMP:
Be generous with the black pepper.

mashed potatoes with garlic and scallion

MAKES 4 SIDE SERVINGS
205 calories per serving; 3.5 grams fat; 16% calories from fat

B oth garlic and scallions are beneficial noontime bracers, gently providing energy by stimulating circulation.

1 ½ pounds potatoes, peeled and chopped into 1-inch pieces

3 cloves garlic, minced

1 shallot, minced

4 scallions, finely minced

1 tablespoon olive oil

pinch of sea salt

STEAM THE POTATOES, garlic, and shallot over boiling water until the potatoes are tender, 12 to 14 minutes. Place in a large bowl and mash by hand, adding the scallions, olive oil, and salt partway through. Serve warm.

IF THE WEATHER IS HOT AND/OR DRY:
Reduce the amount of garlic to 2 cloves and omit the shallot.

IF THE WEATHER IS COLD AND/OR DAMP:
Add freshly ground black pepper while mashing.

asparagus with lemon-garlic paste

calming

MAKES 4 SERVINGS
75 calories per serving: 2 grams fat; 22% calories from fat

Those who feel bloated, either from PMS or from a salty breakfast, will find relief in this tasty salad. Asparagus contains a compound called asparagine, which stimulates kidney function, thus acting as a natural diuretic.

1 pound asparagus, trimmed

2 cloves garlic, peeled and halved

3 tablespoons vegetable stock

2 teaspoons olive oil

2 tablespoons lemon juice

pinch of cayenne pepper

pinch of sea salt

STEAM THE ASPARAGUS and garlic over boiling water until the asparagus is tender, 4 to 5 minutes. Remove the garlic to a spice grinder or mortar, add the stock, olive oil, lemon juice, cayenne, and salt, and grind until you have a smooth paste. Toss with the asparagus and serve warm or chilled.

IF THE WEATHER IS HOT AND/OR DRY:
Serve chilled with lemon wedges for drizzling. Great with chilled poached salmon.

IF THE WEATHER IS COLD AND/OR DAMP:
Serve warm, sprinkling with freshly ground black pepper.

mixed greens with sea herbs and sesame-lime dressing

calming

MAKES 4 SERVINGS

80 calories per serving: 2 grams fat: 22% calories from fat

Sea herbs contain the stress-reducing minerals calcium and magnesium. Sea herbs also are prescribed regularly in Japan to fight obesity.

½ cup very loosely packed dried arame sea herb (see The Savory Pantry. page 422)

1 cup vegetable stock

1 slice fresh ginger

juice of 1 lime

2 teaspoons toasted (dark) sesame oil

1 teaspoon prepared coarse-style mustard

5 cups mixed greens

4 scallions, minced

RINSE THE ARAME well under running water, then combine with the stock and ginger in a small saucepan and bring to a boil. Reduce the heat, cover loosely, and simmer until the arame is tender, 15 to 20 minutes. Drain and discard the ginger.

IN A SMALL bowl, whisk together the lime juice, sesame oil, and mustard, then pour over the cooked arame. Combine well.

IN A SALAD bowl, combine the greens and scallions, add the arame mixture, and toss well to combine, about 30 times.

IF THE WEATHER IS HOT AND/OR DRY:

Add some watercress to the mixed greens or top the salad with a bit of chopped avocado.

IF THE WEATHER IS COLD AND/OR DAMP:

Add some mustard greens to the mixed greens or top the salad with a bit of chopped artichoke heart.

spring greens with pea shoots

calming

75 calories per serving; 2 grams fat; 22% calories from fat

Merely glancing at this sprightly salad may help to relieve stress. Since the color green is neither hot nor cold, it has a calming effect on many people, much like a landscape of gently rolling hills.

4 cups mixed spring greens, such as mustard, dandelion, and watercress

1 cup pea shoots or other sprouts

1 carrot 3 red radishes, thinly sliced

1 tablespoon balsamic vinegar

1 tablespoon lemon juice

2 teaspoons sesame oil

IN A SALAD bowl, combine the greens and pea shoots. Use a cheese slicer or potato peeler to slice the carrot into thin ribbons and add them to the salad along with the radishes.

IN A SMALL bowl, whisk together the vinegar, lemon juice, and sesame oil. Pour over the salad and toss well to combine—about 30 times should do.

IF THE WEATHER IS HOT AND/OR DRY:
Serve with a grilled tofu steak or Chinese Tofu Salad with Honey-Ginger Dressing (page 76).

IF THE WEATHER IS COLD AND/OR DAMP:
Serve with spicy beans, such as Black Bean-Veggie Burgers (page 75).

calming potato salad with tomatoes and fresh basil

MAKES 4 SERVINGS
165 calories per serving; 3.5 grams fat; 19% calories from fat

Eating potatoes, the great American comfort food, is often associated with the soothing of jagged nerves. Although the practice is without scientific validation in the West, in Russia steamed potatoes are a common remedy for nerve-induced asthma.

1 pound new potatoes, cut into 1-inch pieces

1 pound ripe tomatoes (2 large), cut into chunks (including juice)

¼ cup minced fresh basil

1 tablespoon olive oil

pinch of sea salt

freshly ground black pepper

STEAM THE POTATOES over boiling water until tender, 12 to 14 minutes. Drain, pat dry, and place in a large bowl.

ADD THE TOMATOES, basil, olive oil, salt, and pepper and toss well to combine. Serve warm or very slightly chilled.

IF THE WEATHER IS HOT AND/OR DRY:
Use half minced fresh peppermint and half minced fresh basil instead of all basil.

IF THE WEATHER IS COLD AND/OR DAMP:
Add a seeded, cored, and minced fresh jalapeño pepper to the salad before combining.

cucumber spears with citrus and soy

calming

MAKES 4 SERVINGS

54 calories per serving: 1 gram fat: 17% calories from fat

This is a suitable side dish for those who suffer from high blood pressure, as well as those who have noontime stress, since cucumber is a natural diuretic.

1 pound cucumbers, peeled and sliced into spears

1 onion, thinly sliced and separated into rings

juice of 1 orange

juice of 1 lemon

juice of 1 lime

2 teaspoons reduced-sodium soy sauce

1 teaspoon toasted (dark) sesame oil

1 teaspoon hot pepper sauce, or to taste

2 tablespoons rice vinegar

freshly ground black pepper

COMBINE ALL OF of the ingredients in a medium bowl and toss well to combine. Cover and let marinate, refrigerated, for at least 1 hour.

IF THE WEATHER IS HOT AND/OR DRY: *Garnish with minced fresh cilantro before serving.*

IF THE WEATHER IS COLD AND/OR DAMP: *Add 1 clove of minced garlic to the recipe and garnish before serving with minced fresh chives.*

fresh tuna salad with tomato and capers

calming

MAKES 4 SERVINGS
165 calories per serving: 1 gram fat; 6% calories from fat

Fresh onion, such as the Vidalia used here, is recommended by Ayurvedic healers as a stimulant and to promote a clear consciousness.

2 ripe tomatoes, chopped (including juice)

1 Vidalia onion, minced

1 teaspoon balsamic vinegar

pinch of dried hot red pepper flakes

1 teaspoon capers, minced

1 tablespoon minced fresh basil

1 tablespoon prepared Dijon-style mustard

1 tablespoon vegetable stock

1 pound fresh tuna steak, dark part removed

COMBINE THE TOMATOES, onion, vinegar, red pepper flakes, capers, and basil in a medium bowl and let marinate at room temperature for about 1 hour.

MEANWHILE, PREPARE THE grill or preheat the broiler. Whisk together the mustard and stock and paint the mixture onto the tuna. Grill or broil 4½ inches from the heat source until just cooked through, about 4 minutes on each side.

WHEN THE TUNA is cool enough to handle, cut or shred it into bite-sized pieces right into the tomato mixture and toss to combine. Serve warm or very slightly chilled as a sandwich filling or on a bed of interesting lettuces.

IF THE WEATHER IS HOT AND/OR DRY:
Serve chilled with an accompaniment of peppermint or lemongrass tea.

IF THE WEATHER IS COLD AND/OR DAMP:
Serve warm on crusty whole wheat rolls.

aduki bean salad with lemon-ginger dressing

calming

MAKES 4 SERVINGS

140 calories per serving: 2.6 grams fat: 16% calories from fat

Ancient Sanskrit texts say that ginger should be eaten at every meal to balance the mood and encourage digestion.

¹/₂ cup dried aduki beans	juice of ¹/₂ lemon
1¹/₂ cups vegetable stock	2 teaspoons olive oil
1 bay leaf	3 tablespoons minced fresh basil
1 slice fresh ginger	1 teaspoon finely grated fresh ginger
¹/₂ pound green beans, cut into 1-inch pieces and blanched for 1 minute	¹/₄ teaspoon hot pepper sauce, or to taste
1 carrot, coarsely grated	pinch of sea salt
2 scallions, minced	2 cups torn red leaf lettuce

COMBINE THE BEANS, stock, bay leaf, and slice of ginger in a medium saucepan and bring to a boil. Reduce the heat, cover loosely, and simmer until the beans are tender, about 55 minutes. Drain and discard the bay leaf and ginger slice.

PLACE THE COOKED aduki beans in a medium bowl, add the green beans, carrot, scallions, lemon juice, olive oil, basil, grated ginger, hot pepper sauce, and salt and stir well to combine. Serve warm or chilled atop the lettuce.

IF THE WEATHER IS HOT AND/OR DRY:
Serve with lemon wedges for drizzling or garnish with minced fresh cilantro.

IF THE WEATHER IS COLD AND/OR DAMP:
Serve warm, topped with toasted sesame seeds or toasted cumin seeds.

beans and grains

lentils with fragrant spice paste

MAKES 1 3/4 CUPS, OR 14 (2-TABLESPOON) SERVINGS
35 calories per serving; less than 1 gram fat

The turmeric helps to make the lentils nearly gas-free, thus creating a more comfortable afternoon for those who enjoy this fragrant condiment. On the folklore side, Indian sages proclaim turmeric to banish evil spirits, so it is a popular ingredient in ritual tonics.

1/2 cup dried lentils	1/2 teaspoon ground turmeric
1 1/2 cups vegetable stock	1 clove garlic, minced
1 bay leaf	1/4 teaspoon dried lemongrass
1 slice fresh ginger	1 teaspoon reduced-sodium soy sauce
2 teaspoons olive oil	1 tablespoon tomato paste
1 teaspoon coriander seed, crushed	1/3 cup brewed tea
1 teaspoon cumin seed, crushed	

TO COOK THE lentils, place them in a medium saucepan with the stock, bay leaf, and ginger. Bring to a boil, reduce the heat, cover loosely, and simmer until the lentils are tender, about 40 minutes.

MEANWHILE, HEAT A large nonstick sauté pan on medium-high and pour in the oil. Add the coriander seed, cumin seed, turmeric, garlic, lemongrass, soy sauce, and tomato paste and sauté, stirring frequently, until the spices are very fragrant, about 5 minutes. Pour in the tea and boil, stirring constantly, until the spice paste is thick, about 2 minutes.

WHEN THE LENTILS are ready, discard the bay leaf and ginger and drain. Swirl in the spice paste and combine well. Serve as a condiment for such bland foods as grilled tofu.

Note: To turn this into a quick dish to combat a sluggish disposition, serve it with cooked brown rice, using 2 tablespoons of lentils for each 1/2 cup of rice.

IF THE WEATHER IS HOT AND/OR DRY:
Serve with a side dish of sliced cucumbers garnished with minced fresh mint.

IF THE WEATHER IS COLD AND/OR DAMP:
During sautéing, add crushed hot red pepper to taste.

cracked wheat with fresh herbs

calming

MAKES 4 LARGE SERVINGS

141 calories per serving: 3.5 grams fat: 22% calories from fat

Consuming such grains as whole wheat can prevent constipation and nervous disorders associated with stress.

1 cup cracked wheat	$^1/_4$ cup minced fresh basil
2 cups vegetable stock	$^1/_2$ cup minced fresh parsley
$^1/_2$ teaspoon cumin seed	2 tablespoons minced fresh oregano or 1 teaspoon dried
1 bay leaf	
pinch of sea salt	2 tablespoons minced fresh chives
6 asparagus spears, cut into 1-inch pieces	juice of 1 lemon
2 carrots, chopped	1 tablespoon olive oil
1 small zucchini, chopped	freshly ground black pepper to taste

COMBINE THE CRACKED wheat, stock, cumin seed, bay leaf, and salt in a small saucepan and bring to a boil. Reduce the heat, cover loosely, and simmer for about 10 minutes. Add the asparagus, carrots, and zucchini, cover, and continue to simmer until all of the ingredients are tender, about 5 minutes more. Drain if necessary.

STIR IN THE basil, parsley, oregano, chives, lemon juice, olive oil, and pepper and serve warm or very slightly chilled.

IF THE WEATHER IS HOT AND/OR DRY:
Stir in $^1/_4$ cup finely chopped water chestnuts before serving.

IF THE WEATHER IS COLD AND/OR DAMP:
Add $^1/_4$ cup finely chopped fresh cabbage to the steamer when you add the asparagus.

buckwheat with roasted peppers and fresh sage

calming

Buckwheat is considered a restorative in such countries as Russia and Poland. Scientific research concurs, revealing that buckwheat can offer the much-needed B vitamins to a stressed body.

$^1/_2$ cup roasted buckwheat groats

1 cup vegetable stock

1 bay leaf

pinch of sea salt

2 cloves garlic. finely minced

2 teaspoons olive oil

2 large roasted red bell peppers. thinly sliced (see Note. page 89)

juice of 1 lemon

2 teaspoons minced fresh sage or 1 teaspoon dried

2 teaspoons minced fresh thyme or 1 teaspoon dried

$^1/_4$ cup minced fresh parsley

COMBINE THE BUCKWHEAT. stock, bay leaf, and salt in a medium saucepan and bring to a boil. Reduce the heat, cover loosely, and simmer until the buckwheat is tender, about 15 minutes.

STIR IN THE garlic, olive oil, roasted peppers, lemon juice, sage, thyme, and parsley and serve warm or at room temperature.

IF WEATHER IS HOT AND/OR DRY:
Add the garlic to the buckwheat during cooking. as well as a pinch of saffron.

IF THE WEATHER IS COLD AND/OR DAMP:
Add a minced leek to the buckwheat during cooking.

rice rolls

Some Buddhist monks eat brown rice during periods of intense meditation because it makes them relaxed and inspired. One reason may be that brown rice contains nerve-soothing B vitamins that are lacking in the more refined white rice.

2 cups short-grain brown rice

2 1/2 cups water

pinch of sea salt

water and vinegar for stick-free rolling

2 teaspoons *umeboshi* plum paste (see The Savory Pantry, page 426)

3 tablespoons ground dried sea herbs, such as kelp, dulse, nori, or arame (see The Savory Pantry, page 422)

3 tablespoons sesame seeds, toasted (see Note, page 69)

COMBINE THE RICE, water, and salt in a large saucepan and bring to a boil. Reduce the heat, cover, and simmer until the rice is tender, about 50 minutes. Let the rice cool until comfortable to handle.

POUR ABOUT 1 cup of water into a bowl and add 2 tablespoons of vinegar. This mixture, called *tezu* in Japan, will keep the rice from sticking to your hands while you roll it. Dip your hands in the tezu, then grab a handful of rice, about 1/2 cup, and begin to form a firm ball. Use a finger to make a hole in the rice ball, clear to the center, and stick in a bit of plum paste. Plug the hole and re-form the ball.

WHEN ALL THE balls are formed (you'll have 8), spread out a sheet of waxed paper and sprinkle the sea herbs and sesame seed on it. Roll each ball in the mixture until lightly covered. Enjoy with soup, such as Carrot Soup with Light Miso and Ginger (page 62). The rolls will keep, covered and refrigerated, for up to 1 week.

IF THE WEATHER IS HOT AND/OR DRY:
Serve with a cress and cucumber salad.

IF THE WEATHER IS COLD AND/OR DAMP:
Omit the sea herbs and use an equal amount of minced fresh chives.

seitan with sugar snaps

calming

250 calories per serving: 2 grams fat: 7% calories from fat

Seitan, which is a meaty-textured food made from wheat, was created by Buddhist monks as a substitute for beef, pork, and poultry. Because seitan lacks the fats and toxins that many animals products contain, it creates less stress on the immune and digestive systems. In addition, seitan is a good source of stress-soothing B vitamins.

1 teaspoon olive oil

1 small onion, thinly sliced

1 clove garlic, minced

12 ounces seitan, sliced (see The Savory Pantry, page 425)

2 cups sugar snap peas, strings removed

1 tablespoon mirin or dry sherry

1 tablespoon reduced-sodium soy sauce

2 tablespoons lemon juice

2 tablespoons vegetable stock or water

1 teaspoon toasted (dark) sesame oil

1 teaspoon arrowroot

2 scallions, minced

HEAT THE OLIVE oil in a large nonstick sauté pan on medium-high, then add the onion, garlic, and seitan and sauté for about 3 minutes. Toss in the peas and continue to sauté for about 3 minutes more.

MEANWHILE, IN A small bowl, whisk together the mirin, soy sauce, lemon juice, stock, sesame oil, and arrowroot. Pour into the seitan mixture and sauté and stir until the liquid has become shiny and slightly thickened. Remove from the heat and sprinkle with the scallions before serving warm.

IF THE WEATHER IS HOT AND/OR DRY:
Add 1/2 cup of thinly sliced fresh mushrooms when you add the peas.

IF THE WEATHER IS COLD AND/OR DAMP:
Add 1/2 teaspoon grated fresh ginger when you add the garlic.

tempeh-sweet potato stew

energizing

186 calories per serving; 4 grams fat; 18% calories from fat

Tempeh is made from soybeans, sometimes with the addition of such grains as rice and millet, and pressed into meaty slabs for use in stir-fries and kabobs in place of meat. Tempeh was created in Indonesia as a way to provide vegetarians with an agreeable high-energy food.

Another ingredient in this dish is the sweet potato, which in Chinese medicine is said to cool and soothe an irritated stomach.

2 teaspoons olive oil

1 onion, thinly sliced

2 cloves garlic, minced

8 ounces tempeh, thinly sliced (see The Savory Pantry, page 426)

3½ cups vegetable stock

1 large sweet potato (about 10 ounces), cut into ½-inch pieces

4 dried shiitake mushrooms, crumbled

4 dried tomatoes, minced

1 tablespoon reduced-sodium soy sauce

1 tablespoon minced fresh oregano or 1 teaspoon dried

pinch of saffron threads, crumbled

2 teaspoons dried nettle (see The Savory Pantry, page 424)

2 teaspoons arrowroot

1 tablespoon red miso (see The Savory Pantry, page 424)

2 tablespoons water

IN A LARGE soup pot, heat the oil on medium-high. Add the onion, garlic, and tempeh and sauté for 5 minutes. Pour in the stock, then add the sweet potato, mushrooms, tomatoes, soy sauce, oregano, saffron, and nettle. Bring to a boil, reduce the heat, cover loosely, and simmer for about 35 minutes.

MEANWHILE, IN A small bowl, whisk together the arrowroot, miso, and water. When the stew is ready, remove the pot from the heat and stir in the miso mixture. Serve warm.

IF THE WEATHER IS HOT AND/OR DRY:
Add 1 cup of cubed eggplant when you add the stock and increase the stock to 4 cups. Garnish the stew with minced fresh cilantro.

IF THE WEATHER IS COLD AND/OR DAMP:
Garnish the stew with minced fresh scallions.

lemony rice with saffron and fresh peas

calming

220 calories per serving (with soy Parmesan); 5.5 grams fat; 10% calories from fat

Ayurvedic healers recommend saffron to soothe premenstrual tension as well as during meditation to "purify the mind."

1 tablespoon olive oil

1 shallot, finely minced

1 clove garlic, finely minced

$1^{1}/_{4}$ cups arborio rice

$1^{3}/_{4}$ cups vegetable stock

$^{1}/_{4}$ cup lemon juice

pinch of saffron threads

$^{3}/_{4}$ cup shelled fresh peas

$^{1}/_{4}$ cup grated soy Parmesan or regular Parmesan cheese

pinch of sea salt

freshly ground black pepper

$^{1}/_{4}$ cup minced fresh basil

2 scallions, finely minced

PREHEAT A LARGE saucepan on medium-high, then add the oil. When the oil is warm, toss in the shallot and garlic and sauté until wilted and fragrant, about 2 minutes. Add the rice, stock, lemon juice, and saffron and bring to a boil. Reduce the heat, cover loosely, and simmer for about 6 minutes. Add the peas and continue to simmer until tender, about 6 more minutes. Add the Parmesan, sea salt, pepper, and basil and let rest off the heat, covered, for about 4 minutes. Serve warm, sprinkled with the scallions.

IF THE WEATHER IS HOT AND/OR DRY:
Add $^{1}/_{2}$ cup corn kernels when you add the peas.

IF THE WEATHER IS COLD AND/OR DAMP:
Increase the garlic to 2 cloves and add 1 grated carrot when you add the peas.

creamy cucumber and
cracked wheat salad

calming

Fragrant with mint, this mild salad calms and refreshes nerves and digestion.

2 cups hot vegetable stock or water	3 tablespoons minced fresh mint
1 cup cracked wheat	1 tablespoon minced fresh chives
1/4 cup celery, minced	1/2 cup plain low-fat soy yogurt or nonfat regular yogurt
2 cucumbers, peeled, seeded, and finely chopped	1 teaspoon prepared Dijon-style mustard
1 medium tomato, finely chopped	1 clove garlic, very finely minced
1 scallion, minced	pinch of sea salt
2 tablespoons minced fresh parsley	freshly ground black pepper

COMBINE THE STOCK and wheat in a medium bowl, cover, and let stand until the wheat is soft and most of the stock has been absorbed, about 30 minutes.

MEANWHILE, IN A second bowl, combine the celery, cucumbers, tomato, scallion, parsley, mint, chives, yogurt, mustard, garlic, salt, and pepper. When the wheat is ready, drain off any excess stock, top with the yogurt mixture, and toss well to combine. Serve at room temperature or slightly chilled.

IF THE WEATHER IS HOT AND/OR DRY:	IF THE WEATHER IS COLD AND/OR DAMP:
Serve with chilled mint tea.	*Double the mustard and garlic and add 1 teaspoon of hot pepper sauce.*

chilled noodles with miso-basil pesto

260 calories per serving: 8.7 grams fat; 30% calories from fat

Ayurvedic experts prescribe basil to rejuvenate a stressed attitude and promote mental acuity.

4 cups (not packed) fresh basil leaves	$^1/_4$ cup toasted sunflower seeds
1 cup fresh parsley leaves	$^1/_4$ cup vegetable stock or water
2 tablespoons olive oil	1 pound thin whole wheat or buckwheat
2 cloves garlic, minced	spaghetti, cooked and chilled
2 tablespoons light miso, such as chickpea (see The Savory Pantry, page, 424)	

IN A PROCESSOR or blender, combine the basil, parsley, olive oil, garlic, miso, sunflower seeds, and stock and process until smooth.

SCOOP THE PESTO onto the spaghetti and toss well to combine.

IF THE WEATHER IS HOT AND/OR DRY:
Serve with a fresh tomato salad.

IF THE WEATHER IS COLD AND/OR DAMP:
Double the garlic and serve the noodles at room temperature.

elbows with dandelion greens

265 calories per serving (with soy Parmesan): 3 grams fat: 10% calories from fat

Dandelion is often prescribed by European herbalists as a diuretic for people with high blood pressure. Unlike some blood pressure medications, dandelion does not deplete the body's potassium. Although all high blood pressure conditions should be reviewed by a health professional, anyone can enjoy this nutrient-rich dish as a satisfying mid-day boost.

1 teaspoon olive oil

1 large clove garlic, minced

1 teaspoon hot pepper sauce, or to taste

2 tablespoons mirin or dry white wine

2 cups chopped dandelion greens

$1/3$ cup vegetable stock

4 cups cooked whole wheat elbow noodles (about 8 ounces dried)

$1/4$ cup grated soy Parmesan or regular Parmesan cheese

freshly ground black pepper to taste

HEAT A LARGE sauté pan on medium-high and pour in the oil. Add the garlic, hot pepper sauce, mirin, and greens and sauté, stirring constantly, for about 1 minute. Pour in the stock and continue to sauté until the greens are wilted but still bright green, about 2 minutes more. Immediately mix with the noodles, Parmesan, and pepper and serve warm.

IF THE WEATHER IS HOT AND/OR DRY:
Instead of mincing the garlic, peel it, then spear it with a toothpick. Sauté as directed and discard before serving.

IF THE WEATHER IS COLD AND/OR DAMP:
Use a generous amount of hot pepper sauce and black pepper.

sesame-scented couscous

MAKES 4 SERVINGS

220 calories per serving: 7 grams fat: 30% calories from fat

Sesame was used by Vedic sages to relieve nervous tension and as a tonic for the complexion.

1 cup whole wheat or white couscous	1/2 cup fresh green peas
1 1/2 cups vegetable stock	2 tablespoons toasted (dark) sesame oil
2 carrots, coarsely grated	1/4 cup fresh lemon juice
2 shallots, finely chopped	3 scallions, finely minced
2 cloves garlic, finely minced	

IN A SMALL saucepan, combine the couscous and stock and bring to a boil. Reduce the heat, cover loosely, and simmer until the stock has been absorbed, about 5 minutes.

REMOVE THE PAN from the heat and swirl in the carrots, shallots, garlic, peas, sesame oil, lemon juice, and scallions. Serve warm or slightly chilled as a salad on a nest of greens or stuff into a pita with sprouts to make a quick sandwich.

IF THE WEATHER IS HOT AND/OR DRY:
Add 1/4 cup of finely chopped water chestnuts when you add the carrots.

IF THE WEATHER IS COLD AND/OR DAMP:
Substitute 1 teaspoon of chili oil for 1 teaspoon of the sesame oil.

ziti with asparagus and fresh thyme

calming

Since thyme contains volatile oil compounds that can help clear a stuffy nose, this is a fitting dish for those who have experienced congestion during the morning.

1 tablespoon olive oil	³⁄₄ cup vegetable stock
1 medium onion, thinly sliced	1 tablespoon mirin or dry white wine
1 clove garlic, finely minced	8 plum tomatoes, chopped (including juice)
1 pound asparagus, trimmed and cut into 1-inch pieces	¹⁄₂ teaspoon dried hot red pepper flakes, or to taste
3 fresh shiitake mushrooms, stemmed and minced	pinch of sea salt
1 tablespoon minced fresh thyme or 1 teaspoon dried	6 cups cooked ziti (about 1 pound dried)

HEAT THE OIL in a large nonstick sauté pan on medium-high, then add the onion and garlic and sauté until fragrant and just wilted, about 2 minutes.

ADD THE ASPARAGUS, mushrooms, thyme, stock, mirin, tomatoes, red pepper, and salt and bring to a boil. Reduce the heat, cover loosely, and simmer, stirring occasionally, until the mixture is fragrant and saucy, about 5 minutes. Toss with the ziti and serve warm.

IF THE WEATHER IS HOT AND/OR DRY:
Increase the shiitake mushrooms from 3 to 5 and serve the ziti at room temperature or very slightly chilled.

IF THE WEATHER IS COLD AND/OR DAMP:
Add a bay leaf at the time you heat the oil. leaving it in throughout cooking.

whole wheat spaghetti with fresh spinach sauce

MAKES 4 LARGE ENTRÉE SERVINGS

385 calories per serving (with soy Parmesan); 9 grams fat; 21% calories from fat

Since stress can deplete nutrients from the body, this dish may serve as a restorative for those who have had a rough morning. Spinach contains phosphorus, iron, potassium, carotenoids, thiamine, riboflavin, niacin, and vitamin C. On a more mystical level, seventeenth-century astrological herbalists claimed that spinach "cools and soothes" a nervous stomach.

9 ounces fresh spinach leaves, cleaned and stemmed	2 tablespoons olive oil
1 clove garlic, peeled and halved	$^1/_4$ cup grated soy Parmesan or regular Parmesan cheese
1 shallot, peeled and halved	pinch of sea salt
$^1/_3$ cup packed fresh basil leaves	6 cups cooked whole wheat spaghetti (about 10 ounces dried)

STEAM THE SPINACH, garlic, and shallot over boiling water until the spinach is just wilted but still vibrant green, $2^1/_2$ to 3 minutes. Pat the spinach dry and tip into a processor or blender along with the garlic and shallot. Add the basil, olive oil, Parmesan, and salt and whiz until smooth. Toss with the spaghetti and serve warm.

IF THE WEATHER IS HOT AND/OR DRY:

When tossing together the spinach sauce and spaghetti, add 2 chopped fresh tomatoes.

IF THE WEATHER IS COLD AND/OR DAMP:

Increase the garlic to 2 cloves and don't steam—finely mince and add them during pureeing.

soba with tahini-mustard sauce and
pickled red cabbage

MAKES 4 SERVINGS
242 calories per serving: 4 grams fat; 15% calories from fat

Made with buckwheat flour, soba noodles are a good restorative to a stressful morning, since they contain calcium as well as B vitamins.

$1/4$ cup thinly shredded red cabbage

3 tablespoons rice vinegar

1 tablespoon balsamic vinegar

1 tablespoon tahini (sesame paste)

1 tablespoon prepared coarse-style mustard

1 tablespoon fresh lemon juice

2 tablespoons water

8 ounces soba noodles, cooked

2 scallions, minced

IN A SMALL bowl, combine the cabbage, rice vinegar, and balsamic vinegar and let the mixture marinate for 30 minutes.

MEANWHILE, IN A medium bowl, whisk together the tahini, mustard, lemon juice, and water. Toss with the noodles and scallions and divide among 4 bowls. Sprinkle a portion of cabbage atop each bowl.

IF THE WEATHER IS HOT AND/OR DRY:
Serve with chilled lemongrass tea. (To make 1 serving, steep 1 teaspoon of minced fresh lemongrass in 1 cup of boiling water, covered, for 5 minutes. Chill, then serve garnished with fresh lemon wedges.)

IF THE WEATHER IS COLD AND/OR DAMP:
When whisking the tahini mixture, add 1 teaspoon (or to taste) of hot pepper sauce.

mid-afternoon

best time of day for:

Asthmatics, since an attack is least likely to occur

Going to the dentist, because oral pain receptors are at their least sensitive

*f*or three days straight in Santa Fe, I was so shockingly exhausted between three and four in the afternoon that I truly could not keep my eyes open. Consulting with a physician friend, I learned that due to natural rhythms, many people experience a general lack of energy in the mid-afternoon. In fact, physiologically it's natural to want to nap. Some scientists attribute this phenomenon to gradually falling blood sugar levels; others note that the lifeless feeling is far worse in people suffering from allergies, sinus trouble, osteoarthritis, digestive difficulties, menopause, or the lunar rhythms of PMS. In my case, my friend said, the high elevation of Santa Fe exacerbated the exhaustion. I believe he was right, since I react similarly in such lofty places as Denver and Harre, Zimbabwe.

Following my friend's advice, I kept my body hydrated with ten 8-ounce glasses of spring water a day. This, he said, would prevent the lack of alertness that can be caused by dehydrating high elevations, airplane travel, and dry weather. I also avoided such dehydrating substances as salty foods, alcohol, and caffeinated beverages. In addition, I took 2,500 mg of Siberian ginseng (Eleuthero) each morning to energize my body and support my adrenal system. By the second day of my new routine, I had beaten the four o'clock blues and had learned to take Siberian ginseng along wherever and whenever I travel.

Although I didn't realize it at the time, I was not alone in my dreary afternoon mood. In literature mid-afternoon is a metaphor for the latter part of life, or the third stage in the four stages of human existence. To be "afternoony" is to feel listless and worn out. Figuratively, mid-afternoon is associated with autumn, when the year begins to pass into decline. Indeed, it seems that more than one writer has felt the plummet of mental and physical energy that can occur in the mid-afternoon.

People in countries such as Mexico, Spain, and Portugal deal with naturally low mid-afternoon energy by taking a siesta. The workday stops between noon and four o'clock, and people use the time to eat, nap, and become refreshed so they can complete the second half of the workday between four and eight o'clock at night. This system has yet to catch on everywhere, perhaps because it presents its own problems, such as dining at eleven o'clock at night—a habit that can lead to weight gain and poor digestion.

Plummeting afternoon energy and low blood sugar levels may well have prompted the English to adopt the custom of taking afternoon tea. A cup of tea and a slice of toast at four o'clock can be quite fortifying. Like-minded, it seems, were the hard-working Italian housewives who for an afternoon snack combined brewed espresso, whipped cream, sugar, and ladyfingers to make the now famous tiramisù, which literally means "pick-me-up." For your own mid-afternoon vitalizer, and to make this time of day productive and interesting, adopt one or more of the following energizing suggestions.

relief at your fingertips

SEA OF ENERGY

The ancient art of accupressure can be employed as a form of self-massage to help eliminate mid-afternoon fatigue. Try it with a massage point that the Chinese call Sea of Energy, which is said to help strengthen the body and relieve general weariness. First rub the palms of your hands together briskly until they're warm, for about 10 seconds. Relax your shoulders, then locate your navel. Drop three finger widths down to find the Sea of Energy point. Slowly and gently press with the tip of your thumb (if you have long fingernails, use a knuckle) as deep as you can go without feeling discomfort. When you've reached that depth, close your eyes and breath deeply for 1 minute, visualizing a glow of light right where you are pressing. Also note the feeling of a "heartbeat" where you press. Then as you slowly and gently release your finger from the point, open your eyes while feeling the glow travel through your body. You can hold the Sea of Energy point for up to 2 minutes if you wish.

YOGIC BREATHING

To amplify the effects of the Sea of Energy, try a few seconds of yogic breathing before you press the point. First, breathe in through your nose. Then immediately place a thumb on your right nostril to close it, exhaling through your left nostril. Close your left nostril with your index finger while breathing in through your right nostril. Continue breathing for five inhale/exhale cycles, ending by exhaling through your left nostril. Yogic sages have used this technique for centuries before meditation, holding that it helps balance and refresh the mind and body. Indeed, as you will notice, it does make the head feel free and unblocked. Daily yogic breathing may help you to think clearly on a regular basis, sorting out important issues and arriving at decisions.

potent pose

To refresh your mind and body in mid-afternoon, try an energizing yoga posture, or asana, called Rainfall. Lean back against a wall with your feet parallel and about a foot from the wall. Position your shoulders and rear end to touch the wall. Then bend forward from the hips and hang, moving your rear up the wall as far as you can. Tighten your abdominal muscles. Let your arms hang as far down as is comfortable, with your fingers gently curving upward, as if holding little teacups. Close your eyes and breathe deeply until you feel a release in your spine, about 1 minute. As you are breathing, imagine that tension is floating up through your body, like a rainfall, vanishing through your hands. Slowly stand up straight, noticing how the top and bottom of your body have become more balanced. I like this pose when I've been sitting for most of the day, as it helps to stretch and gently energize the neglected lower half of the body.

try a tea

Peppermint is what herbalists call an aromatic, or a substance that acts as a mild, caffeine-free stimulant. To make 1 cup of peppermint tea, steep 2 teaspoons of dried leaf in 1 cup of boiling water, covered, for 4 minutes. Then strain and sip hot if the weather is cold and damp, or chilled if the weather is hot and dry.

You can also add a slice of dried Chinese licorice root (available at Chinese markets and health food stores) to the peppermint tea during steeping and keep it in while you're sipping. Chinese licorice has a tonic effect on the adrenals, meaning it can help relieve fatigue. Proponents of the herb actually chew the dried root like gum (it tastes

BRIGHTENING BREATH

For a quick mid-afternoon restorative, stand with your arms at your sides. Inhale through your nose sharply three times in a row without exhaling. Then exhale through your mouth while quickly raising your arms over your head. Repeat the process three times, for a total of four. Observe the feeling of clarity in your head, neck, and shoulders before continuing with your day.

*Cinnamon, thanks to its
essential oil constituants,
is a mild stimulant that
temporarily increases
vitality. For a quick
dash of energy, add a
cinnamon stick to your
mid-afternoon tea while
it's brewing. (Stash a
package in your desk
drawer for convenience at
work.) Keep the cinna-
mon stick in the tea while
you sip, using it as an
aromatic stirrer.*

sweet and earthy). Since Chinese licorice may aggravate high blood pressure, those with the condition should avoid the herb and stick with straight peppermint.

Green tea, which contains a small amount of caffeine—25 mg or less per cup—becomes a refreshing mid-afternoon bracer when combined with peppermint. Steep 1 teaspoon of each in 1 cup of boiling water, covered, for 2 minutes. Those who are taking any type of homeopathic medications will want to substitute uplifting lemongrass for peppermint, since the menthol in the latter may lessen the effect of the medications.

making scents

According to the science of fragrance psychology, or aromatherapy, inhaling the essences of certain flowers and herbs can help refresh you. One such plant is rose geranium. Aromatherapists hold that its essence is uplifting, as well as useful in treating anxiety. Rose geranium may also be a mild stimulant to the adrenals, which can help restore energy in those who suffer from the four o'clock blues. To try it, drip 2 drops of essential oil of rose geranium (available at herb shops and health food stores) on a tissue and inhale while breathing deeply for 1 to 2 minutes. For a prolonged treatment, tuck the tissue into the breast pocket of your blouse, shirt, or jacket. Essential oils of bergamot, rosemary, and basil will have similar energizing effects.

For a quick and refreshing aromatic mini massage, mix 3 or 4 drops of essential oil of rose geranium (or your choice of energizing oils) with 2 teaspoons of unscented hand lotion. (Take a jar to work in your purse or briefcase.) Lightly dampen your hands and arms with water and rub on the lotion, inhaling the essence as you rub. When you're finished, shake your hands for about 7 seconds, breathing deeply, and afterward, you will note an all-over renewed feeling.

best foods

The recipes in this chapter are designed to revive your mind and body by avoiding saturated fat and refined sugar. Nuts and seeds, as in Tamari Almonds with Fresh Basil and Roasted Pumpkin Seeds with Garlic and Dill, contain quick energy-producing protein and are recommended in small amounts. Fruit-sweetened snack breads and cookies—Almond Date Bars and Cinnamon-Oat Cookies, to name two—contain whole grains to sustain your energy level. And spicy salsas and spreads serve to stimulate your senses with aromatics such as hot peppers, chives, basil, and garlic. For convenience, most of the recipes can be made ahead and packed for an invigorating snack when you need it.

toasted sunflower seeds with miso

MAKES ¹/₂ CUP, OR 8 (1-TABLESPOON) SERVINGS
22 calories per serving: 1.75 grams fat; 70% calories from fat

Sunflower seeds are a good source of B vitamins, which help the body produce the energizing hormone adrenaline. The miso promotes healthy digestion, which can also help restore energy levels. Although the seeds contain what nutritionists call a heart-healthy fat, it's still fat, so be judicious in your portions.

¹/₂ cup hulled raw sunflower seeds

1 teaspoon vegetable stock or water

1 teaspoon balsamic vinegar

¹/₂ teaspoon red miso (see The Savory Pantry, page 424)

TOAST THE SEEDS in a dry nonstick sauté pan, stirring constantly, over medium-high heat. The seeds are done when they turn a rich, medium brown, which should take 2 to 3 minutes.

COMBINE THE STOCK, vinegar, and miso in a small dish and whisk well to combine. When the seeds are done, pour the miso mixture over them and toss well to combine. Let the seeds cool until they are dry to the touch. Store in a tightly covered jar in a cool dark place for up to 2 weeks.

IF THE WEATHER IS HOT AND/OR DRY:
Add ¹/₂ teaspoon of ground coriander to the miso mixture before mixing it with the seeds.

IF THE WEATHER IS COLD AND/OR DAMP:
Add a dash of hot pepper sauce to the miso mixture before mixing it with the seeds.

AVOID THESE FOODS AND BEVERAGES

Some health experts say that consuming these items can zap vitality:

Baked goods made totally of white flour

Products containing refined white sugar

Alcoholic beverages

Caffeine-containing beverages and foods

Fatty and fried foods

roasted soy nuts

MAKES 2 CUPS, OR 8 (¼-CUP) SERVINGS
61 calories per serving: trace of fat

Soybeans are a good source of soluble fiber, which can help regulate blood sugar and energy levels. Additionally, soybeans contain phytochemicals that may help prevent breast cancer.

1 cup dried white soybeans

water for soaking and boiling

1 ½ teaspoons seasonal spice mix (see below)

SOAK THE BEANS overnight in 4 cups of water.

PREHEAT THE OVEN to 400°F.

DRAIN THE BEANS and add fresh water to cover in a large pot. Cover and bring to a boil, then drain immediately and pat dry.

SPREAD THE BEANS out on a large jelly roll pan or cookie sheet, place in the oven, and reduce the oven temperature to 350°F. Roast the beans, stirring frequently, until tender and medium brown, 50 to 60 minutes. Toss immediately with your spice mix of choice. Let cool, then store in a tightly covered glass jar in a cool dry place for up to 1 month.

SEASONAL SPICE MIX IF THE WEATHER IS HOT AND/OR DRY:

Combine ½ teaspoon ground fennel seed. ½ teaspoon ground cumin seed. ½ teaspoon ground turmeric. and a pinch of sea salt. Then toss with the roasted beans.

SEASONAL SPICE MIX IF THE WEATHER IS COLD AND/OR DAMP:

Combine ½ teaspoon ground ginger. ½ teaspoon ground cinnamon. and a pinch each of sea salt and black pepper. Then toss with the roasted beans.

roasted pumpkin seeds with garlic and dill

MAKES 1 1/2 CUPS (THE SEEDS SWELL DURING ROASTING), OR 12 (2-TABLESPOON) SERVINGS
104 calories per serving: 1 gram fat: 9% calories from fat

Roasting your own seeds lets you enjoy them knowing they have been prepared without fatigue-producing fat. As an added bonus, pumpkin seeds are a good source of zinc, a mineral that may help prevent prostate problems.

1 cup raw pumpkin seeds

1 clove garlic, peeled and halved

1 1/2 teaspoons dried dill

TOSS THE PUMPKIN seeds in a large nonstick sauté pan. Spear each garlic half with a toothpick and add them to the pan. Roast over medium-high heat, stirring constantly, until the seeds are puffed up and medium brown, about 4 minutes. Be sure to stand back, because they pop.

DISCARD THE GARLIC and stir in the dill. Store in a tightly covered jar for up to 1 month.

IF THE WEATHER IS HOT AND/OR DRY:
Substitute basil for the dill.

IF THE WEATHER IS COLD AND/OR DAMP:
Double the garlic.

tamari almonds with fresh basil

MAKES 1 CUP, OR ABOUT 15 (2-ALMOND) SERVINGS
50 calories per serving: 4 grams fat: 70% calories from fat

Almonds promote a slow, even rise in blood sugar levels, providing smooth, caffeine-free energy. To avoid excess fat, stick to one serving of these tasty treats.

1 cup raw almonds

1 $^{1}/_{2}$ tablespoons reduced-sodium tamari or soy sauce

3 tablespoons fresh basil

TOAST THE ALMONDS in a large nonstick sauté pan over medium-high heat, stirring constantly, until fragrant and medium-brown, about 4 minutes.

REMOVE THE PAN from the heat and immediately pour in the tamari, swirling it around to coat all of the almonds. Quickly tip the almonds into a glass jar and add the basil. Close the jar and shake about 30 times to bruise the basil and release its aroma into the almonds. Store the jar in the refrigerator for up to 1 week.

IF THE WEATHER IS HOT AND/OR DRY:
Increase the basil to $^{1}/_{4}$ cup.

IF THE WEATHER IS COLD AND/OR DAMP:
Use fresh oregano instead of basil.

easy yeast bread

MAKES 10 SLICES
145 calories per serving: 3.5 grams fat: 21% calories from fat

A diet high in whole grains and seeds, such as this bread provides, can help prevent mid-afternoon fatigue.

1 cup whole wheat bread flour

1 1/2 cups unbleached all-purpose flour

2 teaspoons barley malt or honey

1 tablespoon baking yeast

1/2 teaspoon sea salt

1 cup water

1 tablespoon olive oil, plus extra for brushing

1/2 cup rolled oats

1 tablespoon flaxseed

2 tablespoons sunflower seeds

COMBINE THE FLOURS in a 4-cup measure and microwave on full power until just warmed, about 1 1/2 minutes (heating helps the flours rise better). If you don't have a microwave, heat the flours on medium-low in a large sauté pan, but don't brown.

WHILE THE FLOURS are heating, combine the barley malt, yeast, and salt in a large bowl. When the flours are ready, immediately add them to the bowl and use a fork to combine well. Add the water, olive oil, oats, flaxseed, and sunflower seeds and stir well to combine.

USE YOUR HANDS to form the dough into a ball, then knead for about 3 minutes. Roll the dough out into a rectangle, then roll the rectangle up, jelly-roll style, to form a baguette. Set the baguette on a parchment-lined cookie sheet, seam side down, and let it rest for 30 minutes.

BRUSH THE BAGUETTE with a bit of oil and set it in a cold oven. Set the oven to 350°F and bake until cooked through, 50 to 60 minutes. Let cool before slicing.

IF THE WEATHER IS HOT AND/OR DRY:
Spread a slice of bread with Creamy Basil Spread (page 126).

IF THE WEATHER IS COLD AND/OR DAMP:
Toast a slice and top with Habanero Salsa (page 125).

leek and millet "polenta"

MAKES 8 SERVINGS
135 calories per serving: 2 grams fat: 14% calories from fat

Millet, by offering more protein than any other grain, may temporarily increase alertness. It is also recommended by many nutritionists to gently and evenly lift sagging blood sugar levels.

1½ cups millet. rinsed	3 leeks. trimmed. rinsed. and minced
3 cups vegetable stock	2 teaspoons olive oil
1 bay leaf	1 tablespoon minced fresh rosemary or
pinch of sea salt	1½ teaspoons dried

COMBINE THE MILLET. stock, and bay leaf in a large saucepan and let soak for 2 hours.

ADD THE SALT. leeks, olive oil, and rosemary and bring to a boil. Reduce the heat to low, cover loosely, and let simmer until the millet is tender, about 25 minutes. Stir well and remove bay leaf.

FIRMLY PRESS THE millet mixture into a lightly oiled 9-inch square pan and smooth the top. Let cool completely before slicing into squares.

IF THE WEATHER IS HOT AND/OR DRY:
Top a slice with Creamy Basil Spread (page 126).

IF THE WEATHER IS COLD AND/OR DAMP:
Top a slice with Habanero Salsa (page 125).

spicy orange salsa

MAKES 1½ CUPS, OR 12 (2-TABLESPOON) SERVINGS
10 calories per serving; no added fat

The aroma of fresh oranges can be refreshing and uplifting. Serve this lively sauce with unfried tortilla chips or Pita Chips (page 128). It's also tasty on grilled salmon for dinner.

4 oranges, peeled, seeded, and chopped

1 lime, peeled, seeded, and chopped

1 fresh jalapeño pepper, seeded, cored, and finely chopped

1 scallion, finely minced

1 tablespoon minced fresh cilantro

COMBINE ALL OF the ingredients in a medium bowl and serve at room temperature or slightly chilled. Store, covered and refrigerated, for up to 5 days—the flavor will actually improve over time.

IF THE WEATHER IS HOT AND/OR DRY:
Use 2 oranges instead of 4 and add 1 cup of chopped fresh mango or papaya.

IF THE WEATHER IS COLD AND/OR DAMP:
Use 2 jalapeños instead of 1.

fresh peach salsa

MAKES 2 CUPS, OR 4 (1/2-CUP) SERVINGS
92 calories per serving: 1 gram fat: 10% calories from fat

Peaches are a good source of beta carotene, a nutrient that strengthens the body by enhancing immunity to disease.

1 pound fresh ripe peaches, peeled, pitted, and finely chopped

4 ripe tomatoes, chopped (including juice)

1 fresh serrano pepper, seeded, cored, and minced

1 clove garlic, very finely minced

1 tablespoon lime juice

1 teaspoon olive oil

1 teaspoon hot pepper sauce, or to taste

1/2 cup fresh cilantro leaves

COMBINE ALL OF the ingredients in a processor or blender and whiz until combined but still slightly chunky, 5 to 7 seconds. Store, covered and refrigerated, for up to 5 days—the flavor will actually improve over time.

IF THE WEATHER IS HOT AND/OR DRY:
Use a jalapeño instead of the serrano pepper.

IF THE WEATHER IS COLD AND/OR DAMP:
Use 2 fresh serranos and 2 cloves of garlic.

habanero salsa

MAKES ABOUT 1 CUP, OR 4 ($^1/_4$-CUP) SERVINGS
50 calories per serving: no added fat

Hot peppers, such as the fiery ones used here, are recommended by some health professionals to treat fatigue and sluggish digestion. Enjoy this ballistic brew with unfried tortilla chips or drizzled over a slice of Leek and Millet "Polenta" (page 122) or toasted slices of Easy Yeast Bread (page 121).

juice of 4 limes (about 1 cup)

3 habanero chilies, seeded, cored, and minced (wear plastic gloves)

2 ripe tomatoes, cored and chopped (including juice)

3 scallions, finely minced

1 clove garlic, minced

pinch of sea salt

COMBINE ALL OF the ingredients in a medium bowl. Store, covered and refrigerated, for up to 5 days—the flavor will actually improve over time.

IF THE WEATHER IS HOT AND/OR DRY:
Add $^1/_4$ cup minced fresh cilantro.

IF THE WEATHER IS COLD AND/OR DAMP:
Use 2 cloves of garlic instead of 1.

creamy basil spread

MAKES 1 1/2 CUPS, OR 20 (1-TABLESPOON) SERVINGS
15 calories per serving: trace of fat

The main ingredient in this spread is reduced-fat tofu, a high-protein food that can revive you when you've run out of steam. Enjoy the spread on a slice of whole grain bread or as a dip for fresh vegetables. You can also mix a portion of the spread with an equal amount of water and use as a tasty dressing for green salads or on whole grains such as rice and barley.

10 1/2 ounces reduced-fat tofu (see The Savory Pantry, page 425)

1 tablespoon red miso (see The Savory Pantry, page 424)

2 teaspoons tahini (sesame paste)

1 teaspoon prepared mustard

juice of 1/2 lemon

1/4 cup fresh basil leaves

2 teaspoons fresh thyme leaves or 1 teaspoon dried

1 clove garlic

BLANCH THE TOFU in boiling water for 2 minutes, then drain and pat dry.

COMBINE ALL OF the ingredients in a processor or blender and whiz until very smooth, about 20 seconds. Store, tightly covered and refrigerated, for up to 1 week.

IF THE WEATHER IS HOT AND/OR DRY:
Replace the garlic with 1 tablespoon of minced fresh chives.

IF THE WEATHER IS COLD AND/OR DAMP:
Add 1 teaspoon (or to taste) of hot pepper sauce and double the garlic.

faux ricotta

MAKES 2 ½ CUPS. OR 9 (¼-CUP) SERVINGS
55 calories per serving: 2.5 grams fat: 40% calories from fat

Spread this dairy-free creamy "cheese" on bagels or crackers or use it as a base for dips. The main ingredient, high-protein reduced-fat tofu, can help fight fatigue.

1 pound firm reduced-fat tofu (see The Savory Pantry. page 425)

3 to 4 tablespoons miso (see The Savory Pantry. page 424)

1 tablespoon olive oil

BLANCH THE TOFU in boiling water for 2 minutes, then drain and pat dry. Slice the tofu into 1-inch slices, weight it down (use a heavy pot with an iron inside) and let it drain for 2 hours.

IN A SMALL bowl, mix together the miso and olive oil. Spread the mixture on each tofu slice, covering all the surfaces. Set the slices on a large plate, cover with waxed paper, and let sit at room temperature for at least 8 hours or overnight.

SCRAPE OFF AND discard the miso. Crumble and use the "cheese" as you would regular ricotta. Store, covered and refrigerated, for up to 1 week.

IF THE WEATHER IS HOT AND/OR DRY:
Mix together equal parts of all-fruit orange marmalade or apricot preserves and cheese. Spread on muffins or scones.

IF THE WEATHER IS COLD AND/OR DAMP:
Add 2 tablespoons of minced fresh chives and 1 clove of minced garlic to each ½ cup of cheese.

pita chips

MAKES 32 CHIPS, OR 4 SERVINGS
221 calories per serving: trace of fat

Make these chips ahead and savor them instead of energy-zapping fatty ones.

2 whole wheat pitas

2 cloves garlic, peeled and halved

4 teaspoons prepared mustard

¼ cup lemon juice

2 tablespoons balsamic vinegar

¼ cup grated regular or soy Parmesan cheese

2 tablespoons minced fresh thyme or 1 tablespoon dried

PREHEAT THE OVEN to 400°F.

USE KITCHEN SHEARS to cut each pita into 8 wedges, then pull each wedge apart to make 2. Rub the rough side of each piece with the cut side of a garlic half. Then discard the garlic.

IN A SMALL bowl, combine the mustard, lemon juice, vinegar, cheese, and thyme. Arrange the chips, rough side up, on a cookie sheet and use a pastry brush to paint on the mustard mixture. Bake in the middle of the oven until lightly browned and crisp, 10 to 12 minutes.

IF THE WEATHER IS HOT AND/OR DRY:
Dip the chips into Creamy Basil Spread (page 126).

IF THE WEATHER IS COLD AND/OR DAMP:
As well as rubbing the unbaked chips with garlic, add a minced clove of garlic to the mustard mixture before brushing it on.

warm sweet potato chips

106 calories per serving: 2 grams fat: 17% calories from fat

Sweet potatoes are a good source of beta carotene, a nutrient that can help keep the adrenal and nervous systems tuned up.

3 sweet potatoes (about 1 pound total)

2 teaspoons olive oil

2 teaspoons minced fresh oregano or
1 teaspoon dried

PREHEAT THE OVEN to 500°F.

CUT THE SWEET potatoes into $1/8$-inch or smaller slices and toss them in a bowl with the oil.

SPRAY A COOKIE sheet with nonstick spray and spread the slices out in a single layer. Bake until lightly browned and cooked through, about 15 minutes. They'll be pleasantly chewy. Toss immediately with the oregano and serve warm.

IF THE WEATHER IS HOT AND/OR DRY:
Substitute minced fresh cilantro for the oregano.

IF THE WEATHER IS COLD AND/OR DAMP:
When tossing the chips with the oregano. add freshly ground black pepper to taste.

maple-caramel corn with raisins

MAKES 4 SERVINGS
193 calories per serving: 7 grams fat: 33% calories from fat

This tasty sweet contains no refined sugar, so it will energize you gently rather than joltingly.

2 tablespoons canola oil

$^1/_4$ cup barley malt

$^1/_4$ teaspoon ground cinnamon

6 cups air-popped popcorn

$^1/_4$ cup finely chopped raisins

IN A SMALL saucepan, combine the oil, barley malt, and cinnamon. Bring the mixture to a boil and continue to boil until the syrup darkens in color, 2 to 3 minutes.

PLACE THE POPCORN in a large bowl. When the syrup is ready, pour it in along with the raisins and toss well to coat. Let the caramel corn stand for 20 minutes before serving.

IF THE WEATHER IS HOT AND/OR DRY:
Add $^1/_4$ teaspoon ground fennel seed to the syrup when boiling.

IF THE WEATHER IS COLD AND/OR DAMP:
Add $^1/_4$ teaspoon ground ginger to the syrup when boiling.

almond date bars

MAKES 16 BARS
64 calories per bar: 1 gram fat: 14% calories from fat

Dates and oats combine to give you stamina.

1 cup pitted dried dates

1/4 cup raisins

1/4 cup finely chopped toasted almonds

1/2 cup rolled oats

1/3 cup whole wheat pastry flour

1/4 teaspoon ground cinnamon

1 teaspoon vanilla extract

1/2 cup egg substitute (see Note. page 13)
or 4 egg whites

PREHEAT THE OVEN to 400°F.

COMBINE THE DATES and raisins in a processor and whiz until finely chopped. Stir in the remaining ingredients.

SPRAY A GLASS pie dish with nonstick spray and press in the dough firmly, smoothing the top. Bake in the middle of the oven until cooked through, 15 to 18 minutes. Let cool before slicing.

IF THE WEATHER IS HOT AND/OR DRY:
Substitute ground cardamom for the cinnamon.

IF THE WEATHER IS COLD AND/OR DAMP:
Double the amount of cinnamon.

cinnamon-oat cookies

MAKES 16 COOKIES
60 calories each: 1 gram fat: 15% calories from fat

These treats are sweetened with all-fruit apple butter, a sweetener that promotes an even flow of energy. Additionally, the zip of cinnamon can help rejuvenate your senses.

For the best texture when baking whole grain cookies without refined sugar, make sure all of the ingredients are at room temperature.

1 tablespoon canola oil

1/2 cup all-fruit apple butter

3 tablespoons soy yogurt or plain nonfat yogurt

1 teaspoon vanilla extract

1/4 cup egg substitute (see Note. page 13) or 2 egg whites

1 1/4 cups whole wheat pastry flour

1/2 teaspoon baking soda

1/4 teaspoon baking powder

1 teaspoon ground cinnamon

1 cup rolled oats

PREHEAT THE OVEN to 375°F.

IN A MEDIUM bowl, combine the oil, apple butter, yogurt, vanilla, and egg substitute. Use a hand mixer to beat until well combined.

IN A LARGE bowl, combine the flour, baking soda, baking powder, cinnamon, and oats. Pour in the liquid ingredients and mix well to combine. Don't overmix; about 15 strokes should do.

LINE A LARGE cookie sheet with baking parchment. Drop well-rounded tablespoonfuls of dough onto the sheet, leaving a bit of space between. Bake in the middle of the oven until cooked through, about 14 minutes. Let the cookies cool on a wire rack before enjoying, or store, tightly covered, for about 3 days.

IF THE WEATHER IS HOT AND/OR DRY: *Spread a cookie with an all-fruit jam. such as raspberry. before serving.*

IF THE WEATHER IS COLD AND/OR DAMP: *Add 1/2 teaspoon ground anise seed to the batter before baking.*

apricot-pecan cookies

MAKES 18 COOKIES

90 calories per cookie: 4.5 grams fat; 44% calories from fat

Apricots are a good source of soluble fiber, which can help stabilize blood sugar and energy levels.

3 tablespoons canola oil

³/₄ cup all-fruit apricot preserves

¹/₄ cup egg substitute (see Note, page 13) or 2 egg whites

¹/₂ cup unbleached all-purpose flour

¹/₂ cup whole wheat pastry flour

1 teaspoon baking powder

³/₄ teaspoon freshly grated orange zest

¹/₂ teaspoon ground cinnamon

¹/₂ cup chopped pecans

1 cup chopped dried apricots

PREHEAT THE OVEN to 350°F.

IN A MEDIUM bowl, combine the oil, preserves, and egg substitute, beating with an electric mixer until smooth. Combine both flours and the baking powder in a medium bowl and stir well. Add the orange zest, cinnamon, pecans, and apricots.

POUR THE LIQUID ingredients into the dry and combine well. Don't overmix.

LINE A LARGE cookie sheet with baking parchment. Drop tablespoons of dough onto the sheet. Bake in the middle of the oven until cooked through, 12 to 15 minutes. Let the cookies cool on a wire rack before enjoying, or store in a tightly closed container at room temperature for up to 5 days.

IF THE WEATHER IS HOT AND/OR DRY:
Serve the cookies with iced peppermint tea.

IF THE WEATHER IS COLD AND/OR DAMP:
Double the amount of cinnamon.

strawberry-mango frappé

MAKES 2 SERVINGS
140 calories per serving: no added fat

This rejuvenating beverage is packed with vitamin C and beta carotene for extra nutrition.

1 cup fresh strawberries. hulled

1 mango

1 cup ice cubes

1 tablespoon lemon juice

²/₃ cup cold vanilla soy milk or skim milk

TIP THE BERRIES in a blender. Peel the mango over the blender container to catch the juices, then slice the mango flesh into it. Add the ice cubes, lemon juice, and milk and blend until thick, about 20 seconds.

IF THE WEATHER IS HOT AND/OR DRY:
Add 1 teaspoon of rose water to the brew before blending.

IF THE WEATHER IS COLD AND/OR DAMP:
Use chilled cinnamon-herb tea in place of the milk.

evening

best time of day for:

| Enjoying foods, since taste buds are at their most receptive | Listening to music, because hearing is the sharpest it can be |

*a*t dusk in Cairo, I watched a woman fill eggplant and zucchini with rice as she explained the evening rhythms of Egypt. Try to calm yourself from the day's activities, she advised, especially before you sit down to eat. That way your body will be able to receive nourishment from the food, you'll avoid indigestion, and even sleep better. The woman continued as she slipped the dish of filled vegetables into the oven, saying that to relax, many men heed the call to prayer and head for the mosque, while women pray at home, sing, garden, read, or prepare the evening meal.

Across the globe, twilight in York, England, acquainted me with relaxation Anglican style through Evensong, that church's way of soothing the day's tensions with song and prayer. As my mind was calmed by the melodies around me, I thought they were not so different from the evening sounds coming from an Egyptian mosque or a Buddhist monastery. Similarly, a friend says that after she sings in her

135

Catholic choir she feels pacified and balanced, and what is singing but the prolonged enunciation of vowels, made with back straight and head held high? Isn't that the same as the mantra OHMMMMM in Eastern meditative chanting?

Come evening, it seems, people the world over seek inner peace. I was delighted to discover that modern research concurs, revealing that the body actually seeks a slower pace in the evening. One physiological clue is that body temperatures begin to fall, readying us for eventual sleep. Another is that the sleep-inducing hormone melatonin starts to make its way through our bodies. But when we fight our natural inclinations toward evening relaxation, intentionally or not, we deny our natural rhythms, leaving the door open for digestive problems, sleep disorders, next-day fatigue, and poor concentration.

To that end, much like those who partake in the Islam call to prayer or Anglican Evensong, some people choose to meditate in the evening before dinner. A meditation teacher in France told me that the practice allows the mind to settle down, at which time the body achieves a deep, rejuvenating rest that diminishes stress and anxiety and leads to a healthy-functioning person.

Although there are as many meditation techniques as there are teachers, beginners can start with a Buddhist technique, which focuses on your "breathing mechanism," either through your nose, mouth, or both. Sit in a chair with your hands in your lap, eyes closed, and feel/think the words "in" and "out" as you inhale and exhale deeply, imagining a glow just below your navel. Soon the words will cease to mean anything and merely assist you in the process of relaxing. Start with 5 minutes of this meditation each evening, peeking with one eye to check a clock for time, and add 1 minute each week until you're up to 15 or 20 minutes. For maximum results, meditate twice a day, once in the morning and once in the evening. (For more meditation tips, see page 6 in "Early Morning.")

If thoughts intrude while you are meditating, just treat them as if you were the host at a big party, greeting them, putting them somewhere comfortable, getting back to them later. Meditation teachers call these tips "training wheels," and add that to help eliminate mental static, instead of "in" and "out," count backward from four with every slow inhalation and exhalation. Try it, observing how it intensifies your experience.

flex to relax

An easy technique to soothe the day's stress is Progressive Relaxation. Make a tight fist, hold it for 10 seconds, then release it, noticing the difference in feelings. Then, sitting in a comfortable chair, repeat the flexing-relaxing technique with every muscle group in your body, starting with your head and neck, then shoulders, and all the way down to your toes. Progressive Relaxation will take about 10 minutes to complete, at which time your entire body should feel loose and revived.

Some people use audiotapes to help induce a peaceful, meditative state. Music stores, book shops, and some natural food stores offer a variety of tapes of calming ocean noises, woodland sounds, or voice-guided relaxation. Many meditators have great success with tapes from the Monroe Institute, which are based on the studies of Robert Monroe. In the 1950s Monroe researched the use of sound to influence learning and discovered that certain patterns of sound help induce such states of mind as peacefulness and sleep. He then devised a series of meditation tapes that encourage stress-free states of mind.

Whether it's focused breathing, singing in a choir, Buddhist chanting, or listening to a tape, any kind of meditation that relieves the day's tension and clears the mind is good. There's an old Zen expression that says, "When the fish is caught, the trap is forgotten." What's important in meditation is not how you got there, but the results you feel. Accentuate them by adopting one or more of the relaxing techniques and recipes that follow.

relief at your fingertips

Chinese doctors call stress "disturbed spirit" and advise settling the spirit for the evening with a self-massage point called The Third Eye. First, rub your hands together briskly for 10 seconds. Fold your hands, bringing them up to the bridge of your nose. Completely rest and relax your head on either folded index finger, just at the point where the bridge of your nose meets your forehead. You are literally holding your head up with your hands. (For extra comfort you may rest your elbows on a table.) Breathing deeply, visualize a glow just below your navel for 10 full breaths. Very slowly raise your head, feeling the tension leave it and flow down and out through your neck and shoulders.

Another way to utilize this particular Third Eye technique is during the first minute of meditation, where it serves as a "jump start" to the process of quieting the mind. (For more information on The Third Eye point, see "Mid-Morning," page 35.)

MOBILE MESSAGES

Two recently sighted meditation bumper stickers:

- *"Don't do something… Just sit there."*

- *"Meditation is not what you think."*

potent pose

At a traditional Japanese dinner, diners sit atop their back-folded legs while eating. The pose, a sort of closed kneel, is a custom with practical roots. Japanese healers, like their Chinese counterparts, maintain that energy runs to and from the stomach through a meridian, or channel, along the front of the thigh. By dining while literally stretching that meridian, stomach energy, and thus digestion, will theoretically be clear and unimpeded.

To help ensure your own stress-free digestion, kneel on the floor, legs folded underneath you, rear resting on heels, and arms at your sides. Breathe deeply for 10 full breaths. As you breathe, keep your back very straight, almost arched, feeling the

WORRY-FREE WORD

Egyptians have a word, maalesh, *that means both "sorry" and "so what." If you've had a rotten day, just say, "Maalesh!" and start afresh tomorrow.*

stomach area "open up" and visualizing it filled with a glow of light. Perform this "diner's pose" just before eating your evening meal. Ayurvedic healers say this pose promotes *agni,* or internal energy, and not only calms and strengthens digestion but helps the body absorb nutrients from the meal.

To supplement the effects of the diner's pose, while performing it, locate a point midway between the base of the breastbone and the navel. Using a finger or knuckle, press in gently but firmly and hold the press for as long as you hold the diner's pose, 10 full breaths. The point, called Center of Power, can help banish stomach spasms and indigestion brought on by stress. Center of Power should be performed only on an empty stomach, or at least 2 hours after dining.

try a tea

CATNIP-CHAMOMILE COMBO

To soothe the day's stresses as well as digestive tension, make a fragrant tea from ginger, catnip, and chamomile. Ginger acts as a carminative, aiding digestion, and catnip and chamomile each contain volatile oils that are mild sedatives to the nervous system. To make tea for four, steep 3 slices of fresh ginger and 2 teaspoons each of dried catnip and chamomile in 4 cups of just-boiled water, covered, for 4 minutes. Sip warm or slightly chilled at the cocktail hour, before the evening meal.

SWEDISH BITTERS

German and English herbalists recommend the commercially prepared herbal combination Swedish Bitters to ease tense digestion, including heartburn and gastritis. The formula is more than 100 years old and includes, among other herbs, aloe to stimulate the movement of food through the body, myrrh to prevent gastric inflammation, and angelica root to prevent intestinal colic. There are several brands of Swedish Bitters from which to choose, available at herb shops, natural food stores, and some supermarkets. Buy the liquid form, which looks like a dark, mysterious brew but which tastes surprisingly pleasant, sweet, and only slightly bitter. Herbalists recommend stirring 1 to 3 teaspoons of the liquid version into 1 cup of warm or cool tea or water and sipping prior to your meal. You can also mix liquid Swedish Bitters into 1 cup of slightly chilled club soda or sparkling mineral water and garnish with a twist of lemon or lime or a sprig of fresh peppermint. Herbalists hold that the "bitter"-tasting herbs in Swedish Bitters work because they neutralize digestive acidity. They sometimes call the tonic *"elixir ad longam vitam,"* or elixir for a long life. In one four-month German double-blind study, participants who received 1 tablespoon of Swedish Bitters before meals experienced less flatulence, fewer stomach spasms, and less constipation than those who took a placebo.

Once, after a stressful day had left my digestive system in a such an uproar that I thought I'd never eat again, a Japanese herbalist recommended a brew that included

Swedish Bitters along with several Japanese herbs. Following his instructions, in a small saucepan I combined 2 cups of spring water, 2 tablespoons of *kukicha* twig tea, 1 *umeboshi* plum (see The Savory Pantry, page 426), 1 slice of fresh ginger, and ¹/₂ teaspoon of tamari soy sauce (all available at herb shops, Asian markets, natural food stores, and some supermarkets). I let the mixture boil for 20 minutes, reducing the liquid to almost half. Then I strained the tea into a cup and swirled in 1 tablespoon of Swedish Bitters before sipping. Although the taste was salty and medicinal, the brew did neutralize my upset condition, and I have employed it many times since.

To ease evening digestive distress Chinese style, try a patent herbal formula called Curing Pills, available at Asian markets and pharmacies and at natural food stores. Curing Pills come in vials in a usually red box. One vial is taken, followed by a cup of warm or hot tea or water. Curing Pills contain 15 different herbs, including angelica root and mint. Their therapeutic effect on digestive distress is so potent that, as well as keeping them in my home first-aid kit, I take them along when traveling.

making scents

In scientific scent studies participants were able to tranquilize their minds and bodies in minutes by smelling certain essences, such as lavender and orange. The naturally occurring chemical compositions of these scents create homeostasis in the body, or a balancing, auto-regulation of the nerve system, to help reduce the ravages of a tense day.

A simple way to incorporate soothing scents into your evening is by burning lavender, cedarwood, or sandalwood incense. Inhaling the gentle fragrance while going about your typical evening activities can be relaxing, or you can burn the incense while meditating,

Essential oils of herbs and plants, available in small, opaque bottles at herb shops and natural food stores, can also be employed to create a peaceful atmosphere. Add essential oils of lavender and orange, for instance, to an aromatherapy diffuser—a small machine that emits puffs of calming essence into the air. Alternatively, fill a small bowl with ¹/₂ cup of warm water, add 3 drops each of essential oils of lavender, rose geranium, ylang ylang, and sandalwood, and sprinkle your carpeting with the mixture. If you prefer, use any of the essences singly. Either way, pure essential oils will evaporate, leaving no trace of stain. You can also put the mixture in a spray bottle to spritz around the room.

For a more personal treatment, moisten a tea towel with the mixture in the bowl and apply the warm compress to your bare abdomen. Lie down, close your eyes, and relax for about 5 minutes, or until the towel gets cold. You can also apply the compress while sitting up during meditation.

If you're going out for the evening, you can still immerse yourself in relaxing essences by dotting 3 drops of essential oil of choice—such as lavender or tangerine—on a cotton ball. Tuck the pacifying perfume into your bra or pocket, where it will send soothing trails of fragrance to your nose all evening.

STRESS AND NUTRIENTS

We used to say "You are what you eat," but now we say "You are what you absorb." You can eat the best food in the world and take all the supplements you want, but if your digestive system is stressed, you won't be able to assimilate all those wonderful nutrients, and your efforts will literally go right down the toilet.

best foods

In the days when humans lived in caves, they ate fatty evening meals. Since the caves had no heat, and nights could get quite cold, a fatty dinner helped keep people warm during the night. It was perhaps that very survival technique that prompted our bodies to release an evening hormone, dubbed galanin, that continues to make us want to eat a fatty dinner even though it's no longer required. In fact, for modern humans, a big, fatty evening meal may cause gallbladder complaints, constipation, indigestion, heartburn, insomnia, and eventually weight gain. That's why the recipes in this chapter are lean yet highly satisfying and flavorful, fulfilling our innate desires without overfilling our waistlines.

In addition, these recipes foster relaxation for the evening with soothing complex carbohydrates, as in Whole Wheat Crepes with Spicy Chickpea Filling; Enchiladas with Barley, Squash, and Saffron; Buckwheat with Black Beans; and Red Lentil Cakes with Garlic and Sage. What's more, many of the recipes contain herbs that perfume the ingredients while acting as nerve tonics, as in Mushrooms with Mellowing Herbs (chamomile); Garlic Crostini with Fresh Tomatoes (lemon balm); and Pâté with Olives, Fresh Basil, and Roasted Red Peppers.

Acting as an evening tonic to neutralize the damage that stress may have done to the body during the day, many of the recipes contain immune-strengthening herbs and nutrients, such as garlic, vitamin C, and beta carotene. Try Sweet Potato Cutlets, Chunky Vegetable Pie, Pumpkin Polenta with Black Bean Salsa, Garlicky Flatbread, or Apricot-Banana Mousse. For an additional evening immuno tonic, choose a recipe that contains shiitake mushrooms, like Mushroom-Spinach Spread.

To turn your own recipe into a calming evening soother, make what Ayurvedic healers call a *churna*, or spice mix. Churnas are used to give foods particular energies—in this instance, a relaxing one.

calming evening churna

1 teaspoon dried chamomile flowers	$^{1}/_{4}$ teaspoon whole fennel seeds
2 teaspoons dried basil	$^{1}/_{4}$ teaspoon ground ginger

COMBINE THE CHAMOMILE, basil, and fennel seeds in an electric spice grinder or a mortar and grind until powdered. Stir in the ginger. You'll have about 2 teaspoons. Sprinkle about $^{1}/_{4}$ teaspoon per serving into soups, stews, pasta dishes, bean and rice dishes, or salads before eating. For the best results, make the churna fresh each time.

IF THE WEATHER IS HOT AND/OR DRY: *Add $^{1}/_{2}$ teaspoon coriander seeds when grinding.*

IF THE WEATHER IS COLD AND/OR DAMP: *Add $^{1}/_{4}$ teaspoon ground cinnamon when you stir in the ginger.*

mixed bean pâté

MAKES 5 CUPS, OR 10 (¹/₂-CUP) SERVINGS
106 calories per servings. 3 grams fat; 25% calories from fat

Beans promote relaxation by offering nerve-soothing B vitamins. In addition, beans are a good source of soluble fiber, which, when consumed regularly, may help lower high blood pressure.

¹/₂ cup dried chickpeas

¹/₂ cup dried black beans

¹/₂ cup dried aduki beans

4 cups water

1 bay leaf

2 slices fresh ginger

2 carrots, sliced

2 cloves garlic, minced

¹/₄ cup lemon juice

3 tablespoons tahini (sesame paste)

2 tablespoons balsamic vinegar

1 tablespoon light miso (see The Savory Pantry, page 424)

2 teaspoons hot pepper sauce, or to taste

SOAK THE CHICKPEAS, black beans, and aduki beans in water to cover overnight. Drain in the morning, then place the beans in a pressure cooker along with the 4 cups of water, bay leaf, ginger, and carrots. Cook according to manufacturer's directions until the beans are tender, about 20 minutes. Alternatively, cook the beans in a large soup pot, loosely covered, until tender, about 55 minutes. Drain the beans, pat dry, and discard the bay leaf and ginger.

PLACE THE BEANS in a processor or blender and whiz until pureed, adding the garlic, lemon juice, tahini, vinegar, miso, and hot pepper sauce halfway through. If your processor is small, puree the pâté in batches.

IF THE WEATHER IS HOT AND/OR DRY:
Use the pâté as a filling for roasted red peppers or as a dip for fresh vegetables.

IF THE WEATHER IS COLD AND/OR DAMP:
Mix half and half with Fresh Salsa (page 73) for a dip. Or serve warm as a sandwich spread.

eggplant spread with greek olives and garlic

MAKES 2 CUPS, OR 4 ($^1/_2$-CUP) SERVINGS
120 calories per serving; 7 grams fat; 53% calories from fat

Eggplant contains compounds that absorb cholesterol in the intestines, thus preventing cholesterol from being absorbed into the bloodstream. And while eggplant is not directly associated with the advancement of a calming mood, those who have consumed a fatty lunch may feel easier knowing that the eggplant is diluting the damage.

1$^1/_4$ pounds eggplant, peeled and thinly sliced

2 cloves garlic, thinly sliced

juice of 1 lemon

$^1/_2$ teaspoon cumin seed

$^1/_2$ teaspoon ground turmeric

1 bay leaf

1 cup vegetable stock

6 large purple Greek olives, pitted

3 tablespoons minced fresh parsley

1 to 2 tablespoons minced fresh cilantro

2 tablespoons tahini (sesame paste)

1 teaspoon hot pepper sauce

IN A MEDIUM saucepan, combine the eggplant, garlic, lemon juice, cumin seed, turmeric, bay leaf, and stock. Bring to a boil, reduce the heat, cover loosely, and simmer until the eggplant is very tender, about 10 minutes. Discard the bay leaf.

WHEN THE EGGPLANT mixture is cool enough to handle, transfer it (with the liquid) to a processor or blender and add the olives, parsley, cilanto, tahini, and hot pepper sauce. Whiz until smooth but slightly chunky, about 8 seconds. Serve warm or slightly chilled.

Note: Although the fat in this dish is not the cholesterol-producing, saturated type, it's still fat. If you'd like to reduce the amount of fat, substitute plain nonfat soy or regular yogurt for the tahini. Or use 1 tablespoon of each.

IF THE WEATHER IS HOT AND/OR DRY:
Be sure to use the larger amount of cilantro, then chill the spread and use on crackers or toasted baguette slices. Or hollow out cherry tomatoes and use the spread as a filling, topping each with a sprig of cilantro.

IF THE WEATHER IS COLD AND/OR DAMP:
Increase the amount of garlic to 2 cloves and use the lesser amount of cilantro. Serve warm on spicy slices of cornbread or focaccia.

pâté with olives, fresh basil, and roasted red peppers

MAKES ABOUT 2 ½ CUPS, OR 5 (½-CUP) SERVINGS
150 calories per serving: 5 grams fat: 30% calories from fat

English herbalists use basil to treat anxiety, saying that the volatile oils the herb contains act as a nervine.

Anxious or not, those who believe in love charms agree with the Italian notion that basil's heart-shaped leaves are a symbol of *amore*.

4 red bell peppers

6 large purple Greek or Chilean olives, pitted

2 cloves garlic, finely minced

2 teaspoons olive oil

⅓ cup fresh basil leaves

juice of ½ lemon

1 teaspoon balsamic vinegar

1½ cups cooked chickpeas

pinch of sea salt

freshly ground black pepper

To ROAST THE peppers, core and seed them. Broil about 4 inches from the heat source, turning frequently, until the pepper skins are charred. Arrange the peppers in a single layer in a large bowl and cover with a towel. Let them cool for 20 to 30 minutes. Then use your fingers and a sharp paring knife to peel off and discard the charred skins.

TIP THE PEPPERS (along with the pepper juice at the bottom of the bowl) in a processor or blender, add the olives, garlic, olive oil, basil, lemon juice, vinegar, chickpeas, salt, and pepper, and process until smooth. For the best flavor, let the pâté marinate overnight in the refrigerator.

IF THE WEATHER IS HOT AND/OR DRY:
Serve drizzled with olive oil on Pita Chips (page 128) and top with chopped fresh tomatoes and fresh basil. Or use as a sauce for just-cooked pasta, combining 4 cups of cooked penne with 1 cup of pâté.

IF THE WEATHER IS COLD AND/OR DAMP:
Be liberal with the freshly ground pepper and use the pâté as a dip for crunchy bread sticks or carrot batons.

mushroom-spinach spread

MAKES 1½ CUPS, OR 6 (¼-CUP) SERVINGS
75 calories per serving: 2 grams fat: 24% calories from fat

Stresses of the day can devitalize the body's immunity to disease. But the shiitake mushrooms in this savory spread contain antiviral compounds that help reactivate immunities.

1 tablespoon mirin or white wine

3 tablespoons vegetable stock

1 teaspoon reduced-sodium soy sauce

1 clove garlic, finely minced

1 teaspoon minced fresh sage or
    ½ teaspoon dried

10 ounces fresh shiitake mushrooms,
    stemmed and cut into ½-inch pieces

2 cups (not packed) coarsely chopped
    fresh spinach leaves

3½ ounces Faux Ricotta (page 127) or
    feta cheese

COMBINE THE MIRIN, stock, soy sauce, garlic, sage, and mushrooms in a large nonstick sauté pan and heat on medium-high for about 5 minutes, or until most of the liquid evaporates. Add the spinach and continue to cook, stirring constantly, until the spinach is wilted but still bright green, about 1 minute more.

TIP THE ENTIRE mixture in a processor or blender and whiz until smooth, adding the ricotta halfway through. Serve at room temperature or very slightly chilled.

IF THE WEATHER IS HOT AND/OR DRY:
Use lemon juice instead of the white wine and serve on cucumber or zucchini rounds.

IF THE WEATHER IS COLD AND/OR DAMP:
Add freshly ground black pepper to taste.

mushrooms with mellowing herbs

MAKES 4 SERVINGS
25 calories per serving; no added fat

Chamomile's volatile oil content combines with the supporting herbs of ginger and garlic to make this dish a mild sedative.

2 fresh portobello mushrooms (about 10 ounces), stemmed and thinly sliced

1/2 cup brewed chamomile tea

2 teaspoons reduced-sodium soy sauce

pinch of ground ginger

1 clove garlic, finely minced

1/2 teaspoon crushed dried chamomile flowers

COMBINE ALL OF the ingredients in a large sauté pan and heat on high until the liquid begins to boil. Reduce the heat to medium and simmer, stirring constantly, until the mushrooms are cooked through and the liquid evaporates, about 4 minutes. Serve warm atop crostini or crusty bread.

IF THE WEATHER IS HOT AND/OR DRY:
Add a 2-inch strip of fresh lemon zest during cooking. Discard the zest before serving.

IF THE WEATHER IS COLD AND/OR DAMP:
Sprinkle the mushrooms liberally with freshly ground black pepper.

grilled eggplant in lettuce petals

MAKES 4 SERVINGS
60 calories per serving: 1 gram fat: 15% calories from fat

This is a good starter for those who have nervous stomachs, since eggplant, along with the spearmint and ginger in this recipe, can help soothe tension in the tummy.

$^1/_3$ cup brewed spearmint tea	1 clove garlic, finely minced
1 teaspoon toasted (dark) sesame oil	1 pound eggplant, thinly sliced
2 teaspoons rice vinegar	curly lettuce leaves for serving
2 teaspoons miso (see The Savory Pantry, page 424)	2 tablespoons minced fresh chives
$^1/_4$ teaspoon finely grated fresh ginger	

COMBINE THE TEA, sesame oil, vinegar, miso, ginger, and garlic in a large bowl and add the eggplant, tossing well to coat all the slices. Let the eggplant marinate, stirring a couple of times, for about 30 minutes.

PREPARE THE GRILL or preheat the broiler. Grill the eggplant about 4$^1/_2$ inches from the heat source until cooked through and lightly burnished, 5 to 6 minutes on each side. Serve on the lettuce petals, sprinkled with the chives.

IF THE WEATHER IS HOT AND/OR DRY:
Serve the eggplant chilled with an accompaniment of chilled spearmint tea. To make 1 serving, steep 1 teaspoon of dried spearmint leaves in 1 cup of boiling water, covered, for 4 minutes, then chill.

IF THE WEATHER IS COLD AND/OR DAMP:
Use $^1/_2$ teaspoon of sesame oil and $^1/_2$ teaspoon of chili oil instead of all sesame oil. Serve warm on crusty bread instead of lettuce.

kibbe with sweet potato and sage

MAKES 4 SERVINGS
150 calories per serving: 2.5 grams fat; 15% calories from fat

Kibbe is popular in cuisines of the Middle East, where it usually takes the form of crisp patties made from meat and cracked wheat. In this vegetarian version the cracked wheat is cooked in brewed linden flower tea, which is a popular mild nerve tonic in France.

1 cup cracked wheat

1 1/2 cups hot brewed linden flower tea

1 clove garlic, minced

1 shallot, minced

1 medium sweet potato, peeled, chopped, and steamed

1 teaspoon minced fresh sage or 1/2 teaspoon dried

2 teaspoons olive oil

2 tablespoons whole wheat flour

IN A LARGE bowl, combine the cracked wheat, tea, garlic, and shallot. Cover and let stand until the wheat is soft and most of the tea has been absorbed, about 30 minutes. Discard any excess tea, then tip the cracked wheat mixture in a processor or blender along with the sweet potato, sage, oil, and flour. Whiz until the mixture becomes the texture of ground meat.

WET YOUR HANDS and shape the mixture into firm 3-inch patties. Heat a nonstick or well-seasoned cast-iron skillet on medium-high and cook the patties until lightly browned, about 2 minutes on each side. Serve warm with such condiments as Fresh Salsa (page 73) or Miso Mustard (page 160).

IF THE WEATHER IS HOT AND/OR DRY:
Serve with Chopped Vegetable Salad with Oregano and Lemon (page 88) or chilled fresh lemonade.

IF THE WEATHER IS COLD AND/OR DAMP:
Serve in toasted whole wheat pitas brushed with spicy mustard.

garlicky flatbread

MAKES 6 FLATBREADS
170 calories per flatbread: 5 grams fat: 27% calories from fat

Ayurvedic healers say that garlic and onion create *agni*, a digestive fire that helps the body absorb nutrients from food. Since tension can inhibit nutrient absorption, this crispy bread is a fitting appetizer for those who have experienced a rocky day.

1 cup whole wheat pastry flour

1 cup semolina flour

1 cup unbleached all-purpose flour

pinch of sea salt

1 cup egg substitute (see Note, page 13) or 8 egg whites

2 tablespoons olive oil

2 teaspoons fresh rosemary leaves or 1 teaspoon dried

1/3 cup finely minced onion

2 cloves garlic, finely minced

IN A MEDIUM bowl, combine the flours, salt, egg substitute, and 1 tablespoon of the oil, mixing until you have a smooth dough. Alternatively, you can mix the ingredients in a processor until the dough forms a smooth ball. Then set the dough in a bowl, cover with plastic wrap, and let it relax for 1 hour (it's not supposed to rise).

PREHEAT THE OVEN to 400°F.

DIVIDE THE DOUGH into 6 pieces and roll each as thin as possible into free-form shapes. If you have a pasta maker, it will work well.

SET THE ROLLED dough on parchment-lined baking sheets and pierce all over with a fork. Brush lightly with the remaining oil and sprinkle with the rosemary, onion, and garlic. Bake in the middle of the oven until crisp and lightly browned, about 10 minutes.

IF THE WEATHER IS HOT AND/OR DRY:
Substitute 2 teaspoons of crushed coriander seed for the rosemary.

IF THE WEATHER IF COLD AND/OR DAMP:
Sprinkle with freshly ground black pepper when you sprinkle on the rosemary.

focaccia with oregano

MAKES 8 APPETIZER SERVINGS
150 calories per serving: 2 grams fat: 12% calories from fat

Thanks to the volatile oils and friendly tannins that oregano contains, this fragrant bread can be a relaxing balm to those with tension-induced headaches or stomachaches.

$1/2$ cup warm brewed linden flower tea or vegetable stock

$1/2$ cup warm low-fat soy milk or low-fat cow's milk

1 package active dry yeast

1 tablespoon olive oil

1 cup plus 2 tablespoons whole wheat bread flour

1 cup plus 2 tablespoons unbleached all-purpose flour. plus extra for kneading

pinch of sea salt

2 tablespoons minced fresh oregano or 1 tablespoon dried

COMBINE THE STOCK. milk, and yeast in a large bowl and stir well. Let the mixture stand until foamy, about 10 minutes, then stir in the olive oil.

ADD THE FLOURS. salt, and oregano and stir well to combine. Tip the dough onto a floured surface and knead until smooth and elastic, about 10 minutes.

SET THE KNEADED dough in a large, lightly oiled bowl, turning it to coat all sides. Cover with plastic wrap and let the dough rise until it has doubled in size, about 1 hour.

SET BAKING TILES or a cookie sheet on the middle rack of the oven and preheat to 500°F.

ROLL THE DOUGH into a 12-inch circle and set it on a lightly floured wooden peel or perforated pizza pan. Pierce it with a fork in 4 or 5 places and set it on the baking tiles. Bake until fragrant and lightly browned, 10 to 12 minutes. Slice into wedges with kitchen shears and serve warm.

IF THE WEATHER IS HOT AND/OR DRY:
Serve topped with Grilled Eggplant (minus Lettuce Petals). page 146. or with an accompaniment of cherry tomatoes.

IF THE WEATHER IS COLD AND/OR DAMP:
Sprinkle with crushed dried red pepper to taste. lightly pressing the flakes into the dough before baking.

garlic crostini with fresh tomatoes

MAKES 8 CROSTINI
165 calories per serving: 1 gram fat: 6% calories from fat

The tomatoes are gently perfumed with lemon balm (*Melissa*), which contains essential oils that gently relieve nervous tension.

4 ripe medium tomatoes, cored and chopped

2 tablespoons minced fresh lemon balm

pinch of sea salt

freshly ground black pepper

1 whole grain baguette, cut into 8 slices

2 teaspoons olive oil

2 cloves garlic, peeled and halved

IN A MEDIUM bowl, combine the tomatoes, lemon balm, salt, and pepper and let the mixture marinate for about 30 minutes.

MEANWHILE, LIGHTLY BRUSH one side of each slice of bread with olive oil. Then rub each coated side with the cut side of garlic until the bread is fragrant.

PREHEAT THE BROILER. Set the bread slices on a wire rack and broil until toasted, 2 to 3 minutes. Arrange the toasted slices on a platter and top each with a scoop of the tomato mixture. Serve warm.

IF THE WEATHER IS HOT AND/OR DRY:
Go light on the black pepper.

IF THE WEATHER IS COLD AND/OR DAMP:
Sauté the tomatoes until they are slightly saucy, about 3 minutes, then stir in the lemon balm before serving.

whole wheat crepes with spicy chickpea filling

MAKES 4 SERVINGS
70 calories per serving: 1 gram fat; 13% calories from fat

Cumin seeds, which season this savory filling, are a common Ayurvedic folk remedy for nervous stomach and digestion.

4 egg whites or $^1/_2$ cup egg substitute (see Note, page 13)

$^1/_4$ cup plain low-fat soy milk

1 tablespoon whole wheat pastry flour

1 teaspoon olive oil

2 cloves garlic, minced

$^1/_4$ cup minced onion

2 teaspoons cumin seeds

$^1/_2$ teaspoon finely grated fresh ginger

1 cup cooked chickpeas, mashed coarsely with a fork

3 scallions, minced

To MAKE THE crepe batter, whisk together the egg whites, soy milk, and flour. Cover and refrigerate for 30 minutes.

To MAKE THE filling, heat the olive oil in a large nonstick sauté pan on medium-high, then add the garlic, onion, cumin seeds, and ginger and sauté until fragrant and lightly browned, about 3 minutes. Stir in the chickpeas and scallions and continue to sauté until heated through, about $1^1/_2$ minutes more.

To MAKE THE crepes, spray a 6-inch nonstick sauté pan or well-seasoned cast-iron skillet with nonstick spray and heat on medium-high. Pour in about 3 tablespoons of the crepe batter and let it cook until firm, about 2 minutes on each side. Repeat with the remaining batter until you have 4 crepes.

DIVIDE THE CHICKPEA filling among the crepes and use a cake icing knife to spread it. Roll up the crepes and serve warm.

IF THE WEATHER IS HOT AND/OR DRY:
Serve chilled. Or omit the chickpea filling and use 3 tablespoons goat cheese, 2 teaspoons minced fresh thyme, and 4 roasted red peppers, all pureed in a blender or processor until smooth.

IF THE WEATHER IS COLD AND/OR DAMP:
Add freshly ground black pepper to the crepe batter before chilling, and add crushed dried red pepper to taste to the chickpea filling.

corn crepes with fresh chives

MAKES 16 CREPES
25 calories per crepe: trace of fat

The Delaware Indians believed that corn nourished the spirit as well as the body. How intuitive they were, since it has since been documented that corn contains spirit-soothing B vitamins.

²/₃ cup fresh corn kernels

¹/₄ cup egg substitute (see Note. page 13) or 2 egg whites

¹/₂ cup plain low-fat soy milk or skim milk

1 tablespoon minced fresh chives

¹/₄ cup yellow cornmeal

¹/₄ cup unbleached all-purpose flour

pinch of sea salt

2 teaspoons olive oil

TIP THE CORN kernels in a processor or blender, whizzing until pureed. The pale yellow cream that results is called corn milk, and you should have about ¹/₂ cup. Whisk in the egg substitute, soy milk, and chives.

IN A MEDIUM bowl, stir together the cornmeal, flour, and sea salt. Pour the liquid ingredients in and mix well to combine.

HEAT A NONSTICK crepe pan on medium-high and brush with some of the olive oil. Pour about 2 tablespoons of batter into the pan, swirling the pan around until the batter forms a round crepe. Cook until the crepe is dotted with light brown, about 2 minutes on each side, then repeat with the remaining batter.

IF THE WEATHER IS HOT AND/OR DRY:
Fill the crepes with Eggplant Spread with Greek Olives and Garlic (page 142) or serve with Chopped Vegetable Salad with Oregano and Lemon (page 88).

IF THE WEATHER IS COLD AND/OR DAMP:
Serve with Fresh Salsa (page 73) or Spicy Orange Salsa (page 123).

sweet potato cutlets

MAKES 4 CUTLETS

170 calories per cutlet; 2 grams fat; 11% calories from fat

On-the-job stresses can increase the amount of age-promoting, damaging molecules in the body. But these cutlets give you a big dose of free radical–fighting beta carotene, helping to decrease the effects of the day's tensions.

1 pound sweet potatoes, peeled, cubed, and steamed	1/4 cup egg substitute (see Note, page 13) or 2 egg whites
1 carrot, grated	1/3 cup bread crumbs
4 scallions, minced	2 teaspoons olive oil
1 1/2 teaspoons good-quality curry powder	2 tablespoons minced fresh cilantro

IN A PROCESSOR or blender, combine the steamed sweet potatoes, carrot, scallions, curry powder, and egg substitute, whizzing until smooth. Shape the dough into 4 firm patties and press into the bread crumbs.

BRUSH A LARGE nonstick sauté pan with the oil and heat on medium-high. Set the cutlets in and sizzle until fragrant and heated through, about 2 1/2 minutes on each side. Sprinkle with the cilantro and serve warm.

IF THE WEATHER IS HOT AND/OR DRY:
Serve with Creamy Basil Spread (page 126) and sliced fresh cucumber.

IF THE WEATHER IS COLD AND/OR DAMP:
Substitute fresh parsley for the cilantro and add freshly ground black pepper when you add the salt. Serve with prepared Dijon-style mustard.

red lentil cakes with garlic and sage

MAKES 12 CAKES, OR 4 SERVINGS
180 calories per serving: 1.5 grams fat: 7% calories from fat

Cherokee healers prescribed sage, as a tea and in foods, for the treatment of nervous debility—a practice that is still being used to make commercial calming tea blends, which are often enhanced by the clean taste of this aromatic herb.

1 teaspoon olive oil	3½ cups vegetable stock
1 small onion, minced	½ teaspoon minced fresh lemongrass
1 clove garlic, minced	1 teaspoon minced fresh sage
1 cup small dried red lentils	2 teaspoons reduced-sodium soy sauce
½ cup whole wheat or white couscous	

HEAT A MEDIUM saucepan on medium-high then add the olive oil, onion, and garlic. Sauté until fragrant and slightly wilted, about 2½ minutes. Add the lentils, couscous, stock, lemongrass, sage, and soy sauce and bring to a boil. Reduce the heat and simmer uncovered for 10 minutes, then remove the pan from the heat. Cover the pan and let it sit for 10 minutes.

TRANSFER THE MIXTURE to a processor or blender, whizzing until pureed. When the puree is cool enough to handle, in about 4 minutes, form it into 12 firm 2-inch cakes. (To reheat, sizzle the cakes in a lightly oiled nonstick sauté pan for about 1 minute on each side.)

IF THE WEATHER IS HOT AND/OR DRY:
Serve with a side of sliced avocado sprinkled with fresh lime juice.

IF THE WEATHER IS COLD AND/OR DAMP:
Increase the garlic to 2 cloves and serve the cakes with a spicy mango chutney or Plum Chutney (page 155).

plum chutney

MAKES 1 1/2 CUPS, OR 6 (1/4-CUP) SERVINGS
135 calories per serving: no added fat

Many health systems, including Chinese, Vietnamese, and Ayurvedic, maintain that eating very spicy food can aggravate existing stress and anxiety. But using this thick and soothing condiment to complement fiery dishes lets you enjoy some spice without losing your cool.

12 medium-ripe red plums, pitted and chopped

1/3 to 1/2 cup barley malt

1 lime, sliced (including peel) and seeded

1/2 cup orange juice

1 tablespoon balsamic vinegar

IN A MEDIUM saucepan, combine the plums, barley malt, lime, and orange juice and bring to a boil. If the plums are sweet, use the lesser amount of barley malt. If they are tart, use more.

REDUCE THE HEAT to medium and let the plums simmer until they appear to have dissolved, about 10 minutes, stirring frequently to prevent burning. Stir in the balsamic vinegar and chill until ready to serve. The chutney can be stored in a covered jar, refrigerated, for up to 1 month.

IF THE WEATHER IS HOT AND/OR DRY:
Use the chutney as an accompaniment to chili, curry, or sandwiches with spicy fillings.

IF THE WEATHER IS COLD AND/OR DAMP:
Add 1 teaspoon ground cinnamon to the plums during cooking. Enjoy the chutney with spicy stews and other pungent entrées.

sauces dips and condiments

dilled red onion

MAKES 4 SERVINGS
58 calories per serving: 1 gram fat; 16% calories from fat

Dill contains the volatile oils carvone and limonene, combining to make the herb a carminative, or a substance that can settle nervous stomach spasms.

4 red onions, peeled, thinly sliced, and separated into rings

2/3 cup vegetable stock or water

1 tablespoon balsamic vinegar

1 teaspoon olive oil

1 tablespoon minced fresh dill

2 scallions, finely minced

freshly ground black pepper

COMBINE THE ONIONS and stock in a medium saucepan and bring to a boil. Reduce the heat and simmer, stirring frequently, until the onions are wilted and the liquid has nearly evaporated, about 9 minutes.

PAT THE ONIONS dry, place in a bowl, and add the vinegar, oil, dill, scallions, and pepper. Serve warm or chilled as an accompaniment to grilled or baked tofu, tempeh, or fish.

IF THE WEATHER IS HOT AND/OR DRY: *Serve the onions slightly chilled.*

IF THE WEATHER IS COLD AND/OR DAMP: *Stir in a pinch of ground cayenne pepper and serve the onions warm.*

warm tomato relish with basil and pine nuts

MAKES 2 CUPS, OR 4 (¹/₂-CUP) SERVINGS
66 calories per serving: 2 grams fat: 27% calories from fat

Many health experts hold basil to be an effective and gentle nerve tonic. In India, where basil is called *tulsi*, stems of the fresh herb are woven together and hung around the neck, where the aroma bestows calmness and clarity to the wearer.

1 tablespoon pine nuts

1 clove garlic, peeled

¹/₄ cup packed fresh basil leaves

1 pound ripe tomatoes, cored and finely chopped

1 teaspoon balsamic vinegar

pinch of sea salt

TO TOAST THE nuts, tip them into a nonstick sauté pan and heat on medium-high, stirring frequently, until lightly browned, about 2¹/₂ minutes.

TIP THE NUTS into a processor or blender and add the garlic, basil, tomatoes, vinegar, and salt. Whiz until combined but not completely smooth, about 5 seconds.

SCOOP THE MIXTURE into the sauté pan and heat on medium until just fragrant, about 2 minutes. Serve with rice or corn-based entrées.

IF THE WEATHER IS HOT AND/OR DRY:
Serve the relish slightly chilled on cold poached salmon.

IF THE WEATHER IS COLD AND/OR DAMP:
After sautéing, stir in 1 teaspoon (or to taste) of hot pepper sauce.

onion gravy with rosemary
(for tofu and tempeh)

MAKES 4 SERVINGS
45 calories per serving: 1 gram fat: 20% calories from fat

Savory cooked onions in a thick, rosemary-scented sauce help make soothing soy foods more delicious and digestible.

1 teaspoon olive oil

1 large onion, thinly sliced

1 clove garlic, finely minced

1 bay leaf

$^1/_2$ teaspoon minced fresh rosemary

$^3/_4$ teaspoon minced fresh lemongrass

$1^1/_4$ cups vegetable stock

2 teaspoons red miso (see The Savory Pantry, page 424)

1 tablespoon plus 1 teaspoon arrowroot

1 teaspoon minced fresh chives

HEAT THE OLIVE oil in a large nonstick sauté pan on medium-high. Add the onion, garlic, and bay leaf and sauté until the onion is fragrant and lightly browned, about 4 minutes. Add the rosemary, lemongrass, and stock and boil until the liquid has been reduced by half, about 4 minutes. Remove the pan from the heat.

WORKING QUICKLY, SCOOP about $^1/_4$ cup of the liquid into a small dish and add the miso, arrowroot, chives, and about $^1/_4$ cup water. Whisk well to combine. Pour into the pan and stir constantly until the arrowroot has become shiny and has thickened the gravy. Serve warm on baked or grilled tofu, tempeh, or seitan.

IF THE WEATHER IS HOT AND/OR DRY:
Add $^1/_4$ teaspoon grated fresh ginger when whisking the miso mixture.

IF THE WEATHER IS COLD AND/OR DAMP:
Add $^1/_4$ teaspoon ground ginger and freshly ground black pepper to taste when whisking the miso mixture.

lemony dipping sauce
(for tofu and tempeh)

MAKES ENOUGH FOR DIPPING 1 POUND (OR 4 ENTRÉE SERVINGS) OF COOKED TOFU OR TEMPEH
10 calories per serving: less than 1 gram fat

The miso in this savory condiment serves as an evening restorative by relaxing the body and aiding digestion.

1 tablespoon miso (see The Savory Pantry. page 424)

1 tablespoon fresh lemon juice

3 tablespoons vegetable stock

dash of hot pepper sauce. or to taste

WHISK TOGETHER ALL of the ingredients and serve at room temperature.

IF THE WEATHER IS HOT AND/OR DRY:
Add 1 teaspoon of minced fresh cilantro to the recipe before serving.

IF THE WEATHER IS COLD AND/OR DAMP:
Add 1/2 teaspoon (or to taste) of prepared hot mustard to the recipe before serving.

miso mustard

MAKES ABOUT ¼ CUP, OR 4 (1-TABLESPOON) SERVINGS
15 calories per serving: no added fat

This zesty condiment illustrates how balancing flavors leads to a balanced disposition. Think of how a dense, fried Chinese egg roll tastes better when paired with the snappy flavor of mustard. Not only is the balance of taste improved, but the mustard actually helps make the oily egg roll easier for the body to assimilate, thus preventing a grumpy bout with indigestion. Use this condiment in the same way, to balance such before-meal fatty tidbits as cheeses or deep-fried vegetables.

1 tablespoon miso (see The Savory Pantry, page 424)

3 tablespoons prepared coarse-style mustard

1 teaspoon balsamic vinegar

WHISK TOGETHER ALL of the ingredients and serve at room temperature.

IF THE WEATHER IS HOT AND/OR DRY:
Use the mustard in a marinade for fresh vegetables by mixing 1 tablespoon with 2 tablespoons of fresh lemon juice for every 2 cups of veggies.

IF THE WEATHER IS COLD AND/OR DAMP:
Add ½ teaspoon (or to taste) of prepared horseradish to the recipe before whisking.

nerimiso

MAKES ABOUT 7 (1-TABLESPOON) SERVINGS
35 calories per serving; less than 1 gram fat; 20% calories from fat

This name means "simmered" miso, from a concept originating in ancient Japanese Zen temples. *Nerimiso* is used as a table condiment for rice-based dishes, cooked tofu, and steamed vegetables. This particular variation contains garlic, carrot, ginger, and thyme to help replenish the body after a stressful day.

5 tablespoons miso (see The Savory Pantry, page 424)

1 tablespoon barley malt

1 tablespoon mirin, white wine, or lemon juice

1 tablespoon finely grated carrot

1/2 teaspoon finely grated fresh ginger

1 small clove garlic, mashed through a garlic press

1/2 teaspoon minced fresh thyme

COMBINE ALL OF the ingredients in a small nonstick sauté pan on medium heat. Simmer, stirring frequently, until slightly thickened, about 2 minutes. Serve warm or slightly chilled, or store in a covered jar, refrigerated, for up to 1 month.

IF THE WEATHER IS HOT AND/OR DRY:
Substitute a finely minced shallot for the garlic.

IF THE WEATHER IS COLD AND/OR DAMP:
Increase the garlic to 2 cloves.

ginger-carrot marinade

MAKES 4 SERVINGS
30 calories per serving: no added fat

Jamu practitioners, or Indonesian herbalists, prescribe ginger to aid in the digestion of fatty meats, especially in the evening when there will be little activity to work off the fat before sleep. You can also enjoy this zippy marinade with tofu, tempeh, seitan, or lean fish.

1/4 cup very finely grated carrot

2 tablespoons very finely grated fresh ginger

2 cloves garlic, finely minced

1 tablespoon reduced-sodium soy sauce

2 tablespoons lemon juice

1 tablespoon cider vinegar

2 tablespoons vegetable stock

1 teaspoon tomato paste

COMBINE ALL OF the ingredients and use as a marinade for 1 pound of meat, fish, poultry, or tofu, allowing the food of choice to marinate for about 30 minutes.

IF THE WEATHER IS HOT AND/OR DRY:
Omit the garlic and use the marinade for baked or grilled tofu.

IF THE WEATHER IS COLD AND/OR DAMP:
Use the marinade for roasted root vegetables, such as parsnips, carrots, and turnips.

broccoli with black bean sauce

MAKES 4 SERVINGS
80 calories per serving: no added fat

Broccoli is a good source of the calming mineral calcium.

- 1 head broccoli (about 1 pound), cut into florets
- 1 tablespoon Chinese fermented black beans (see The Savory Pantry, page 423), rinsed and minced
- 1 teaspoon mirin or dry sherry
- 2 teaspoons reduced-sodium soy sauce
- ½ teaspoon miso (see The Savory Pantry, page 424)

- ⅓ cup vegetable stock
- 1 clove garlic, peeled
- 2 teaspoons arrowroot
- 1 tablespoon water
- 2 teaspoons minced fresh chives

STEAM THE BROCCOLI over boiling water until bright green and just tender, about 7 minutes.

MEANWHILE, TO MAKE the sauce, combine the black beans, mirin, soy sauce, miso, stock, and garlic in a small saucepan over high heat and boil until reduced by half, 4 to 5 minutes. Discard the garlic.

IN A SMALL bowl, combine the arrowroot, water, and chives, pour into the sauce, and stir constantly until slightly thickened, about 25 seconds. Remove the sauce from the heat and toss with the broccoli. Serve warm.

IF THE WEATHER IS HOT AND/OR DRY:
Toss the broccoli with an equal amount of cooked thin rice noodles and serve at room temperature or very slightly chilled.

IF THE WEATHER IS COLD AND/OR DAMP:
Mince the garlic and leave it in the dish.

side dishes and salads

quick gingered peas

MAKES 4 SERVINGS
42 calories per serving: less than 1 gram fat; 18% calories from fat

Peas contain the soluble type of fiber that helps stabilize energy levels and, when consumed regularly, may even help lower stress-related high blood pressure.

2 slices fresh ginger	$1/2$ teaspoon balsamic vinegar
9 ounces snow peas, strings removed	pinch of sea salt
$1/2$ teaspoon toasted (dark) sesame oil	freshly ground black pepper

COMBINE THE GINGER and some water in a medium pot, and bring to a boil. Steam the peas over the ginger water until bright green and just tender, 2 to 3 minutes.

TOSS THE PEAS with the sesame oil, balsamic vinegar, salt, and pepper and serve warm or very slightly chilled.

IF THE WEATHER IS HOT AND/OR DRY:
Substitute 1 teaspoon of lemon juice for the $1/2$ teaspoon of balsamic vinegar. Serve the peas slightly chilled as a side salad.

IF THE WEATHER IS COLD AND/OR DAMP:
Add a pinch of good-quality curry powder when you add the salt and pepper.

corn on the cob with miso

MAKES 4 SERVINGS
93 calories per serving: 1.5 grams fat; 14% calories from fat

Corn is a good source of the stress-soothing B vitamins, as well as the mineral potassium, which is important for normalizing high blood pressure.

4 ears of corn, shucked	1½ teaspoons miso (see The Savory Pantry, page 424)

STEAM THE CORN over boiling water until tender, about 12 minutes. Then mix 1½ teaspoons of the steaming water with the miso and, using a pastry brush, spread it on the corn before serving warm.

IF THE WEATHER IS HOT AND/OR DRY:
Mix the miso with 1½ teaspoons of tomato juice instead of the steaming water.

IF THE WEATHER IS COLD AND/OR DAMP:
Add ½ teaspoon of prepared mustard to the miso when mixing.

steamed corn on the cob with garlic paste

MAKES 4 SERVINGS
105 calories per serving: 2 grams fat: 17% calories from fat

Daily doses of aspirin and antacids can deplete your stores of immune-enhancing, blood-building folate. But since corn is a good source of the nutrient, an ear a day may keep the doctor away.

4 ears of corn, shucked

1 bay leaf

2 large cloves garlic, peeled and halved

1 tablespoon vegetable stock

1 teaspoon olive oil

pinch of sea salt

ARRANGE THE EARS in a steamer basket over boiling water, tucking the bay leaf under them. Add the garlic, cover, and steam until the ears are tender, about 4 minutes. Discard the bay leaf.

IN A SMALL bowl, use a fork to mash the steamed garlic with the stock, olive oil, and salt. Rub the paste lightly over each ear before serving warm.

IF THE WEATHER IS HOT AND/OR DRY:
Add a pinch of ground coriander to the garlic paste when mashing.

IF THE WEATHER IS COLD AND/OR DAMP:
Add freshly ground pepper to taste or a pinch of curry powder to the garlic paste when mashing.

nishime-style vegetables

MAKES 4 SERVINGS
85 calories per serving; 1 gram fat; 11% calories from fat

This is one way that seasonal vegetables are prepared and served in small Japanese villages. The gentle cooking style of slow simmering in water is reputed to be restorative and calming.

⅓ pound broccoli florets	2 scallions, minced
2 carrots, sliced into coins	1 teaspoon toasted (dark) sesame oil
⅓ pound snow peas, strings removed	1 tablespoon lemon juice

BRING ABOUT 2 inches of water to a boil in a medium saucepan. Add the broccoli and carrots, cover loosely, reduce the heat to medium, and cook until the vegetables are almost tender, about 5 minutes. Add the snow peas and continue to simmer until tender, 2 to 3 minutes more. Remove the vegetables from the water, reserving about 2 tablespoons of the cooking water.

IN A SMALL bowl, mix together the reserved cooking water, scallions, sesame oil, and lemon juice, then toss with the vegetables.

IF THE WEATHER IS HOT AND/OR DRY:	IF THE WEATHER IS COLD AND/OR DAMP:
Serve the vegetables slightly chilled as a salad on a bed of mixed greens.	*Mix the scallions, oil, and lemon juice with the entire amount of cooking water and serve as a vegetable soup garnished with freshly ground black pepper.*

curried red potatoes

MAKES 4 SERVINGS.
140 calories per serving: 2 grams fat: 12% calories from fat.

A useful dish for those who want to "de-tox" their systems gently, this curry contains turmeric, which in India is prescribed to help cleanse a stressed liver. In China, where turmeric is called *yu jin*, it is taken as a tea to help treat liver congestion and gallstones.

2 teaspoons olive oil	1 pound potatoes, steamed and cubed
1 small onion, minced	$^1/_4$ cup vegetable stock
1 clove garlic, minced	1 tablespoon minced fresh chives
1 teaspoon flavorful curry powder	

HEAT THE OIL in a large nonstick sauté pan on medium-high. Add the onion, garlic, and curry powder and sauté until the vegetables are wilted and fragrant, about $2^1/_2$ minutes. Add the potatoes and stock and heat, stirring constantly, until most of the stock has evaporated, about 2 minutes. Sprinkle with the chives before serving.

IF THE WEATHER IS HOT AND/OR DRY:
Instead of mincing the garlic, spear it with a toothpick for sautéing and discard it before serving. Then substitute minced fresh cilantro for the chives.

IF THE WEATHER IS COLD AND/OR DAMP:
Double the amount of garlic and stir in a pinch of cayenne pepper before serving.

collards with black pepper and red wine

MAKES 4 SERVINGS
40 calories per serving: trace of fat

These homey greens, when eaten three times a week, may comfort colons that are spastic and stressed.

$^1/_2$ teaspoon olive oil

lots of freshly ground black pepper

1 clove garlic, minced

1 bunch fresh collards (about 7 ounces), rinsed and sliced

2 tablespoons dry red wine or lemon juice

HEAT THE OIL in a large nonstick sauté pan on high heat. Add the pepper, garlic, and collards and sauté on high heat until the collards are bright green and just wilted. When the collards just begin to look dry, add the wine and sauté until it appears to have evaporated, about 1 minute.

IF THE WEATHER IS HOT AND/OR DRY:
Serve slightly chilled as a salad, accompanied by Garlic Crostini with Fresh Tomatoes (page 150).

IF THE WEATHER IS COLD AND/OR DAMP:
Double the garlic and serve warm.

carrot and burdock, kinpira style

MAKES 4 SERVINGS
42 calories per serving: trace of fat

Kinpira is a Japanese method of cooking root vegetables for maximum flavor. The vegetables are sautéed, then simmered. In this recipe carrot and burdock are featured, acting as "skin savers" for people who spend their days in harsh weather or polluted atmospheres, since both vegetables contain compounds that tonify the complexion.

$1/2$ teaspoon olive oil

3 medium carrots, julienned

2 fresh burdock roots (see The Savory Pantry, page 422), julienned

1 medium onion, sliced

1 teaspoon dried nettle (see The Savory Pantry, page 424) or 1 tablespoon minced fresh parsley

$1/2$ to 1 cup vegetable stock

HEAT THE OIL in a medium saucepan over medium-high. Add the carrots, burdock roots, onion, and nettle and sauté until fragrant, about 3 minutes. Add $1/2$ cup of the stock and bring the mixture to a boil. Cover loosely, reduce the heat, and continue to simmer until the vegetables are tender, 12 to 15 minutes, adding more stock if you need it.

IF THE WEATHER IS HOT AND/OR DRY: *Reverse the quantities of carrot and burdock by using 2 carrots and 3 burdock roots.*

IF THE WEATHER IS COLD AND/OR DAMP: *Add 1 clove of minced garlic when you add the onion.*

stuffed peppers with arugula and olives

MAKES 4 SERVINGS

170 calories per serving: 1.5 grams fat: 8% calories from fat

This recipe is a whole-body restorative to help end the day on a healthful note. The peppers, arugula, and carrots replenish the body with vitamin C and beta carotene, which act as guards against cell damage due to internal and environmental stresses.

4 large red bell peppers (8 to 10 ounces each), cored and seeded

1 1/2 cups vegetable stock

1 cup whole wheat or white couscous

1 bay leaf

1 clove garlic, minced

1 carrot, grated (about 1/2 cup)

1/2 cup finely chopped arugula

2 scallions, minced

3 tablespoons chopped green olives

1/4 cup tomato salsa, such as Fresh Salsa (page 73)

1/4 cup grated nonfat soy mozzarella or part-skim mozzarella cheese

PREHEAT THE OVEN to 375°F.

COVER THE PEPPERS with boiling water and simmer until just tender, 3 to 3 1/2 minutes. Then drain and pat dry.

MEANWHILE, IN A small saucepan, combine the stock, couscous, bay leaf, and garlic and bring to a boil. Reduce the heat, cover loosely, and simmer until all of the stock has been absorbed, about 5 minutes. Discard bay leaf.

STIR THE CARROT, arugula, scallions, olives, salsa, and mozzarella into the couscous. Pack the couscous mixture into the peppers. Then set the peppers in a baking pan and bake until warmed through and the cheese has melted, about 15 minutes.

IF THE WEATHER IS HOT AND/OR DRY:
Serve the peppers in a pool of tomato sauce.

IF THE WEATHER IS COLD AND/OR DAMP:
Double the garlic and serve the peppers drizzled with extra salsa.

chilled steamed vegetables with yogurt-dill dressing

MAKES 4 SERVINGS
85 calories per serving: 1 gram fat: 11% calories from fat

Both broccoli and cauliflower are cruciferous vegetables, a plant family that modern science believes can help prevent cancer when consumed regularly. Since daily tensions can diminish our defenses against cancer and other illnesses, this salad serves as a fitting tonic.

1 small head cauliflower
  (about 1 1/4 pounds), cut into florets

1 cup broccoli florets (4 to 5 ounces)

2 medium carrots, sliced into coins

1 teaspoon olive oil

1 teaspoon cumin seeds

1 clove garlic, finely minced

4 scallions, minced

2 teaspoons minced fresh dill or
  1 teaspoon dried

1/2 cup plain nonfat yogurt or soy yogurt

STEAM THE CAULIFLOWER, broccoli, and carrots over boiling water until tender, 7 to 8 minutes.

HEAT THE OIL in a small sauté pan on medium-high, then add the cumin seed and garlic. Sauté until fragrant, 2 to 3 minutes. The seeds will pop, which is okay. Remove the pan from the heat and stir in the scallions, dill, and yogurt. When the vegetables are ready, pat them dry and toss with the dressing. Chill for at least 1 hour before serving.

IF THE WEATHER IS HOT AND/OR DRY:
Omit the carrots and add 1 cup of chopped cherry tomatoes when you combine the steamed vegetables with the dressing.

IF THE WEATHER IS COLD AND/OR DAMP:
Add 1 teaspoon (or to taste) of hot pepper sauce to the dressing and serve the dish warm with a side of garlic bread or a cup of hot soup.

grilled vegetable salad with tomato-rosemary dressing

MAKES 4 SERVINGS
75 calories per serving: 1 gram fat: 12% calories from fat

A diet rich in high-fiber vegetables plays an important role in strengthening digestion, especially in the wake of a chaotic day. This salad is a good example of how a vegetable-based dish can be satisfying when perfumed with robust rosemary and garlic.

3 yellow summer squash (about 9 ounces total), thinly sliced lengthwise

3 zucchini (about 9 ounces total), thinly sliced lengthwise

2 thin purple Asian eggplant (about 9 ounces total), thinly sliced lengthwise

1 onion (about 8 ounces), thinly sliced

1/4 cup lemon juice

1 tablespoon balsamic vinegar

1 teaspoon olive oil

2 medium tomatoes, chopped

2 teaspoons minced fresh rosemary or 1 teaspoon dried

1 clove garlic, minced

2 tablespoons minced fresh chives

lemon wedges for serving

PREPARE THE GRILL or preheat the broiler.

COMBINE THE YELLOW squash, zucchini, eggplant, and onion in a large bowl and stir in the lemon juice, vinegar, oil, tomatoes, rosemary, and garlic. Let the vegetables marinate for 20 minutes, then grill or broil about 4 inches from the heat source, turning frequently, until mottled with brown and tender, about 15 minutes. Sprinkle with the chives before serving warm or at room temperature with the lemon wedges.

IF THE WEATHER IS HOT AND/OR DRY:
Serve the salad slightly chilled on a bed of mixed greens.

IF THE WEATHER IS COLD AND/OR DAMP:
Double the garlic and add a minced fresh jalapeño along with it.

brussels sprouts with shiitakes and shallots

MAKES 4 SERVINGS
50 calories per serving: 1 gram fat: 18% calories from fat

People who eat a steady diet of Brussels sprouts, such as residents of Russia and Poland, have a comparatively low incidence of gastrointestinal diseases, including colon cancer. Those who have a family history of such disorders may benefit from adding Brussels sprouts to three evening meals a week.

³/₄ pound small Brussels sprouts

¹/₄ pound fresh shiitake mushrooms (about 12), stemmed and sliced

1 shallot, minced

2 tablespoons lemon juice

1 teaspoon olive oil

1 teaspoon minced fresh rosemary

pinch of sea salt

STEAM THE SPROUTS and mushrooms over boiling water until the sprouts are tender, about 12 minutes. Toss with the shallot, lemon juice, olive oil, rosemary, and salt and serve.

IF THE WEATHER IS HOT AND/OR DRY:
Serve the sprouts slightly chilled on a bed of curly red leaf lettuce.

IF THE WEATHER IS COLD AND/OR DAMP:
Use 2 cloves of minced garlic instead of the shallot and sprinkle the dish with freshly ground black pepper before serving.

yellow beans with asparagus

MAKES 4 SERVINGS
45 calories per serving; 1 gram fat; 21% calories from fat

A bracer for the immune system, the asparagus in this dish contains phytochemicals, which can help the body fight disease.

²/₃ pound asparagus, trimmed	1 teaspoon cumin seed
¹/₂ pound yellow wax beans, trimmed	1 teaspoon fennel seed
¹/₂ teaspoon olive oil	1 teaspoon lemon juice
¹/₂ teaspoon mustard oil	2 tablespoons minced fresh basil
1 teaspoon ground coriander	pinch of sea salt

STEAM THE ASPARAGUS and beans over boiling water until tender, about 5 minutes.

MEANWHILE, IN A medium sauté pan, heat the oils on medium-high heat. Add the coriander, cumin seed, and fennel seed and sauté until fragrant and lightly browned, about 1¹/₂ minutes. The seeds will pop, which is okay.

WHEN THE VEGETABLES are ready, add them to the sauté pan with the lemon juice, basil, and salt and toss well to combine.

IF THE WEATHER IS HOT AND/OR DRY:
Serve chilled with lemon or lime wedges for drizzling.

IF THE WEATHER IS COLD AND/OR DAMP:
Mix 1 teaspoon of prepared mustard with the lemon juice before adding to the dish.

blanched asparagus with citrus-cider dressing

MAKES 4 SERVINGS
90 calories per serving: 3 grams fat: 30% calories from fat

To retain valuable nutrients in such delicate vegetables as asparagus and leafy greens, Japanese cooks prepare them "*ohitashi* style," or blanched. As well as being healthful, ohitashi is quick, allowing you to prepare a fresh and wholesome dish on even the busiest of weekdays.

1 ¼ pounds fresh asparagus, trimmed

2 tablespoons cider vinegar

1 tablespoon olive oil

¼ teaspoon prepared mustard

¼ teaspoon freshly grated orange zest

IN A SAUTÉ pan, cover the asparagus with boiling water and simmer until bright green and just tender, 1 to 2 minutes for thin spears and longer for thicker ones. Pat dry.

IN A SMALL bowl, whisk together the vinegar, oil, mustard, and orange zest. Toss well with the asparagus and serve.

IF THE WEATHER IS HOT AND/OR DRY:
Serve the asparagus slightly chilled on a nest of arugula or fresh spinach.

IF THE WEATHER IS COLD AND/OR DAMP:
Serve the asparagus warm with an accompaniment of crusty garlic bread.

squash and sugar snaps
with black bean sauce

MAKES 4 SERVINGS
67 calories per serving: 1 gram fat: 14% calories from fat

Those who are susceptible to colds and flu may find this dish a health booster. The beans and the sugar snap peas are good sources of protease inhibitors, which are thought to help deter viral infections.

1 1/2 cups chopped green and yellow beans	1 clove garlic, minced
1 1/2 cups sugar snap peas, strings removed	1/4 cup cooked black beans
1 yellow squash, cut into 1/2-inch slices	2 tablespoons lime juice
2 teaspoons olive oil	1 teaspoon hot pepper sauce
1/4 teaspoon ground turmeric	3 tablespoons minced fresh cilantro or parsley
1/2 teaspoon ground cumin	

STEAM THE GREEN and yellow beans, sugar snaps, and squash over boiling water until tender, about 6 minutes. Pat dry.

HEAT THE OLIVE oil in a large nonstick sauté pan over medium-high and add the turmeric, cumin, and garlic. Sauté until fragrant, about 2 minutes. Toss with the steamed vegetables, black beans, lime juice, hot pepper sauce, and cilantro.

IF THE WEATHER IS HOT AND/OR DRY:
Serve slightly chilled and use the cilantro rather than the parsley.

IF THE WEATHER IS COLD AND/OR DAMP:
Serve warm, using the parsley rather than the cilantro.

warm red potatoes with tomato and scallion

MAKES 4 SERVINGS
130 calories per serving: no added fat

Potatoes contain strong antiviral properties, making them the perfect dinner partner when a seasonal virus is making the rounds.

3 medium waxy red potatoes (about 1 pound), thinly sliced

2 medium tomatoes, chopped

2 cloves garlic, very finely minced

2 teaspoons minced fresh oregano or 1 teaspoon dried

2 tablespoons minced fresh basil

3 scallions, finely minced

pinch of sea salt

STEAM THE POTATOES over boiling water until tender, 10 to 12 minutes.

MEANWHILE, IN A medium bowl, combine the tomatoes, garlic, oregano, basil, scallions, and salt. When the potatoes are ready, toss them in and mix well.

IF THE WEATHER IS HOT AND/OR DRY:
Serve the potatoes slightly chilled with an extra tablespoon of basil.

IF THE WEATHER IS COLD AND/OR DAMP:
Substitute 3 tablespoons of minced raw onion for the scallions.

braised baby squash with garam masala

MAKES 4 SERVINGS

95 calories per serving: 1 gram fat: 10% calories from fat

In India, where this dish is called *tinda*, the garam masala spice paste is said to soothe digestion and aid the assimilation of nutrients.

2 teaspoons olive oil

2 cloves elephant garlic, minced

1 teaspoon garam masala spice paste
(see The Savory Pantry, page 424)

3 cups chopped tomatoes

1 fresh jalapeño pepper, minced

1 teaspoon reduced-sodium soy sauce

1 pound baby squash, small zucchini, or
pickling cucumbers, thinly sliced

minced fresh cilantro for garnish

HEAT THE OLIVE oil in a large sauté pan on medium-high. Add the garlic and garam masala and sauté until fragrant and lightly cooked, about 3 minutes. Add the tomatoes and jalapeño and bring to a boil. Continue to boil for 2 minutes, then add the soy sauce and squash. Reduce the heat, cover loosely, and let the mixture simmer for about 20 minutes. Sprinkle with cilantro before serving.

IF THE WEATHER IS HOT AND/OR DRY:
Reduce the garlic to 1 clove and serve the dish slightly chilled.

IF THE WEATHER IS COLD AND/OR DAMP:
Serve the dish warm, garnished with minced fresh parsley instead of cilantro.

gratin of leeks and brussels sprouts

MAKES 4 SERVINGS
160 calories per serving: 3 grams fat; 16% calories from fat

Those who have difficulty digesting Brussels sprouts will experience a more sociable evening with this dish, since nutmeg eases the intestinal turmoil sometimes associated with the health-giving vegetable.

2 teaspoons olive oil	$^1/_4$ teaspoon freshly grated nutmeg
2 large leeks, trimmed, rinsed, and chopped	$^1/_4$ teaspoon freshly ground black pepper
$^1/_2$ pound Brussels sprouts, trimmed and quartered	$^1/_4$ cup grated nonfat soy mozzarella or part-skim mozzarella cheese
2 tablespoons flour	1 heaping tablespoon minced fresh parsley
1 cup plain low-fat soy milk or skim milk	1 plum tomato, thinly sliced

PREHEAT THE OVEN to 375°F.

HEAT THE OLIVE oil in a large sauté pan on medium-high. Add the leeks and Brussels sprouts and sauté until slightly soft and fragrant, about 3 minutes. Add the flour, then whisk in the milk, nutmeg, pepper, cheese, and parsley. Spoon the mixture into a lightly oiled 8-inch quiche dish and top with the tomato. Bake in the middle of the oven until the top is lightly browned, about 25 minutes.

IF THE WEATHER IS HOT AND/OR DRY: *Sprinkle with fresh watercress leaves before serving.*

IF THE WEATHER IS COLD AND/OR DAMP: *Add 1 clove of minced garlic when you sauté the leeks and garnish the dish with minced scallion before serving.*

broccoli with lemon sauce

MAKES 4 SERVINGS
30 calories per serving; trace of fat

Traditional Chinese medicine holds that lemon helps to dispel any angry feelings that have amassed during the day by regulating the liver energy, or liver *chi*. Western medicine has yet to comment on this theory, but it's certain that the lemony sauce in this dish has a pleasing effect on the broccoli.

1 pound broccoli florets

3 tablespoons fresh lemon juice

$1/2$ teaspoon tahini (sesame paste)

dash of hot pepper sauce

STEAM THE BROCCOLI over boiling water until bright green and tender, 7 to 9 minutes.

MEANWHILE, IN A small bowl, whisk together the lemon juice, tahini, and hot pepper sauce. When the broccoli is done, pour on the sauce and toss well.

IF THE WEATHER IS HOT AND/OR DRY:
Serve the broccoli slightly chilled with lemon wedges for drizzling.

IF THE WEATHER IS COLD AND/OR DAMP:
Serve the broccoli warm and increase the hot pepper sauce to $1/2$ teaspoon (or to taste).

coleslaw with roasted peppers

MAKES 4 SERVINGS
44 calories per serving: 1 gram fat; 21% calories from fat

Stomach ulcer sufferers may wish to add this dish to their dinner menu because cabbage encourages the stomach lining to release stomach mucins, which protect the stomach itself against acidity.

2 cups shredded white cabbage	2 scallions, finely minced
2 roasted red bell peppers, chopped	$1/4$ cup fresh lemon juice
1 stalk celery, finely chopped (including leaves)	1 teaspoon olive oil
	1 tablespoon vegetable stock
2 tablespoons minced fresh parsley	1 teaspoon prepared mustard

IN A SALAD bowl, combine the cabbage, peppers, celery, parsley, and scallions.

IN A SMALL bowl, whisk together the lemon juice, olive oil, stock, and mustard. Pour the dressing over the slaw and toss well.

IF THE WEATHER IS HOT AND/OR DRY:	IF THE WEATHER IS COLD AND/OR DAMP:
Serve the slaw slightly chilled with grilled foods such as fish or tofu.	*Add a pinch (or to taste) of cayenne pepper to the lemon mixture before whisking.*

warm onion salad with
toasted sesame seeds

MAKES 4 SERVINGS

71 calories per serving: 2.75 grams fat: 32% calories from fat

Onions have an antibacterial effect on the mouth and intestines, making this salad a helpful balm to banish disease-producing germs you may have encountered during the day.

1 large onion, thinly sliced

2 large carrots (about 8 ounces total), thinly sliced

1/4 cup green beans cut into 1-inch pieces

1 leek, trimmed, rinsed, and thinly sliced

1/2 lemon, sliced

2 teaspoons olive oil

2 teaspoons balsamic vinegar

1/4 teaspoon prepared mustard

dash of hot pepper sauce

pinch of sea salt

2 teaspoons sesame seeds, toasted (see Note, page 69)

STEAM THE ONION, carrots, beans, leek, and lemon slices over boiling water until just tender, 7 to 8 minutes.

MEANWHILE, IN A small bowl, whisk together the olive oil, vinegar, mustard, hot pepper sauce, and salt.

WHEN THE VEGETABLES are ready, discard the lemon slices and toss with the dressing. Garnish with the sesame seeds.

IF THE WEATHER IS HOT AND/OR DRY:
Substitute 1 large cucumber, peeled, seeded, and thinly sliced, for the carrot. Don't steam the cucumber, just toss it with the steamed onion mixture when you add the dressing. Serve the salad slightly chilled.

IF THE WEATHER IS COLD AND/OR DAMP:
Serve the salad on a bed of dandelion greens.

butternut squash with leeks

MAKES 4 SERVINGS
75 calories per serving: 2.5 grams fat; 30% calories from fat

Those who smoke, or who spend the day around people who do, may benefit from a steady diet of winter squash. This sweet and tasty vegetable contains a potent amount of beta carotene, which can help protect the lungs from diseases, including cancer.

1 ¼ pounds butternut squash, peeled, seeded, and cut into 1-inch pieces

1 leek, trimmed, rinsed, and minced

½ cup teaspoon olive oil

½ cup vegetable stock

¼ teaspoon balsamic vinegar

2 tablespoons sesame seeds, toasted (see Note, page 69)

2 tablespoons minced fresh chives

PREHEAT THE OVEN to 375°F.

COMBINE THE SQUASH, leek, olive oil, stock, and vinegar in a 1-quart casserole dish. Cover and bake in the middle of the oven until the squash is tender, 20 to 25 minutes, removing the cover after 10 minutes. Garnish with the sesame seeds and chives before serving.

IF THE WEATHER IS HOT AND/OR DRY:
Substitute sliced toasted almonds for the sesame seeds.

IF THE WEATHER IS COLD AND/OR DAMP:
Add 1 clove of minced garlic to the dish before baking.

green beans with fresh ginger

MAKES 4 SERVINGS

55 calories per serving; 2 grams fat; 32% calories from fat

Japanese scientists have discovered that ginger decreases gastric secretions in the stomach, making this spicy dish a suitable tonic for those who have had a "gut-wrenching" day.

1 pound fresh green beans, trimmed	1 teaspoon toasted (dark) sesame oil
1/2 lemon, sliced	8 thin slices fresh ginger, cut into threads
1 teaspoon olive oil	pinch of sea salt

STEAM THE BEANS and lemon slices over boiling water until tender, about 5 minutes for medium to large beans, less for slender beans. Discard the lemon slices.

IN A SMALL bowl, whisk together the oils, ginger, and salt. When the beans are ready, add the dressing and toss well.

IF THE WEATHER IS HOT AND/OR DRY:
Serve the beans slightly chilled, sprinkled with minced fresh peppermint.

IF THE WEATHER IS COLD AND/OR DAMP:
Whisk 1/2 teaspoon of prepared mustard into the dressing and serve the beans warm.

braised red cabbage with balsamic vinegar

MAKES 4 LARGE SERVINGS
73 calories per serving: 1 gram fat; 12% calories from fat

One Japanese study reveals that families consuming the most cabbage have the lowest cancer rates. So, as well as being tasty, a side
dish like this, eaten at least three times a week, may give you one
less thing to worry about.

1 medium red cabbage (about 2 pounds), chopped into 1-inch pieces	$\frac{1}{3}$ cup vegetable stock
1 medium onion, finely chopped	5 tablespoons balsamic vinegar
1 teaspoon olive oil	2 tablespoons barley malt
1 cooking apple, grated	pinch of sea salt

IN A LARGE pot, combine the cabbage, onion, olive oil, apple, and stock and bring to
a boil. Reduce the heat, cover loosely, and simmer until the cabbage is soft, about 15
minutes. Stir in the vinegar, barley malt, and salt and continue to simmer until the
cabbage is very wilted, 10 to 15 minutes more.

IF THE WEATHER IS HOT AND/OR DRY:
*Serve the cabbage slightly chilled as an
accompaniment to a sandwich.*

IF THE WEATHER IS COLD AND/OR DAMP:
*Serve the cabbage warm as a side dish with
grilled tempeh or fish.*

mushroom salad with fresh greens and toasted pine nuts

MAKES 4 SERVINGS
98 calories per serving: 4 grams fat; 35% calories from fat

Try this savory salad to deter colds, flu, and other viruses you may come in contact with throughout the day. The shiitake mushrooms stimulate the body's production of interferon, which is a natural defense against infection.

1/2 pound green beans, trimmed

1/4 pound fresh shiitake mushrooms, stemmed and sliced

4 scallions, sliced

2 teaspoons olive oil

1 tablespoon balsamic vinegar

1 clove garlic, minced

1 teaspoon minced fresh rosemary

pinch of sea salt

freshly ground black pepper

3 cups mustard greens or arugula

2 tablespoons pine nuts, toasted (see Note)

PREHEAT THE OVEN to 400°F.

IN A LARGE baking dish, combine the beans, mushrooms, scallions, and olive oil. Bake in the middle of the oven, stirring occasionally, until tender, about 20 minutes. Toss with the vinegar, garlic, rosemary, salt, pepper, and greens and sprinkle with the nuts.

Note: To toast the pine nuts, heat them in a nonstick sauté pan over medium-high heat, stirring constantly, until lightly browned, about 2 minutes.

IF THE WEATHER IS HOT AND/OR DRY:
For half of the greens, use Chinese bok choy, including stems.

IF THE WEATHER IS COLD AND/OR DAMP:
When tossing in the greens, add 1/4 cup of minced red onion.

chilled somen noodles with snow peas and sesame sauce

MAKES 4 SERVINGS
135 calories per serving: 2 grams fat: 13% calories from fat

Unlike some whole wheat pasta, these slender noodles are easy to digest and won't feel like a lump in your stomach for the rest of the night.

8 ounces somen noodles (see Noodles, Japanese, The Savory Pantry, page 425)

3 slices fresh ginger

1 cup snow peas

2 tablespoons lemon juice

2 tablespoons vegetable stock

1 tablespoon tahini (sesame paste)

pinch of sea salt

freshly ground black pepper

2 scallions, minced

COMBINE THE SOMEN and ginger in a large pot of boiling water and cook until almost tender, about 4 minutes. Add the snow peas and continue to boil until the somen and peas are tender, about 1 minute more. Drain, pat dry, and discard the ginger.

MEANWHILE, COMBINE THE lemon juice, stock, tahini, salt, and scallions. When the somen and snow peas are ready, add the dressing and toss well. Chill for at least 30 minutes before serving.

IF THE WEATHER IS HOT AND/OR DRY:
The very texture of the somen noodles makes this a traditional hot-weather dish, but to make it even "cooler," sprinkle with minced fresh cilantro before serving.

IF THE WEATHER IS COLD AND/OR DAMP:
When mixing the dressing, add 1 teaspoon (or to taste) of hot pepper sauce and serve the somen warm.

limas with garlic and fennel

MAKES 4 SERVINGS
180 calories per serving: 3.5 grams fat; 17% calories from fat

Beans contain complex sugars that defy digestion by the stomach. Consequently, when they arrive in the intestines, they are digested by the "friendly" bacteria residing there, a by-product of which is gas. Fennel, however, can diminish the problem, thus creating a more pleasant evening.

1 tablespoon olive oil	2 tablespoons lemon juice
1 teaspoon fennel seed	1/4 cup minced fennel bulb
2 cloves garlic, minced	pinch of sea salt
1 shallot, minced	freshly ground black pepper
2 cups lima beans, cooked	

HEAT THE OLIVE oil in a medium sauté pan on medium-high. Add the fennel seed, garlic, and shallot and sauté until the mixture is fragrant and the garlic and shallot are lightly browned, 3 to 4 minutes.

IN A MEDIUM bowl, combine the limas with the garlic mixture, lemon juice, fennel bulb, salt, and pepper.

IF THE WEATHER IS HOT AND/OR DRY:
Serve the limas slightly chilled with chopped tomatoes and whole wheat pitas.

IF THE WEATHER IS COLD AND/OR DAMP:
Serve the limas warm with minced fresh jalapeño garnish and crusty garlic bread.

spinach salad with tempeh croutons

MAKES 4 SERVINGS
106 calories per serving: 4.5 grams fat: 38% calories from fat

Controversy raged for years over spinach as a source of iron because some scientists believed that our bodies were unable to absorb the plant-based mineral. But recent research reveals that if vitamin C is absorbed along with spinach's iron (as is found in the lemon juice in this recipe), the mineral then becomes available to the body, thus helping to avert such evening conditions as exhaustion and fatigue.

4 ounces tempeh (see The Savory Pantry, page 426). cut into ½-inch cubes

1 clove garlic, minced

1 tablespoon toasted (dark) sesame oil

1 teaspoon honey

dash of hot pepper sauce, or to taste

1 tablespoon lemon juice

1 teaspoon reduced-sodium soy sauce

1½ teaspoons grated fresh ginger

3 cups spinach leaves, rinsed

1 cup torn pieces romaine lettuce

2 scallions, minced

TO MAKE THE croutons, heat the tempeh in a large nonstick sauté pan on medium-high, stirring constantly, until lightly browned, 2½ to 3 minutes. Remove the croutons from the heat and let them relax while you prepare the salad.

IN THE BOTTOM of a salad bowl, combine the garlic, sesame oil, honey, hot pepper sauce, lemon juice, soy sauce, and ginger, and whisk well. Add the spinach, romaine, and scallions and toss until all of the leaves are lightly bathed with the dressing. Serve the salad on chilled plates and garnish with the croutons.

IF THE WEATHER IS HOT AND/OR DRY:
Substitute 1 cup of julienned zucchini or summer squash for the romaine.

IF THE WEATHER IS COLD AND/OR DAMP:
Substitute 1 cup of dandelion leaves for the romaine.

romaine with lime-anchovy dressing

MAKES 4 SERVINGS

36 calories per serving: less than 1 gram fat

Several health systems, including Chinese and Ayurvedic, maintain that eating light foods at the evening meal helps promote good digestion and a good mood. This crisp salad, with its low-oil dressing, is just such a dish.

1 anchovy fillet

1 clove garlic, peeled

2 tablespoons fresh lime juice

dash of Worcestershire sauce

dash of hot pepper sauce

freshly ground black pepper

1 head romaine lettuce, torn into pieces

IN A SMALL bowl, combine the anchovy, garlic, lime juice, Worcestershire sauce, hot pepper sauce, and black pepper, using a fork to mash the mixture into a paste.

PUT THE ROMAINE into a salad bowl, pour the dressing on top, and toss well, about 30 times, to combine.

IF THE WEATHER IS HOT AND/OR DRY:
Add a chopped ripe tomato to the romaine before tossing with the dressing.

IF THE WEATHER IS COLD AND/OR DAMP:
Increase the garlic to 2 cloves.

lentil salad with red wine vinaigrette

MAKES 4 SERVINGS
152 calories per serving: 4 grams fat: 23% calories from fat

This dish eliminates the ever-present concern of what to make for dinner. It's wholesome and healthful, and the lentils take a mere 20 minutes to cook.

²/₃ cup dried green lentils

1 small carrot, minced

1 celery stalk, minced (including leaves)

1 onion, minced

1 bay leaf

2 tablespoons red wine vinegar

1 tablespoon olive oil

pinch of cayenne pepper

pinch of sea salt

1 teaspoon minced fresh thyme or ¹/₂ teaspoon dried

4 scallions, minced

2 cups chicory, thinly sliced

COMBINE THE LENTILS, carrot, celery, onion, and bay leaf in a large saucepan and add water to cover. Bring the mixture to a boil. Then reduce the heat to medium, cover loosely, and simmer until the lentils are just tender, about 20 minutes. Discard the bay leaf.

MEANWHILE, WHISK TOGETHER the vinegar, oil, cayenne, salt, and thyme. When the lentils are ready, drain them and immediately stir in the scallions, chicory, and dressing. Let the salad rest for about 5 minutes to give the chicory time to wilt slightly.

IF THE WEATHER IS HOT AND/OR DRY:
Substitute thinly sliced collard greens for the chicory.

IF THE WEATHER IS COLD AND/OR DAMP:
Add 1 or 2 cloves of minced garlic to the dressing before tossing.

spicy white bean salad with spinach

MAKES 4 SERVINGS
107 calories per serving; 1.5 grams fat; 13% calories from fat

Those who are irregular may want to include beans with their evening meal two or three times a week. Beans contain insoluble fiber, a potent anti-constipation medicine.

2 cups cooked white beans

2 cups fresh spinach, chopped and blanched

juice of 1 lemon

1 tablespoon olive oil

dash of hot pepper sauce, or to taste

1 teaspoon balsamic vinegar

pinch of sea salt

1 clove garlic, finely minced

2 teaspoons minced fresh cilantro

COMBINE ALL OF the ingredients in a large bowl and toss well, about 30 times, to combine.

IF THE WEATHER IS HOT AND/OR DRY:
Serve the salad slightly chilled, accompanied by iced mint tea.

IF THE WEATHER IS COLD AND/OR DAMP:
Double the garlic and serve the salad warm.

barley salad with roasted peppers

MAKES 4 SERVINGS
275 calories per serving: 4 grams fat: 13% calories from fat

If you worry about your family's health, barley may help to relieve your fears. This sweet and nutty grain interferes with the liver's ability to produce cholesterol, making barley a tasty tonic for the prevention of stroke and heart attacks. In addition, barley contains protease inhibitors that can help prevent certain types of cancer.

1 cup pearled barley, rinsed

1 bay leaf

3 cups vegetable stock

4 large dried shiitake mushrooms, stemmed and crumbled

2 scallions, minced

2 cups chopped fresh spinach

1 carrot, grated

2 roasted red bell peppers, chopped (see Note, page 89)

$^1/_4$ cup lemon juice

1 tablespoon olive oil

1 teaspoon prepared mustard

2 teaspoons minced fresh rosemary

1 shallot, minced

pinch of sea salt

freshly ground black pepper

HEAT THE STILL-WET barley in a large soup pot on medium-high, stirring constantly, until lightly toasted, about 3 minutes. Add the bay leaf, stock, and mushrooms and bring the mixture to a boil. Reduce the heat, cover loosely, and simmer until the barley is tender, about 55 minutes. Drain off any excess liquid and discard the bay leaf. Stir in the scallions, spinach, carrot, and roasted peppers.

IN A SMALL bowl, whisk together the lemon juice, olive oil, mustard, rosemary, shallot, salt, and pepper, then pour over the barley and toss well.

IF THE WEATHER IS HOT AND/OR DRY:
Serve the salad slightly chilled on a bed of red oak lettuce.

IF THE WEATHER IS COLD AND/OR DAMP:
Substitute 2 cloves of minced fresh garlic for the shallot and serve the salad warm.

green rice with shallots and parsley

MAKES 6 SERVINGS
180 calories per serving: 2.5 grams fat: 13% calories from fat

Parsley, being a gentle diuretic, can be a balm to those who feel bloated from eating overly salted foods at lunch.

2 scallions. minced

2 shallots. minced

1/4 cup egg substitute (see Note. page 13) or 2 egg whites

1 cup soy milk or skim milk

1/3 cup grated fat-free soy mozzarella or part-skim mozzarella cheese

1/2 cup minced fresh parsley

pinch of saffron

3 cups cooked brown and wild rice

PREHEAT THE OVEN to 375°F.

COMBINE ALL OF the ingredients in a lightly oiled 1 1/2-quart soufflé dish and mix well. Press the top down to level it, then bake in the middle of the oven until cooked through and slightly firm, about 20 minutes.

IF THE WEATHER IS HOT AND/OR DRY:
Serve the rice as an accompaniment to poached trout or salmon.

IF THE WEATHER IS COLD AND/OR DAMP:
Substitute 2 cloves of minced fresh garlic for the shallots.

cucumbers with sushi rice (chirazushi)

MAKES 4 SERVINGS
157 calories per serving: 3 grams fat: 17% calories from fat

Japanese cooks prize this light and tangy dish as relaxant to the digestive system.

1 cup short-grain Japanese-style rice

1 1/4 cups vegetable stock

1 tablespoon rice vinegar

1 tablespoon mirin or dry sherry

2 teaspoons reduced-sodium soy sauce

1 teaspoon toasted (dark) sesame oil

1 large cucumber. peeled. seeded. and julienned

2 tablespoons sesame seeds. toasted (see Note. page 69)

2 tablespoons minced fresh chives

COMBINE THE RICE and stock in a large saucepan and soak for 30 minutes. Bring the rice to a boil, reduce the heat, cover loosely, and simmer until the rice is tender and all of the stock has been absorbed, about 15 minutes.

TRANSFER THE RICE to a large shallow bowl so it can begin to cool. This will prevent it from becoming gummy. Stir in the vinegar, mirin, soy sauce, sesame oil, cucumber, sesame seeds, and chives.

IF THE WEATHER IS HOT AND/OR DRY:
Serve the chirazushi slightly chilled.

IF THE WEATHER IS COLD AND/OR DAMP:
Stir in a minced jalapeño instead of the cucumber. and serve the chirazushi warm.

"un-chicken" salad with chinese vinaigrette

MAKES 4 ENTRÉE SERVINGS
241 calories per serving; 3.5 grams fat; 13% calories from fat

Some health experts believe that eating too much commercially raised chicken can make us nervous. They hold that since a chicken's life is spent pecking, scratching, and clawing, these mannerisms can exhibit themselves in poultry-eating humans as irritability, agitation, and unpredictable physical movements. Indeed, this is a highly controversial concept, but if you tend to be wound a bit too tight, this seitan-based dish may well be worth trying in place of the usual chicken salad.

1 pound seitan (see The Savory Pantry, page 425)

1 tablespoon toasted (dark) sesame oil

pinch of cayenne pepper, or to taste

1 tablespoon balsamic vinegar

1 tablespoon reduced-sodium soy sauce

1 clove garlic, minced

$^1/_2$ teaspoon finely minced fresh ginger

1 teaspoon barley malt

2 teaspoons prepared mustard

1 small carrot, grated

2 scallions, finely minced

romaine lettuce leaves for serving

PLACE THE SEITAN in a medium bowl. In a small bowl, whisk together the sesame oil, cayenne, vinegar, soy sauce, garlic, ginger, barley malt, and mustard. Pour onto the seitan and add the carrot and scallions as you mix well. It may not look like there is enough dressing, but toss the salad 30 times and it will be fine. Serve the salad rolled in the romaine leaves and eat it with the hands, Chinese style.

IF THE WEATHER IS HOT AND/OR DRY: *Sprinkle the salad with finely chopped tomato before serving.*

IF THE WEATHER IS COLD AND/OR DAMP: *Omit the romaine leaves and serve the salad in toasted whole wheat pitas.*

"un-chicken" salad with watercress

MAKES 4 SIDE SERVINGS
125 calories per serving: less than 1 gram fat

Brazilian healers use watercress as a remedy for nervous digestion.

7 ounces seitan (see The Savory Pantry, page 425), shredded into bite-sized pieces

2 tablespoons Faux Ricotta (page 127)

1 tablespoon lemon juice

1 tablespoon vegetable stock or water

$^1/_2$ cup watercress leaves

PLACE THE SEITAN in a medium bowl. In a small bowl, combine the cheese, lemon juice, and stock, and whisk well. Pour over the seitan, add the watercress, and mix well.

IF THE WEATHER IS HOT AND/OR DRY:
Serve the salad with a chilled soup.

IF THE WEATHER IS COLD AND/OR DAMP:
Serve the salad with a warm spicy soup.

black bean salad with corn
and creamy basil dressing

MAKES 4 ENTRÉE SERVINGS
397 calories per serving: 9.6 grams fat: 21% calories from fat

If you've gotten a cut or scratch during the day, this dish may help it heal. The pumpkin seeds it contains are a good source of zinc, a mineral that scientists have verified to be helpful in wound recovery.

1 cup bulgur

3 cups vegetable stock or water

1 bay leaf

1 cup cooked black beans

³/₄ cup corn kernels

2 tablespoons pumpkin seeds, toasted (see Note)

¹/₂ cup (not packed) fresh basil leaves

2 tablespoons olive oil

2 cloves garlic, minced

3 tablespoons Faux Ricotta (page 127) or nonfat ricotta cheese

3 tablespoons lemon juice

3 tablespoons grated soy Parmesan or regular Parmesan cheese

1 tablespoon balsamic vinegar

pinch of sea salt

freshly ground black pepper

COMBINE THE BULGUR, stock, and bay leaf in a saucepan and bring to a boil. Loosely cover the pan, reduce the heat, and simmer for about 10 minutes. Cover the pan tightly and remove from the heat. Let the bulgur sit until tender and all of the liquid has been absorbed, about 15 minutes. Discard the bay leaf.

MEANWHILE, COMBINE THE beans, corn, pumpkin seeds, and basil in a medium bowl. When the bulgur is ready, stir it in. In a small bowl, whisk together the oil, garlic, ricotta, lemon juice, Parmesan, vinegar, salt, and pepper. Spoon onto the bean mixture and mix well.

Note: To toast pumpkin seeds, heat them in a nonstick sauté pan over medium-high heat, stirring constantly, until fragrant and lightly browned, about 2¹/₂ minutes.

IF THE WEATHER IS HOT AND/OR DRY:
Serve the salad slightly chilled with tomato salsa and minced fresh cilantro.

IF THE WEATHER IS COLD AND/OR DAMP:
Serve the salad at room temperature or gently warmed, garnished generously with minced scallion.

warm orzo salad with pine nuts and fresh thyme

MAKES 4 ENTRÉE SERVINGS
335 calories per serving: 11 grams fat: 30% calories from fat

Symptoms of colds, sinus, or allergies can become worse in the evening. This salad can help by offering such natural decongestants as onion, garlic, carrot, hot pepper sauce, and thyme.

1 medium onion, finely chopped

5 fresh shiitake mushrooms, stemmed and finely chopped

1 large handful (6 ounces) green beans, trimmed and finely chopped

2 cloves garlic, minced

4 cups cooked orzo (about 12 ounces dried)

2 medium carrots, coarsely grated

1/4 cup pine nuts, toasted (see Note, page 187)

1/4 cup raisins

2 tablespoons minced fresh thyme or 2 teaspoons dried

pinch of sea salt

freshly ground black pepper

2 tablespoons olive oil

2 tablespoons vegetable stock

1 tablespoon balsamic vinegar

1 tablespoon lemon juice

1 teaspoon hot pepper sauce, or to taste

3 tablespoons grated soy Parmesan or regular Parmesan cheese

STEAM THE ONION, mushrooms, green beans, and garlic over boiling water until just tender, 6 to 7 minutes. Remove to a large bowl and add the orzo, carrots, pine nuts, raisins, and thyme.

IN A SMALL bowl, whisk together the salt, pepper, oil, stock, vinegar, lemon juice, hot pepper sauce, and Parmesan. Pour over the orzo mixture and toss well.

IF THE WEATHER IS HOT AND/OR DRY:
Substitute zucchini for the green beans and serve the salad slightly chilled.

IF THE WEATHER IS COLD AND/OR DAMP:
Serve the salad warm with a generous amount of freshly ground black pepper.

savory cauliflower pâté

MAKE 3 CUPS, OR 6 (½-CUP) SERVINGS
189 calories per serving: no added fat

This dish may remind you of mashed potatoes or polenta, but the secret ingredient is millet, a grain that Russian folklore says can soothe anxiety and the nervous stomach that accompanies it.

1 cup yellow millet

½ cup chopped cauliflower
(about 5 ounces)

4 cups vegetable stock

1 bay leaf

1 shallot, sliced

1 tablespoon *umeboshi* plum paste
(see The Savory Pantry, page 426)

IN A MEDIUM saucepan, combine the millet, cauliflower, stock, bay leaf, and shallot and bring the mixture to a boil. Reduce the heat, cover loosely, and simmer until the millet and cauliflower are soft, 25 to 30 minutes. Discard the bay leaf.

SCOOP THE MIXTURE (including liquid) into a processor and whiz until pureed, adding the plum paste halfway through. Pureeing the mixture will take about 10 seconds, so be patient. Serve warm.

IF THE WEATHER IS HOT AND/OR DRY:
Add a pinch of saffron threads before cooking.

IF THE WEATHER IS COLD AND/OR DAMP:
Add 1 or 2 cloves of peeled, halved garlic before cooking.

spring vegetable stock

MAKES 1 QUART, OR ENOUGH FOR 4 SERVINGS
About 10 calories per cup; no added fat

Use this stock as a base for any of the lighter soups in this section.

5 cups water

1/2 cup chopped fresh spinach

1 onion, quartered (including skin)

1 leek, trimmed, rinsed, and sliced

1/2 cup coarsely chopped celery
   (including leaves)

1/2 cup fresh parsley

1 bay leaf

1 clove garlic, halved (including skin)

5 whole peppercorns

COMBINE ALL OF the ingredients in a large soup pot and bring to a boil. Reduce the heat, cover loosely, and simmer gently until the stock is very fragrant, 25 to 30 minutes. Strain before using. Or make the stock ahead and refrigerate for up to 5 days.

IF THE WEATHER IS HOT AND/OR DRY:
Substitute a halved shallot for the garlic, and 5 whole coriander seeds for the peppercorns. If you have it on hand, add 2 slices of dried Chinese licorice root.

IF THE WEATHER IS COLD AND/OR DAMP:
Increase the amount of garlic to 2 cloves and add 1 dried hot pepper before boiling.

winter vegetable stock

MAKES 1 QUART, OR ENOUGH FOR 4 SERVINGS
About 10 calories per cup: no added fat

This is a flavorful base for the thick soups and stews in this section.

5 cups water

2 carrots, coarsely chopped

2 onions, quartered (including skins)

2 parsnips, coarsely chopped

5 cloves garlic, halved (including skins)

1 stalk celery, coarsely chopped
(including leaves)

1 bay leaf

1 dried hot red pepper

COMBINE ALL OF the ingredients in a large soup pot and bring to a boil. Reduce the heat, cover loosely, and simmer until the stock is fragrant, about 30 minutes. Strain before using. Or make the stock ahead and refrigerate for up to 5 days.

IF THE WEATHER IS HOT AND/OR DRY:
Substitute 1 chopped leek for all of the garlic and replace the hot pepper with about 1/4 cup of fresh parsley.

IF THE WEATHER IS COLD AND/OR DAMP:
Use 2 hot peppers instead of 1.

soups and stews

white bean stew with fresh basil

MAKES 4 SERVINGS
270 calories per serving: 2 grams fat: 7% calories from fat

This stew is similar to the type of evening soup a practitioner of Chinese medicine might recommend for a patient feeling feverish with muscle aches and a stiff neck. The basil, onion, garlic, and scallions are known as "surface-relieving herbs" because they help disperse symptoms that are generally associated with the beginning stages of colds and flu.

2 cups cooked white beans	4 cups vegetable stock
2 teaspoons olive oil	2 medium tomatoes, chopped
4 dried shiitake mushrooms, stemmed and crumbled	$^1/_2$ pound waxy-type potatoes, finely chopped
2 medium carrots, finely chopped	2 cups chopped mustard greens or dandelions
1 stalk celery, finely chopped (including leaves)	$^1/_4$ cup minced fresh basil
1 medium onion, finely chopped	4 scallions, minced
2 cloves garlic, minced	pinch of sea salt
1 medium zucchini, finely chopped	freshly ground black pepper

TIP HALF OF the beans (1 cup) into a processor or blender and whiz until smooth. Set aside.

HEAT THE OIL in a large soup pot on medium-high. Add the mushrooms, carrots, celery, onion, garlic, and zucchini and sauté until fragrant and just wilted, about 5 minutes. Add the stock, tomatoes, potatoes, and processed beans. Reduce the heat, cover loosely, and simmer until the vegetables are tender, about 15 minutes. Stir in the remaining beans, mustard greens, and basil and continue to simmer until heated through, about 3 more minutes. Serve warm, garnished with the scallions, salt, and pepper.

IF THE WEATHER IS HOT AND/OR DRY:
Add 1 teaspoon of minced fresh cilantro to each serving when you add the scallions.

IF THE WEATHER IS COLD AND/OR DAMP:
Substitute $^1/_2$ cup of finely chopped winter squash for the zucchini and be generous with the black pepper.

black bean stew with butternut squash

MAKES 4 ENTRÉE SERVINGS
180 calories per serving: 3 grams fat: 14% calories from fat

Black mung beans, such as those offered here, are a staple medicine in India for restoring and detoxifying the body after a long day.

6 cups vegetable stock

¹/₂ cup black mung beans (available at Indian markets)

3 cups butternut squash, cut into ¹/₂-inch pieces

1 bay leaf

1 tablespoon minced fresh thyme or 1 teaspoon dried

1 tablespoon minced fresh oregano or 1 teaspoon dried

1 slice fresh ginger

1 clove garlic, peeled, seeded, and speared with a toothpick

2 tablespoons dried black sea herb such as arame or hijiki (see The Savory Pantry, page 422)

2 tablespoons shredded dried daikon radish (see The Savory Pantry, page 423)

2 tablespoons dried Chinese mushrooms, crumbled

2 dried shiitake mushrooms, stemmed and crumbled

1 medium onion, chopped

3 tablespoons rolled oats

1 tablespoon miso (see The Savory Pantry, page 424)

2 teaspoons olive oil

1 teaspoon balsamic vinegar

IN A LARGE soup pot, combine the stock, beans, squash, bay leaf, thyme, oregano, ginger, garlic, sea herb, daikon, Chinese mushrooms, shiitake mushrooms, onion, and oats and bring to a boil. Reduce the heat, cover loosely, and simmer until the beans are very tender, about 1 hour. Discard the bay leaf, garlic, and ginger.

IN A SMALL dish, combine the miso, oil, and vinegar and stir it into the hot stew. Immediately remove the stew from the heat and serve.

IF THE WEATHER IS HOT AND/OR DRY:
Add a 4-inch piece of burdock root (see The Savory Pantry, page 422), thinly sliced, when adding the squash, or add 1 teaspoon of fennel seed when adding the thyme.

IF THE WEATHER IS COLD AND/OR DAMP:
Instead of discarding the garlic, mince it and add it to the dish. When adding the garlic, also add ¹/₂ teaspoon of dry mustard.

vegetable soup with relaxing herbs

MAKES 4 SERVINGS

61 calories per serving: no added fat

Chamomile, a mild nerve tonic, enlivens the flavors of the squash, carrots, and onion in this fragrant soup.

$^1/_2$ pound butternut squash, chopped

2 medium carrots, sliced

1 large onion, sliced

2 cloves garlic, peeled

2 cups vegetable stock (or water used for steaming vegetables)

1 tablespoon fennel seeds, toasted (see Note)

2 teaspoons dried chamomile flowers

7 fresh shiitake mushrooms, stemmed and sliced

1 tomato, chopped

1 teaspoon reduced-sodium soy sauce

dash of hot pepper sauce, or to taste

STEAM THE SQUASH, carrots, onion, and garlic over boiling water until tender, about 9 minutes. Tip the vegetables into a processor or blender, whizzing until smooth. You'll have about 2 cups of puree.

COMBINE THE PUREE, stock, fennel seed, chamomile, mushrooms, tomato, soy sauce, and hot pepper sauce in a soup pot and heat gently until fragrant and the mushrooms are cooked through, about 10 minutes.

Note: To toast fennel seeds, tip them into a large, dry sauté pan and heat on high, stirring constantly, for about 2 minutes.

IF THE WEATHER IS HOT AND/OR DRY:
Use only 1 carrot and add $^1/_4$ cup of chopped water chestnuts.

IF THE WEATHER IS COLD AND/OR DAMP:
Be generous with the hot pepper sauce.

lentils in white wine with mild garlic

MAKES 8 SERVINGS
145 calories per serving: 4.6 grams fat: 27% calories from fat

According to Ayurveda, saffron tones a jumpy digestive system.

2 cups dried lentils

4 cups vegetable stock

1 bay leaf

2 cloves elephant garlic, peeled and halved

1/2 teaspoon saffron threads

2 tablespoons olive oil

10 ounces reduced-fat tofu, cut into 1-inch slices (see The Savory Pantry, page 425)

2 tablespoons flour

pinch of sea salt

freshly ground black pepper

1 2-inch sprig fresh rosemary

1/4 cup dry white wine

1 large carrot, finely chopped

PREHEAT THE OVEN to 350°F.

IN A LARGE flameproof casserole dish, combine the lentils, stock, bay leaf, garlic, and saffron and bring to a boil. Reduce the heat, cover loosely, and simmer for 20 minutes.

MEANWHILE, HEAT THE olive oil in a large sauté pan on medium-high. Toss the tofu with the flour, salt, and pepper and sauté in the oil until it has browned, 6 to 7 minutes.

ADD THE TOFU to the lentils along with the rosemary, wine, and carrot. Cover and bake in the middle of the oven until the lentils are tender, about 1 1/4 hours.

IF THE WEATHER IS HOT AND/OR DRY:
Serve the lentils slightly chilled. If you eat eggs, serve the lentils as an accompaniment to an omelet or scrambled eggs.

IF THE WEATHER IS COLD AND/OR DAMP:
Serve the lentils warm with a side of crusty garlic bread.

spicy lentil chili

MAKES 8 SERVINGS
135 calories per serving: 3.5 grams fat: 23% calories from fat

Pungent hot pepper is used in parts of Africa as an evening rejuvenator for the heart, lungs, and nerves.

2 tablespoons olive oil	2 cups bulgur
2 medium onions, chopped	7 cups vegetable stock
2 to 3 cloves garlic, minced	3 tablespoons good-quality chili powder
1½ cups dried lentils	pinch of sea salt

HEAT THE OIL in a large pot on medium-high, then add the onions and garlic. Sauté until lightly browned, about 5 minutes. Add the lentils, bulgur, stock, chili powder, and salt and bring to a boil. Reduce the heat, cover loosely, and simmer until the lentils are tender and most of the liquid has been absorbed, about 40 minutes.

IF THE WEATHER IS HOT AND/OR DRY:
Add 1 teaspoon of ground coriander when you add the chili powder. Then garnish with minced fresh cilantro and serve with chilled mint tea.

IF THE WEATHER IS COLD AND/OR DAMP:
Use the larger amount of garlic and add 1 or 2 minced fresh jalapeño peppers when you add the lentils.

posole (dried corn stew)

MAKES 4 ENTRÉE SERVINGS
135 calories per serving; 2.5 grams fat; 16% calories from fat

Corn is a Japanese folk remedy for soothing heartache, and it is also used in the same way by the Tewa Indians of North America. Although heartache is a very subjective ailment, interestingly enough, modern science has discovered that corn can help regulate blood cholesterol levels, thus helping to prevent a heart attack.

2 teaspoons olive oil	1 bay leaf
1 onion, chopped	2 carrots, minced
2 cloves garlic, minced	1 tablespoon flavorful chili powder
2 shallots, minced	2 teaspoons tomato paste
1 cup whole dried corn	1 teaspoon minced fresh rosemary or $^1/_2$ teaspoon dried
2 quarts vegetable stock	
5 dried chestnuts (see Notes)	1 heaping tablespoon preserved cabbage (see Notes)

HEAT THE OIL in a large soup pot on medium-high. Add the onion, garlic, and shallots and sauté until fragrant and lightly browned, about 5 minutes. Add the corn, stock, chestnuts, bay leaf, carrots, chili powder, tomato paste, rosemary, and preserved cabbage and bring to a boil. Reduce the heat, cover loosely, and simmer until the corn pops open and is tender, about $3^1/_2$ hours.

Notes: The dried chestnuts, which give the posole a meat-free smoky taste, are available at health food stores and Asian markets. The preserved cabbage comes in stout round crocks and is available at Asian markets.

IF THE WEATHER IS HOT AND/OR DRY:
Serve the posole with garnishes of plain soy or regular yogurt and minced scallions.

IF THE WEATHER IS COLD AND/OR DAMP:
Add freshly ground black pepper before serving.

spicy minestrone with fresh and dried tomatoes

MAKES 4 SERVINGS

145 calories per serving: 3.5 grams fat: 22% calories from fat

Although this soup has a robust flavor, the low-fat ingredients make it a light dish that won't "sit on your stomach" all night.

1 tablespoon olive oil

2 cloves garlic, minced

1 onion, chopped

2 large carrots, chopped

1 stalk celery, chopped (including leaves)

1 medium potato, chopped

1/3 cup chopped cauliflower

1 medium zucchini, chopped

4 plum tomatoes, sliced

5 large slices of dried tomatoes

2 teaspoons balsamic vinegar

1/2 teaspoon dried hot red pepper flakes, or to taste

2 tablespoons cooked chickpeas

2 tablespoons dried orzo or other tiny pasta

4 cups vegetable stock

pinch of sea salt

freshly ground black pepper

1/4 cup minced fresh cilantro

HEAT THE OIL in a large soup pot on medium-high. Add the garlic and onion and sauté until fragrant and just wilted, about 3 minutes. Add the carrots, celery, potato, cauliflower, zucchini, plum tomatoes, dried tomatoes, vinegar, red pepper, chickpeas, orzo, stock, salt, and pepper and bring to a boil. Reduce the heat, cover loosely, and let the soup simmer until the vegetables are fragrant and tender and the pasta is cooked through, 15 to 20 minutes. Garnish with the cilantro before serving.

IF THE WEATHER IS HOT AND/OR DRY:
Reduce the garlic to 1 clove.

IF THE WEATHER IS COLD AND/OR DAMP:
Stir in a pinch (or to taste) of cayenne pepper before serving.

summer vegetable soup with
miso and fresh herbs

MAKES 8 SERVINGS
90 calories per serving: 1.5 grams fat: 15% calories from fat

Unwind from your day with this vitamin-pill-in-a-soup, containing beta carotene, vitamin C, immune-enhancing polysaccharides, iron, calcium, and potassium.

2 teaspoons olive oil

1 onion, chopped

2 cloves garlic, minced

$^{1}/_{2}$ teaspoon cumin seed

1 bay leaf

2 tablespoons dry white wine or mirin

$^{3}/_{4}$ cup cubed potatoes (about 4 small)

1 large carrot, sliced

1 cup cauliflower florets

$1^{1}/_{2}$ cups broccoli florets

2 medium tomatoes, chopped

4 dried shiitake mushrooms, stemmed and crumbled

2 tablespoons shredded dried daikon radish (see The Savory Pantry, page 423)

4 cups vegetable stock

2 cups (not packed) chopped spinach

$^{1}/_{4}$ cup minced fresh basil

1 tablespoon minced fresh parsley

1 tablespoon minced fresh cilantro

1 tablespoon lemon juice

1 tablespoon miso (see The Savory Pantry, page 424)

1 tablespoon minced fresh chives

freshly ground black pepper

grated soy Parmesan or regular Parmesan cheese for serving

HEAT THE OLIVE oil in a large soup pot on medium-high. Add the onion, garlic, cumin, bay leaf, and wine and sauté until the onion is browned, 8 to 10 minutes. Add the potatoes, carrot, cauliflower, broccoli, tomatoes, mushrooms, daikon, and stock and bring to a boil. Reduce the heat, cover loosely, and simmer until the vegetables are just tender, about 15 minutes. Discard the bay leaf. Stir in the spinach, basil, parsley, and cilantro.

IN A SMALL dish, whisk together the lemon juice and miso, then stir into the soup along with the chives. Sprinkle with the pepper and Parmesan before serving.

IF THE WEATHER IS HOT AND/OR DRY:
Serve with a chilled green salad such as Romaine with Lime-Anchovy Dressing (page 191) and whole wheat rolls.

IF THE WEATHER IS COLD AND/OR DAMP:
Omit the cilantro, double the amount of parsley, and sprinkle liberally with freshly ground black pepper. Serve the soup with a spicy, crusty bread such as Garlicky Flatbread (page 148).

spinach gazpacho with fresh basil

MAKES 4 SERVINGS
47 calories per serving: no added fat

Spinach is recommended in Ayurveda to deter the effects of the often fatty, nutrient-poor daily Western diet.

2 1/2 cups (not packed) chopped fresh spinach

2 cloves garlic, minced

2 cups vegetable stock

2 tablespoons lemon juice

2 small cucumbers, peeled, seeded, and chopped

2 medium tomatoes, chopped

1 medium red onion, minced

1/4 cup minced fresh basil

COMBINE THE SPINACH, garlic, and stock in a medium saucepan and bring to a boil. Reduce the heat, cover loosely, and simmer until the spinach is just tender, about 3 minutes. Place in a large bowl, cover, and refrigerate for at least 30 minutes.

IN A PROCESSOR or blender, combine the spinach mixture with the lemon juice, cucumbers, tomatoes, onion, and basil and whiz until smooth.

IF THE WEATHER IS HOT AND/OR DRY:
Serve the soup with a crisp green salad such as Mushroom Salad with Fresh Greens and Toasted Pine Nuts (page 187).

IF THE WEATHER IS COLD AND/OR DAMP:
Garnish the soup with chopped fresh green chilies.

onion soup with rosemary and miso

MAKES 4 SERVINGS
90 calories per serving: 2.5 grams fat; 24% calories from fat

Egyptians believe that onions restore strength to the body and keep us healthy. In fact, in Egypt it's not unusual for every dish at a meal to contain onions.

2 teaspoons olive oil

3 large onions, thinly sliced

2 leeks, rinsed, trimmed, and thinly sliced

2 shallots, thinly sliced

2 cloves garlic, thinly sliced

1 bay leaf

1 3-inch sprig fresh rosemary

4 cups vegetable stock

4 teaspoons red miso (see The Savory Pantry, page 424)

6 tablespoons grated soy Parmesan or regular Parmesan cheese

HEAT THE OLIVE oil in a large soup pot on high heat. Add the onions, leeks, shallots, garlic, and bay leaf and sauté until the vegetables are fragrant and browned, about 5 minutes. Don't let the garlic burn.

ADD THE ROSEMARY and stock and bring to a boil. Reduce the heat, cover loosely, and simmer until the vegetables are tender, about 15 minutes. Discard the bay leaf. Place the miso in a small strainer, dip the strainer into the soup, and push the miso through with a spoon. Remove the soup from the heat, swirl in the cheese, and serve.

IF THE WEATHER IS HOT AND/OR DRY:
Add 1/2 teaspoon of dill seed or fennel seed when sautéing the onions. Or serve the soup with an accompaniment of sliced blanched bulb fennel.

IF THE WEATHER IS COLD AND/OR DAMP:
Add 1/4 teaspoon of ground cloves when sautéing, then sprinkle the soup with freshly ground pepper before serving.

quick homemade soup for one

MAKES 1 LARGE SERVING
150 calories: no added fat

For those who have had a harried day, this fresh repast serves as a great evening restorative by offering both beta carotene and vitamin C. What's more, it takes a mere 20 minutes to prepare and cook.

1¾ cups vegetable stock

1 rounded tablespoon dried daikon radish (see The Savory Pantry, page 423)

1 shallot, minced

½ cup grated carrot

1 bay leaf

½ cup chopped mustard greens or kale

5 tablespoons cooked beans, rice, or pasta

1 teaspoon red miso (see The Savory Pantry, page 424)

1 scallion, finely minced

IN A SAUCEPAN, combine the stock, daikon, shallot, carrot, and bay leaf and bring to a boil. Reduce the heat, cover loosely, and simmer for about 7 minutes. Add the greens and beans and continue to simmer until the greens are bright green and just tender, about 2 minutes more. Remove the soup from the heat and whisk in the miso. Discard the bay leaf. Serve warm, sprinkled with the scallion.

IF THE WEATHER IS HOT AND/OR DRY: *Substitute grated fresh radish (daikon or other) for the dried.*

IF THE WEATHER IS COLD AND/OR DAMP: *Substitute 1 or 2 cloves of minced garlic for the shallot and swirl in a pinch of ground cayenne pepper before serving.*

savoy cabbage soup with chinese licorice root and white miso

MAKES 8 SERVINGS
110 calories per serving: 2 grams fat: 17% calories from fat

The sulfur compounds present in cabbage help to fight infectious bacteria and viruses, making this a smart soup to sip when you spend the day with someone who is coming down with a cold or the flu. The soup is flavored with Chinese licorice root, an herb said to help relieve aches, pains, and tension due to stress.

1 tablespoon olive oil

4 medium onions (about 1 pound), thinly sliced

3 cloves garlic, minced

4 cups vegetable stock

1 pound potatoes, diced

1 bay leaf

4 cups (about 1/2 pound) thinly sliced savoy or white cabbage

3 slices dried Chinese licorice root (available at natural food stores and Asian markets)

1 tablespoon dried nettle (see The Savory Pantry, page 424) or 1 tablespoon minced fresh parsley

1/4 cup white miso (see The Savory Pantry, page 424)

HEAT THE OIL in a large soup pot over medium-high. Add the onions and garlic and sauté until they are fragrant and lightly browned, about 5 minutes.

ADD THE STOCK, potatoes, bay leaf, cabbage, licorice root, and nettle and bring to a boil. Reduce the heat, cover loosely, and simmer until the vegetables are tender, about 40 minutes.

REMOVE THE SOUP from the heat and discard the bay leaf. Scoop the miso into a small strainer, dip the strainer into the soup, and push the miso through with a spoon, mixing well with the soup.

Notes: If you have arthritis and are avoiding the potatoes because the solanine they contain aggravates your condition, substitute half parsnips and half carrots for the potatoes. If you have high blood pressure, omit the licorice and use the parsley instead of the nettle.

IF THE WEATHER IS HOT AND/OR DRY:
Add a pinch of saffron threads before simmering.

IF THE WEATHER IS COLD AND/OR DAMP:
Garnish the soup with minced scallion before serving.

zucchini puree with roasted pepper and marjoram

MAKES 4 SERVINGS

90 calories per serving: 2.25 grams fat: 22% calories from fat

Marjoram is used by Mediterranean and Asian herbalists to compose nerves and digestion.

1 medium onion, chopped

1 clove garlic, minced

2 small zucchini, sliced

2 teaspoons olive oil

8 ripe plum tomatoes, quartered

1 roasted red bell pepper, sliced
(see Note, page 89)

juice of 1 lemon

1/8 teaspoon finely grated lemon zest

2 tablespoons chopped fresh marjoram or
2 teaspoons dried

STEAM THE ONION, garlic, and zucchini over boiling water until tender, about 6 minutes. Transfer the vegetables to a processor or blender along with the olive oil, tomatoes, roasted pepper, lemon juice, lemon zest, and marjoram and whiz until pureed. Chill before serving.

IF THE WEATHER IS HOT AND/OR DRY:
Garnish the soup with thinly sliced radishes and serve with chilled chrysanthemum tea (available dried at natural food stores and Asian markets).

IF THE WEATHER IS COLD AND/OR DAMP:
Increase the garlic to 2 cloves and garnish the soup with chopped fresh green chilies.

red lentil chili with tomato-caper salsa

MAKES 4 ENTRÉE SERVINGS
186 calories per serving: 2.75 grams fat; 13% calories from fat

The folklore of many lands maintains that legumes, such as lentils, can alleviate depression. Modern science may concur, since lentils contain the mood-lifting B vitamins, iron, and magnesium. Red lentils are especially appropriate for busy people because they require no soaking and take a mere 15 minutes or less to cook. The zatar, as well as being tasty, makes the lentils more digestible.

2 teaspoons olive oil

1 onion, minced

2 cloves garlic, minced

1 bay leaf

1 tablespoon tomato paste

1 tablespoon flour

2 teaspoons dried zatar (available at Middle Eastern markets and some specialty stores) or thyme

1 to 2 minced fresh jalapeño peppers

²/₃ cup dried red lentils

3 cups vegetable stock

2 tablespoons minced fresh parsley

1 teaspoon reduced-sodium soy sauce

1 teaspoon hot pepper sauce, or to taste

2 cups chopped tomatoes

1 green bell pepper, seeded, cored, and minced

2 scallions, minced

1 tablespoon balsamic vinegar

1 tablespoon capers, minced

HEAT THE OIL in a large soup pot on medium-high, then add the onion, garlic, and bay leaf. Sauté until the onion is fragrant and lightly browned, about 4 minutes.

STIR IN THE tomato paste, flour, zatar, jalapeño, lentils, and stock and bring to a boil. Reduce the heat, cover loosely, and simmer until the lentils are tender, about 15 minutes. Stir in the parsley, soy sauce, and hot pepper sauce and heat through. Discard the bay leaf.

MEANWHILE. TO MAKE the salsa, combine the tomatoes, green pepper, scallions, vinegar, and capers. Serve the chili in shallow bowls with a pool of salsa atop each serving.

IF THE WEATHER IS HOT AND/OR DRY:
Swirl a spoonful of plain soy yogurt or regular yogurt into the chili when you spoon in the salsa.

IF THE WEATHER IS COLD AND/OR DAMP:
Add 1 or 2 cloves of minced fresh garlic to the salsa.

avocado soup with lemon, orange, and lime

MAKES 4 SERVINGS
225 calories per serving; 15 grams fat; 60% calories from fat

People who work and live in polluted areas, as well as those who are stressed, may want to add an avocado or two per week to their diets. The creamy-fleshed fruit is one of the rare food sources of vitamin E, a nutrient that can help reverse the damaging effects of living hectic lives in less than pristine environments.

2 cloves garlic. minced	1 1/4 teaspoons finely grated lemon zest
1 tablespoon lemon juice	1 1/2 cups chilled vegetable stock
1 tablespoon orange juice	3/4 cup plain soy yogurt or regular yogurt
2 ripe avocados. peeled and cubed (about 2 cups)	1 lime. cut into wedges

COMBINE THE GARLIC, lemon juice, orange juice, avocados, lemon zest, stock, and yogurt in a processor or blender and whiz until smooth. Serve in chilled bowls with the lime wedges for squeezing.

Note: You can see from the amount of fat that avocado is not a food to serve at every meal. But on an occasional basis the monounsaturated fat the fruit offers can actually reduce the risk of heart attack. What's more, avocado's fat is a good internal tonic for dry skin and hair. Be sure to rub the inside of the shell on damp hands for an emollient skin conditioner.

IF THE WEATHER IS HOT AND/OR DRY:
Serve with an iced lemony-herb tea.

IF THE WEATHER IS COLD AND/OR DAMP:
Add 1 teaspoon (or to taste) of hot pepper sauce to the salsa.

chilled potato soup with leek and fennel

MAKES 4 SERVINGS
146 calories per serving: no added fat

Fennel is an antispasmodic, which means it naturally soothes indigestion due to stress. In addition, fennel can help stimulate appetites in those who are too tense to dine enjoyably.

1 large leek, white part only, rinsed and chopped

¼ cup chopped onion

1 large fennel bulb, chopped

2 medium potatoes, peeled and chopped

2 cloves garlic, minced

1 cup plain soy milk or skim milk

1 cup vegetable stock

pinch of sea salt

freshly ground black pepper

watercress leaves for garnish

STEAM THE LEEK, onion, fennel, potatoes, and garlic over boiling water until tender, about 12 minutes. Tip the vegetables to a processor or blender and whiz until smooth. Stir in the milk and stock and chill for at least 30 minutes. Add salt and pepper to taste and garnish with the cress before serving.

IF THE WEATHER IS HOT AND/OR DRY:
Serve with a fresh tomato-basil salad as an accompaniment.

IF THE WEATHER IS COLD AND/OR DAMP:
Replace the cress with chopped fresh oregano and serve with hot crusty garlic bread.

mixed vegetable soup with fresh thyme and miso

MAKES 4 SERVINGS
92 calories per serving: 1.5 grams fat: 15% calories from fat

This soup was designed to fill nutritional gaps for those who have missed their daily dose of vegetables. Providing such nutrients as beta carotene, iron, and calcium, the soup contains a diverse group of vegetables—root, ground-growing, and leafy. Some nutritionists say it encourages a balanced energy in those who partake.

1 teaspoon olive oil

1 large shallot, finely minced

1 carrot, finely diced

7 ounces bok choy, chopped, stems and leaves separated

$4^1/_4$-inch slices daikon radish (see The Savory Pantry, page 423), finely diced

1 teaspoon dried nettle (see The Savory Pantry, page 424)

1 tablespoon minced fresh thyme

1 bay leaf

2 dried shiitake mushrooms, stemmed and crumbled

5 cups vegetable stock

3 ounces soba noodles

$^1/_4$ cup minced fresh garlic chives or regular chives

4 teaspoons miso (see The Savory Pantry, page 424)

HEAT THE OIL in a large soup pot on medium-high. Add the shallot and carrot and sauté until the shallot is fragrant and lightly browned, about 3 minutes.

ADD THE BOK choy stems, daikon radish, nettle, thyme, bay leaf, mushrooms, and stock and bring to a boil. Boil for 5 minutes, add the noodles and bok choy leaves, then boil until the noodles are tender, about 5 minutes more. Discard the bay leaf.

REMOVE THE POT from the heat and stir in the chives. Place the miso in a small strainer, dip the strainer into the soup, and push the miso through with a spoon, mixing well with the soup.

IF THE WEATHER IS HOT AND/OR DRY:
Use regular chives instead of garlic chives.

IF THE WEATHER IS COLD AND/OR DAMP:
Substitute mustard greens or dandelion greens for the bok choy, adding the full amount with the noodles.

aduki-carrot soup with sage

MAKES 4 SERVINGS
130 calories per serving: no added fat

Chinese and Japanese healers consider aduki beans to be a potent tonic for the kidneys. And since they also hold that healthy kidneys are the key to all manner of human energy and that the kidneys suffer during periods of stress, this soup becomes an important evening restorative.

1 quart vegetable stock or brewed roasted barley tea (see Note)

5 medium carrots, diced

2 medium onions, chopped

1/4 cup dried aduki beans (see The Savory Pantry, page 422)

1/4 cup loosely packed shredded dried daikon radish (see The Savory Pantry, page 423)

4 dried shiitake mushrooms, stemmed and crumbled

1 bay leaf

1 teaspoon minced fresh sage or 1/2 teaspoon dried

1 tablespoon miso (see The Savory Pantry, page 424)

2 tablespoons minced fresh chives

IN A LARGE soup pot, combine the stock, carrots, onions, beans, daikon, mushrooms, and bay leaf and bring the mixture to a boil. Reduce the heat, cover loosely, and simmer until the beans are very tender, about 50 minutes.

MEANWHILE, IN A small bowl, combine the sage, miso, and chives with 2 tablespoons of water. When the soup is ready, remove the pot from the heat and stir in the miso mixture.

Note: Roasted barley is available at health food stores, Asian markets, and some supermarkets. It's barley that has been roasted to a deep, rich brown and makes a fragrant tea, or stock, that looks like beef bouillon. Some Japanese and Chinese healers hold that roasted barley tea is tonifying to an overindulged liver. Korean healers use the tea to help treat stomach cancer.

IF THE WEATHER IS HOT AND/OR DRY:
Substitute 1 sweet potato, finely chopped, for 3 of the carrots.

IF THE WEATHER IS COLD AND/OR DAMP:
Garnish liberally with freshly ground black pepper.

chunky vegetable pie with whole wheat crust

MAKES 4 SERVINGS
263 calories per serving; 7.5 grams fat; 27% calories from fat

The vegetables in this savory pie are excellent sources of vitamin C, which boosts immunity to stress-induced diseases.

3 large carrots (about 1 pound), cut into 1-inch chunks

$^3/_4$ pound Brussels sprouts, stemmed and halved

$^1/_2$ pound cauliflower, broken into small pieces

1 small onion, finely chopped

2 cloves garlic, minced

3 tablespoons coarsely crushed dried porcini mushrooms

$^1/_2$ cup unbleached all-purpose flour

$^1/_2$ cup whole wheat pastry flour, plus extra

2 tablespoons olive oil

pinch of sea salt

$^1/_4$ cup plain soy milk or buttermilk

$^1/_2$ cup chopped tomatoes

2 tablespoons dry white wine or lemon juice

2 teaspoons minced fresh oregano or 1 teaspoon dried

$^1/_2$ teaspoon good-quality curry powder

$^1/_4$ cup grated soy Parmesan or regular Parmesan cheese

PREHEAT THE OVEN to 375°F.

STEAM THE CARROTS, Brussels sprouts, cauliflower, onion, garlic, and mushrooms over boiling water until tender, about 15 minutes.

MEANWHILE, TO MAKE the crust, combine the flours in a processor, adding the olive oil, salt, and buttermilk while the motor is running. Whiz until the dough forms a ball, about 10 seconds. Alternatively, you can add the oil, salt, and buttermilk to the flours and mix well with a large fork. Lightly sprinkle a dry work surface with flour and set the dough ball in the middle. Use a lightly floured rolling pin to roll the dough out to a 10-inch circle.

WHEN THE VEGETABLES are ready, spoon them into a lightly oiled 9-inch deep-dish pie pan and stir in the tomatoes, wine, oregano, and curry powder. Cover the vegetables with the pie dough, tucking it in at the sides and poking a few air holes in the top with the tip of a knife. Bake in the middle of the oven until the crust is lightly browned and the vegetables are tender and bubbly, about 25 minutes. Serve in shallow bowls, sprinkled with the Parmesan.

IF THE WEATHER IS HOT AND/OR DRY:
Serve the pie with a salad of mixed greens dressed with lemon juice and olive oil.

IF THE WEATHER IS COLD AND/OR DAMP:
Increase the curry powder to 1 teaspoon and add ground cayenne to taste.

savory potato-leek cobbler

MAKES 4 SERVINGS

365 calories per serving. 4 grams fat; 10% calories from fat

Anxiety can be a symptom of potassium deficiency, a mineral found in abundance in this satisfying vegetarian entrée.

1 pound potatoes, peeled and chopped into 1-inch chunks

1 large onion, chopped

3 leeks, rinsed, trimmed, and sliced

2 tablespoons arrowroot

1/4 cup vegetable stock

1 tablespoon minced fresh dill or 1 teaspoon dried

pinch of sea salt

freshly ground black pepper

1/2 cup unbleached all-purpose flour

1/2 cup whole wheat pastry flour

1 teaspoon baking powder

1 teaspoon dillseed

1 tablespoon olive oil

1/4 to 1/3 cup plain soy milk or skim milk

PREHEAT THE OVEN to 400°F.

STEAM THE POTATOES, onion, and leeks over boiling water until the potatoes are not quite tender, about 10 minutes. Place the vegetables in a lightly oiled 1 1/2-quart casserole dish.

WHISK TOGETHER THE arrowroot, stock, dill, salt, and pepper and pour over the potato mixture; stir well.

TO MAKE THE crust, combine the flours, baking powder, and dillseed and gradually stir in the oil and milk, starting with the 1/4 cup and adding more if necessary. Use your hands to shape the dough into a ball, then flatten it into a round slightly larger than the top of the baking dish. Set the dough on the vegetables, tucking it in around the edges and poking in a few air holes with the tip of a knife.

BAKE IN THE middle of the oven until the vegetable mixture is bubbly and the crust is lightly browned, 20 to 25 minutes.

IF THE WEATHER IS HOT AND/OR DRY:
Serve with iced hibiscus tea and lemon sorbet for dessert.

IF THE WEATHER IS COLD AND/OR DAMP:
Add 2 cloves of garlic to the steaming pot and substitute cumin seed for dillseed in the crust.

millet croquettes with warm onion relish

MAKES 5 SERVINGS
120 calories per serving: trace of fat

Since millet is an alkaline food, it's balancing for people whose diet contains too many acid-forming foods, such as white sugar and meats. Some nutritionists believe that acid-forming foods eventually cause such illnesses as colds, flu, and even cancer, and so millet is a good evening repast for those prone to fast-food lunches.

1 cup yellow millet

2 cups vegetable stock

8 slices of dried tomatoes. julienned

½ cup chopped onion

1 carrot. grated

½ cup minced mustard greens or spinach

1 tablespoon minced fresh thyme or
  1 teaspoon dried

1 clove garlic. minced

¼ cup egg substitute (see Note.
  page 13). 2 egg whites. or 1 egg

2 teaspoons prepared mustard

pinch of sea salt

dash of hot pepper sauce. or to taste

FOR THE RELISH:

½ cup chopped onions

2 tablespoons mirin or white wine

1 teaspoon reduced-sodium soy sauce

COMBINE THE MILLET. stock, and dried tomatoes in a medium saucepan and bring to a boil. Reduce the heat, cover loosely, and simmer until the millet is very tender and all of the liquid has been absorbed, 25 to 30 minutes.

STIR IN THE onion, carrot, mustard greens, thyme, garlic, egg substitute, prepared mustard, salt, and hot pepper sauce. Wet your hands and form the mixture into 5 very firm balls, pressing each about 30 times. Flatten the balls slightly.

TO COOK THE croquettes, heat a lightly oiled large cast-iron or nonstick pan on medium heat. Add the croquettes and sizzle until heated through, about 5 minutes on each side.

TO MAKE THE onion relish, combine the onions, mirin, and soy sauce in a medium pot saucepan and bring to a boil. Cook on high, stirring constantly, until the onions are fragrant and almost caramelized, about 15 minutes, adding splashes of water to moisten the onion if needed.

SERVE THE CROQUETTES warm, accompanied by the relish.

IF THE WEATHER IS HOT AND/OR DRY:
Serve with chilled lemon-spiked tomato juice.

IF THE WEATHER IS COLD AND/OR DAMP:
Increase the garlic to 2 cloves and be liberal with the hot pepper sauce.

enchiladas with barley, squash, and saffron

MAKES 5 SERVINGS
140 calories per serving: 1.8 grams fat; 12% calories from fat

Some nutritionists recommend barley to help activate the lymph system, thus prompting toxic substances to be eliminated from the body. For those who have overindulged in junk food during the day, these enchiladas may be the perfect evening antidote.

1/2 cup pearled barley

1 jalapeño pepper, seeded, cored, and minced

1 small onion, finely chopped (about 1/2 cup)

1/2 cup coarsely grated buttercup or butternut squash

1 red bell pepper, finely chopped

1/2 teaspoon saffron threads

1/2 teaspoon hot pepper sauce, or to taste

3 cups vegetable stock

1/3 cup minced fresh cilantro

pinch of sea salt

1/4 cup (not packed) grated nonfat soy mozzarella or part-skim mozzarella cheese

5 large whole wheat tortillas

2 teaspoons olive oil

2 teaspoons cumin seed

IN A LARGE saucepan, combine the barley, jalapeño, onion, squash, bell pepper, saffron, hot pepper sauce, and stock and bring to a boil. Reduce the heat, cover loosely, and continue to simmer until the barley is tender and all of the stock has been absorbed, about 1 1/4 hours. Let the barley rest, uncovered, for about 5 minutes, then stir in the cilantro, salt, and mozzarella.

LAY THE TORTILLAS on a work surface and place an equal amount of barley filling on the edge of each. Then roll up each enchilada.

HEAT THE OIL and cumin seed in a large sauté pan on medium-high. Arrange the enchiladas in the pan and sizzle until brown, about 2 minutes on each side. If your pan is not big enough, sizzle the enchiladas in batches.

IF THE WEATHER IS HOT AND/OR DRY:
Serve the enchiladas with chopped fresh tomatoes garnished with lemon and minced cilantro.

IF THE WEATHER IS COLD AND/OR DAMP:
Use 2 jalapeños when cooking the barley and add 2 cloves of minced fresh garlic. Serve the enchiladas with a spicy salsa.

barley with sun-dried tomatoes, mushrooms, and pine nuts

MAKES 4 SERVINGS
190 calories per serving: 5.75 grams fat: 27% calories from fat

A Chinese doctor I know recommends barley (1/2 cup twice a week) as a restorative for overworked women, saying it "tones the liver and rejuvenates the complexion." Western medicine validates at least half the claim by noting that barley contains folate and niacin, both needed for healthy liver function.

1/2 cup pearled barley

3 cups vegetable stock

1 clove garlic, minced

pinch of sea salt

5 large slices sun-dried tomatoes, finely chopped

5 dried porcini mushrooms, finely chopped

juice of 1 lemon

1 tablespoon balsamic vinegar

1 tablespoon olive oil

3 scallions, minced

2 tablespoons pine nuts, toasted (see Note, page 187)

COMBINE THE BARLEY, stock, garlic, and salt in a large saucepan and bring to a boil. Reduce the heat, cover loosely, and simmer until the barley is tender and all of the liquid has been absorbed, 55 to 60 minutes.

STIR IN THE dried tomatoes, mushrooms, lemon juice, vinegar, olive oil, scallions, and pine nuts.

IF THE WEATHER IS HOT AND/OR DRY:
Serve the barley slightly chilled on a nest of mixed greens.

IF THE WEATHER IS COLD AND/OR DAMP:
Increase the garlic to 2 cloves and add a pinch of dried hot red pepper flakes to the cooking barley. Garnish the barley with chopped green chilies.

buckwheat with black beans

MAKES 4 SERVINGS

158 calories per serving: 2.5 grams fat: 14% calories from fat

If the strains of the day have elevated your blood pressure, eating buckwheat may help to normalize it. Buckwheat is a good source of magnesium, and low levels of magnesium in the body are associated with hypertension.

1/2 cup roasted buckwheat groats	1 teaspoon hot pepper sauce, or to taste
1 cup vegetable stock	1 cup cooked black beans
1 cloves garlic, finely minced	2 scallions, minced
1/4 cup minced onion	1 tablespoon fresh lime juice
2 teaspoons olive oil	pinch of sea salt
1/2 teaspoon dried hot red pepper flakes	

IN A MEDIUM saucepan, bring the buckwheat, stock, garlic, and onion to a boil. Reduce the heat, cover loosely, and simmer until the buckwheat is tender, about 15 minutes.

STIR IN THE oil, red pepper flakes, hot pepper sauce, beans, scallions, lime juice, and salt.

IF THE WEATHER IS HOT AND/OR DRY:
Serve the buckwheat slightly chilled with a chilled soup such as Avocado Soup with Lemon, Orange, and Lime (page 218).

IF THE WEATHER IS COLD AND/OR DAMP:
Serve the buckwheat warm with an accompaniment of roasted vegetables.

grilled falafel with lemony tahini sauce

MAKES 4 SERVINGS
300 calories per serving: 5 grams fat: 15% calories from fat

Fresh lemon juice is an accepted home remedy for relief of the symptoms of colds, coughs, and upset stomach. Even if you don't suffer from these ills, its fresh taste is rejuvenating after a long day.

2 1/2 cups cooked chickpeas	2 tablespoons reduced-sodium soy sauce
2 large cloves garlic, chopped	2 teaspoons olive oil
2 shallots, chopped	1 tablespoon tahini (sesame paste)
1/2 teaspoon ground coriander	2 tablespoons lemon juice
1/2 teaspoon ground cumin	1 tablespoon water
pinch of cayenne pepper, or to taste	dash of hot pepper sauce, or to taste
pinch of ground cinnamon, or to taste	1 small cucumber, chopped
2 tablespoons parsley leaves	2 large whole wheat pitas, halved
1/2 cup vegetable stock	

COMBINE THE CHICKPEAS, garlic, shallots, coriander, cumin, cayenne, cinnamon, parsley, stock, and soy sauce in a processor and whiz until the mixture is the consistency of ground meat. Alternatively, you can run the mixture through a meat grinder. Wet your hands and shape the mixture into 4 firm balls, pressing each about 30 times between your hands. Flatten each ball into a thick patty, then cover and refrigerate overnight.

WHEN YOU'RE READY, preheat the broiler or prepare the grill. Use the back of a spoon to coat each patty on both sides with the oil. Broil or grill the falafel patties until browned, about 6 minutes on each side.

MEANWHILE, TO MAKE the sauce, whisk together the tahini, lemon juice, water, and hot pepper sauce. Sprinkle some cucumber into each pita half, set in a falafel patty, and top with sauce and more cucumbers.

IF THE WEATHER IS HOT AND/OR DRY:
Add an equal portion of chopped tomato when you add the cucumber. Serve the falafel with iced peppermint tea.

IF THE WEATHER IS COLD AND/OR DAMP:
Omit the cucumber and substitute mustard greens, dandelion greens, or chopped green bell pepper.

spicy tofu pie with ricotta crust

MAKES 4 SERVINGS

283 calories per serving; 12 grams fat; 37% calories from fat

Tofu is a decent source of iron, the absence of which may cause fatigue and weakness, especially in the evening hours.

1 pound reduced fat tofu, cut into 2-inch chunks (see The Savory Pantry, page 425)

1 1/2 tablespoons flour

1 tablespoon dry white wine or nonalcoholic wine

2 cloves garlic, minced

1 large shallot, finely chopped

1/3 cup finely chopped onion

3 tomatoes, chopped (including juice)

1/2 teaspoon hot pepper sauce, or to taste

1/4 teaspoon dried hot red pepper flakes, or to taste

2 teaspoons minced fresh tarragon or 1 teaspoon dried

FOR THE CRUST:

1/2 cup whole wheat pastry flour

1/2 cup unbleached all-purpose flour

2 tablespoons olive oil

1/4 cup nonfat ricotta cheese or grated soy mozzarella cheese

freshly ground black pepper

PREHEAT THE OVEN to 350°F.

PLACE THE TOFU in a lightly oiled 9-inch deep-dish pie pan, sprinkle with the flour and wine, and stir well. Stir in the garlic, shallot, onion, tomatoes, hot pepper sauce, red pepper flakes, and tarragon.

TO MAKE THE crust, place the flours, oil, cheese, and pepper in a processor and whiz until the mixture forms a ball of dough, adding a splash of water if necessary. Alternatively, you can mix the dough in a bowl using a large fork to combine the ingredients, then finish the mixing with your hands.

ROLL THE DOUGH out to a 10-inch circle, then lay it on top of the pie, crimping the edges. Poke a few air holes in the dough with the tip of a sharp knife. Bake in the middle of the oven until the tomatoes are bubbly and the edges of the crust are lightly browned, 25 to 30 minutes.

IF THE WEATHER IS HOT AND/OR DRY:
Serve the pie with iced fresh lemonade.

IF THE WEATHER IS COLD AND/OR DAMP:
Serve the pie with warm lemon-spiked apple cider.

grilled tofu salad with fresh sage dressing

MAKES 4 SERVINGS
150 calories per serving: 1 gram fat: 6% calories from fat

Sage is used by Welsh and English herbalists to prevent and treat anxiety-induced flatulence and indigestion.

¾ pound firm reduced-fat tofu
(see The Savory Pantry, page 425)

1 tablespoon reduced-sodium soy sauce

1 tablespoon prepared mustard

2 cups broccoli florets

4 red radishes, sliced

4 scallions, minced

3 cups torn romaine lettuce

½ cup chopped peeled tomatoes

1 tablespoon balsamic vinegar

1 teaspoon minced fresh sage or
½ teaspoon dried

pinch of sea salt

freshly ground black pepper

CUT THE TOFU into ½-inch slabs, set them on a plate, cover with waxed paper, and set a heavy object on top to press out the liquid. Leave the tofu pressed for about 25 minutes. Drain.

PREPARE THE GRILL or preheat the broiler. When the tofu is ready, combine the soy sauce and mustard and use the back of a spoon to spread the mixture lightly over all the surfaces. Grill or broil about 4½ inches from the heat source until the tofu is cooked through, about 4 minutes on each side. Cut the tofu into 1-inch pieces.

MEANWHILE, STEAM THE broccoli over boiling water until tender, about 5 minutes. Toss with the tofu, radishes, scallions, and romaine.

COMBINE THE TOMATOES, vinegar, sage, salt, and pepper in a processor or blender and whiz until smooth. Pour over the tofu mixture and toss well.

IF THE WEATHER IS HOT AND/OR DRY:
Garnish the salad with alfalfa sprouts.

IF THE WEATHER IS COLD AND/OR DAMP:
Garnish the salad with minced fresh parsley.

grilled tofu with lemon and capers

MAKES 4 SERVINGS
130 calories per serving: 4.5 grams fat: 30% calories from fat

Tofu is a good source of the B vitamins, a group of nutrients that can help avert nervous disorders and digestive distress.

1 pound firm reduced-fat tofu, cut into 4 slabs

juice of 1 lemon

1 clove garlic, minced

2 teaspoons prepared mustard

2 teaspoons capers, minced

freshly ground black pepper

2 tablespoons minced fresh chives

ARRANGE THE TOFU on a plate, cover with waxed paper, and set a heavy object on top to press out the liquid. Leave the tofu pressed for about 25 minutes.

MEANWHILE, COMBINE THE lemon juice, garlic, mustard, capers, and pepper and whisk together. When the tofu is ready, drain it and brush the marinade over all the surfaces. Let the tofu marinate for about 20 minutes.

PREPARE THE GRILL or preheat the broiler. Grill or broil the tofu about $4^{1}/_{2}$ inches from the heat source until lightly browned and cooked through, about $4^{1}/_{2}$ minutes on each side. Sprinkle with the chives before serving.

IF THE WEATHER IS HOT AND/OR DRY: Serve with a side dish such as Blanched Asparagus with Citrus-Cider Dressing (page 176).

IF THE WEATHER IS COLD AND/OR DAMP: Serve with a warm soup such as Spicy Minestrone with Fresh and Dried Tomatoes (page 210).

baked tofu with sesame-basil salsa

MAKES 4 SERVINGS
180 calories per serving: 10 grams fat: 47% calories from fat

Prized by herbalists for its aromatic properties, basil is recommended as a soothing stomach tonic.

1 pound firm reduced-fat tofu, cut into 4 slabs

2 cups fresh basil leaves

1 fresh jalapeño pepper, cored, seeded, and chopped

1 clove garlic, minced

1 plum tomato, chopped

2 teaspoons reduced-sodium soy sauce or *nam pla* (Thai fish sauce)

1 tablespoon toasted (dark) sesame oil

¼ cup fresh orange juice

PREHEAT THE OVEN to 375°F.

ARRANGE THE TOFU slabs in a lightly oiled pan and bake in the middle of the oven until cooked through and lightly browned, about 20 minutes.

MEANWHILE, IN A processor or blender, combine the basil, jalapeño, garlic, tomato, soy sauce, sesame oil, and orange juice and whiz to combine. Spoon over the tofu before serving.

IF THE WEATHER IS HOT AND/OR DRY:
Serve the tofu slightly chilled on a nest of mixed greens dressed with a lemony vinaigrette.

IF THE WEATHER IS COLD AND/OR DAMP:
Serve the tofu warm with crusty garlic bread.

grilled tofu with indian curry paste and mixed greens

MAKES 4 SERVINGS
132 calories per serving; 3.5 grams fat; 24% calories from fat

The bouquet of spices that perfumes the tofu has a dual role. It lends an appetizing flavor to the tofu and also serves as a remedy for jittery digestion.

1 pound firm reduced-fat tofu, cut into 4 slabs

1 teaspoon coriander seeds

1 teaspoon cumin seeds

pinch of cayenne pepper, or to taste

2 cloves garlic, minced

1 teaspoon finely grated fresh ginger (including juice)

1/2 teaspoon tamarind paste (available at Indian markets and some supermarkets)

juice of 1 lemon

6 cups mixed greens, such as mustard, arugula, and red oak lettuce

juice of 1 lime

lime wedges for serving

ARRANGE THE TOFU on a plate, cover with waxed paper, and set a heavy object on top to press out the liquid. Leave the tofu pressed for about 25 minutes.

MEANWHILE, COMBINE THE coriander seed, cumin seed, cayenne, garlic, ginger, tamarind paste, and lemon juice. When the tofu is ready, drain it and coat all sides with the paste. Let the tofu marinate for about 15 minutes.

PREPARE THE GRILL or preheat the broiler. Grill or broil the tofu about 4½ inches from the heat source until cooked through and lightly browned, about 5 minutes on each side.

ARRANGE THE GREENS among 4 plates and sprinkle with the lime juice. When the tofu is ready, set a slice on each plate of greens and serve with the lime wedges.

IF THE WEATHER IS HOT AND/OR DRY:
Garnish the dish with minced fresh cilantro.

IF THE WEATHER IS COLD AND/OR DAMP:
Add hot pepper sauce to taste to the curry paste and be sure to serve the tofu warm.

baked tofu with lemon-miso sauce

MAKES 4 SERVINGS

134 calories per serving: 4.5 grams fat: 30% calories from fat

When combined with beta carotene, riboflavin, a B vitamin, can improve stressed digestion. In this quick and savory dish, tofu contributes the riboflavin and parsley provides the beta carotene.

1 tablespoon red miso (see The Savory Pantry, page 424)

juice of 1 lemon

¹/₄ teaspoon finely minced fresh ginger

1 clove garlic, finely minced

¹/₂ teaspoon toasted (dark) sesame oil

1 tablespoon minced red onion

1 pound firm reduced-fat tofu (see The Savory Pantry, page 425), cut into ¹/₂-inch slices

2 tablespoons minced fresh parsley

2 scallions, minced

IN A GLASS pie dish, whisk together the miso, lemon juice, ginger, garlic, sesame oil, and onion. Add the tofu, bathing all sides of the slices in the marinade. Cover and refrigerate, allowing the tofu to marinate for at least 1 hour or overnight.

PREHEAT THE OVEN to 350°F.

BAKE THE TOFU in the middle of the oven until fragrant and cooked through, 25 to 30 minutes. Serve sprinkled with the parsley and scallions.

IF THE WEATHER IS HOT AND/OR DRY: *Serve the tofu Sang Chu (Korean) style, wrapped in lettuce leaves, with lemon wedges for squeezing.*

IF THE WEATHER IS COLD AND/OR DAMP: *Serve the tofu warm in a mustard-lined toasted pita.*

basmati pilaf with asparagus and shiitakes

MAKES **4** SERVINGS

181 calories per serving: 3.5 grams fat; 17% calories from fat

Few foods contain as many stress-fighting nutrients as asparagus; vitamin C, beta carotene, and selenium, which can become depleted from tension, are replaced with asparagus. Not only that, but the savory spears offer folic and nucleic acids, which help rebuild a stress-depleted immune system.

1 tablespoon olive oil

1 clove garlic, minced

1 medium onion, finely chopped

2 teaspoons ground fennel seed

1/2 teaspoon good-quality curry powder

2 cups vegetable stock

8 dried shiitake mushrooms, stemmed and crumbled

1 cup basmati rice

1 pound asparagus, trimmed and chopped

2 tablespoons grated nonfat soy mozzarella or part-skim mozzarella cheese

pinch of sea salt

freshly ground black pepper

HEAT THE OLIVE oil in a large saucepan on medium-high, then add the garlic, onion, fennel, and curry powder. Sauté until the vegetables are fragrant and slightly softened, about 3 minutes.

ADD THE STOCK, mushrooms, and rice and bring the mixture to a boil. Reduce the heat, cover loosely, and cook until the rice is not quite tender, about 12 minutes. Add the asparagus, cover, and continue to cook until the rice is tender and the asparagus is bright green and slightly softened, 2 to 3 minutes more. Stir in the mozzarella, salt, and pepper.

IF THE WEATHER IS HOT AND/OR DRY:
Serve the pilaf very slightly chilled with a salad of mixed greens.

IF THE WEATHER IS COLD AND/OR DAMP:
Double the garlic and serve the pilaf warm.

saffron-scented beans and rice

MAKES 4 SERVINGS
334 calories per serving: 6 grams fat: 16% calories from fat

In Sanskrit, saffron is called *nagakeshara*, and it is said to be *sattvic*, or capable of evoking peace and enlightenment to those who partake of it. Although Western medicine has not studied this claim, Western herbalists do prescribe saffron to make peace in an otherwise tumultuous digestive system, which may indeed be a good idea when dining on beans and rice.

2 teaspoons olive oil

1/2 cup finely minced onion

2 cloves garlic, finely minced

1/2 teaspoon saffron threads

1 1/2 cups basmati rice

1/2 cup dried red lentils

3 1/2 cups vegetable stock

1 cup salsa, such as Habanero Salsa (page 125) or Spicy Orange Salsa (page 123), plus extra for serving

pinch of sea salt

1 avocado, peeled and sliced

8 whole wheat tortillas

HEAT THE OLIVE oil in a large saucepan on medium-high, then add the onion, garlic, and saffron. Sauté until the onion is fragrant and wilted, about 3 minutes.

ADD THE RICE, lentils, and stock and bring the mixture to a boil. Reduce the heat, cover loosely, and simmer until the ingredients are tender and all of the stock has been absorbed, 14 to 15 minutes. Stir in the salsa, salt, and avocado and wrap a scoop of the mixture in each of the tortillas. Serve drizzled with extra salsa.

IF THE WEATHER IS HOT AND/OR DRY:
Use 2 avocados instead of 1 and serve with iced lemon-mint tea.

IF THE WEATHER IS COLD AND/OR DAMP:
Add 1/2 teaspoon of whole black or yellow mustard seed to the onion mixture when sautéing.

jambalaya with green and wax beans

MAKES 4 SERVINGS
180 calories per serving; 2.25 grams fat; 12% calories from fat

A tried-and-true remedy, hot peppers such as these jalapeños act as a digestive tonic and stimulator of the immune system. They are an especially useful evening nostrum for those who are just coming down with a cold.

2 teaspoons olive oil

½ cup minced onion

2 cloves garlic, finely minced

1 to 2 fresh jalapeño peppers, cored, seeded, and minced

½ cup basmati rice

1 cup vegetable stock

2 teaspoons minced fresh thyme or 1 teaspoon dried

1 bay leaf

¾ pound green and wax beans, trimmed and chopped

3 tablespoons minced fresh parsley

½ cup finely chopped fresh tomatoes (including juice)

HEAT THE OLIVE oil in a large saucepan on medium-high, then add the onion, garlic, and jalapeños. Sauté until the onion is fragrant and soft, about 3 minutes.

ADD THE RICE, stock, thyme, and bay leaf and bring the mixture to a boil. Reduce the heat, cover loosely, and simmer for about 8 minutes. Add the beans and continue to simmer until the rice and beans are tender, about 7 minutes more. Discard the bay leaf and stir in the parsley and tomatoes.

IF THE WEATHER IS HOT AND/OR DRY:
Increase the tomatoes to 1 cup.

IF THE WEATHER IS COLD AND/OR DAMP:
Add another chopped jalapeño to the tomatoes when you stir them in.

italian rice with zucchini and fresh sage

MAKES 4 SERVINGS

313 calories per serving; 2.75 grams fat; 8% calories from fat

Sage is purported to be an antihydrotic, or a substance that reduces and suppresses perspiration. This process begins about two hours after ingestion, making sage a perfect preventative for night sweats in menopausal women.

2 teaspoons olive oil

1 small onion, finely chopped

1 clove garlic, minced

1 tablespoon minced fresh sage or
    1 teaspoon dried

1 6-ounce zucchini, coarsely grated

1 6-ounce yellow summer squash, coarsely grated

1 1/4 cups arborio rice

2 1/2 cups hot vegetable stock

1 bay leaf

2 tablespoons minced fresh parsley

2 tablespoons grated soy Parmesan or
    regular Parmesan cheese

HEAT THE OIL in a large saucepan on medium-high, then add the onion, garlic, and sage. Sauté until the onion is fragrant and soft, 2 to 3 minutes.

ADD THE ZUCCHINI, squash, rice, stock, and bay leaf and bring the mixture to a boil. Reduce the heat, cover loosely, and simmer until the rice is tender and creamy and all of the liquid has been absorbed, about 17 minutes. Discard the bay leaf and stir in the parsley and Parmesan. Let the rice rest for 5 minutes before serving.

IF THE WEATHER IS HOT AND/OR DRY:
Serve with an eggplant dish such as Grilled Eggplant in Lettuce Petals (page 146).

IF THE WEATHER IS COLD AND/OR DAMP:
Increase the garlic to 2 cloves and serve the rice with a spicy side dish such as Braised Baby Squash with Garam Masala (page 179).

italian rice with black beans and mushrooms

MAKES 4 SERVINGS

317 calories per serving: 2.75 grams fat; 8% calories from fat

For two thousand years, shiitake mushrooms have been touted in China and Japan as a longevity tonic. Modern medicine concurs, reporting that shiitakes contain a friendly virus that helps the body fight infection and controls anxiety-induced high blood pressure.

2 teaspoons olive oil	2 1/2 cups hot vegetable stock
1 onion, finely chopped	1 slice dried Chinese licorice root (available at herb shops, natural food stores, and Asian markets) (see Note)
2 cloves garlic, finely minced	
6 fresh shiitake mushrooms, stemmed and thinly sliced	1 teaspoon hot pepper sauce, or to taste
	1 teaspoon (toasted) dark sesame oil
1 teaspoon Chinese fermented black beans, rinsed and minced	1 tablespoon reduced-sodium soy sauce
1 1/4 cups arborio rice	3 tablespoons grated soy Parmesan or regular Parmesan cheese

HEAT THE OIL in a large saucepan on medium-high and add the onion, garlic, mushrooms, and black beans. Sauté until the onion is fragrant and soft, about 3 minutes.

ADD THE RICE, stock, and licorice root and bring the mixture to a boil. Reduce the heat, cover loosely, and simmer until the rice is tender and creamy, about 17 minutes. Discard the licorice root and stir in the hot pepper sauce, sesame oil, soy sauce, and Parmesan. Let the rice rest for about 5 minutes before serving.

Note: If you have high blood pressure, omit the licorice, which may aggravate the condition.

IF THE WEATHER IS HOT AND/OR DRY:
Garnish the rice with minced fresh cilantro.

IF THE WEATHER IS COLD AND/OR DAMP:
Garnish the rice with minced fresh parsley.

seitan with portobello mushrooms and fresh basil

MAKES 2 SERVINGS

146 calories per serving; 3.25 grams fat; 19% calories from fat

Early American herbalists used basil as an antispasmodic to treat nerve-induced stomach spasms and headaches.

2 teaspoons olive oil	2 tablespoons flour
1 bay leaf	1 1/2 teaspoons reduced-sodium soy sauce
1 onion, sliced	1 teaspoon prepared mustard
1 clove garlic, minced	1 teaspoon tomato paste
1 4-ounce portobello mushroom, stemmed and sliced	1/3 cup vegetable stock
	1/4 cup minced fresh basil
1/2 pound seitan (see The Savory Pantry, page 425), cut into 1/3-inch slices	

HEAT THE OIL in a deep sauté pan on medium-high and add the bay leaf, onion, garlic, mushroom, and seitan. Sauté until the onion is soft and fragrant, about 3 minutes.

SPRINKLE THE FLOUR on top, then stir it in. Add the soy sauce, mustard, tomato paste, and stock and stir well to combine. Bring the mixture to a boil and continue to boil until the mixture is thick and saucy, about 3 minutes. Swirl in the basil before serving.

IF THE WEATHER IS HOT AND/OR DRY:
Serve the dish in a shallow bowl over a mound of short-grain rice.

IF THE WEATHER IS COLD AND/OR DAMP:
Increase the garlic to 2 cloves and serve the dish in a shallow bowl over a mound of barley or buckwheat.

seitan satay with garlicky peanut sauce

MAKES 4 SERVINGS
276 calories per serving: 6 grams fat: 20% calories from fat

A Peruvian cook taught me that adding peanuts to vegetarian dishes increases the digestibility by lightly lining the stomach and preventing the plant-based foods from fermenting.

2 large cloves garlic, finely minced

$1/4$ cup lime juice

2 tablespoons peanut butter

2 teaspoons reduced-sodium soy sauce

dash of hot pepper sauce

1 tablespoon vegetable stock or water

1 pound seitan (see The Savory Pantry, page 425), cut into 1-inch chunks

1 cucumber, halved and thinly sliced

2 teaspoons balsamic vinegar

pinch of sea salt

1 teaspoon sesame seeds, toasted (see Note, page 69)

romaine lettuce leaves for serving

COMBINE THE GARLIC, lime juice, peanut butter, soy sauce, hot pepper sauce, and stock in a glass pie dish, add the seitan, and stir until all of the pieces are well coated. Let the seitan marinate for about 30 minutes.

PREPARE THE GRILL or preheat the broiler. Thread the seitan pieces onto bamboo skewers and grill about $4\frac{1}{2}$ inches from the heat source until cooked through, 4 to 5 minutes on each side.

MEANWHILE, COMBINE THE cucumber, vinegar, salt, and sesame seeds. Serve the seitan on the romaine leaves, sprinkled with the cucumber mixture. Diners can remove the seitan from the skewers and eat the dish with their fingers.

IF THE WEATHER IS HOT AND/OR DRY:
Reduce the garlic to 1 clove and garnish the dish with minced fresh cilantro.

IF THE WEATHER IS COLD AND/OR DAMP:
Be liberal with the hot pepper sauce and garnish the dish with minced scallion.

seitan with green beans, garlic, and ginger

MAKES 4 SERVINGS
216 calories per serving: 3.5 grams fat; 15% calories from fat

Substances that prevent the formation of gas (stress-induced or other) in the intestines are called carminatives. Ginger is a treasured carminative in the healing arts of Japan, China, and India because of its effectiveness and delicious flowery-citrus aroma.

$^1/_2$ pound green beans, trimmed

1 small onion, thinly sliced

1 teaspoon olive oil

1 large slice fresh ginger

1 clove garlic, peeled

12 ounces seitan (see The Savory Pantry, page 425), thinly sliced into strips

$^1/_4$ cup vegetable stock

2 teaspoons arrowroot

2 teaspoons reduced-sodium soy sauce

1 teaspoon toasted (dark) sesame oil

STEAM THE GREEN beans and onion over boiling water until the beans are bright green and just tender, about 3$^1/_2$ minutes for medium-sized beans.

HEAT THE OIL in a large sauté pan on medium-high, then add the ginger, garlic, and seitan. Sauté until the seitan is lightly browned, about 4 minutes.

MEANWHILE, WHISK TOGETHER the stock, arrowroot, soy sauce, and sesame oil.

WHEN THE BEANS are ready, add them to the seitan. Pour in the stock mixture and cook until it thickens slightly, 1 to 2 minutes. Remove the ginger and garlic and serve warm.

IF THE WEATHER IS HOT AND/OR DRY:
Serve with chilled sliced cucumbers.

IF THE WEATHER IS COLD AND/OR DAMP:
Mince the ginger and garlic before adding and leave it in the dish.

burritos with quinoa and jalapeño

MAKES 4 SERVINGS

281 calories per serving: 5 grams fat: 16% calories from fat

Quinoa, an excellent vegetable source of protein, was the staple of the entire ancient Inca civilization. It is now known that the tasty little kernels also contain a good amount of magnesium, a mineral that can help regulate anxiety-induced high blood pressure.

2 teaspoons olive oil

1 medium onion, chopped

1 clove garlic, minced

1/2 teaspoon dried hot red pepper flakes, or to taste

pinch of ground cayenne pepper

1/2 teaspoon ground turmeric

1/2 teaspoon cumin seed

1 jalapeño pepper seeded, cored, and finely minced

1 1/2 cups cooked quinoa

1/4 cup cooked chickpeas, mashed lightly with a fork

4 whole wheat tortillas

1/4 cup grated fat-free soy mozzarella or part-skim regular mozzarella cheese

1 cup salsa (see Habanero Salsa, page 125)

HEAT THE OIL in a large sauté pan on medium-high, then add the onion, garlic, red pepper flakes, cayenne, turmeric, cumin seed, and jalapeño. Sauté the mixture until fragrant and the onion is soft, about 5 minutes.

ADD THE QUINOA and chickpeas and continue to sauté until heated through, about 4 minutes more.

LAY THE TORTILLAS out on a work surface and place a mound of quinoa filling on each. Sprinkle with the mozzarella and roll up to make burritos. Serve with the salsa.

IF THE WEATHER IS HOT AND/OR DRY:
Add 1 tablespoon of minced fresh cilantro to the filling when you sprinkle on the cheese.

IF THE WEATHER IS COLD AND/OR DAMP:
Add 1 tablespoon of minced fresh oregano to the filling when you sprinkle on the cheese.

soft tacos with spicy summer vegetables

MAKES 4 SERVINGS
115 calories per serving: 2.5 grams fat: 19% calories from fat

Think of this dish as a premenstrual tonic, containing iron to help prevent anemia and vitamin C to help the body absorb the plant-based iron. Additionally, the oregano helps to abate the digestive distress that can occur at this time of the month. Although these low-fat tacos are a fine female balm, they are a tasty meal for men as well.

2 teaspoons olive oil

1 medium onion, thinly sliced

2 cloves garlic, minced

1 green bell pepper, seeded and finely chopped

2 medium zucchini, thinly sliced into half moons

3 tomatillos, husked and thinly sliced into half moons

1 cup chopped green beans

2 tomatoes, chopped

dash of hot pepper sauce, or to taste

1 tablespoon minced fresh oregano or 1 1/2 teaspoons dried

2 tablespoons grated fat-free soy mozzarella or part-skim regular mozzarella cheese

4 soft 6-inch corn tortillas

HEAT THE OLIVE oil in a large sauté pan on medium-high, then add the onion, garlic, green pepper, zucchini, tomatillos, green beans, and tomatoes. Sauté until the vegetables are fragrant, tender, and saucy, 8 to 10 minutes. Swirl in the hot pepper sauce, oregano, and cheese.

PLACE EACH TORTILLA on a plate, spoon an equal amount of filling on each, and fold in half.

IF THE WEATHER IS HOT AND/OR DRY:
Serve the tortillas with minted lemonade.

IF THE WEATHER IS COLD AND/OR DAMP:
Serve the tortillas with steaming cinnamon tea.

pumpkin polenta with black bean salsa

MAKES 4 SERVINGS

185 calories per serving: 1.5 grams fat: 7% calories from fat

A rejuvenator for the nervous system, this corn-based dish is a good source of tension-taming B vitamins.

2 cups water

2 cups chilled vegetable stock

1 cup yellow cornmeal

1 bay leaf

pinch of sea salt

1 cup grated pie pumpkin or butternut squash

2 ripe tomatoes, chopped

1 jalapeño pepper, seeded, cored, and minced

1 clove garlic, minced

1 tablespoon lemon juice

1 tablespoon red wine vinegar

$^1/_2$ cup cooked black beans

BRING THE WATER to a boil in a large frypan.

WHISK TOGETHER THE stock and cornmeal, then add it to the boiling water along with the bay leaf, sea salt, and pumpkin. Reduce the heat and simmer, stirring frequently, until the polenta has thickened, 12 to 15 minutes. Discard the bay leaf.

MEANWHILE, COMBINE THE tomatoes, jalapeño, garlic, lemon juice, vinegar, and black beans. Serve the polenta in shallow bowls, topped with about 3 tablespoons of the salsa on each serving. Pass the rest of the salsa in a bowl.

IF THE WEATHER IS HOT AND/OR DRY:
Add 1 tablespoon of minced fresh cilantro to the salsa.

IF THE WEATHER IS COLD AND/OR DAMP:
Increase the garlic to 2 cloves and add 1 tablespoon of minced fresh oregano to the salsa.

polenta with garlicky greens

MAKES 4 SERVINGS
178 calories per serving: 2.25 grams fat: 12% calories from fat

The arugula in this recipe is an agreeable evening rejuvenator for those who have had an action-packed day. It contains beta carotene, which serves as a nerve tonic and helps prevent the premature aging that comes from a stressful life.

2 cups water

2 cups chilled vegetable stock

1 cup yellow cornmeal

pinch of sea salt

2 tablespoons finely chopped sun-dried tomatoes

1 teaspoon olive oil

2 cloves garlic, minced

4 cups arugula or other dark leafy greens, rinsed but not dried

2 tablespoons lemon juice

2 tablespoons grated fat-free soy mozzarella or part-skim regular mozzarella cheese

BRING THE WATER to a boil in a large frypan.

WHISK TOGETHER THE stock, cornmeal, and salt, then add it to the boiling water. Reduce the heat, add the tomatoes, and simmer, stirring frequently, until the polenta has thickened, about 12 to 15 minutes.

MEANWHILE, HEAT THE oil in a large sauté pan on medium-high. Add the garlic and damp arugula and sauté until the arugula is bright green and wilted, about 2 to 3 minutes. Sprinkle with the lemon juice and sauté for about 30 seconds more.

STIR THE GREENS into the polenta along with the cheese.

IF THE WEATHER IS HOT AND/OR DRY:
Omit the dried tomatoes and stir in 2 chopped fresh tomatoes when you add the greens to the cooked polenta.

IF THE WEATHER IS COLD AND/OR DAMP:
Add a whole dried hot pepper when you sauté the garlic and greens.

bulgur with asparagus, green beans, and soy-mustard vinaigrette

MAKES 4 SERVINGS
196 calories per serving: 3.75 grams fat: 18% calories from fat

This easy entrée is an antidote to junk food eaten throughout the day. Bulgur wheat is a good source of dietary fiber, which helps to quickly rid the digestive system of waste, thus preventing digestive problems, including cancer.

1 cup bulgur

2 cups boiling vegetable stock

1 bay leaf

1 clove garlic, finely minced

10 slices sun-dried tomatoes, chopped

6 ounces asparagus, trimmed and cut into 1-inch pieces

4 ounces green beans, trimmed and cut into 1-inch pieces

1 carrot, coarsely grated

2 scallions, finely minced

1 tablespoon balsamic vinegar

1 tablespoon reduced-sodium soy sauce

1 teaspoon prepared mustard

1 tablespoon olive oil

COMBINE THE BULGUR, stock, bay leaf, garlic, and dried tomatoes in a medium bowl. Let the mixture stand for about 30 minutes, until all of the liquid has been absorbed and the bulgur is tender. Discard the bay leaf.

MEANWHILE, STEAM THE asparagus and green beans over boiling water until just tender, 3½ to 4 minutes.

WHEN THE BULGUR is ready, stir in the asparagus, beans, carrot, and scallions. In a small bowl, whisk together the vinegar, soy sauce, mustard, and oil. Pour over the bulgur and toss well.

IF THE WEATHER IS HOT AND/OR DRY:
Omit the carrot and add ½ cup of finely chopped artichoke hearts. Serve the bulgur on a bed of chilled lettuce.

IF THE WEATHER IS COLD AND/OR DAMP:
Increase the garlic to 2 cloves and serve warm in toasted pita halves.

tangy wheat pilaf

MAKES 4 SERVINGS
184 calories per serving; 4 grams fat; 19% calories from fat

Rhubarb, which is used here as a vegetable, is a good source of potassium, a mineral that can help normalize blood pressure levels.

2 teaspoons olive oil

1 small onion, minced

1 clove garlic, minced

1 bay leaf

1 cup finely chopped rhubarb

1 cup bulgur

1 ³/₄ cups vegetable stock

pinch of sea salt

¹/₄ cup minced fresh parsley

2 tablespoons finely chopped almonds,
toasted (see Note)

HEAT THE OIL in a large sauté pan on medium heat, then add the onion, garlic, bay leaf, and rhubarb. Sauté until fragrant and the onion is slightly softened, 4 to 5 minutes. Discard the bay leaf.

COMBINE THE BULGUR, stock, and salt in a medium saucepan and bring to a boil. Reduce the heat, cover loosely, and simmer until the bulgur is tender and all of the stock has been absorbed, about 7 minutes. Stir in the rhubarb mixture along with the parsley and garnish with the almonds before serving.

Note: To toast the almonds, heat them in a dry sauté pan on medium-high, stirring constantly, until lightly browned, about 2 minutes.

IF THE WEATHER IS HOT AND/OR DRY:
Serve the pilaf slightly chilled with a side of Grilled Eggplant in Lettuce Petals (page 146).

IF THE WEATHER IS COLD AND/OR DAMP:
Serve the pilaf warm with a side of Garlicky Flatbread (page 148).

spicy grilled tempeh on skewers

MAKES 2 SERVINGS

210 calories per serving: 5 grams fat: 21% calories from fat

Tempeh is an excellent source of dietary fiber, acting as an intestinal tonic.

juice of 1 lemon	1/4 teaspoon freshly ground black pepper
2 teaspoons reduced-sodium soy sauce	1/4 teaspoon ground cayenne pepper. or to taste
1/2 teaspoon prepared mustard	2 cloves garlic. minced
1/4 teaspoon ground coriander	8 ounces tempeh (see The Savory Pantry. page 426). cut into 1-inch cubes
1/4 teaspoon ground cumin	

IN A LARGE shallow bowl, combine the lemon juice, soy sauce, mustard, coriander, cumin, black pepper, cayenne, and garlic. Add the tempeh and marinate for about 1 hour.

PREPARE THE GRILL or preheat the broiler. Thread the tempeh onto bamboo skewers and grill or broil about 4½ inches from the heat source until cooked through, about 4 minutes on each side.

IF THE WEATHER IS HOT AND/OR DRY:
Serve the tempeh with lemon wedges for drizzling and a chilled cucumber salad on the side.

IF THE WEATHER IS COLD AND/OR DAMP:
Serve the tempeh with a spicy salsa. such as Habanero Salsa (page 125).

tempeh with lemon, garlic, and parsley

MAKES 2 SERVINGS

260 calories per serving; 5 grams fat; 18% calories from fat

All of the seasonings in this savory dish—lemon, garlic, and parsley —are considered digestive tonics and can freshen a system that's been disrupted by daily tensions.

¼ cup lemon juice	2 tablespoons whole wheat flour
2 cloves garlic, minced	2 tomatoes, minced (including juice)
1 teaspoon reduced-sodium soy sauce	2 tablespoons minced fresh parsley
8 ounces tempeh (see The Savory Pantry, page 426), sliced thinly on the diagonal	

COMBINE THE LEMON juice, garlic, and soy sauce in a glass pie dish and add the tempeh. Marinate for about 15 minutes, making sure that all sides of the tempeh have been bathed in the marinade.

DRAIN THE TEMPEH, reserving the marinade, and lightly dust each slice with flour. Heat the tomatoes in a large sauté pan on medium-high and add the tempeh. Simmer until the tempeh is cooked through and lightly browned, about 5 minutes, adding the marinade toward the end. Sprinkle with the parsley before serving.

IF THE WEATHER IS HOT AND/OR DRY:
Serve with a side dish of corn, such as Corn on the Cob with Miso (page 165).

IF THE WEATHER IS COLD AND/OR DAMP:
Serve with a warm vegetable salad, such as Warm Onion Salad with Toasted Sesame Seeds (page 183).

tempeh with roasted peppers
and rosemary

MAKES 2 SERVINGS
225 calories per serving: 7.5 grams fat: 28% calories from fat

This dish may vanquish a tension headache. Rosemary contains a compound that acts on headaches like aspirin but without irritating the stomach lining.

2 teaspoons olive oil

1 clove garlic, minced

1 2-inch sprig fresh rosemary

8 ounces tempeh (see The Savory Pantry. page 426), halved and cut on a severe diagonal

4 roasted red bell peppers (see Note. page 89), sliced

1 tablespoon balsamic vinegar

$^1/_3$ cup vegetable stock or water

3 tablespoons minced fresh parsley

HEAT THE OIL in a large sauté pan on medium-high, then add the garlic, rosemary, and tempeh. Sauté until the tempeh is lightly browned, about 3 minutes.

ADD THE PEPPERS, vinegar, and stock and bring to a boil. Reduce the heat to low, cover loosely, and simmer for about 7 minutes. The peppers should still be brightly colored. Discard the rosemary and sprinkle with the parsley before serving.

IF THE WEATHER IS HOT AND/OR DRY:
Don't mince the garlic: instead. skewer it on a toothpick and remove it from the dish when you remove the rosemary.

IF THE WEATHER IS COLD AND/OR DAMP:
Double the amount of garlic.

baked tempeh cutlets with ginger and lemongrass

MAKES 2 SERVINGS
175 calories per serving: 5 grams fat: 26% calories from fat

In Indonesia, Jamu herbalists claim that lemongrass improves digestion, allowing the body to absorb maximum nutrition from foods.

3 tablespoons (not packed) grated fresh ginger

1 tablespoon reduced-sodium soy sauce

¼ teaspoon prepared mustard

1 teaspoon toasted (dark) sesame oil

2 tablespoons vegetable stock

1 teaspoon minced fresh lemongrass

8 ounces tempeh (see The Savory Pantry. page 426). cut into triangles

2 scallions. minced

USING YOUR HANDS. squeeze the ginger over a glass pie dish to obtain about 1 teaspoon of ginger juice. Discard the squeezed gratings. Add the soy sauce, mustard, sesame oil, stock, and lemongrass and stir to combine. Add the tempeh, making sure that all surfaces have been bathed in the marinade. Let the tempeh marinate, covered and refrigerated, for at least 1 hour or up to 8 hours, turning the cutlets halfway through.

PREHEAT THE OVEN to 375°F.

BAKE THE MARINATED tempeh right in the marinating dish until cooked through, about 25 minutes, turning the cutlets halfway through. Sprinkle with the scallions before serving.

IF THE WEATHER IS HOT AND/OR DRY:
Serve the cutlets with Lemony Dipping Sauce (page 159).

IF THE WEATHER IS COLD AND/OR DAMP:
Add 1 clove of minced garlic to the marinade and serve the cutlets with Onion Gravy with Rosemary (page 158).

fusilli with sage and fresh mushrooms

MAKES 4 SERVINGS

397 calories per serving: 2.5 grams fat: 6% calories from fat

The shiitake mushrooms in this dish contain vitamin B$_6$, which helps soothe the nerves and fight depression.

2 teaspoons olive oil

14 fresh sage leaves

1 clove garlic, speared with a toothpick

4 fresh shiitake mushrooms, stemmed and sliced

12 ounces fresh plum tomatoes, cored, seeded, and coarsely chopped

pinch of sea salt

freshly ground black pepper

1 teaspoon balsamic vinegar

dash of hot pepper sauce, or to taste

7 cups cooked fusilli pasta (about 1 pound dried)

HEAT THE OIL in a large sauté pan on medium-high, then add the sage leaves, garlic, and mushrooms. Sauté until the mushrooms are cooked through and lightly browned, about 3 minutes. Add the tomatoes and sauté on high, stirring constantly, until the mixture is saucy, about 3 more minutes. Discard the garlic and swirl in the salt, pepper, vinegar, and hot pepper sauce. Toss well with the fusilli.

IF THE WEATHER IS HOT AND/OR DRY:
Serve with a salad of crisp greens, such as Romaine with Lime-Anchovy Dressing (page 191).

IF THE WEATHER IS COLD AND/OR DAMP:
Instead of skewering the garlic, mince it and leave it in the dish and use 2 cloves instead of 1.

penne with roasted garlic and artichokes

MAKES 4 SERVINGS
459 calories per serving: 5 grams fat: 10% calories from fat

Although raw garlic provides the strongest medicine when it comes to the immune system, roasted garlic is nonetheless a potent digestion enhancer, often prescribed to treat chronic nervous stomachs and colons.

2 garlic bulbs

1 tablespoon olive oil

8 artichoke hearts, chopped

1 teaspoon dried hot red pepper flakes, or to taste

pinch of sea salt

$^1/_4$ cup grated fat-free soy mozzarella or part-skim regular mozzarella cheese

7 cups hot cooked penne pasta (about 1 pound dried)

PREHEAT THE OVEN to 400°F.

SLICE OFF THE pointed tops of the garlic bulbs, then wrap them loosely in foil. Bake in the middle of the oven until very soft, about 25 minutes.

WHEN THE BULBS are cool enough to handle, use your fingers to pinch the garlic from each clove. Use a fork to mash the garlic with the olive oil to make a paste. If it's too thick, add 1 or 2 tablespoons of hot water. Scoop the paste into a large pasta bowl with the artichoke hearts, red pepper flakes, salt, cheese, and pasta and toss well.

IF THE WEATHER IS HOT AND/OR DRY:
Sprinkle the pasta liberally with minced fresh mint.

IF THE WEATHER IS COLD AND/OR DAMP:
Increase the amount of red pepper flakes and sprinkle the pasta with freshly ground black pepper.

rotini with cumin-tomato sauce

MAKES 4 SERVINGS
257 calories per serving: 1 gram fat; 4% calories from fat

Ayurvedic herbalists hold that cumin helps tonify touchy digestion. In India cumin is sautéed in oil, sometimes with mustard seed, to create a soothing spiced elixir that serves as a base for sautéed foods. This base, called *vagar,* is said to help the body assimilate nutrients from ingested foods. In this low-fat version of vagar, the cumin seeds are simmered with aromatics, such as garlic, and tomatoes.

1 tablespoon cumin seeds

2 ½ cups chopped tomatoes

2 mild green chilies, sliced

2 cloves garlic, minced

2 tablespoons dry red wine or non-alcoholic wine

dash of hot pepper sauce, or to taste

4 cups cooked hot whole wheat or regular rotini pasta (about 12 ounces dried)

HEAT THE CUMIN seeds in a large sauté pan on medium-high until lightly toasted, about 2 minutes. They'll begin to pop, which is okay. Add the tomatoes, chilies, garlic, wine, and hot pepper sauce and bring the mixture to a boil. Reduce the heat, cover loosely, and simmer until slightly thick and saucy, about 15 minutes. Toss with the pasta and serve.

IF THE WEATHER IS HOT AND/OR DRY:
Serve a lemony sorbet or Cool Melon Ice (page 274) for dessert.

IF THE WEATHER IS COLD AND/OR DAMP:
Use chopped fresh hot chilies, such as serrano or jalapeño, instead of the mild green ones.

penne puttanesca

MAKES 4 SERVINGS
447 calories per serving; 4 grams fat; 8% calories from fat

Those who avoid spicy tomato sauce because it gives them indigestion may want to try this version. The oregano contains compounds that make it a digestive soother and revitalizer.

10 pitted black olives

25 fresh mushrooms, cleaned and halved

2 tablespoons capers

2 cloves garlic, halved

2 teaspoons balsamic vinegar

4 anchovy fillets

2 pounds fresh plum tomatoes, chopped, or 2 large cans chopped tomatoes

1 teaspoon olive oil

1 tablespoon minced fresh oregano

1/2 teaspoon dried hot red pepper flakes, or to taste

1 teaspoon hot pepper sauce, or to taste

7 to 8 cups hot cooked penne pasta (about 1 pound dried)

COMBINE THE OLIVES, mushrooms, capers, garlic, vinegar, and anchovies in a processor or blender and whiz until smooth. Scoop the mixture into a large sauté pan and add the tomatoes, olive oil, oregano, red pepper flakes, and hot pepper sauce. Bring the mixture to a boil, reduce the heat, cover loosely, and simmer until the sauce is thick and slightly orange, 15 to 20 minutes. Toss with the pasta and serve.

IF THE WEATHER IS HOT AND/OR DRY:
Reduce the garlic to 1 clove and add 1 tablespoon of minced fresh mint when you add the oregano.

IF THE WEATHER IS COLD AND/OR DAMP:
Serve with a warm spicy bread such as garlic bread or Focaccia with Oregano (page 149).

ravioli with basil sauce

MAKES 4 SERVINGS

419 calories per serving: 4 grams fat: 9% calories from fat

Aromatherapists prescribe basil to treat nervous fatigue and digestive spasms due to stress.

50 small vegetable-filled ravioli, cooked
(reserve water)

4 ounces fresh basil leaves

1 large clove garlic, halved

3 tablespoons pine nuts, toasted
(see Note, page 187)

$^1/_2$ cup nonfat ricotta cheese or
Faux Ricotta (page 127)

2 tablespoons grated soy Parmesan or
regular Parmesan cheese

2 tablespoons ravioli cooking water

freshly ground black pepper

TIP THE RAVIOLI in a shallow pasta bowl and keep it handy.

IN A PROCESSOR or blender combine the basil, garlic, pine nuts, ricotta, Parmesan, cooking water, and black pepper and whiz until smooth. Scoop onto the ravioli and toss well but gently to avoid breaking the ravioli.

IF THE WEATHER IS HOT AND/OR DRY:
*Substitute 1 tablespoon of lemon juice for
1 tablespoon of the cooking water.*

IF THE WEATHER IS COLD AND/OR DAMP:
*Increase the garlic to 2 cloves and be
liberal with the black pepper.*

ravioli with mushroom sauce

MAKES 4 SERVINGS
417 calories per serving: 5 grams fat: 11% calories from fat

The mushrooms contain immune-building folate, making this dish an evening rejuvenator.

1 tablespoon olive oil

2 cloves garlic, minced

¾ cup vegetable stock

1 tablespoon minced fresh thyme or
    1½ teaspoons dried

1 teaspoon tomato paste

dash hot pepper sauce

6 dried shiitake mushrooms, stemmed and
    crumbled

12 slices sun-dried tomatoes, chopped

50 vegetable-filled ravioli, cooked

2 tablespoons grated soy Parmesan or
    regular Parmesan cheese

HEAT THE OLIVE oil in a large sauté pan on medium-high and add the garlic, stock, thyme, tomato paste, hot pepper sauce, mushrooms, and dried tomatoes. Bring the mixture to a boil, reduce the heat, and simmer until the mushrooms and tomatoes are tender, about 6 minutes. Toss with the ravioli and Parmesan, then serve.

IF THE WEATHER IS HOT AND/OR DRY:
Substitute 4 chopped plum tomatoes for the dried ones.

IF THE WEATHER IS COLD AND/OR DAMP:
Sprinkle the pasta with freshly ground black pepper before serving.

couscous salad with sesame dressing

MAKES 4 SERVINGS
190 calories per serving: 6 grams fat: 28% calories from fat

Couscous, especially the whole wheat variety, is a decent source of folate, a nutrient whose absence is associated with depression and anxiety.

1 1/2 cups vegetable stock	juice of 1 lemon
1 cup whole wheat or white couscous	1 tablespoon rice vinegar
1/2 teaspoon olive oil	1 tablespoon toasted (dark) sesame oil
5 slices sun-dried tomatoes, finely chopped	4 purple cabbage petals
1/2 cup chopped green beans	3 scallions, minced

BRING THE STOCK to a boil in a medium saucepan and add the couscous, oil, dried tomatoes, and beans. Stir one time, cover loosely, remove from the heat, and let the mixture stand until the couscous is tender and all of the liquid has been absorbed, about 5 minutes.

COMBINE THE LEMON juice, vinegar, and sesame oil, whisking well. Pour over the couscous and toss well, being careful not to mash the couscous. Serve the couscous in the cabbage petals sprinkled with the scallions.

IF THE WEATHER IS HOT AND/OR DRY:
Replace the scallions with 3 tablespoons of minced fresh mint.

IF THE WEATHER IS COLD AND/OR DAMP:
Add 2 cloves of minced fresh garlic when you add the couscous to the boiling water.

braised vegetables with couscous

MAKES 4 SERVINGS
256 calories per serving: 2.5 grams fat: 9% calories from fat

Thyme, which perfumes this hearty meal, is employed by English and Welsh herbalists to treat sluggish and stressed digestion.

1 medium onion, chopped

2 large carrots, cut into $1/2$-inch slices

$1/2$ pound potatoes, cut into $1/2$-inch chunks

2 medium tomatoes, finely chopped (including juice)

2 fresh jalapeño peppers, seeded, cored, and minced

2 cloves garlic, minced

1 tablespoon minced fresh thyme or $1^1/2$ teaspoons dried

1 tablespoon minced fresh rosemary or $1^1/2$ teaspoons dried

1 bay leaf

1 tablespoon minced fresh oregano or $1^1/2$ teaspoons dried

2 teaspoons reduced-sodium soy sauce

2 teaspoons olive oil

1 cup vegetable stock

1 cup water

$3/4$ cup whole wheat or white couscous

3 whole cloves

$1/4$ teaspoon fennel seed

$1/4$ cup minced fresh parsley

3 scallions, minced

COMBINE THE ONION, carrots, potatoes, tomatoes, jalapeños, garlic, thyme, rosemary, bay leaf, oregano, soy sauce, olive oil, and stock in a large saucepan and bring to a boil. Reduce the heat, cover loosely, and simmer until the vegetables are fragrant and very tender, 45 to 50 minutes. Discard the bay leaf.

MEANWHILE, COMBINE THE water, couscous, cloves, and fennel seed in a saucepan and bring to a boil. Cover, remove the pan from the heat, and let stand until all of the liquid has been absorbed, at least 5 minutes.

TO SERVE, DIVIDE the couscous among 4 shallow bowls. Spoon the vegetables on top and garnish with the parsley and scallions.

IF THE WEATHER IS HOT AND/OR DRY:
Omit the parsley garnish and use $1/4$ cup of minced fresh cilantro.

IF THE WEATHER IS COLD AND/OR DAMP:
Sprinkle each serving with hot red pepper flakes to taste.

pumpkin cheesecake

MAKES 12 SERVINGS
137 calories per serving: 4.5 grams fat: 30% calories from fat

The low-fat nature of this normally rich dessert promotes more relaxed digestion and easier sleep than its fattier cousins do.

1 pack (about 5½ ounces) whole wheat graham crackers

3 tablespoons canola oil

1 tablespoon barley malt

1 pound low-fat tofu or low-fat cottage cheese

½ cup plain soy yogurt or low-fat regular yogurt

¾ cup pumpkin puree

¼ cup flour

¾ cup egg substitute (see Note, page 13) or 6 egg whites

1 teaspoon vanilla extract

⅓ cup pure maple syrup

½ teaspoon pumpkin pie spice

PREHEAT THE OVEN to 325°F.

WRAP THE OUTSIDE of an 8-inch springform pan with aluminum foil, shiny side out, and spray the inside of the pan with nonstick spray.

COMBINE THE GRAHAM crackers, oil, and barley malt in a processor or blender and whiz until you have evenly ground crumbs. Use your hands to press the mixture firmly onto the bottom and 1½ inches up the sides of the pan, then refrigerate.

COMBINE THE TOFU, yogurt, pumpkin puree, flour, egg substitute, vanilla, maple syrup, and pumpkin pie spice in a processor or blender and whiz until smooth. Scoop into the chilled crust.

BAKE IN THE middle of the oven until firm, about 50 minutes. Let the cheesecake cool completely before slicing and serving.

IF THE WEATHER IS HOT AND/OR DRY: *Garnish each serving of cheesecake with fresh raspberries.*

IF THE WEATHER IS COLD AND/OR DAMP: *Add ½ teaspoon of ground cinnamon when you add the pumpkin pie spice, and garnish each slice of cheesecake with sliced poached pears or Plum and Pear Compote (page 269).*

strawberry-rhubarb crisp

MAKES 4 SERVINGS
147 calories per serving: no added fat

Although the berries in this recipe are cooked, they still retain some vitamin C—a boon to those who have downed aspirin during the day, since the medication can deplete the body of vitamin C.

3 cups chopped fresh rhubarb	$^1/_3$ cup barley malt
2 cups chopped fresh strawberries	1 cup rolled oats
2 tablespoons arrowroot	2 tablespoons pure maple syrup
3 tablespoons apple juice	pinch of ground cinnamon

PREHEAT THE OVEN to 375°F.

COMBINE THE RHUBARB, berries, arrowroot, apple juice, and barley malt in a 1½-quart casserole dish.

TIP THE OATS in a dry large sauté pan and heat on medium-high, stirring constantly, until lightly browned, about 2½ minutes. Immediately stir in the maple syrup and cinnamon, then spoon the mixture evenly on top of the berry mixture.

COVER WITH ALUMINUM foil and bake in the middle of the oven until the fruit is bubbly, about 20 minutes. Remove the foil and continue to bake until the topping is medium brown, about 5 minutes more.

IF THE WEATHER IS HOT AND/OR DRY:
Top each serving with nonfat vanilla soy yogurt or regular yogurt and sliced fresh strawberries.

IF THE WEATHER IS COLD AND/OR DAMP:
Serve the crisp with a cup of hot spicy cinnamon tea.

raspberry filling for a tart or pie

MAKES 6 SERVINGS
210 calories per serving; 4.6 grams fat; 20% calories from fat

Each serving of this dish contains a healthy 4 grams of dietary fiber, or one-fifth of what experts recommend we need each day to promote healthy digestion.

4 cups fresh raspberries

3 tablespoons barley malt, or to taste

1 tablespoon lemon juice

$^1/_4$ cup unbleached, all-purpose flour

1 9-inch baked tart or pie shell (or use the crust in Chunky Vegetable Pie, page 222, baked blind at 350°F for 18 minutes)

COMBINE THE BERRIES, barley malt, lemon juice, and flour in a saucepan and bring to a boil, stirring constantly. Continue to boil until the mixture is thick but the berries are still bright in color, 4 to 5 minutes. Let the filling cool for about 8 minutes before scooping it into the shell. Chill completely before serving.

IF THE WEATHER IS HOT AND/OR DRY:
Top each serving with sliced fresh apricots and a sprig of fresh mint.

IF THE WEATHER IS COLD AND/OR DAMP:
Drizzle each slice with a bit of hot cinnamon-spiked maple syrup.

apricot-banana mousse

MAKES 4 SERVINGS
197 calories per serving: no added fat

Apricots are a great source of the body-guarding nutrient beta carotene. In fact, the luscious fruit may be the best way to get children to ingest it, since apricot is a more popular flavor than yellow vegetables.

$^1/_2$ cup dried apricots (12 to 14)	2 ice cubes
$^1/_2$ cup apple juice	1 tablespoon lemon juice
2 small bananas, peeled	4 fat-free oatmeal cookies
1 cup plain nonfat soy yogurt or regular yogurt	fresh mint sprigs for garnish

COMBINE THE APRICOTS and juice in a small saucepan and bring to a boil. Reduce the heat, cover loosely, and simmer until the apricots are very tender, about 10 minutes. Let the apricots cool.

TIP THE APRICOTS (including juice), bananas, yogurt, ice cubes, and lemon juice in a processor or blender and whiz until smooth and creamy. Let the mousse chill for at least 1 hour, then set a cookie in each of 4 dessert dishes and spoon the mouse on top. Garnish with the mint and serve.

IF THE WEATHER IS HOT AND/OR DRY:
Garnish the mousse with fresh raspberries or sliced fresh apricots.

IF THE WEATHER IS COLD AND/OR DAMP:
Add a 2-inch cinnamon stick when simmering the apricots in the juice.

vanilla custards with almonds and fresh oranges

MAKES 4 SERVINGS

175 calories per serving: 2 grams fat: 11% calories from fat

Aromatherapists maintain that the scent of vanilla is calming and soothing to the nerves.

1 1/2 cups vanilla soy milk

1 tablespoon arrowroot

2 tablespoons egg substitute
  (see Note, page 13)

1 1/2 teaspoons vanilla extract

1/4 cup pure maple syrup

2 oranges, peeled, seeded, and sectioned

2 tablespoons slivered almonds, toasted
  (see Note, page 248)

WHISK THE MILK and arrowroot in a small saucepan and boil until just thick, 1 to 2 minutes.

IN A MEDIUM bowl, beat the egg substitute, vanilla, and maple syrup with a hand mixer. Beat in a little of the hot milk and continue beating while you slowly add the rest of the milk. Let the bubbles die down.

POUR THE MIXTURE into 4 custard cups or ramekins and steam over boiling water until firm but a bit jiggly, 5 to 6 minutes. Garnish with the oranges and almonds before serving.

IF THE WEATHER IS HOT AND/OR DRY:
Chill the custards before serving.

IF THE WEATHER IS COLD AND/OR DAMP:
Serve the custards warm.

bread pudding with cinnamon and apricots

MAKES 4 SERVINGS

228 calories per serving: 3.75 grams fat: 14% calories from fat

Japanese healers recommend whole wheat to treat digestion problems caused by stress and poor eating habits. This dessert may be a corrective measure for any junk food eaten throughout the day.

6 slices whole wheat bread, torn into pieces

1/3 cup chopped dried apricots (about 12)

1/4 cup egg substitute (see Note, page 13) or 2 egg whites

1 1/2 cups low-fat vanilla soy milk or skim milk

1/4 cup all-fruit apricot jam

1/2 teaspoon vanilla extract

1/2 teaspoon ground cinnamon

12 almonds, chopped and toasted (see Note, page 248)

PREHEAT THE OVEN to 375°F.

ARRANGE THE BREAD pieces and apricots in a 1 1/2-quart soufflé dish.

IN A MEDIUM bowl, combine the egg substitute, milk, jam, vanilla, and cinnamon, using a hand mixer to blend well. Pour the mixture over the bread, pushing the bread down and mixing gently. Cover and bake in the middle of the oven until the consistency is thick and pudding-like, about 25 minutes. Sprinkle with the almonds before serving.

IF THE WEATHER IS HOT AND/OR DRY:
Serve the pudding topped with nonfat vanilla soy yogurt or regular yogurt.

IF THE WEATHER IS COLD AND/OR DAMP:
Serve the pudding warm, sprinkled with extra cinnamon.

apple-scented rice pudding with dates

MAKES 4 SERVINGS
250 calories per serving: trace of fat

The apple flavor in this homey dish is enhanced by chamomile flowers, an herb containing volatile oils that relax both the nervous and the digestive systems.

2 cups apple cider	1 3-inch cinnamon stick
2 teaspoons dried chamomile tea	1 bay leaf
1¼ cups arborio rice	pinch of sea salt
3 whole cloves	4 large pitted dried dates, finely chopped

IN A SMALL saucepan, bring the apple cider to a boil, then remove it from the heat and add the chamomile. Cover and let the brew steep for 4 minutes. Strain and discard the chamomile.

IN A MEDIUM saucepan combine the scented cider, rice, cloves, cinnamon stick, bay leaf, salt, and dates and bring to a boil. Cover loosely, reduce the heat, and simmer until the rice is tender and all of the cider has been absorbed, 17 to 18 minutes. Remove the cinnamon stick and bay leaf before serving.

IF THE WEATHER IS HOT AND/OR DRY:
Serve the pudding with crisp fresh apple slices.

IF THE WEATHER IS COLD AND/OR DAMP:
Serve the pudding warm, topped with toasted sunflower seeds.

creamy date pudding with cinnamon and coconut

MAKES 4 SERVINGS
180 calories per serving: 2.5 grams fat: 13% calories from fat

Since dates are one of the few fruits that can be dried without the use of sulfites, they make a wholesome choice. In addition, dates are a decent source of fatigue-fighting iron, made more bio-available by the vitamin C in the limes.

1/2 cup finely chopped dried dates

1/4 cup unsweetened dried shredded coconut

2 cups low-fat vanilla soy milk or skim milk

1/2 teaspoon vanilla extract

1 tablespoon pure maple syrup

1/2 teaspoon ground cinnamon

1/4 cup unbleached all purpose flour

1 lime, quartered

IN A MEDIUM saucepan, combine the dates, coconut, milk, vanilla, maple syrup, cinnamon, and flour and bring to a boil, whisking frequently. This may take 2 to 3 minutes. Continue to boil and whisk until the mixture has thickened slightly, about 2 minutes more. Refrigerate until thickened, about 1 hour. Serve in dessert bowls, accompanied by the lime quarters for drizzling.

IF THE WEATHER IS HOT AND/OR DRY:
Serve the pudding with chilled orange segments.

IF THE WEATHER IS COLD AND/OR DAMP:
Top the pudding with toasted pumpkin seeds.

plum and pear compote

MAKES 4 LARGE SERVINGS
120 calories per serving: no added fat

Plums are a good source of potassium, a mineral whose presence in the diet may help avert a stroke.

4 large ripe plums (about 1 pound), pitted and thinly sliced

2 ripe Bartlett pears (about ½ pound), cored and thinly sliced

½ lemon, seeded and thinly sliced (including rind)

3 pitted dried dates, minced

1 cup brewed cinnamon-herb tea

COMBINE ALL OF the ingredients in a medium saucepan and bring to a boil. Reduce the heat and simmer until the fruit is tender and the liquid has been reduced to about ½ cup, about 10 minutes.

IF THE WEATHER IS HOT AND/OR DRY:
Serve the compote slightly chilled, topped with fresh mint sprigs. Or use the compote as a topping for soy or regular frozen yogurt.

IF THE WEATHER IS COLD AND/OR DAMP:
Serve the compote warm atop such baked goods as Spicy Apple Bread (page 47).

baked summer fruits with maple-cinnamon topping

MAKES 4 LARGE SERVINGS
181 calories per serving: 3.5 grams fat; 16% calories from fat

Those who smoke cigarettes or live in areas where the air is polluted may want to end their evening meal with this vitamin C–packed dessert, since vitamin C helps to prevent lung disease and infection.

1 pound (about 4) ripe nectarines, pitted and thinly sliced

1 pound (about 6) ripe red plums, pitted and thinly sliced

1 tablespoon fresh lemon juice

1 tablespoon all-fruit raspberry preserves

2 teaspoons arrowroot

1 cup rolled oats

2 tablespoons hulled raw unsalted sunflower seeds

$1/4$ cup raisins

3 tablespoons pure maple syrup

1 teaspoon canola oil

pinch of ground cinnamon

PREHEAT THE OVEN to 375°F.

IN A $1^1/2$-QUART casserole dish, combine the nectarines, plums, lemon juice, preserves, and arrowroot.

IN A LARGE sauté pan, heat the oats and sunflower seeds on medium-high, stirring constantly, until lightly toasted, 2 to 3 minutes. Stir in the raisins, maple syrup, oil, and cinnamon, then spread the mixture evenly over the fruit. Cover and bake in the middle of the oven until the fruit begins to bubble, about 15 minutes. Remove the cover and continue to bake for about 5 minutes more.

IF THE WEATHER IS HOT AND/OR DRY:
Serve the dish slightly chilled alone or atop a frozen treat such as Low-Fat Blueberry Ice Cream (page 277).

IF THE WEATHER IS COLD AND/OR DAMP:
Serve the dish warm alone or atop halved muffins, such as Carrot-Raisin Muffins (page 45).

peaches in red wine

MAKES 4 SERVINGS

48 calories per serving; no added fat

Peaches were revered in ancient China, where they remain symbolic of a happy life. For another bright note, the fruit is a good source of vitamin C, which can help prevent such infections as colds and flu.

4 peaches, halved and pitted

$^1/_2$ cup orange juice

$^1/_2$ cup red wine or nonalcoholic red wine

fresh mint sprigs for garnish

IN A DEEP frypan, combine the peaches, orange juice, and wine and bring to a boil. Reduce the heat and simmer for about 5 minutes. Refrigerate the peaches in the liquid until chilled, at least 1 hour. Serve the peaches in shallow bowls, topped with 1 or 2 tablespoons of the liquid and garnished with the mint.

IF THE WEATHER IS HOT AND/OR DRY:
Add 2 lemon slices to the liquid during simmering.

IF THE WEATHER IS COLD AND/OR DAMP:
Add a 2-inch cinnamon stick to the liquid during simmering. Instead of refrigerating, let the peaches sit in the liquid at room temperature for about 15 minutes before serving. Omit the mint and garnish with a sprinkle of ground cinnamon.

pears in cider with rosemary

MAKES 4 LARGE SERVINGS
210 calories per serving; no added fat

Rosemary, having both aromatic and carminative properties, makes this dish the perfect evening tonic for those with nervous digestion.

2 pounds Bartlett pears, peeled, cored, and thinly sliced

1 4-inch sprig fresh rosemary or 2 teaspoons dried rosemary leaves

²⁄₃ cup apple cider

COMBINE THE PEARS, rosemary, and cider in a wide frypan and bring to a boil. Cover loosely, reduce the heat, and simmer until the pears are fragrant and just tender, about 5 minutes. Strain and discard the rosemary. Serve the pears in shallow bowls, drizzled with the rosemary-scented cider.

IF THE WEATHER IS HOT AND/OR DRY:
Serve the pears chilled alone or atop frozen yogurt, such as Frozen Cinnamon-Pumpkin Yogurt (page 278).

IF THE WEATHER IS COLD AND/OR DAMP:
Serve the pears warm alone or atop baked goods such as Three-Grain Scones (page 18).

frozen fruit freeze

MAKES 2 SERVINGS
215 calories per serving: trace of fat

Banana, which contains the natural relaxant tryptophan, makes this satisfying dessert a mild nerve tonic.

$^1/_4$ cup all-fruit raspberry preserves

1 frozen banana, sliced (about $^1/_2$ cup)

$^1/_2$ cup sliced frozen strawberries

$^1/_2$ cup cold low-fat vanilla soy milk or skim milk

1 tablespoon lemon juice

$^1/_2$ teaspoon vanilla extract

pinch of ground cinnamon

COMBINE ALL OF the ingredients in a processor or blender and whiz until smooth. Serve in chilled milkshake glasses.

IF THE WEATHER IS HOT AND/OR DRY:
Substitute $^1/_2$ cup of fresh mango pulp for the strawberries. Omit the cinnamon, using a pinch of ground cardamom instead.

IF THE WEATHER IS COLD AND/OR DAMP:
When adding the cinnamon, also add a pinch each of ground cloves, nutmeg, and ginger.

cool melon ice

Containing good amounts of vitamin C, beta carotene, and folate, this refreshing repast is a great evening tonic for the immune system.

1 cup brewed peppermint tea, cooled

1/3 cup barley malt

1 pound cucumbers, peeled, seeded, and chopped

1/2 medium cantaloupe, peeled and chopped

2 tablespoons fresh lime juice

USING A HAND mixer, combine the tea and barley malt in a small bowl.

COMBINE THE CUCUMBERS, cantaloupe, and lime juice in a processor or blender and whiz until pureed. Add the tea mixture and freeze in an ice cream maker according to the manufacturer's directions.

IF THE WEATHER IS HOT AND/OR DRY:
Replace the lime juice with orange juice.

IF THE WEATHER IS COLD AND/OR DAMP:
You may want to choose one of the more naturally warming desserts in this section, such as Strawberry-Rhubarb Crisp (page 262). But if you have your heart set on this icy dessert, warm it up a bit by substituting 2 tablespoons of ginger juice for the lime juice.

watermelon ice

MAKES 4 SERVINGS
90 calories per serving: no added fat

Watermelon is one of the best food sources of chromium, a trace mineral valued for its ability to help regulate blood sugar levels and assimilate fat. Those whose daily diets are high in such refined foods as white flour and white sugar may be deficient in chromium.

2 pounds peeled and seeded watermelon

$^1/_2$ cup apple juice

$^1/_2$ cup white grape juice

1 tablespoon lemon juice

COMBINE THE WATERMELON and juices in a processor or blender and whiz until smooth. Chill the mixture, then freeze in an ice cream maker according to the manufacturer's directions.

IF THE WEATHER IS HOT AND/OR DRY:
Serve the ice in chilled dessert dishes and enjoy as is.

IF THE WEATHER IS COLD AND/OR DAMP:
This is not the smartest dessert choice for cold or damp days. but if your mind is made up. warm up the recipe a bit by adding 1 teaspoon of cinnamon during processing.

peppermint ice

MAKES 4 LARGE SERVINGS
64 calories per serving: no added fat

Peppermint is prized as a stomach tonic, used to treat nervousness and poor digestion due to stress or headaches.

1 1/2 cups strong brewed peppermint tea, chilled

1 1/2 cups white grape juice

1 tablespoon lemon juice

COMBINE ALL OF the ingredients, then freeze in an ice cream maker according to the manufacturer's directions.

IF THE WEATHER IS HOT AND/OR DRY:
Use orange juice instead of lemon juice.

IF THE WEATHER IS COLD AND/OR DAMP:
This is a very cooling dessert, but if you crave it, perhaps for soothing a dry throat, add 5 whole cloves to the peppermint tea during brewing and remove them before proceeding with the recipe.

low-fat blueberry ice cream

MAKES 1 QUART, OR 4 LARGE SERVINGS
98 calories per serving: no added fat

Women on a daily dose of birth control pills, as well as anyone who has had a stressful day, may benefit from this frozen delight. The blueberries contain a good amount of vitamin C, which is diminished by taking the "pill" and by stress.

2 cups blueberries

2 cups low-fat vanilla soy milk or skim milk

$1/4$ cup pure maple syrup

$1/2$ teaspoon ground cinnamon

PUREE THE BERRIES in a processor or blender, adding the milk, maple syrup, and cinnamon halfway through. Freeze the mixture in an ice cream maker according to the manufacturer's directions.

IF THE WEATHER IS HOT AND/OR DRY:
Omit the cinnamon and substitute $1/2$ teaspoon of ground cardamom.

IF THE WEATHER IS COLD AND/OR DAMP:
Add $1/2$ teaspoon of ground ginger when you add the cinnamon.

frozen cinnamon-pumpkin yogurt

MAKES 4 SERVINGS
119 calories per serving: trace of fat

Those who refuse to eat their vegetables will be pleased to partake of this tasty treat, getting a big dose of immune-enhancing beta carotene in spite of themselves.

2 cups finely chopped fresh pumpkin
(about 1 pound)

$^1/_4$ teaspoon freshly grated orange zest

1 teaspoon vanilla extract

$^1/_2$ teaspoon pumpkin pie spice

$^1/_4$ cup pure maple syrup

2 cups plain nonfat soy yogurt or regular yogurt

STEAM THE PUMPKIN over boiling water until tender, about 9 to 10 minutes. When the pumpkin is cool enough to handle, tip it into a processor or blender and whiz until smooth.

COMBINE THE PUMPKIN, orange zest, vanilla, pumpkin pie spice, maple syrup, and yogurt in an ice cream maker and freeze according the manufacturer's directions. For the best textural results, serve at once and don't refreeze.

IF THE WEATHER IS HOT AND/OR DRY:
Serve in chilled dessert bowls with juicy segments of fresh orange.

IF THE WEATHER IS COLD AND/OR DAMP:
Add $^1/_2$ teaspoon of ground cinnamon when you add the pumpkin pie spice. and garnish each serving with toasted pumpkin seeds (see Note. page 199).

night

night

WHERE DREAMS ARE MADE

best time of day for:

Revitalizing your mind and
body

*A*t two in the morning in Taipei, visions of eviscerated snakes hung in
my mind, much as I had seen them in the famous "snake alley" earlier
that day. A reptilian pharmacopoeia, snake alley is where locals go to
buy the body parts and fluids of the slithery serpents to heal what ails
them. Crocks of snake hearts, vats of snake bile, and unimaginable
smells made a lasting impression on this Westerner. As I lay sleepless,
the last straw was thinking I heard footsteps approaching my door, only
to realize it was the anxious pounding of my own heart.

Consulting the next day with a Taiwanese physician, I learned that
insomnia, or the inability to fall asleep or stay asleep, is not a condition
in itself, but a symptom. The key to solving insomnia, he explained, is
in identifying the problem that is preventing sleep and solving it. As the
old Chinese saying goes, "To conquer an enemy, you have to know him
first."

Conditions that can cause insomnia include hyperthyroidism, pain from arthritis, diabetes, excessive caffeine consumption, excessive alcohol consumption, cigarette smoking, changes in weather, breathing problems, and a diet high in refined white sugar. But experts say that 75 percent of all insomnia is psychological, usually brought about by anxiety-causing events such as my encounter in snake alley.

The physician assuaged my anxiety, explaining that the Taiwanese look to snakes for healing because they are thought of as cunning, wise, heroic, and a symbol of renewal. Knowing that, I could understand why snake heart soup, for instance, might be an apt tonic for those who believe. Although I did not adopt the snake healing diet for myself, the new information on this exotic custom removed the heart-pounding horrors from my imagination, enabling me to sleep again peacefully.

Since after four days of poor sleep humans lose their ability to think clearly, I was lucky that my insomnia lasted for only one night. Others are not so fortunate: there are 250 sleep clinics in the United States alone, and more than 30 million insomniacs suffer from the lack of profound healing and rejuvenating that sound sleep brings. My Taiwanese physician said that many Americans have too much anxiety, preventing them from paying attention to, and taking control of, their daily rhythms. These rhythms should work in symphony, he noted, much like musicians in an orchestra. When every musician follows the conductor, each one plays his part at just the right time. "But when there's no conductor, the beat becomes erratic." Each person needs to conduct his own daily rhythms, being mindful of diet, exercise, work schedule, sleep, and even how these rhythms respond to seasonal and weather changes. "In summer in old China," he continued, "at two o'clock in the afternoon it was so hot that everyone pulled down the shades and rested. But now, with air conditioning, everyone just keeps on working, right through the heat. Often people become fatigued and irritable, not sleeping well, from what we call summer insomnia. It's because air conditioning has disrupted their natural rhythms."

Television, the physician went on, also disrupts sleep rhythms when watched just before retiring. Watching screeching police chases, shootings, or graphic medical emergencies is not conducive to restful sleep.

Activities that nourish restful sleep, according to him and other physicians, are such calm-promoting practices as:

- Listening to soothing music while concentrating on forgetting the day's tensions. The music physiologically slows your heartbeat and breathing, making you more relaxed.

- Taking a warm bath while meditating or reading relaxing poetry. The warm water works by relaxing tense muscles, especially if a handful of Epsom salts is added.

- Having a massage. Warm rubbing with the hands eases stressed muscles, encouraging a calm state of mind. Try it right now, using your right hand to rub the left side of your neck and shoulders for 10 seconds, then repeating with your left hand on your right side. Notice the soothing warmth that suffuses the areas.

- Avoiding such stimulants as television, alcohol, caffeine, cigarettes, and foods containing refined sugar.
- Exercising during the day, not before bedtime. Exercise increases the metabolism, which is not good just before bed.
- Eating foods throughout the day that are high in the nerve-soothing B vitamins, such as the whole grain offerings in the preceding chapters. Also try to eat foods like broccoli and leafy greens, high in calming calcium, and soybeans (including tofu, soy cheese, and tempeh), which contain mellowing magnesium.
- Sleeping on all-cotton sheets to inspire bodily comfort. Look for labels that say the sheets have at least 230 threads per inch. These sheets can be expensive, so you may want to check linen outlets. The good news is they last a long time.
- Going to bed at the same time each night to encourage your mind and body to adopt a regular sleep pattern.

relief at your fingertips

The classic accupressure point for soothing insomnia, called Spirit Gate, promotes deep, restful sleep. Spirit Gate has been used for centuries to treat all types of insomnia in both men and women. To try it you'll need two firm-fitting wrist bands, such as the kind you use when exercising, and two roundish uncooked dried beans, such as kidney or garbanzo. An hour before bedtime, put the bands on your wrists, then tuck a bean under each at the indentation just under the wrist bone, straight down from the pinky. The beans work all night, gently pressing on the Spirit Gate points. As well as helping to relieve insomnia due to anxiety, Spirit Gate can help prevent menopausal night sweats. To increase the effectiveness of Spirit Gate, dot a small drop of essential oil of lavender on the skin before putting each bean in place. (For a non-bean alternative, see page 372, but note the different locations of the pressure points.)

potent pose

The Corpse is a passive but powerful yoga posture that invokes harmony and deep relaxation. Use it to encourage a recuperative night's sleep. First, lie on the floor on your back, stretching your whole body, arms over your head and toes pointed. Breathe into the stretch a couple of times, observing your breathing, as anxiety can make it shallow. Then separate your feet a comfortable distance apart and place your arms at your sides, palms facing skyward. Beginning with your head, notice the force of gravity as you acquiesce to its gentle pull. Start with your head and move downward, noting the same sensation in every part of your body that is touching the floor, such as shoulders, upper back, elbows, knuckles, calves. All the while, breathe deeply, feeling a glow just below your navel. When you're finished, arise very, very slowly and head for bed.

PASS ON PILLS

Research reveals that prescription sleeping pills prevent you from sleeping well because they interfere with the normal sleep rhythms we must experience in order to have a truly restful sleep. Also, when used over long periods of time, sleeping pills can actually cause insomnia.

DARK OF THE NIGHT

To ensure a good night's sleep, be sure your room is completely dark. Melatonin, the hormone that lulls us into slumber, is most actively secreted when there is no illumination. Even a night light can disrupt a sensitive sleeper's rest.

Another way to use the Corpse to help induce sleep is to assume the pose and, instead of concentrating on body parts, repeat a meditative chant to yourself while breathing deeply. Normally meditation is performed sitting up because its intense relaxing effect can lull one to sleep, making the Corpse and meditation perfect partners in the pursuit of slumber. To try it, simply repeat a meditation chant or mantra. If you don't know one, repeat "sleep" with each deep inhale and exhale.

SOCKS FOR SLEEP

An Ayurvedic physician told me that many of his sleepless patients have been lulled into slumber by sleeping in, of all things, wet socks! The idea is to soak a pair of medium-weight socks and wring them out before putting them on your feet. Then climb into bed, wrapping your feet in a towel to protect the bed linens. Those who practice this ritual say that, amazingly, the socks don't feel wet and cold, just normal. More important, the socks help them get to sleep and stay asleep. One way the sock treatment may work is by helping lower the body temperature, a natural rhythm that should occur automatically at night but may not in those who have trouble sleeping.

try a tea

In medical herbalism, nerve relaxants are a classification of plants that soothe anxiety. They are used to induce sleep, yet do not interfere with natural sleep rhythms, as most synthetic sleeping pills do.

Valerian root, for instance, contains a volatile oil, valerianic acid, that gives the herb its nervine properties. Skullcap, another relaxant, contains a flavonoid compound, scutellarin, making it a nerve tonic. Similarly, the leaves of passionflower offer passiflorine, an alkaloid that acts as a mild sedative. In Germany and England the three herbs are often combined to make a relaxing tea to combat insomnia. To make a cup, steep 1 teaspoon each of dried valerian root, skullcap, and passionflower in 1 cup of just-boiled water, covered, for 5 minutes. Because the taste is slightly medicinal, many sippers include 1 teaspoon of chamomile or catnip during steeping to zip up the brew.

Dried hops flowers can also help induce sleep. Make a tea by steeping 2 teaspoons in 1 cup of just-boiled water, covered, for 8 minutes. Hops can also be combined with tilia (linden flower, lime flower). All of these herbs are available at herb shops, natural food stores, and some supermarkets.

Also available from these sources are herbs in liquid tincture form. You'll see them in small brown glass bottles containing either alcohol, vegetable glycerine, or vinegar in which the herb or herbs have been steeped. Always follow the manufacturer's instructions, but for most brands, add 1 eyedropper of tincture (about 1 teaspoon) to 1 cup of warm water and sip. Motherwort (*Leonurus cardiaca*) is one extremely soothing tincture to try that's not commonly available in dried form for tea.

making scents

There are many theories on how certain scents help relax us into sleep. One theory often subscribed to by fragrance scientists begins with a fragrance molecule, such as one of lavender, breaking off from a carrier. A carrier could be a lavender-scented cream you've just rubbed on your feet, for instance. The fragrance molecule winds up in the nose, where fragrance-receiver cells decode the molecule so they can tell the brain what to do about it. In the case of lavender, the fragrance cells discover that it is a nerve soother, and send the message on to the brain via neurotransmitters. Once in the brain, the proper nerve-soothing chemicals are emitted into the body, and you begin to feel relaxed.

To make such a calming cream, combine 2 tablespoons of unscented body lotion with 10 drops of essential oil of lavender and 2 drops of essential oil of marjoram (available at herb shops and natural food stores). Before bed, rub the cream on your feet, legs, hands, arms, and abdomen, breathing in the tranquilizing essences as you rub. To intensify the treatment, place 1 drop each of essential oil of lavender and marjoram on your pillow.

Other soothing essences include neroli, extracted from the flower of the bitter orange tree; ylang-ylang, a sweet and seductive scent from a tropical flower; vanilla; and tangerine. Substitute any one of them for the marjoram in the calming cream, or dot a drop or two on your pillow.

You can also add calming essences to a warm bath. Try lavender and orange or ylang-ylang and tangerine, putting 5 drops of each into a drawn bath before soaking. Or make a foot bath, filling a basin with about 1 gallon of warm water and adding 2 drops of each essence. As a treat for your skin after bathing, rub on the calming lavender cream while your skin is still damp from the bath, since skin is more receptive to emollient properties when warm and moist.

Nighttime is the best time to refresh and rejuvenate your skin, since cell division is most active between 1:00 and 4:00 A.M. What you apply to your skin at this time is critical. Avoid any face or body creams that contain mineral oil or petroleum products. These products don't penetrate the skin, block skin's respiration, and eventually clog pores and cause dehydration. As an alternative, buy face and body creams that use such nut and seed oils as sunflower, safflower, hazelnut, and jojoba. Many such products contain skin-nourishing essential oils, like lavender, neroli, and ylang-ylang— conveniently, the same ones that help lull you to sleep.

These products are available at herb shops, natural food stores, and some department stores, but you can easily make your own scented skin oil. In an opaque glass bottle, combine 2 tablespoons of hazelnut or jojoba oil with 5 drops each of pure essential oils of neroli and sandalwood. To preserve the mixture, add 2 drops of wheat germ oil. To use, lightly rub about $\frac{1}{8}$ teaspoon of the mixture onto a damp face and throat, as well as under the eyes. For a calming and nourishing scalp massage, dot a tiny drop on each finger, burrow your fingers through your hair to your scalp, and rub briskly all around your head. The mixture is also an enriching night nostrum for skin all over the body, but since neroli is a bit costly, most people reserve it for the face. Neroli and sandalwood each contain compounds that soothe and heal all skin types, and as a bonus, when inhaled, the orangy, woodsy aroma is a mild sedative.

As a partner to the neroli-sandalwood night oil, make your own smoothing facial toner by combining $\frac{1}{2}$ cup of distilled water, $\frac{1}{4}$ cup of liquid witch hazel, 2 tablespoons of aloe vera gel, and 12 drops of essential oil of lavender. Pour the mixture into a spray bottle and mist your cleansed face before applying the night oil. Lavender has a tonic effect on all skin types. It also helps prevent itchy skin, which for those who suffer is the worst at about 11 o'clock at night.

If you are feeling ambitious, you may want to prepare an exfoliating, moisturizing, full-body scrub to ease your skin into nighttime rejuvenation. In a small bowl, combine $\frac{1}{3}$ cup of Epsom salts, 2 tablespoons of canola oil, and 3 drops each of essential oils of lavender and orange. While in the shower or bath, gently rub small handfuls of the fragrant scrub into the body skin for silky-smooth results. Rinse well before moisturizing your damp skin with the calming lavender cream.

best foods

For the soundest sleep, it's best to avoid eating a meal for at least three hours before bedtime. During the night the body is busy processing food and assimilating nutrients in the lower part of the digestive system. That's why when you eat a big, fatty meal before going to bed, it feels like it's "sitting on your stomach." It really is. There are, however, certain light nighttime nourishers that can help lull the body to slumber.

steamed milk with nutmeg

MAKES 1 SERVING
110 calories per serving: no added fat

Milk (if you're using the variety from cows) offers sleep-coaxing calcium and tryptophan. In addition to inducing sleep, tryptophan had an added effect in one sleep study: depressed alcoholics who ingested it before retiring reported lower levels of daytime depression than their counterparts who did not. (If you're off dairy and looking for a food-based source of tryptophan, eat a banana instead of preparing this recipe.)

In this recipe, the nutmeg may be calming, too, since the freshly grated spice has mild nervine properties.

1 cup skim milk or nonfat soy milk   1/2 teaspoon freshly grated nutmeg

1 teaspoon honey

BRING THE MILK to a boil in a small saucepan. Remove from the heat and whisk in the honey and nutmeg. Sip warm.

IF THE WEATHER IS HOT AND/OR DRY:
Add 1/2 teaspoon of rose water when whisking in the honey and nutmeg.

IF THE WEATHER IS COLD AND/OR DAMP:
Increase the nutmeg to 3/4 teaspoon.

ayurvedic almond milk

MAKES 1 SERVING
346 calories per serving: 46 grams fat; 98% calories from fat

This nondairy recipe is based on a 3,000-year-old Ayurvedic formula for insomnia. Almonds, Ayurvedics hold, have rejuvenating and healing properties. They and the poppy seeds in this recipe are good sources of magnesium, a mineral that is deficient in many people who suffer from anxiety and sleeplessness.

This may be a good before-bedtime choice for sleepless children (over the age of 2), since some physicians hold that the condition may be caused by dairy milk intolerance. Half the recipe is the correct amount for children under 12.

2 tablespoons raw unsalted pumpkin seeds	8 ounces distilled water
20 blanched almonds	2 teaspoons honey
1 tablespoon poppy seeds	1/4 teaspoon ground ginger, or to taste

IN THE MORNING, soak the pumpkin seeds, almonds, and poppy seeds in the water and let them sit all day. An hour before bedtime, pour the mixture into a blender and whiz until smooth. Stir in the honey and ginger, then sip.

Note: Because of the high fat content, this is not a potion you want to drink nightly. As a variation, to lower the fat content, do not puree; strain out the nuts and seeds instead. Then stir the honey and ginger into the soaking water. When the recipe is prepared in this manner, the nuts and seeds may be reused one more time.

IF THE WEATHER IS HOT AND/OR DRY:	IF THE WEATHER IS COLD AND/OR DAMP:
Add 1 teaspoon of lemon juice when stirring in the honey.	*Add a pinch of freshly ground nutmeg when you add the ginger.*

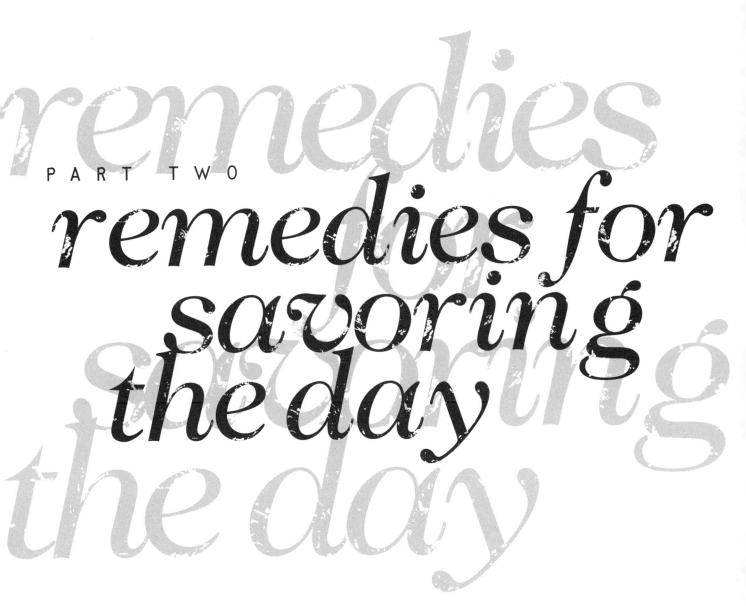

PART TWO

remedies for savoring the day

easing arthritis pain

when symptoms may occur:

In the evening. for osteoarthritis

In the morning. for rheumatoid arthritis

If the weather is cold and/or damp

My father, who is in his eighties, had such painful arthritis in his lower back and left hip that he couldn't walk a mere 50 feet. For an active person who exercised daily, riding an exercise bike and working with weights, the disability was devastating. Surgery was suggested, but learning that the odds of recovery are poor for back operations, he embarked on a more natural approach.

First he bought a pair of well-made, supportive walking shoes, and amazingly, in two days he was once again walking everywhere. He then commenced his daily exercise routine, which included a series of hand, arm, and neck stretches that for years had eased the minor arthritic pain in those areas. This time, however, he added some leg and hip stretches to "increase circulation and feel limbered up." He cut down on red meats, cheeses, and fatty desserts and kept his weight down to minimize joint strain. In addition, he exercised the mind as well as the body, noting that sitting idly feeling sorry about your pain never cured anyone.

Arthritis, a condition that can be caused by more than 100 different diseases, is the inflammation of a joint or joints. Arthritis causes pain and soreness, sometimes progressing into handicapping disability. Sixteen million Americans suffer from osteoarthritis, which is caused by wear and tear on the joints. It's most common in women of advancing years but can occur in men or in younger people, especially those who lift, haul, or stand on hard surfaces all day. An additional one million Americans suffer from rheumatoid arthritis, which is caused by a virus and which may affect surrounding tissue as well as joints, producing fever, weakness, and fatigue. Heredity and a toxic environment are suspected as causes of the virus. If you have either type of arthritis, your pain may be soothed by trying the stretches, teas, penetrating rubs, and foods that follow.

potent poses

These stretches are based on my father's flexibility routine, gleaned from experts at Northwestern University, the University of Chicago, the University of California–Berkeley, and family members. (Be sure to consult with a health professional before starting.) It's best to begin slowly, increasing the repetitions and intensity of the stretches gradually. After you perform the stretches, notice that the areas you've worked feel warm and more limber, a sign of increased circulation.

SEVEN-STEP LIMBERING FOR FINGERS. HANDS. ARMS. AND NECK

1. While still in bed. sit up and separately wiggle each finger and thumb up and down 30 times. While wiggling a finger. it's okay if the surrounding fingers move.

2. While still in bed. bend both hands. from the wrists. up and down 50 times.

3. Standing. wave both hands downward from the wrists 50 times. (If your legs and feet are too stiff to stand. skip to the feet- and leg-limbering exercises below before continuing with this group.)

4. Press the four fingers of your right hand against the palm of your left hand. pushing them back as far as you can go. 20 times. Repeat the process with the fingers of your left hand on the palm of your right hand.

   It is also advised that. to keep your hands and wrists limber. you use a device called hand grips. They look like V-shaped rubber-coated kitchen tongs and are available in light. medium. and heavy tensions. The idea is to squeeze them on a daily basis. much as you would squeeze a tennis ball. With the grips the goal is to work each hand by squeezing the large end of the V at least 50 times and squeezing the small end 50 times.

5. Concentrating now on your neck. press your chin toward your chest. then tilt your head back as far as you can. repeating the back and forth movement 20 times.

6. Very, very slowly, circle your head around to the right 5 times, then repeat the movement to the left 5 times.

7. Standing on your right foot, wiggle your left foot side to side 20 times, then repeat by standing on your left foot and wiggling your right foot.

THE COLD SHOULDER

A gymnast who competed at the 1976 Montreal Olympics told me that cold, in the form of ice packs, produces more permanent relief from arthritis pain than heat. Try it by applying an ice pack to the inflamed area for 10-minute intervals (any longer could freeze the skin). For an even more potent treatment, apply the ice pack for 10 minutes, then heat for 10 minutes, finishing with 10 minutes of ice. Always finish with ice to avoid inflammation.

NINE-STEP LIMBERING FOR FEET, LEGS, HIPS, AND WAIST

1. Lying in bed, keeping your feet still, wiggle your toes up and down 50 times.

2. Lying flat, bending your knees slightly, lift your right leg as high as is comfortable, then lower 15 times. Repeat the sequence 3 times with the same leg, then perform the exercise with the left leg.

3. Lying flat, knees straight and locked, lift your right leg as high as is comfortable, clasping your hands behind your knee or thigh for support if necessary, and lower 40 times. Repeat the exercise with your left leg.

4. Now with knees bent, raise both legs this time, hands clasped behind the knees for support. Once raised, straighten and bend your legs 15 times.

5. Sitting on the side of the bed, stretch out your legs in a V shape. Drop the left leg, keeping the right one out. Then raise the left leg while dropping the right leg. Repeat raising and dropping for a total of 30 times.

6. Stand up straight, then bend forward from your waist as far as you can (back curled over), stretching your lower back, arms hanging, then straightening up immediately. Repeat the exercise 50 times.

7. Repeat #6, but when bending from your waist, hold the pose for 10 counts before straightening up. Repeat the exercise 5 times.

8. Standing with hands on hips, bend over as far to the right as you can, feeling the left side of your waist stretch. Straighten up. Repeat 9 times for a total of 10 side stretches. Then bend to the left 10 times. Repeat the entire sequence for a total of 40 side bends.

9. Standing, with hands on hips, twist torso to the right and back ten times; twist to the left and back ten times. Repeat entire sequence for a total of forty twists.

Once you have warmed up your joints and muscles, you can ride a bike, use a ski machine or treadmill, walk, or swim, since regular exercise can help abate arthritis pain by improving agility and circulation. In addition, many people who suffer from arthritis have regular therapeutic massage treatments to improve joint and muscle flexibility. In Swedish massage, for instance, therapists soothingly knead and tap the muscles, as well as stretch the joints. To find a massage therapist, ask friends, ask your doctor, or find certified massage therapists in the yellow page listings in the phone book. Call to inquire about training, years of experience, and success with inflamed joints.

For another option, you may wish to seek the services of a chiropractor. One two-year British study concluded that if chiropractic care for back pain were employed instead of surgery, it would save the United Kingdom over £30 million annually. A U.S. study reported that patients receiving chiropractic back care recover four times faster than those treated surgically, especially if the chiropractic treatments occur within the first month of symptoms. Chiropractors maintain that the spine is the basis of health and that misalignments can cause a number of ills, aches, and pains. To that end, they "adjust" the spine into alignment. Although a chiropractic adjustment can't mend worn joints, it can, for instance, realign the neck with the shoulders to lessen arthritic pain and help prevent the condition from progressing. Chiropractors can "adjust" knees, elbows, hands, and feet in addition to the spine.

NONSURGICAL SUCCESS

In 1992 I opted for chiropractic treatments, three times a week for three months, to prevent the progression of a painful degenerating disc in my neck. Concurrently, as advised by my chiropractor, I began using one-pound hand-held weights while doing my daily aerobics, gently toning the supportive muscles in my neck and shoulder area. The treatments were not always comfortable, and sometimes I felt so lightheaded afterward that I had to sit for a while to rebalance myself. But to this day, having one "tune-up" treatment a month, I am virtually pain-free and have excellent range of motion in my neck.

try a tea

CHINESE BLEND

The classic Chinese tea to ease arthritis pain is composed of a 2-inch stick of cinnamon, 2 slices of fresh ginger, 2 Chinese (jujube) dates, and 2 slices of dried astragalus root. The dates and the astragalus are available at herb shops and Chinese markets, but the blend is so popular that you can often buy it prepackaged. To make the tea, combine all of the ingredients in 2 cups of water and boil until the water has been reduced by half. Then strain and sip once a day. The herbs may be used a second time. One reason the blend may work is that the cinnamon and ginger contain compounds that warm the body and increase circulation, thus helping to relieve pain. The astragalus, according to modern Western research, helps restore immune function, which is especially important to those suffering from rheumatoid arthritis.

GINGER TEAS

Ayurvedic herbalists believe that rheumatoid arthritis is caused by the accumulation of toxins in the system and, like the Chinese, recommend ginger to restore the body to a nontoxic state. They suggest grating 1 tablespoon of fresh ginger (including the juice) into 1 cup of brewed black or green tea and sipping two or three times a day. Although scientific research has not commented on the Ayurvedic toxin theory, ginger does help diminish pain by increasing blood flow to the area. As an extra tonic to fight arthritis, add 1 tablespoon of just-crushed celery seed to the tea when adding the ginger. Celery seed contains antirheumatic volatile oils and consequently is commonly used by herbalists to treat arthritis. In addition, 1 tablespoon of celery seed contains 127 mg of calcium, a mineral that is critical to bone and joint health.

BLACK COHOSH

For pain, a long-established nostrum is the North American herb black cohosh. Among its antiarthritic compounds is salicylic acid, the active ingredient in aspirin. Black cohosh is available at natural food stores and herb shops. It also comes in dried tea form, but the taste is awful, so buy a liquid tincture instead. A normal dose is one eyedropper of tincture (about 28 drops) in a bit of warm water, taken three to four times a day, but check with a health professional about what dose is right for you.

BLS BANISHES PAIN

Arthritis sufferers in the Philippines make their own antipain potion, called BLS, which means bawang *(garlic),* luya *(ginger), and* siling labuyo *(hot pepper). They chop 1 cup of each (fresh) ingredient and heat the mixture gently in 2 cups of coconut oil or olive oil for about 20 minutes. After allowing the steeping mixture to cool, they strain and discard the BLS ingredients and massage the resulting oil onto painful areas. It works by stimulating circulation, much like commercially produced "deep heat" products.*

making scents

Herb-scented rubs, available at pharmacies, natural food stores, and herb shops, help increase circulation in inflamed areas, thus temporarily relieving pain. Among the best are Tiger Balm, containing penetrating camphor; Triflora, a nearly scentless gel that

ANTIPAIN POTIONS

The most-prescribed medication for arthritis, aspirin, is effective for 22 hours if taken in the morning, as opposed to 17 hours of effectiveness when taken at other times of the day. Many people can't take aspirin orally, however, because it causes stomach problems. If that is your case, ask your doctor for similar anti-inflammatory compounds in rectal suppository form or transdermal patches.

RECIPES TO HELP
EASE ARTHRITIS

Rice Cereal, Chinese Style (page 21)

Cherry Jam with Walnuts (page 28)

NOURISHING
NUTRIENT

People have reported easing of aches and pains after supplementing their diets with glucosamine sulfate. Available at natural food stores; for best absorption the nutrient is often combined with tyrosine and vitamin C.

includes wild rosemary and comfrey; and a cream, made of the anti-inflammatory methyl salicylate, warming capsaicin from hot peppers, and boswellia (a type of frankincense) extract. Boswellia is what herbalists call a rubefacient, or substance that stimulates blood flow to the area on which it is rubbed. Use any of these rubs on the spot to soothe arthritic pain or before exercise to prevent later aches.

A more unusual arthritis treatment is one you prepare yourself from a Tibetan incense called Aquilaria, available at Tibetan shops and some East Indian shops. It's made from 31 different aromatic herbs. To help soothe sore joints, finely grind one stick in a mortar or with the back of a spoon, adding about 1 tablespoon of untoasted (light) sesame oil, or enough to make a lotion. Then rub the potion into sore areas. It smells woody and floral as it subdues the pain.

best foods

Many people report relief from arthritic pain with the addition of essential fatty acids (EFAs) to their diets. EFAs help reduce inflammation and can be obtained from several sources. Flaxseed oil, available in liquid from the refrigerated sections of natural food stores and some supermarkets, can be swirled into morning oatmeal, used as a replacement for oil on salads, or drizzled on a muffin or toast. The usual dose is 1 to 2 tablespoons a day, but be aware that it is a fat, so if you don't want to gain weight, substitute it for an equal amount of another fat in your daily diet. Alternatively, you can eat two to three 4-ounce servings of salmon a week, since the fish contains substances similar to EFAs. For EFAs in supplement form, try evening primrose oil in 1,500-mg capsules, taking one a day. (Women with breast cancer should not take evening primrose oil, as it may aggravate the condition.)

Other foods offering anti-inflammatory action are alfalfa sprouts, pineapple, and turmeric, the spice that gives curry powder its golden hue. Add the sprouts to a salad, for instance, to help diminish evening pain. Including spicy flavorings in your meals, such as ginger, hot peppers, and garlic, also may help alleviate arthritis pain by increasing circulation.

Foods to avoid include dairy products, since vitamin D may increase the soreness in joints. Some people also report less pain when they avoid eating members of the nightshade family, such as bell peppers, tomatoes, eggplant, and white potatoes. The same goes for foods containing refined white sugar and white flour. Abstaining from red meat has also been linked to less painful joints, especially in those suffering from rheumatoid arthritis.

RESOURCES FOR PAINLESS JOINTS

· American Chiropractic Association (referrals): 1-800-986-4636
· American Massage Therapy Association (referrals to therapists): 708-864-0123
· Arthritis Foundation Information (answers questions): 1-800-238-7800
· *Arthritis Magazine* (subscription information): 1-800-933-0032
· Arthritis Consulting Services (information on holistic approaches): 1-800-327-3027
· Roger Wyburn-Mason & Jack M. Blount Foundation for the Eradication of Rheumatoid Disease (information on dietary control; physician referral): 615-646-1030
· *The Complete Guide to Exercise Videos* (catalog with over 250 videos, including some specific to arthritis): 1-800-433-6769

SEE ALSO
· Lulling LOW BACK Pain (page 362)
· Taming NECK and SHOULDER Tension (page 374)
· Surmounting SORE MUSCLES (page 399)
· Coddling TIRED FEET (page 413)

adjusting anxiety

adjusting anxiety

when symptoms may occur:

During extreme weather conditions, especially on very hot, cold, or dry days

At the change of seasons

While driving to New York, I was distressed about Cyrus, my seriously ill, beautiful, 15-year-old Siamese cat. Approaching the George Washington Bridge at 65 miles an hour, I felt suddenly closed in by a tall construction median on my left and a huge truck on my right. My breathing became shallow, my mouth dry, and I was alarmingly lightheaded. Noting my discomfort, my husband told me to "floor it," thus getting beyond the situation.

It was perfect advice. For anxiousness (such as my feeling of being "closed in" by my circumstances), fear of flying, or fear of heights, for example, experts recommend trying to "look beyond the frightening situation." With fear of flying, for instance, that means thinking about pleasant adventures upon landing, not focusing on the flight itself.

Psychiatrists also advise getting control of your breathing to eliminate the uncomfortable feelings associated with anxiety. Sit down and close your eyes as soon as possible. Noticing your shallow breathing, focus on making your breaths longer and deeper. As you're working on your breathing, for deeper relaxation try an accupressure point, yoga pose, tea, or calming essence mentioned in this section. Note, however, that frequent anxiety attacks should be discussed with a health professional, since they may be a sign of such medical conditions as hyperthyroidism, adrenal tumors, diabetes, or mitral valve prolapse.

relief at your fingertips

To help promote calm, perform an accupressure point called The Third Eye. Rub your hands together briskly for about 10 seconds, then put your palms together in a prayer position. Rest the area where the bridge of your nose meets your forehead on the tips of your index or third fingers (if you have long nails, bend your fingers and rest the area on your knuckles.) Let the weight of your head rest on your fingers while you breathe fully, visualizing a glow expanding through your lungs. Continue this exercise for 2 minutes or until your breathing returns to normal.

potent pose

To help increase lung capacity while getting control of your breath, sit down and lace your hands behind your back, then straighten your arms as best you can. Gently arch your back, letting your head fall as far back as is comfortable, feeling your chest muscles expand as you breathe fully for five breaths. Rest for a count of 10, then repeat.

try a tea

RESCUE REMEDY

The Bach Flower Remedies is a system of 38 botanical essences that balance various uncomfortable states of mind. Developed in the 1930s by a Welsh doctor, Edward Bach, the essences are said to work gently on a very deep, or spiritual, level, eliminating negative states of mind. For anxiety, practitioners recommend a premixed combination of five flowers called Rescue Remedy, available at natural food stores and herb shops. Four drops are taken in $1/4$ cup of water prior to such anxiety-producing activities as dental visits or airplane travel. Although Rescue Remedy has not been scientifically investigated in the United States, I am never without a bottle, both for home and for travel. In fact, I was grateful for its soothing effects after my George Washington Bridge episode, as well as when my Cyrus died. I also employed Rescue Remedy

ALL IN A NAME

Anxiety *is Latin for* *"twisted rope."*

ESSENTIAL ADVICE

"Disease is in essence the result of conflict between Soul and Mind, and will never be eradicated except by spiritual and mental effort."

—Edward Bach, M.D.

three weeks later, when Cy's life-long love, our 17-year-old female Siamese, Vanessa, died of a broken heart.

CATNIP-CHAMOMILE TEA

For a more traditional anxiety-chasing tea, combine 1 teaspoon each of dried catnip and chamomile in 1 cup of just-boiled water. Cover for 4 minutes, then sip. Both herbs contain volatile oils that act as nervines on an anxious system. If you have predictably anxious times of the day, brew a double batch and keep it in the refrigerator for when you need it or tote it to work in a thermos. The tea can be sipped warm in cold seasons and slightly chilled in hotter months.

making scents

If you are working on controlling your breath, fill a sink, basin, or large bowl with warm water and add 3 drops of tincture of benzoin, available at pharmacies, natural food stores, and herb shops. Positioning your head about 8 inches above the sink, inhale the rich, sweet, resiny essence for 5 to 10 minutes. Tent a towel over your head and shoulders to capture the aroma. The deep aroma is what aromatherapists call "grounding." In much the same way as grounding safely guides electrical currents, benzoin provides our emotions with a connection to the earth, making our behavior once again effective and organized.

best foods

ANTIANXIETY
RECIPES

Warm Tomato Relish with Basil and Pine Nuts (page 157)

Calming Evening Churna (page 140)

Pâté with Olives, Fresh Basil, and Roasted Red Peppers (page 143)

To help prevent anxiety attacks, nutritionists recommend a diet high in foods containing B vitamins, such as barley, brown rice, whole wheat, soybeans, lentils, and chickpeas. In addition, calcium, from such sources as broccoli and leafy greens, acts as a natural nerve tonic, as does dill seed, which contains 100 mg of calcium per tablespoon. Fresh vegetables and fruits, especially when eaten raw, are also good sources of vitamin C, a nutrient that becomes depleted in times of stress. Lastly, be sure to add magnesium to your diet. This nerve-soothing mineral is available in prepared mustard —1 tablespoon providing about a tenth of the daily recommendation.

Avoid such nerve-jangling foods as caffeine, alcohol, refined sugar, colas, fried foods, and salty foods.

RESOURCES TO SOOTHE ANXIETY

- · Anxiety Hotline: 919-785-7069
- · Anxiety Disorders of America (information line): 900-737-3400
- · National Anxiety Center (educational information): 201-763-6392
- · Pass-Group (phone counseling for panic disorders): 716-689-4399
- · TERRAP (information, counseling, and a publication for those with phobias): 1-800-2-PHOBIA
- · Phobics Anonymous (12-step recovery program for anxieties): 619-322-COPE
- · The Monroe Institute (meditation tapes): 1-800-541-2488

SEE ALSO

- · Meditation: Early Morning (page 6) and Evening (page 136)
- · Prepping for PRESENTATIONS (page 380)
- · Managing STRESS (page 406)

abating asthma

WHEN SYMPTOMS MAY OCCUR

when symptoms may occur:

| In the night

| During the allergy season.
May through November

"*i* couldn't go to a restaurant because sulfites in the food might cause an asthma attack. I couldn't go to a mall because of the smoke. I couldn't travel because of the poor quality of air on the plane. I couldn't go anywhere. I was making out my will."

That's how a former asthma sufferer described his life to me. For him and for one in forty people the world over, the condition can be a nightmare. Physically, asthma is the temporary narrowing of the bronchial muscles, accompanied by the swelling of their mucous linings, caused by exposure to allergic irritants or—especially in adult asthmatics—emotional stress. In addition to coughing and wheezing, sufferers experience shortness of breath, obstructed breathing, and the inability to exhale fully. It's easy to imagine the fear and anxiety that must accompany having asthma. If the anxiety is not managed, it can actually bring on an attack. What's worse, since asthma can flare up at night, sufferers sometimes remain sleepless with dread, only to spend their waking hours fatigued.

The happy ending for the aforementioned man was finding a bronchodilator called Severent, a prescription inhaler drug taken in two small puffs twice a day. With it he doesn't get "the shakes" that can be a side effect of some other bronchial inhalers. In addition, he tries to avoid dust, smoke, feathers, animal dander, pollen, and emotional upsets. He now feels "just about normal" for the first time in years.

Other asthma sufferers report fewer and shorter attacks by employing one or more of the suggestions below. Note that asthma, which is Greek for "panting," is a serious condition and should be treated with the help of a health professional. Five thousand people die yearly from the condition because they fail to seek professional treatment in time.

relief at your fingertips

At the onset of an asthma attack, try to relax your chest muscles by sitting down and letting your shoulders drop to an untensed position. Rub your hands together for about 10 seconds, then, using your thumbs, trace your collarbone from your shoulders toward your breastbone. Stop when you come to the indentations just under the collarbone, above the breastbone, and apply light pressure. Closing your eyes and breathing slowly, envision a glow of warm light throughout your lungs. Continue until you are relaxed and breathing more freely. The points that you are pressing were named Elegant Mansion by ancient Chinese acupuncturists, gently reminding users of the importance of abundant lung capacity. The Elegant Mansion pressure points may be utilized as often as needed, with or without medications.

BETTER BREATHING

A Russian teacher of stress management told me that breath control is the most powerful method for managing asthma. This can be accomplished through regular meditation (see pages 6 and 136) or through biofeedback. In the latter, machines called incentive respirators are blown into, visually indicating to asthmatics that their breathing is becoming fuller as they become more relaxed.

try a tea

A time-tested tea to relieve asthma symptoms—and sometimes eliminate the condition altogether—is ephedra, or *ma huang*, as it is known to the Chinese. The herb dilates the bronchial tubes and soothes mucous membranes. Some former asthmatics who take ephedra daily say they now don't even need an inhaler. To make an ephedra-based tea, place 2 teaspoons of dried ephedra and 1 teaspoon of dried lemon balm (*Melissa*) or valerian root (available at herb shops and natural food stores) in 2 cups of

KIDS AND ASTHMA

Statistics show that almost 7 percent of children in the United States have asthma, but some experts feel the number is low because many cases go unnoticed or untreated.

*Tempting as it may be to
keep a window cracked
open at night, physicians
advise against it, since
allergens and irritants can
easily enter the sleeping
space and cause an
asthma attack.*

water and bring to a boil. Cover loosely and boil until the liquid has been reduced by half, about 10 minutes. Then strain and sip warm. (Cold beverages may cause bronchial spasms.) Generally, 3 cups of the tea are recommended daily, but check with a health professional about what is right for you. Since ephedra is a hypertensive (that is, it elevates blood pressure), it should not be taken by people with high blood pressure. Pregnant women should avoid ephedra because it may cause uterine contractions.

TEA FROM TIBET

Many asthmatics report complete relief from the condition by drinking 8 ounces a day of a tea made from the Tibetan kombucha mushroom. The fungus, available from "kombucha breeders," may well be the asthma panacea of the century, but its preparation must be precise for the best results. If you are interested in trying kombucha tea, seek the advice of an expert breeder, one who has studied sanitary, safe, mold-free methods. To find such a person, ask at natural food stores or herb shops, or seek a referral from a holistic health practitioner. Alternatively, kombucha is available in capsule form, as well as a liquid extract, from natural food stores.

making scents

Essential oils of eucalyptus, bergamot, and/or lavender (available at herb shops and natural food stores) contain volatile oils that help open and relax bronchial pathways. For a simple treatment, place a drop of each of the essences on a tissue and inhale while trying to relax and get your breath back. If you choose only one oil, make it eucalyptus, since it is the strongest cough suppressant of the three. At night, when asthma attacks are most likely to occur, place 3 drops of the essence on your pillow before you retire. Take the essence with you when traveling to use on hotel pillows. In addition, to combat the stale air in planes, offices, or malls, combine 20 drops of essential oil of eucalyptus and $1/2$ cup of distilled water in a spray bottle and mist around your face and head when you feel the air getting stale. To intensify the mist, add 5 drops of calming essential oil of lavender for the evening, and 5 drops of energizing essential oil of bergamot for the day. You can also put 10 drops of essential oil of eucalyptus in the bottom of your shower. When you turn on the hot water, you will create a penetrating, bronchial-soothing steam room.

best foods

Asthmatics, including those on Severent and other prescription drugs, are often advised to eat foods high in the immune-stimulating B vitamins, such as brown rice, chickpeas, soybeans, avocado, banana, barley, and lean fish. Magnesium is also recommended, since low levels of the mineral are associated with asthma. Prepared mustard is a good source of magnesium, as are soybeans, black-eyed peas, and lentils. Also, when planning your menu, add foods high in mucus-cutting beta carotene, such as broccoli, carrots, winter squash, dark leafy greens, and sweet potatoes. These vegetables, especially when eaten raw, also provide immune-boosting vitamin C. One nutrient that is not readily available from food is the vitamin E-like CO Q 10, which helps oxygenate lung and bronchial (and other) tissues. Some physicians recommend taking a 30-mg capsule a day for fortification whether you're on asthma medication or not.

Experts advise avoiding mucus-producing dairy products, as well as sulfite-containing wines. In addition, steer clear of processed junk foods that contain preservatives, artificial colors, and flavors, as they may cause an asthma attack.

RECIPE FOR EASY BREATHING

Potato Salad with Tomatoes and Fresh Basil (page 94)

RESOURCES FOR BREATHING EASY
- Sulfitest (sulfite test strips to detect the chemical in foods): 1-800-645-6335
- House of Hezekiah (catalog offering ephedra and other antiasthmatic herbs): 816-753-3312
- Asthma and Allergy Foundation of America (educational materials and monthly publication): 1-800-7-ASTHMA
- The Lung Hot Line (information on chronic respiratory diseases): 1-800-222-LUNG
- National Allergy and Asthma Network (help for parents with asthmatic kids): 1-800-878-4403
- Respiratory Health Association (conducts Better Breathing Classes): 201-848-5875
- Care for Life (educates public on issues facing those with long-term disabilities): 312-883-1018
- American Lung Association (public education and programs): 1-800-LUNG-USA
- Asthma Information Center (list of support groups): 1-800-727-5400

SEE ALSO
- Adjusting ANXIETY (page 296)
- Kicking a COUGH (page 321)
- Healing HAY FEVER (page 342)
- Managing STRESS (page 406)

banishing breakouts and rashes

when symptoms may occur:

| As hormonal rhythms change. for example. during puberty. menstruation, or menopause | At the change of seasons and during hot. humid weather | At night. for hot. itchy rashes |

While doing research on healthy skin and hair, a team of researchers and I tested a dozen skin care product lines. Along with the good things we learned, all of us experienced various welts, rashes, and pimples.

Consequently, I now know that to prevent breakouts, you should avoid cleansers, toners, moisturizers, and other skin care products containing pore-clogging mineral oil and petroleum products. In addition, avoid facial products containing large concentrations of such potentially irritating essences as lemongrass, sage, bergamot, and peppermint. Glycolic acid treatments, as well as products containing hydroxy acids, may also cause rashes and breakouts, so people with sensitive skin may wish to avoid them. Be sure to rinse your face 20 times after cleansing to wash away potentially clogging residues. To avoid unnecessary bacterial contact, keep your hands off your face throughout the day.

Pimples occur when pores become blocked and inflamed, either from oil buildup or by external irritants. In addition, pimples and rashes can be caused by hormonal changes, lack of exercise, birth control pills, allergies, stress, and reactions to environmental pollution. Pimples and rashes are also one way the body rids itself of an overload of internal toxins, such as those produced by junk food and alcohol. So it's as important to "eat clean" as it is to keep your face clean. These suggestions will help.

relief at your fingertips

For an exfoliating daily cleanser that removes debris from clogged pores, combine 1 tablespoon of oat bran with 1 tablespoon of warm water and stir well. For very dry skin, use milk instead of water because it has moisturizing properties; for very oily skin, use the more astringent cooled brewed black tea. To apply, first rinse your face with warm water a few times. (If you're prone to breakouts and rashes, never steam your face, because steaming creates exactly the hot and humid atmosphere that creates flare-ups.) Then spread the oat bran cleanser on your damp face and throat and use your hands to massage it lightly into the skin, making circular motions for about 2 minutes while avoiding the sensitive skin of the under-eye area. Let the cleanser sit on your skin for 2 minutes, then rinse with room temperature water 20 times before applying a moisturizer while your skin is still damp. (If your skin is extremely oily, omit the moisturizer and apply a chamomile or calendula herbal water, as described below.) Use the cleanser day or night, but it is especially effective in the morning, since during the night the body releases toxins through the skin, which need to be removed to prevent pimples and rashes.

try a tea

Chamomile and calendula contain compounds that, when made into strong teas and applied topically, reduce inflammation and help healthy new skin form. Place 1 tablespoon of each dried herb (or 2 tablespoons of the single herb of your choice) in 1 cup of just-boiled water and steep until cool, about 20 minutes. The result, called an herbal water, can be applied to the skin with a cotton ball as a soothing toner. Or pour the herbal water into a spray bottle and mist the face soothingly as needed. For itchy, flaky hot rashes, fill your spray bottle with half herbal water and half aloe vera juice. Either way, the potion will keep, refrigerated, for 5 days.

BARE IS BETTER

To avoid pimples and rashes from clogged pores, never wear foundation or powder on your face while exercising.

THE BRUSH-OFF

To avoid unnecessary rashes and breakouts, wash makeup brushes weekly in mild shampoo, rinsing well.

If you're prone to breakouts and rashes, keep a tube of Ayurvedic Turmeric cream handy. Available at herb shops, natural food stores, and Indian markets, the soothing, anti-infective, antibacterial balm contains sandalwood as well as turmeric, helping to prevent and cure skin eruptions.

making scents

Essential oil of lavender, available at herb shops and natural food stores, is anti-infective and stimulates new skin growth. Use it to make a soothing compress for blemished or rashy skin by adding 3 drops of pure essence to $1/2$ cup of warm water. Dip in a clean face cloth and apply it to the inflamed area for about 5 minutes, repeating as necessary. Undiluted essential oil of lavender (or tea tree) can be dotted on facial blemishes to help them heal.

In combination with lavender or by itself, essential oil of immortelle (everlasting flower; *Helichrysum*) can help soothe any type of skin inflammation. Available at herb shops and natural food stores, immortelle smells faintly burned and currylike. Add 1 or 2 drops to the lavender compress water. To keep my skin smooth in hot weather, I make an herbal spray by combining about 20 drops of essential oil of immortelle and $1/2$ cup of distilled water in a spray bottle and mist my face before and during exercise. When I'm in a polluted area, I do it even over makeup. Be sure to use only pure, steam-distilled essential oil of immortelle, as "absolute" of immortelle has been extracted with a solvent and is not suitable for use on the skin. To tell the difference, the essential oil is a liquid tinged with red, and the absolute is a solid, pasty substance.

RASH DECISION

For fun, I rubbed a fake tattoo on my husband's chest near his armpit. The next day he developed a hot, red rash under his arm, and because it was near lymph nodes, he saw a doctor. All was well, but the point is, if you have a rash near lymphs, in the armpits or groin, or if your rash lasts longer than a week, see a health professional.

best foods

To help keep your skin clear, drink eight 8-ounce glasses of water and eat two $1/2$ cup servings of dark, leafy greens each day. In addition to skin-enriching beta carotene and vitamin C, greens contain chlorophyll, which helps rid the blood and intestines of toxins that could otherwise show up as breakouts.

Foods that can lead to pimples and rashes include alcohol, dairy products, foods containing caffeine, shellfish, junk food, processed foods, fried foods, foods made from white flour, and chocolate. A steady diet of refined white sugar, some experts advise, can lead to enlarged pores.

RECIPE FOR
SMOOTH SKIN

*Carrot and Burdock,
Kinpira Style (page 170)*

smart supplements

Although it is always wise to check with a health professional before introducing a new supplement to your system, some skin experts recommend the following nutrients for glowing skin:

· Evening primrose oil (500 to 1,500 mg a day) contains essential fatty acid compounds that help skin heal.

· Vitamin E (at least 400 IUs a day) prevents free-radical damage due to stress and environmental factors.

· CO Q 10 (30 mg a day) is a vitamin E-like compound that helps oxygenate the skin.

· Vitamin C (2 teaspoons a day of chavanprash, available at natural food stores, herb shops, and Indian markets) helps fight infection.

· Acidophilus, taken on an empty stomach before breakfast, supplies the digestive system with friendly bacteria so that food and nutrients will be easily assimilated, aiding skin health.

· Kelp (500 to 660 mg a day) supplies trace minerals that help tonify the skin.

· Chromium (200 mcg a day) helps reduce skin infections.

· Zinc (10 mg 3 times a day) aids skin healing. Note that those prone to yeast infections should not take zinc, since it may exacerbate the condition.

· Pycnogenol (50 mg a day) helps prevent breakouts.

RESOURCES FOR HEALTHY SKIN
· Kiehl's (handmade, botanically based skin care products): 1-800-KIEHLS-1
· Nature's Symphony (pure, botanically based skin care products): 407-393-0065
· The Aromatherapy Catalog (essential oils by mail): 610-775-4403; 1-800-898-PURE

SEE ALSO
· Smoothing DRY SKIN (page 332)
· Managing STRESS (page 406)

calming
caffeine
tremors

when symptoms may occur:

Mid-afternoon to evening.
when caffeinated bever-
ages are consumed in the
afternoon

Years ago I worked at a newspaper, and I admit that the archetypal image of the coffee-guzzling, cigarette-smoking American journalist was true at that time. Our news deadline was two in the afternoon, and by then many of the reporters had downed 10 or 12 cups of coffee, resulting in scattered concentration, jitters, and the inability to focus.

Happily, today's newsrooms have become somewhat more health-conscious, offering decaf as an alternative. Unlike coffee drunk in the morning, afternoon sipping may not perk you up but merely give you the shakes. One theory is that in the mid-afternoon the body naturally starts to slow down for the day. In fact, some scientists say it's natural to want to nap. Drinking such caffeinated beverages as coffee, tea, or cola at that time of day literally works against your body's natural rhythms. If you have overimbibed, however, these suggestions can help.

try a tea

To soothe jangled nerves, combine 2 teaspoons each of dried chamomile, lavender, and linden flower (tilia), available at herb shops and natural food stores, in a large teapot. Pour in 4 cups of just-boiled water, cover, and let the brew steep for 4 minutes. Then strain and drink it all. These herbs contain volatile oils that help soothe nerves, but if you don't have them on hand, drink 4 cups of plain warm water to help flush the caffeine out of your system.

making scents

Essential oil of lavender contains compounds that help relax the jitters, even those made worse by caffeine. Shake 2 or 3 drops of the essence onto a tissue and inhale, breathing deeply, for about 5 minutes. At the same time, fill a basin with warm water, adding 5 drops of essential oil of lavender. Put your feet in, cover them with a towel to keep the heat in, and try to relax while you soak, inhaling the calming floral aroma. If you can't accommodate your feet, fill a sink with the water, add the essence, and rinse your arms, face, and neck.

best foods

Warm low-fat foods such as vegetable soup or defatted chicken soup may help to soothe and rebalance your rhythms. Steamed broccoli works too, by replacing the calcium that the caffeine has stolen from your body, a mineral that tonifies edgy nerves. If you order Chinese take-out, request that no MSG or sulfites be added to the food, since the chemicals may aggravate your already-tense condition. Also, keep drinking warm water to flush the caffeine from your system.

RESOURCES FOR CALM COFFEE DRINKING:
· First Colony Tea and Coffee (organically grown decaf): 804-622-2224
· Frontier Coffee (organically grown decaf): 319-227-7996
· Food & Drug Administration (pamphlet on caffeine jitters): 301-443-3170

SEE ALSO
· Adjusting ANXIETY (page 296)
· Curing a HEADACHE (page 346)
· Securing SOUND SLEEP (page 402)
· Managing STRESS (page 406)

MOVE IT

An hour of aerobics, tennis, gardening, walking, or swimming may calm you down. Since caffeinated beverages are dehydrating, be sure to drink plenty of water during and after whichever activity you select.

comforting
a cold

comforting a cold

when symptoms may occur:

| At the change of seasons, especially from fall to winter | During the evening and night, when runny nose and aches may worsen |

One winter, instead of a flu shot, my doctor gave me homeopathic antiviral pills containing minute doses of herbs and other plants, including echinacea, red onion, eucalyptus, and boneset. I took one pill four times a day every other Sunday, letting each pill dissolve under my tongue. Despite sometimes working seven days a week, 12 hours a day; being coughed on and sneezed on from one end of the United States to the other; and breathing almost daily doses of stale, virus-abundant airplane air, I avoided catching a cold or the flu.

In addition, twice a day I took 1 teaspoon of the Ayurvedic herbal preparation chavanprash, available at herb shops, natural food stores, and Indian markets. Made from the Indian gooseberry, also called amla, chavanprash is a potent source of immune-enhancing, viral-destroying vitamin C. Each amla, which is about the size of a small plum, contains 3,000 stable mg of the vitamin. I also exercised and meditated daily to strengthen my immunities. When I felt exhausted and thus more susceptible to catching something, I placed 28 drops of echinacea tincture (available at herb shops and natural food stores) in ¼ cup of warm water ot tea. Echinacea acts on a cellular level to protect the body from viruses. If these preventive measures, however, have found you too late, and you now have a cold, the following suggestions may help soothe your discomfort.

GOING FOR THE THROAT

If the first sign that you're catching a cold shows up as a sore throat, you may be able to avert the cold by taking 28 drops of echinacea tincture three or four times a day. If you have a sore throat along with a cold, help it heal by chewing on a small piece of fresh ginger, letting its stimulating, anti-infective juices bathe your sore throat. If your throat is dry and scratchy, drink a tea made of slippery elm, which soothes inflamed throat linings. Slippery elm is gooey and difficult to brew, so buy tea bags of a blend containing the herb, available at herb shops and natural food stores.

relief at your fingertips

To temporarily open a stuffy nose, employ a Chinese accupressure point called Fragrant Perfume. Rub your hands together briskly 10 times, then press an index finger firmly next to the outside edge of each nostril. (If you have long fingernails, use your knuckles.) Close your eyes and breathe deeply through your nose, envisioning a flow of golden warmth soothing and opening your nasal passages. Hold the point for about 2 minutes, repeating as necessary.

try a tea

According to French herbalists, thyme contains volatile oils that promote free breathing. To brew it into a tea, steep 1 teaspoon of the dried herb or 2 teaspoons of the fresh herb in 1 cup of just-boiled water, covered, for 5 minutes. To make a stronger brew, grate 1 tablespoon of fresh ginger, then squeeze the gratings to make juice right into the thyme tea.

For a more exotic ginger-based potion, try *trikatu*, which is a Hindi word for "three spices." Available in capsule form at natural food stores, herb shops, and Indian markets, trikatu is usually composed of two kinds of dried hot peppers plus dried ginger. Break a capsule into a cup of tea, or swallow a capsule, chased with a cup of tea, thyme, or otherwise. Trikatu warms the body, increases sluggish circulation, and helps heal mucous membranes.

If your cold lasts longer than 2 weeks, if you have a fever over 102°F, or if you have a green mucus nasal discharge, you may have a more serious infection and should see a health professional.

*To prevent reinfecting
yourself (and infecting
others), when you're fin-
ished blowing your nose,
flush the tissue; don't
reuse it. Then wash your
hands to remove germs.*

*Saline nose sprays, which are made of salt and water (available at pharmacies),
moisten uncomfortably dry nasal passages and are nonaddictive. Homeopathic
saline sprays (available at natural food stores, herb shops, and some pharmacies)
are soothing too, containing the herb euphorbia, a natural anti-inflammatory.
Avoid decongestant sprays that dry the nasal passages. Unpleasant as it may
seem, letting the mucus flow rids the body of infection.*

making scents

To open your head in a hurry, add 5 drops of essential oil of eucalyptus or thyme (available at herb shops and natural food stores) to a basin of warm water. Tent a towel over
your head and breathe the healing inhalation for about 7 minutes, repeating as necessary. Place a bowl of eucalyptus-scented warm water on a heating vent (or add eucalyptus to the water in a humidifier) to keep your bedroom humid, since dry air makes
cold symptoms worse.

To alleviate morning congestion, sprinkle 10 drops of essential oil of eucalyptus
or thyme in the bottom of your shower before turning on the hot water.

ADVICE FROM THE COUNTRY

*A farmer in Boone County, Missouri, told me that he had avoided getting a cold
for almost 40 years by rinsing his head with cold water at the end of his morning
shower. He said it "cooled his head down" so it wouldn't be shocked by coming
out of the hot shower into cold air. I do employ the practice (and it may well
work), but I do it mainly because it makes my hair shiny.*

best foods

Spicy, stimulating foods that warm the body, encouraging the flow of mucus, can help
ease cold symptoms. Try garlic, ginger, hot pepper, and black pepper added to such
warming foods as soups, stews, and casseroles. In addition, eating foods rich in beta
carotene, such as broccoli, sweet potatoes, carrots, dark greens, and acorn squash, can
help soothe the mucous membranes. Avoid such mucus-forming foods as dairy products and chocolate.

RESOURCES FOR NATURAL COLD PREPARATIONS

· Shanah Azee (catalog offering homeopathic sprays and pills): 1-800-945-0409
· Gaia Herbs (catalog offering fresh botanical extracts): 1-800-831-7780
· International Foundation of Homeopathy (provides public with homeopathy information): 206-324-8230

SEE ALSO

· Kicking a COUGH (page 321)
· Healing HAY FEVER (page 342)
· Curing a HEADACHE (page 346)
· Releasing SINUS PRESSURE (page 392)

spicy squash soup with scallions

MAKES 4 SERVINGS
105 calories per serving: no added fat

In this aromatic soup, ginger, garlic, hot pepper, black pepper, and scallions help clear the head.

1 pound butternut squash, peeled and chopped into 1-inch chunks

$1/4$ cup mirin or dry sherry

2 cloves garlic, finely minced

1 teaspoon finely minced fresh ginger

$1/2$ cup sliced fresh shiitake mushrooms

3 cups fish stock or vegetable stock

1 teaspoon dried hot red pepper flakes, or to taste

freshly ground black pepper to taste

RECIPE FOR COLD PREVENTION

Morning Immune-Boost Spread (page 32)

IN A MEDIUM soup pot, combine the squash, mirin, garlic, ginger, mushrooms, stock, and red pepper flakes. Bring to a boil, reduce the heat, and simmer until the squash is cooked through, about 5 minutes. Swirl in the black pepper and scallions and serve hot.

IF THE WEATHER IS HOT AND/OR DRY:
Swirl a dash of toasted (dark) sesame oil into each bowl before serving.

IF THE WEATHER IS COLD AND/OR DAMP:
Swirl a dash of hot pepper sauce into each bowl before serving.

correcting confusion and memory loss

when symptoms may occur:

| In the evening

| During extreme hot, cold, dry, or windy weather

*h*aving a cat diagnosed as senile, I observed that her confusion and disorientation became worse in the evening. Likewise, humans who are senile or who have conditions making them prone to confusion experience a worsening of their symptoms in the evening, a phenomenon known as "sundowning." One theory is that as the human body automatically slows down in the evening, preparing for sleep, our sharpness decreases also. (My cat, unlike many felines, had never been nocturnal, always following a human schedule.) Confusion and faltering memory, however, can come at any time from depression, overwork, stress, aging, excessive worry, poor diet, or lack of exercise. If symptoms become debilitating, seek the advice of a health professional. But for minor bouts of mental fuzziness, these suggestions may help.

relief at your fingertips

To balance and focus the mind, apply an accupressure point called The Third Eye. Rub your hands together briskly for about 10 seconds. Closing your eyes, breathe in slowly and fully, and use an index finger to press firmly on the area where the bridge of your nose meets your forehead. Exhale as if you were blowing out a candle. Continue pressing The Third Eye and breathing as instructed for one full minute. Confused dogs and cats benefit by your pressing their Third Eye point too, but for the best results, be sure you are calm and focused while doing so.

try a tea

Ginkgo leaves eliminate confusion and improve memory by increasing circulation and blood flow to the brain. Ginkgo is generally prescribed in 400-mg capsules, available at herb shops and natural food stores, to be taken three times a day. The capsules can be broken open and swirled into warm water. Note, however, that people with high blood pressure should not take ginkgo, since it may aggravate the condition. An alternative is rosemary tea made by steeping 1 teaspoon of dried rosemary in 1 cup of just-boiled water, covered, for 4 minutes. Although the results are not yet in, rosemary's volatile oils are being studied as a possible relief for people who are confused, senile, or have Alzheimer's disease.

making scents

To further employ rosemary's potentially focusing fragrance, combine 20 drops of essential oil, available at herb shops and natural food stores, and ½ cup of distilled water in a spray bottle. Mist the bracing brew around your head to sharpen your attention. Try it also just prior to or while pressing The Third Eye point, as described above.

best foods

Eating foods containing choline, an amino acid, increases your body's supply of a compound called acetylcholine, which helps transmit clear messages to and from the brain. Good sources of choline are soybeans, lentils, rice, and cashews. Another good source of choline is lecithin. Try 1 tablespoon twice a day sprinkled onto cereals, salads, soups, or stews. Available at natural food stores, pharmacies, and some supermarkets, lecithin comes from soybeans but tastes buttery and rich.

HAVE A DRINK

Dehydration studies indicate that people who are well hydrated are more alert than their less hydrated counterparts. For maximum alertness, be sure to drink at least eight 8-ounce glasses of fresh water a day, especially if you partake of such dehydrating activities as drinking alcohol and caffeinated beverages and eating salty junk foods.

B vitamins help transform choline into acetylcholine and are available in such foods as brewers yeast (some cats love this sprinkled on food or given in tablet form as a treat), barley, brown rice, dried beans (especially lentils), and soybeans. To improve brain circulation, be sure to add vitamin C–rich foods to your diet in the form of broccoli, red bell peppers, oranges, strawberries and the C-packed herbal chavanprash, a medicinal jam made from the Indian gooseberry, available at natural food stores, herb shops, and Indian markets.

smart supplement

CO Q 10, available at natural food stores and some supermarkets, is a vitamin E-like compound that improves oxygenation in the brain, thus helping to eliminate confusion. Experts advise taking 30 to 60 mg a day, but check with a health professional before adding supplements to your diet, especially if you are on medication of any kind.

Foods that may cause confusion and memory loss by clogging blood flow to the brain include junk food, processed foods, fried foods, fatty meats, dairy products, and foods containing refined white flour.

RESOURCES FOR CLEAR THINKING

- New Jersey Neurological Institute (assesses and treats memory problems): 201-992-3300
- National Council on Aging (provides directory of support groups): 1-800-424-9046
- National Alzheimer's Disease and Related Disorders Association (provides support for family members): 1-800-272-3900
- International Institute for Clear Thinking (teaches coping skills): 414-739-8311

SEE ALSO

- Adjusting ANXIETY (page 296)
- Disarming DEPRESSION (page 324)
- Curing a HEADACHE (page 346)
- Managing STRESS (page 406)

correcting constipation

correcting constipation

when symptoms may occur:

| In extreme cold or in hot and dry weather | If daily rhythms are disrupted by stress or travel |

*b*erks County, Pennsylvania, home of Pennsylvania Dutch cooking, offers some of the fattiest, fiber-void foods in the entire country. Consequently, some residents tend to be constipated. My friend who owns a bulk food store there hears regular reports of residents' irregularity as they chat at the register with chocolates in one hand and bran in the other.

Thyroid problems, diabetes, stress, pregnancy, iron pills, and many prescription drugs can cause constipation, but usually the culprit is a lack of fiber and fluids in the diet. As well as being an uncomfortable condition, constipation can be dangerous—if food doesn't move through the intestines regularly, toxins can accumulate and eventually be reabsorbed into the body, causing such problems as fatigue, irritability, skin problems, and headaches.

In addition to the suggestions offered here, adding a regular exercise routine to your life can help move waste through the intestines. Walking, dancing, bicycling, swimming, yoga, tai chi, or work on a treadmill or ski machine can help prevent and cure constipation. Or check local television listings for exercise shows and make a point of tuning in at least three times a week.

potent pose

To help tone and energize your digestive system, try a yoga asana, or posture, called the Locust. In the morning before eating, lie face down on the floor, hands made into fists and tucked below your hip bones, on your abdomen. Resting your forehead on the floor, raise your legs (knees as straight as you can make them, engaging the muscles in your rear) and keep them raised for five deep, full breaths. Release the pose, noting a warm, slightly energized feeling in your abdomen.

try a tea

The chlorophyll in such "green" drinks as wheat grass juice or barley grass juice can help cleanse and energize a sluggish digestive system. Fresh wheat grass juice, which tastes sweet and green, is available at juice bars and natural food cafés. Powdered wheat and barley grass juices, available at natural food stores, can be mixed with warm water at home and taken as needed, one to three servings a day. Alternatively, food-grade aloe vera juice, available at natural food stores, 1/4 cup taken twice daily, has a calming, healing effect on the intestines and helps to soften stools. Don't rely on these beverages, however, to cure constipation for more than 2 weeks—a low-fat, high-fiber diet with plenty of fresh water is the best method. Also, don't become dependent on such herbal laxative teas as senna and cascara. Just because they're "natural" doesn't mean they're not every bit as addictive as over-the-counter laxatives. One woman told me she has been addicted to senna for 12 years!

smart supplement

One capsule of acidophilus, available in the refrigerated sections of natural food stores and some supermarkets, taken daily in the morning 20 minutes before eating, replenishes the "friendly flora" in the intestines, thus allowing the smooth passage of food. Additionally, a regular dose of acidophilus may make the nutrients in your foods more readily absorbed.

best foods

To prevent and cure constipation, eat a high-fiber diet that includes at least three servings of fresh fruits a day. Those with edible skins and seeds, such as apples, raspberries, blueberries, strawberries, pears, and figs, contain the most fiber. Dried fruits, like prunes, are also a good fiber source. So are vegetables such as peas, corn, broccoli, cabbage, and dark greens like collards. Cooked dried beans and whole grains such as oats, barley, brown rice, and millet are also good sources of fiber. For the smoothest results, as you add these foods to your diet, be sure to increase your consumption of fresh water, drinking at least eight 8-ounce glasses a day.

Avoid such clogging foods as white flour products, refined white sugar, fried foods, fatty foods, dairy products, alcohol, and meats, especially fatty ones.

RESOURCES FOR HEALTHY DIGESTION
- Glaxo Institute for Digestive Health Information Center (sends literature): 1-800-232-4434
- National Digestive Diseases Information Clearinghouse (patient education materials): 301-654-3810

SEE ALSO
- Disarming DEPRESSION (page 324)
- Overcoming JET LAG (page 358)
- Lulling LOW BACK PAIN (page 362)
- Pacifying the PROSTATE (page 384)
- Managing STRESS (page 406)
- Settling an UPSET STOMACH (page 415)

oat muffins with apricots and figs

MAKES 12 MUFFINS
155 calories per muffin: 2 grams fat: 12% calories from fat

Be sure to drink a full 8-ounce glass of water with this high-fiber breakfast or snack.

1 1/2 cups rolled oats

1/2 cup all-fruit apricot juice

2 fresh apricots. pitted and finely chopped

4 dried figs. finely chopped

2 teaspoons finely grated fresh ginger

1/2 cup nonfat apricot yogurt or soy yogurt

1/4 cup all-fruit apricot butter or apple butter

1/4 cup barley malt

2 large egg whites or 1/4 cup egg substitute
(see Note. page 13)

1 tablespoon canola oil

1 cup unbleached all-purpose flour

1/4 cup whole wheat pastry flour

2 teaspoons baking soda

1 teaspoon ground cinnamon

PREHEAT THE OVEN to 400°F.

IN A MEDIUM bowl, combine the oats, juice, apricots, figs, and ginger and let the mixture soak for about 10 minutes. Then stir in the yogurt, apricot butter, barley malt, egg whites, and oil.

IN ANOTHER MEDIUM bowl, combine the flours, baking soda, and cinnamon. Pour the liquid ingredients into the flour mixture and use a large rubber spatula to combine well. Don't overmix; about 15 strokes should do.

LIGHTLY OIL 12 muffin cups and divide the batter among them. Bake in the middle of the oven until cooked through, 18 to 20 minutes.

IF THE WEATHER IS HOT AND/OR DRY:
*Use finely chopped fresh figs instead of
dried. or serve each muffin with a tall glass
of room-temperature peppermint tea.*

IF THE WEATHER IS COLD AND/OR DAMP:
*Serve each muffin with a steaming mug of
cinnamon-herb tea.*

kicking
a cough

kicking
a cough

when symptoms may occur:

| *At night* | *When the weather is cold and dry* | *At the change of seasons* |

*R*eturning from Russia with a nagging cough left my husband susceptible to six months of recurring bronchial and lung infections. He then resolved to rebuild his immune system by:

1. Eliminating mucus-causing dairy products from his diet

2. Increasing his daily intake of lung-soothing beta carotene by eating at least two carrots a day

3. Taking 2 teaspoons a day of vitamin C-rich, anti-infective chavanprash, available at natural food stores, herb shops, and Indian markets

4. Increasing his aerobic activity from 3 to 5 days a week, helping to oxygenate his lungs and bronchials

He has not caught a cough since 1991.

try a tea

To amplify his anticough routine, my husband also employed a tincture of the herb mullein (available at herb shops and natural food stores), taking 30 drops in 1 cup of hot water three times a day. A North American native, mullein contains compounds

*Since cold beverages can
constrict and tighten
bronchials, coughers
should drink the more
quelling warm and hot tea
choices.*

that relax and soothe bronchial and lung tissues. He also discovered the English cough remedy of thyme, an herb containing volatile oils that relax the lungs enough to promote the flow of mucus, thus helping to eliminate infection. To make a cup, steep 2 teaspoons of fresh thyme or 1 teaspoon dried in 1 cup of just-boiled water, covered, for 4 minutes. Then strain and sip. For cough curing Chinese style, add a slice of fresh ginger— to stimulate warmth in the lungs and bronchials—during the steeping. Unani, or Middle Eastern herbalists, recommend adding 1 teaspoon of anise seed to the thyme mixture during steeping. Anise seed acts as a demulcent, or soother, to inflamed tissue. Note that since thyme and ginger are mild stimulants, for peaceful slumber you should opt for plain anise seed tea at night.

making scents

To make a penetrating sauna that opens the lungs, promoting free breathing, sprinkle 10 drops of essential oil of eucalyptus (available at herb shops and natural food stores) in the bottom of your shower. Turn on the water and step in, deeply breathing the healing steam for 5 to 10 minutes. Alternatively, use essential oil of thyme or a combination of thyme and eucalyptus. To intensify the treatment, sip a cup of thyme tea (see above) while enjoying the medicating steam. You can also take advantage of the running water and take a soothing shower!

best foods

Nutrient-rich fresh vegetables and fruits, such as apples, oranges, peaches, plums, papayas, mangoes, broccoli, spinach, Brussels sprouts, kale, carrots, sweet potatoes, and winter squash, provide vitamin C and beta carotene, which bolster the immune system, helping to prevent and cure lung infection. Hot dairy-free soups and stews also encourage clearing of the lungs and bronchials, as do spicy flavorings such as garlic, ginger, and hot peppers.

Onions, an old German folk remedy for coughs, also promote free breathing and fight infection, thanks to the volatile oil and sulfur compounds they contain. To make your own onion cough syrup, peel and finely chop one medium onion and arrange the pieces in a shallow bowl. Pour on honey to cover, cover the bowl with plastic wrap, and let it sit at room temperature overnight. During that time the onion will release its penetrating juices into the honey. In the morning, strain and discard the onion. Take 1 tablespoon of the soothing syrup three times a day until your cough subsides.

RESOURCES FOR HEALTHY LUNGS

· National Jewish Center for Immunology and Respiratory Medicine (educates the public):
   1-800-222-LUNG
· American Institute for Preventive Medicine (programs to stop smoking): 1-800-345-AIPM
· Nicotine Anonymous World Services (12 steps to quit): 415-922-8575
· Smokenders (programs to quit): 1-800-828-4357

SEE ALSO

· Abating ASTHMA (page 300)
· Comforting a COLD (page 310)

ten-vegetable stew

MAKES 8 SIDE SERVINGS, OR 4 ENTRÉE SERVINGS
117 calories per serving (for each side serving): 2 grams fat: 15% calories from fat

This nutrient-packed recipe is based on a *fanesca*, a spring vegetable soup popular in Ecuador. The beta carotene offered by the vegetables can soothe irritated lungs and bronchials, as can the thyme.

2 cups vegetable stock

1 cup chopped onions

1 tablespoon minced fresh thyme or
   1 1/2 teaspoons dried

1 teaspoon ground cumin

2 cloves garlic, minced

1/2 teaspoon freshly ground black pepper,
   or to taste

1 bay leaf

1 cup corn kernels

1 cup shelled fresh or frozen peas

1 cup shredded white cabbage

1 cup sliced celery

1 cup chopped red bell peppers

1 cup sliced carrots

1 cup chopped green beans

1 cup chopped zucchini

2 cups low-fat soy milk or skim milk
   2 tablespoons peanut butter

dash of hot pepper sauce, or to taste

IN A LARGE pot, combine the stock, onions, thyme, cumin, garlic, black pepper, and bay leaf and bring the mixture to a boil. Reduce the heat and simmer for 5 minutes. Then add the corn, peas, cabbage, celery, bell peppers, carrots, green beans, and zucchini and continue to simmer until the vegetables are tender, about 12 minutes.

MEANWHILE, IN A large bowl, whisk together the soy milk, peanut butter, and hot pepper sauce. When the vegetables are tender, stir the mixture into the soup and simmer for an additional 5 minutes. Discard the bay leaf. Serve warm.

IF THE WEATHER IS HOT AND/OR DRY:
Garnish each serving with minced fresh mint.

IF THE WEATHER IS COLD AND/OR DAMP:
Garnish each serving with minced scallion.

MORE RECIPES TO
CALM A COUGH

*Brussels Sprouts with
Shiitakes and Shallots
(page 174)*

*Aduki-Carrot Soup with
Sage (page 221)*

disarming
depression

when symptoms may occur:

| In winter, when days are shorter | During the mid-afternoon | When the weather is dreary and drizzly |

*f*or five years Barbara hated her job. Refusing to seek other employment because of a fear of the unknown, she developed frequent headaches and digestive problems and became distracted and frequently weepy, especially when the weather was rainy. On her days off, Barbara barely rose from her bed. It was a classic case of depression.

Latin for "to press down," depression can be caused by major stress, allergies, seasonal affective disorder (SAD, a reaction to lack of daylight in fall and winter seasons), diabetes, hypothyroidism, birth control pills, steroids, lack of exercise, or a combination of these things. Women are more frequently diagnosed as depressed, perhaps because they may be more apt to seek professional help than men. Depression can cause withdrawn behavior, anguish, guilt, crying jags, headaches, backaches, sleep disorders, eating disorders, fatigue, apathy, lethargy, substance abuse, lack of interest in sex, and thoughts of suicide. Barbara began to lift herself out of depression by adopting a program of daily meditation (see pages 6 and 136), giving up caffeine, walking for exercise, and massage therapy. In addition, with the help of a therapist, Barbara practiced changing her point of view, learning to think more positively. One exercise that helped when she had a depressing thought was to ask herself, "Is this thought helping me or hurting me?" She eventually turned the corner, learning to accept her positive thoughts and reject her depressing ones—skills that helped her gain the confidence to seek a new job and thus a fresh beginning.

"MISERY IS OPTIONAL."

—Dr. Anthony Dallman-Jones

try a tea

A Chinese doctor in Seattle told me that after his father died, his mother went into a deep, immobilizing depression that lifted only when she began drinking daily doses of *dong quai* tea. According to Chinese herbalists, dong quai, the root of the Chinese angelica plant, contains vitamin B12, a natural mood enhancer. Indeed, dong quai has been prescribed for thousands of years to women who become depressed during menstruation and menopause. It is available in capsule or tincture form at herb shops, natural food stores, and Chinese markets. Three times a day, break one capsule into a cup of warm water (or use about 30 drops of tincture, or one eyedropper full) and sip. Alternatively, purchase sliced dried dong quai root at a Chinese market and chew on a sweet and earthy 1-inch piece three times a day. Women with uterine fibroids should avoid dong quai, as it may cause bleeding.

For a more Western approach, steep 1 teaspoon each of dried lavender and rosemary in 1 cup of just-boiled water, covered, for 4 minutes. Then strain and sip three times a day. Lavender contains volatile oil compounds that may lighten the mood, and rosemary's piney scent is delightfully uplifting.

One German study maintains that many cases of depression, especially in the elderly, are linked to poor blood circulation in the brain. To that end, half of the participants in the study took 80 mg of ginkgo herb extract, in water as a tea, three times a day, subsequently showing marked improvement in four weeks' time. Those who took the placebo did not improve. Note that since ginkgo may aggravate high blood pressure, those with the condition should avoid it.

making scents

For a mood-enhancing way to start the morning, sprinkle 5 drops each of essential oil of bergamot (a zesty orange scent) and rose geranium (both available at herbs shops and natural food stores) on the bottom of your shower. Turning on the water creates a lively, pleasant, and aromatic steam.

To enhance the effect, use an orange or rose geranium-scented shower gel, available at herb shops and natural food stores. Be sure to rinse yourself off with cool water,

SEEDS OF JOY

Planting a garden, especially one containing fragrant herbs and colorful flowers, may help lift depression. Caring for and observing plants as they grow brings enjoyment, as well as a positive feeling for the future. If you don't have a garden plot, a pot of rosemary on the windowsill is a buoyant beginning.

WASH YOUR TROUBLES AWAY

Taking your car through a car wash—the kind where you remain inside the car—may elevate your mood. Observe the water whoosh the grime away, adopting the experience as a metaphor for your woes.

Help overcome depression by volunteering your services. Take a pot of soup to the local homeless shelter. Deliver meals to shut-in elderly people. No matter how low you're feeling, there's always someone else who's in worse shape.

HERE COMES
THE SUN

Depression studies show that being in the sun, even just sitting in a sunny window or driving in a car, for two hours a day may improve your mood. The reason is that sunlight encourages the production of the hormone cortisol, which makes us lively.

PETTING ALLOWED

Depressed people feel happier and more connected to the world where they care for other creatures instead of dwelling in their own low moods. Cats, dogs, even a goldfish in a bowl can make you smile.

thus energizing the nerve endings in the skin. While your skin is still damp, moisturize it with an uplifting body lotion you can make yourself by combining 5 drops of essential oil of rose geranium with 1 tablespoon of unscented body lotion. Make an extra batch in a small bottle to use throughout the day, rubbing it on your hands and earlobes, especially in mid-afternoon, when possible low blood sugar and fatigue may spur a glum mood.

best foods

To increase alertness if your mood is low, eat such lean protein foods as broiled fish or low-fat tofu. Eating protein helps raise energy levels by increasing the production in the brain of the stimulating hormones dopamine and norepinephrine.

Conversely, if depression has caused anxiety, complex carbohydrates such as whole wheat pasta, barley, or brown rice will increase the production of soothing serotonin in the brain to help balance your mood. In addition, to help banish depression, avoid alcohol, caffeine, refined white sugar, soft drinks, junk foods, and fatty foods. They rob the body of mood-enhancing B vitamins and calcium.

smart supplements

To help lift depression, taking 100 mg a day of B vitamin complex will assist you in achieving and maintaining proper brain and nerve function, as will taking 1,000 mg of vitamin C and 400 IUs of vitamin E per day.

RESOURCES FOR A GOOD MOOD
- National Foundation for Depressive Illness (provides information to the public): 1-800-248-4344
- National Depressive and Manic-Depressive Association (provides information to the public; lists of support groups): 1-800-826-3632
- National Mental Health Association (provides information to the public; lists of support groups): 1-800-969-6642
- National Alliance for the Mentally Ill (provides information to the public; lists of support groups): 1-800-950-6264
- Depression After Delivery (provides information and support for postpartum depression): 1-800-944-4773
- Post-Partum Support International: 805-967-7636
- Depressives Anonymous (self-help through weekly meetings): 212-689-2600
- Depressed Anonymous (12-step program; newsletter and phone support): 502-969-3359
- National Counseling Center of the Humanistic Foundation (referrals to professional help): 1-800-333-4444
- Emotions Anonymous (provides literature, information, and local referrals): 612-647-9712

SEE ALSO
· Correcting CONFUSION AND MEMORY LOSS (page 314)
· Fighting FATIGUE (page 339)
· Mending MENSTRUAL CRAMPS (page 366)
· Managing STRESS (page 406)

fragrant corn chowder with fresh herbs

MAKES 6 LARGE ENTRÉE SERVINGS
220 calories per serving: no added fat

The vibrant combination of thyme, oregano, and tarragon in this nutritious soup may help brighten a dreary mood. On the folklore side, some Japanese herbalists hold that corn acts as a tonic for a heavy heart.

2 quarts water

2 tablespoons dried nettle (see The Savory Pantry, page 424)

3 carrots, finely chopped

1 pound red new potatoes, finely chopped

1 fresh hot pepper, cored, seeded, and finely chopped

1/4 cup shredded dried daikon radish (see The Savory Pantry, page 423)

2 tablespoons arame sea herb (see The Savory Pantry, page 422)

3 1/2 cups corn kernels

2 cups low-fat soy milk or skim milk

1 tablespoon minced fresh thyme

1 tablespoon minced fresh oregano

2 teaspoons minced fresh tarragon
pinch of sea salt

freshly ground black pepper

minced fresh chives for garnish

IN A LARGE soup pot, combine the water, nettle, carrots, potatoes, hot pepper, daikon, arame, and corn and bring the mixture to a boil. Reduce the heat to medium-low, cover loosely, and simmer until the vegetables are tender, about 20 minutes.

ADD THE MILK, thyme, oregano, tarragon, salt, and pepper and simmer for about 1 minute more. Serve warm, sprinkled with the chives.

Note: If you have high blood pressure, replace the nettle with 1/4 cup of minced fresh parsley.

IF THE WEATHER IS HOT AND/OR DRY:
Serve with dill-sprinkled sliced cucumbers.

IF THE WEATHER IS COLD AND/OR DAMP:
Use 3 jalapeños and be liberal with the freshly ground pepper.

relieving diarrhea

relieving diarrhea

when symptoms may occur:

| In hot, humid weather | Anytime that stress is not managed |

*a*dear friend who is an artist and professor remembers as a student being so panicked before a math final that she wound up in the school infirmary with diarrhea. By taking paregoric to calm down and completing the test in the infirmary, she felt free from the pressures of the classroom and passed the test. Realizing that the diarrhea was stress-induced, she made a plan for subsequent situations. She now gets control of her body through deep, deliberate breathing, often going outside into fresh air, away from people. Splashing her face with cold water, as well as running cold water across her wrists, also helps. If a towel is available, a cold compress on the back of her neck provides soothing comfort.

Peristalsis, the muscular contractions that move food through the body, is controlled by the nervous system. This is why unmanaged stress can interfere with the normal flow of intestinal contractions, disrupting their natural rhythms.

Medications such as antibiotics are also responsible for bouts of diarrhea. AAD (antibiotic-associated diarrhea) occurs as the drug destroys not only the bacteria that may be making you sick but also the "friendly flora" that keep intestines healthy. To replace the friendly flora, take a capsule of acidophilus (available in the refrigerated sections of natural food stores) 20 minutes before eating in the morning. Avoid AAD in the first place by abstaining from antibiotics unless they are absolutely necessary.

Viral infections such as the flu can also cause diarrhea, but if the condition lasts for more than a day or two, the cause may be bacteria or parasites, and you will need to see a health professional.

try a tea

Plain black tea, 1 teaspoon or bag steeped in 1 cup of just-boiled water for 4 minutes, contains tannins that have a tonifying effect on overenergized intestines. Peppermint and chamomile teas, brewed the same way, are also soothing, as is the Japanese twig tea called *kukicha* (available at Japanese markers and natural food stores). Note, however, that experts say diarrhea is the body's way of ridding itself of toxins and therefore should not be suppressed.

best foods

Toast and plain crackers are mild foods that can soothe a hyper digestive system. Even if you don't feel hungry, eating a cracker can keep you from feeling dizzy. Peppermint and ginger candy contain volatile oil compounds that may help soothe diarrhea. Avoid overly sugary foods, oily foods, fried foods, alcohol, bran, beans, garlic, hot peppers, and coffee, which can exacerbate the condition.

RESOURCES FOR HEALTHY DIGESTION
· National Digestive Diseases Information Clearinghouse (pamphlets, catalogs, and guides): 301-654-3810
· Digestive Disease National Coalition (educational material): 202-544-7497

SEE ALSO
· Adjusting ANXIETY (page 296)
· Settling an UPSET STOMACH (page 415)
· Managing STRESS (page 406)

defeating dry hair

*n*oting the drying effect that constant airplane travel has on my hair, I've gotten resourceful about keeping it healthy in spite of my lifestyle. The best advice is to get a great haircut regularly so that you can avoid using such damaging styling appliances as curling irons, hot curlers, and dryers. A cut that suits your hair type and is easy to manage will allow you simply to towel-dry your hair and go. Also, to prevent damage from chemical treatments, have coloring and perms done by a well-recommended professional—don't do them yourself. As for the sun, stay out of it. Many people think that wearing a hat will protect their hair, but the heat that the hat produces simply depletes the scalp of moisture, leading to lackluster locks.

Dry hair also can result from sudden weight loss, aging, thyroid disease, and poor diet. To restore or retain your mane, try these suggestions.

To prevent dry hair, avoid shampoos containing the harsh cleanser sodium lauryl sulphite. Shampoos containing the cleansers coconut oil or sodium laureth sulphite are more gentle. Also, your shampoo label should say the product is pH balanced. Shampoos that are too acidic can dry out the hair.

relief at your fingertips

Massaging the scalp stimulates circulation, making hair more lustrous. To try it, combine 2 drops of essential oil of rosemary with 1 teaspoon of jojoba oil, available at natural food stores and herb shops. (Rosemary contains volatile oils that warm and activate the scalp.) Dot the tips of each finger with the mixture, then burrow your fingers beneath your hair and massage your scalp with firm, circular motions. To avoid irritation, be sure to use your fingertips, not your fingernails, and massage for about 5 minutes. Since heat helps open the hair shaft, to make an intensifying conditioning treatment, rub your hair with the rosemary mixture, then wrap your head in plastic wrap so your body heat is retained. Wait for about 20 minutes before shampooing (do some yoga stretches or meditate while you're waiting). After shampooing, rinse your hair with cold water, which helps to smooth and close the outer layer, promoting shine.

best foods

When a smart Hollywood horse trainer gambled, and won, that flaxseed oil added to his animals' diets would promote shiny coats, human hair experts adopted the plan with similar success. Flaxseed oil contains compounds called essential fatty acids, which promote strong, healthy hair. Experts recommend taking 1 to 2 tablespoons a day, swirled into oatmeal or drizzled on a muffin or toast. Note that flaxseed oil contains the same calories and fat as other oils, so be sure to adjust your total intake of fat accordingly or you will gain weight. Also, for best effects, avoid cigarettes, alcohol and caffeine, salty junk foods, and processed meats; they are dehydrating, drawing moisture away from the scalp.

RESOURCES FOR LUSTROUS HAIR
- Kiehl's (catalog of handmade, botanically based hair care): 1-800-KIEHLS-1
- Sebastian's Hotline (advice on hair care): 1-800-829-7322

SEE ALSO
- Smoothing DRY SKIN (page 332)

smoothing dry skin

smoothing dry skin

when symptoms may occur:

| *In dry weather, hot or cold* | *At the change of seasons*

𝒲hen two weeks in the upper Sonoran Desert left my usually normal skin parched, I consulted with a skin care expert who helped me resoften my complexion. Most people who think they have dry skin, he said, really have dehydrated skin from environmental factors such as dry air and pollution. True dry skin may also be dehydrated, he continued, but it's different in that dry skin is aged and very lined. Problems arise when people with dehydrated skin slather on oily creams meant for dry skin; dehydrated skin needs moisture, not oil.

To that end, as instructed, I made sure to drink eight to ten 8-ounce glasses of water a day and misted my face with distilled water hourly as well as before applying a nut oil–based moisturizer (petroleum-based moisturizers can dehydrate the skin). To prevent or cure your own dehydrated or dry skin, adopt these smoothing suggestions.

try a tea

To smooth dry and dehydrated skin, Egyptian herbalists recommend topical treatments with calendula flower tea, containing essential oils that soothe and hydrate skin, as well as help new skin form. In addition, calendula offers vitamin C and beta carotene to nourish the skin, which is especially helpful if you are in polluted areas. To try it, steep 2 fresh or dried calendula flower heads (minus the green parts) in 1 cup of just-boiled water, covered, until cool, at least 20 minutes, then strain. Treat your skin daily with the brew by wiping a saturated cotton pad over your face and throat before applying moisturizer. For a take-along tonic, combine $1/4$ cup of the calendula tea with $1/4$ cup of hydrating rose water in a $1/2$-cup spray bottle. Mist your face with the revitalizer throughout the day, even over makeup.

For a skin-saving tea to take internally, try nettle. Many skin experts believe that dry and dehydrated conditions should be treated with herbs that support the body with nutrients. A cup of nettle tea provides calcium for supple skin; silica to help our bodies absorb calcium; beta carotene to prevent early aging; and iron to combat the exhaustion that may eventually cause unsightly facial lines. To make a cup, steep 1 tablespoon of dried nettle (available at natural food stores and herb shops) in 1 cup of just-boiled water, covered, for 10 minutes. Then strain and enjoy nettle's parsley-like flavor. Although nettle is safe for most people to take daily, it may aggravate high blood pressure, so those with the condition should avoid it.

Another option is the Chinese herb dong quai, available at herb shops, natural food stores, and Chinese markets. Although not documented in the West, Chinese scientists maintain that dong quai, taken internally, promotes smooth skin, and devotees swear by it. Dong quai is available in capsule form, or buy the dried sliced root at a Chinese market and chew on a 1-inch piece of the sweet and earthy-tasting root three times each day as needed.

Another herb from the Orient, Chinese licorice root, has a hydrating effect on the skin when taken internally. Buy Chinese licorice at herb shops, natural food stores, and Chinese markets and boil 3 dried slices in 2 cups of water until the liquid has been reduced to $1 1/2$ cups. Strain and discard the licorice, then drink as needed. Since the herb hydrates the entire body, those who naturally retain water should avoid Chinese licorice. It is also hypertensive, so those with high blood pressure should avoid it.

From ancient Manchuria and Tibet comes the hydrating skin tonic *kombucha*. Many people who sip the tea daily—4 ounces 15 minutes before breakfast—report that it corrects dry and dehydrated skin conditions. Made from a mushroom-like fungus (available at Asian markets and natural food stores), kombucha has not been scientifically tested in the United States, but German, Chinese, and Japanese research verifies the skin-smoothing claim. One way it may work is that kombucha contains glucuronic acid, which is normally produced by the liver to help rid the body of toxins. The introduction of the compound from kombucha may put less stress on the liver, thus benefiting the complexion.

making scents

For extra hydration, smooth your complexion with a moisture mask made of honey, a natural humectant that softens the skin. Tie or comb your hair back, then splash your face with warm water. Combine 2 tablespoons of honey with 1 teaspoon of moisturizing, aromatic rose water and rub the mixture into your face and throat with gentle, circular motions. Relax while you let the mask soak in for 10 minutes. (You can make a double batch, rubbing the extra into your hands.) Rinse well, about 20 times, then moisturize while your skin is still damp. As an alternative, use 1 teaspoon of revitalizing kombucha tea (available at some natural food stores), instead of the rose water. The kombucha helps correct the pH in the skin, thus promoting hydration.

Essential oil of neroli (an orange-scented flower available at herb shops and natural food stores) contains compounds that help regenerate dry and dehydrated skin. To make your own face cream, combine about 10 drops of neroli with 2 tablespoons of good-quality nut oil–based skin lotion, applying about 1 teaspoon morning and night to damp skin, including the skin under the eyes. For an extra emollient treatment, dampen your skin with cooled chamomile tea before applying the neroli lotion. To make the tea, steep 1 teaspoon of dried chamomile in 1 cup of just-boiled water, covered, for 4 minutes. Then strain the tea and let it cool before using. For convenience, pour the tea into a spray bottle to mist your face.

For an overnight treatment to soften weathered, dry, or dehydrated hands, combine 1 drop each of essential oil of rose geranium, sandalwood, and chamomile (available at herb shops and natural food stores) with 1 teaspoon of canola oil and rub the mixture into warm, damp hands. Put on cotton or disposable gloves to help the scented oil penetrate, and go to sleep. The essences contain compounds that help heal skin and help fresh skin form.

best foods

Members of the allium genus—namely, garlic, onion, leeks, and chives—contain sulfur compounds that, when eaten regularly, help keep skin soft and youthful. In addition, including such dark leafy greens as mustard, kale, and dandelion in your diet contributes beta carotene, to help new skin tissue form, and chlorophyll, which aids in immune support. Add to the list 1 tablespoon of pumpkin seeds a day to supply enough zinc to help skin heal. And simply for their juicy hydrating powers, be sure to eat such fresh fruits as mangoes, papayas, oranges, grapefruits, peaches, and plums.

Slice and pack them into a container to take to work or on airplane flights, to help with hydration.

To retain a lustrous complexion, avoid such dehydrating items as fried foods, animal fat, salty junk foods, preserved meats and fish, alcohol, caffeine, and foods containing refined sugar. Smoking is drying and dehydrating as well.

smart supplements

Some skin experts recommend:

· Kelp, a sea herb, containing compounds that help maintain good skin tone. Kelp is available in capsule form at natural food stores and herb shops and can be taken daily.

· Evening primrose oil (1,500 mg a day), which contains linoleic acid for moisturization of the skin. (Women who have breast cancer should not take evening primrose but can opt for linoleic-containing black currant oil capsules instead.)

· At least 400 IUs of vitamin E a day to protect against premature aging.

· Royal Bee Jelly (1 teaspoon a day), available in a honey solution from natural food stores, to help smooth and moisturize the complexion.

· At least, 1,000 mg of vitamin C a day to protect against premature aging. A good source is 2 teaspoons a day (morning and evening) of the Ayurvedic Indian gooseberry jam, chavanprash, available at Indian markets and some natural food stores.

SOURCES FOR HEALTHY SKIN
· Kiehl's (catalog of handmade, botanically based skin care products): 1-800-KIEHLS-1
· Nature's Symphony (plant-based skin care): 407-393-0065
· Kombucha source: 1-800-555-7580
· The Aromatherapy Catalog (pure essential oils): 1-800-898-PURE

SEE ALSO
· Defeating DRY HAIR (page 330)
· Halting HOT FLASHES (page 350)
· Pacifying the PROSTATE (page 384)
· Alleviating WATER RETENTION (page 418)

RECIPES FOR
SMOOTH SKIN

Sesame-Scented Couscous (page 108)

Carrot and Burdock, Kinpira Style (page 170)

easing an earache

when symptoms may occur:

At the change of seasons,
when head colds, sore
throats, and sinus pressure
may be rampant

*a*pediatrician with three earache-prone kids of her own told me her secret for curing the common ailment. Dip a small cotton swab in hydrogen peroxide, she advised, then, tilting the head to the side, ear up, very gently insert the swab and count slowly to 10. She chants, "One no earache, two no earache," and on to 10. After 10 seconds, fizzy sounds are heard as wax and other clogging debris are being dissolved. Then repeat with the other ear, cleaning out the ears with the cotton swab.

Similarly, in Arizona I learned a Navajo ear-soothing remedy called ear candles. Twelve-inch hollow muslin cones coated in pure beeswax, called ear candles, must be administered by another person, since the end of the candle that is not in the ear burns a small flame. Heat from the flame creates a little vacuum that draws wax and debris out of the ear. I was shocked to see the amount of wax that emerged from the ear following this procedure. Ear candles are available at natural food stores and herb shops. When you make your purchase, be sure to obtain accompanying written instructions for their safe use.

Earaches are the most frequently heard complaint by pediatricians and family physicians. The most common cause of earaches in children is a condition called otitis media, or middle ear infection, often marked by fever and crankiness. Children who frequent the local public pool are also susceptible to swimmer's ear, otitis externa.

Half of adult earaches come from injury or from pressure changes due to such activities as air travel or scuba diving. The latter condition, called barotrauma, can be aggravated by head colds and sinus pressure. The remaining half of adult earaches are referred ear pain, actually originating from the head, neck, teeth, sinuses, or heart problems.

To ease an earache, experts recommend avoiding activities that cause pressure in the eardrum, such as swimming and air travel. And since ear infections can originate in the throat, spreading up to the ear through the eustachian tube, tincture of the anti-infective herb echinacea, available at herb shops and natural food stores, is often advised, 28 drops (about one eyedropper) taken orally three times a day. In addition, you may find relief from these soothing suggestions.

relief at your fingertips

Earache sufferers report immediate respite from pain by applying hot compresses. Rinse a face cloth with hot water, wring it out, and apply it over the ear and adjoining jawbone area, or wherever there is pain, for 10 minutes twice a day. For an intensified approach, heat the damp cloth for 30 seconds on full power in the microwave before applying. (For children, test the cloth first, making sure it's not too hot for their delicate skin.) Another approach is to wet the cloth with a product called glycothymoline, available at natural food stores or see the source listed below. Originally formulated as a mouthwash, it contains a number of penetrating herbs, including thyme, pine, mint, and eucalyptus. When applied soaked on a face cloth, it is an effective balm, especially for earaches due to sinus pressure.

Whether you use plain water or glycothymoline, when applying the compress, relax by closing your eyes and concentrate on breathing deeply. To avoid any unneeded pressure in the area, relax your jaw, keeping your lips together and teeth apart. Using your finger to press on painful areas while applying the compress may also help alleviate pain.

making scents

To make an effective (and highly aromatic!) anti-infective ear oil, heat $\frac{1}{4}$ cup of olive oil or canola oil in a small saucepan until hot but not boiling, then remove from the heat. Meanwhile, peel 5 garlic cloves. When the oil is ready, mash the garlic through a press, dropping the pulp and juice right into the oil. Stir well and strain away any pieces. Test the oil on the inside of your wrist. If it feels too hot there, it's too hot for your ear also, and you should let it cool slighty before using. To apply, tilt your head to one side, ear up, and use an eyedropper to drip 3 to 5 drops of the warm oil into the ear. Remain in the tilted position for about 3 minutes to allow the oil to penetrate. Repeat with the other ear if necessary. The oil can be gently reheated in the microwave (don't boil) and applied twice a day.

best foods

If an earache is caused by sinus pressure or a head cold, hot, spicy soups and stews containing chilies, garlic, and ginger may provide temporary relief. Chewing on hard candies or ice can aggravate an earache, so opt for softer, less noisy repasts. In addition, some experts maintain that avoiding dairy products can help prevent earaches.

SOURCES FOR EARACHE RELIEF
- Home Health (source of glycothymoline): 1-800-284-9123
- Ear Foundation (public education and information): 805-569-1111

SEE ALSO
- Comforting a COLD (page 310)
- Healing HAY FEVER (page 342)
- Curing a HEADACHE (page 346)
- Releasing SINUS PRESSURE (page 392)

fighting
fatigue

when symptoms may occur:

| In the mid-afternoon | At the change of seasons and in very hot weather | When the weather is dreary |

While polling experts for tips on how to combat lack of energy, I was attracted to the wise advice one physician gave his patient. Find out what is sapping your energy in the first place—perhaps some unpleasant circumstance, he instructed. Addressing the cause of fatigue is a lot more important than treating its symptoms.

Certainly, if conditions such as worry, stress, guilt, depression, or grief are causing fatigue, they must be addressed and healed on their own emotional terms. Part of that therapy, though, as well as for fatigue caused by the more obvious physical manifestations of arthritis, digestive problems, medications such as antibiotics, and menopause, includes the suggestions offered here.

BASIC BACH

The system of Bach Flower Remedies, created by a Welsh physician, is based on the theory that minute doses of certain flower and plant essences can correct such conditions as fatigue. Of the 38 essences, available at natural food stores and herb shops, olive is slated to help restore energy.

relief at your fingertips

Massage energizes the entire body by stimulating circulation and helping to fortify the immune system. When combined with a nutritious diet and regular exercise, massage can revitalize the weary. To find a massage therapist, ask friends, inquire at natural food stores, ask your doctor, or check the source at the end of this section, deciding before you go whether you would be more comfortable with a male or female therapist. Basically, you'll find that there are two types, of massage: Western and Eastern. Western-style massages are what some people call Swedish or deep muscle, characterized by kneading and tapping on lightly oiled skin. For the Eastern style, no oil is used and clients wear light clothing, helping the therapist not to slip while using thumbs, elbows, hands, and sometimes knees to press and activate various energy channels on the body. These days most massage therapists have knowledge of both Western and Eastern styles of massage, enabling the client to receive the benefits of both worlds. Those who are unsure about having a full-body massage can opt for a rejuvenating facial massage, usually found at day spas and full-service salons.

Once, just after I had received an Ayurvedic face massage, the therapist taught me an invigorating self-massage technique. To try it, begin by briskly rubbing your hands together for 10 seconds. Then, using both sets of fingertips, locate the point below each knee where it meets the shin bone. Then move an inch or so toward the outside of each leg. Check to make sure your fingertips are in the right place by wiggling your feet up and down. If you feel the muscle move, you're on the right spot; if not, adjust your fingers. Breathing in fully, close your eyes. As you breathe out, begin briskly rubbing the leg area, continuing to rub for 1 to 2 minutes. When you've finished, open your eyes, noting a gentle energy moving through your body.

try a tea

Experts hold that stimulants such as coffee eventually deplete our energy reserves. One reason this may be true is that the caffeine in such beverages as coffee, strongly brewed tea, chocolate, and some colas depletes our B vitamin reserves, which can lead to fatigue. Adaptagenic herbs, however, help our bodies adapt to stress as well as to generate and conserve energy. One widely studied tonic is Siberian ginseng (Eleuthero, not Chinese Panax ginseng). Chinese herbalists classify Siberian ginseng as a chi (energy) tonic that increases stamina on a deep, internal level. The herb, which contains essential oils that promote vitality and stamina, is usually taken in the morning in 2,500-mg capsules, available at herb shops and natural food stores. Alternatively, from the same sources you can purchase a tincture of Siberian ginseng and take it according to the instructions on the bottle. For the best results, take Siberian ginseng for 6 days a week, letting your body relax on the seventh. Then begin again as needed.

Some people take the herb for 2 weeks at the change of seasons to invigorate themselves during this transitional period.

best foods

Fresh foods, such as seasonal fruits and vegetables, contain energizing vitamins, as well as enzymes and fiber to aid proper digestion (some fatigue is caused by constipation). Also be sure to drink at least eight 8-ounce glasses of water a day, since fluids help flush out energy-robbing wastes and toxins, which can cause stagnation and lethargy.

Eating fatty and fried foods, as well as overeating, can be fatiguing because they put a great deal of stress on the digestive system. Extra digestive acids, enzymes, and bile must be secreted, and the body can't always meet those demands. Moreover, when the digestive system is stressed, the body is less able to assimilate vitalizing nutrients.

RESOURCES FOR FIGHTING FATIGUE
- American Massage Therapy Association (referrals to therapists): 1-800-986-4636
- National Chronic Fatigue Syndrome Association, Inc. (support groups, seminars, literature): 816-931-4777
- CFIDS Association, Inc. (fatigue newsletter and information): 1-800-442-3437

SEE ALSO
- Mid-Afternoon (page 113)
- Disarming DEPRESSION (page 324)
- Lulling LOW BACK PAIN (page 362)
- Securing SOUND SLEEP (page 402)
- Managing STRESS (page 406)

healing
hayfever

when symptoms may occur:

| In the morning | March through November

O ne spring in Cairo, Egypt, the dust, pollution, and pollen combined to give me a whopping attack of hay fever, complete with runny nose, weepy eyes, and itchy ear canals. A doctor suggested I stay in the hotel, windows closed, to eliminate exposure to the irritants. He also recommended I take oral homeopathic allergy drops containing minute doses of botanicals, including euphorbia, which eliminates nasal congestion and watery eyes. To the treatment I added a soothing warm facial compress made by dipping a face cloth in hot water and using it to cover and rejuvenate my entire face.

Hay fever, also called seasonal rhinitis, occurs when stimuli, usually pollen, animal hair, molds, or pollution, adversely affect the mucous membranes of the eyes, ears, and air passages. Stress, some experts say, may worsen hay fever conditions, especially in those people who simultaneously suffer from asthma (tightening of the bronchials) and skin rashes. The strategies that follow can help prevent hay fever attacks or may assuage existing conditions.

relief at your fingertips

To help soothe red, itchy eyes, make eye packs by steeping 1 teaspoon of fresh chervil and 1 teaspoon of dried chamomile in 1 cup of just-boiled water, covered, until cool (at least 20 minutes), then discarding the herbs. Dip two cotton pads into the soothing brew, set them on closed eyes, and lightly press the pads on the sides, bottom, and top of the eyes for 10 minutes. Since chervil is a seasonal herb, growing only in early spring, make an extra batch of the comforting mixture and pour it into an ice cube tray to freeze. Once frozen, transfer the cubes to a freezer bag, then melt one as you need it throughout the 8-month hay fever season.

To help drain nasal congestion while applying the chervil-chamomile eye pack, use both index fingers to press firmly next to the jawbone just under the ear. The points may be sensitive, so assert pressure accordingly. Some people claim that while pressing the points they can actually feel the congestion in their face draining down their throat. If this happens to you, to help prevent a sore throat, sip a cup of aromatic tea, such as the one mentioned below.

try a tea

The Chinese herb *ma huang*, called ephedra in the West, contains a compound called ephedrine, which acts as a tonic to inflamed respiratory passages. Ma huang is available at herb shops, natural food stores, and Chinese markets. To make a tea, boil ten 1-inch twigs in 2 cups of water for 10 minutes. Then add a slice of fresh ginger and continue to boil for an additional 5 minutes before straining and sipping. It tastes sweet and zippy. Since ma huang is a mild stimulant, the tea should not be taken before bed, and daily doses should be limited to 2 cups. As a historical note, in ancient China ma huang tea was sipped by Buddhist monks before meditation to "clear the head."

making scents

To make a head-clearing morning sauna, sprinkle 10 drops of essential oil of tea tree (available at herb shops and natural food stores) in the bottom of your shower before turning on the water. Then shower as usual, breathing in the penetrating aroma. Tea tree contains volatile oil compounds that help clear stuffy respiratory passages, so for treatments throughout the day, drip 2 drops of tea tee oil on a tissue and inhale. Or

BE A MASKED MAN

In the cosmetic section of pharmacies, you'll find a blue liquid-filled plastic mask called "hot or cold eye mask." Hay fever sufferers should keep one handy. During a hay fever attack, soak the mask in hot, not boiling, water for 10 minutes and apply to the face for 15 minutes. For a quicker fix, heat the mask on medium power in the microwave for 30 seconds.

RECIPES TO EASE
HAY FEVER
*Apricot-Almond Granola
with Coconut (page 27)*

*Warm Orzo Salad with
Pine Nuts and Fresh
Thyme (page 200)*

mix 25 drops of tea tree oil into ½ cup of distilled water for a decongestant spray that also purifies office or home air. People who are allergic to molds can eliminate them by misting this spray around baseboards and other mold-prone areas of the home every 2 days. In addition, spray office and home air filters to prevent pollen from entering the environment.

RX FOR HAY FEVER

Some physicians report that their hay fever patients find relief by taking an under-the-tongue homeopathic pill made of minute doses of arsenicum album, available at natural food stores and some pharmacies. Check with your doctor about what dose is right for you, and note that for best results with this treatment you must eliminate peppermint (even toothpaste flavored by peppermint) from your life because it may block absorption.

best foods

Adding foods rich in beta carotene to your diet, such as dandelion, sorrel, mustard greens, carrots, sweet potatoes, apricots, mangoes, and papayas, may help fight hay fever, since the nutrient helps to soothe mucous membranes. Spicy flavors such as garlic, hot peppers, and ginger may help to temporarily clear your head, as will such high-calcium offerings as broccoli, kale, and dill seed, which help tone nerves and reduce immune-robbing stress. For the best respiratory results, avoid dairy products, foods containing artificial colors and flavors, junk foods, and cigarette smoking.

smart supplements

Some experts maintain that hay fever can be abated by boosting the immune system. To that end, these supplements are recommended:

· CO Q 10, a vitamin E-like substance that helps to oxygenate respiratory tissues; 30 mg a day.

· Vitamin B complex, to tonify stressed nerves; 100 mg a day.

· Vitamin C, to help boost the body's production of immune-enhancing interferon; 1 teaspoon twice a day of the Indian Ayurvedic jam, chavanprash, made from the vitamin C-rich Indian gooseberry (available at Indian markets and natural food stores).

· Acidophilus (available in the refrigerated sections of natural food stores), to strengthen immunity by enriching the digestive system with friendly flora; 1 capsule 20 minutes before breakfast.

RESOURCES FOR CLEAR BREATHING

· American Allergy Association (information on diet and environmental control): 415-322-1663
· Arrowroot Natural Pharmacy (homeopathic hay fever preparations): 1-800-234-8879

SEE ALSO

· Early Morning (page 3)
· Abating ASTHMA (page 300)
· Banishing BREAKOUTS AND RASHES (page 304)
· Releasing SINUS PRESSURE (page 392)

curing a headache

curing headache

when symptoms may occur:

In the morning, if associated with hay fever and sinus pressure	Mid-afternoon, if associated with stress

*b*othered by a headache above my left jaw and ear, I consulted both a dentist and a periodontist, thinking the problem might be referred pain from a toothache. My teeth were fine, they told me, but the headache was caused by my unconsciously grinding my teeth. If I didn't stop, they cautioned, the pain would worsen and my teeth would eventually suffer.

Unconvinced at first of the diagnosis, I nonetheless became more mindful of relaxing my jaw, repeating what I now call the mandible mantra of "Lips together, teeth apart." I then became aware of situations in which I tensed my jaw and ground my teeth, such as sitting in a traffic jam, giving an ill pet an injection, performing tough moves during exercise. Luckily, by repeating the mantra to myself, I was easily able to prevent further headaches.

Common headaches can be caused by poor diet, dehydration, sinus pressure, hay fever, sleep apnea, red wine, birth control pills, constipation, and often, as in my case, just plain stress. What happens is that tension causes involuntary muscle contractions around the face and head, resulting in pain in those areas, particularly the back of the head, neck, eyes, and forehead. Some people describe the pain as a vise gripping the skull. Headaches may last for days, eventually causing fatigue and depression. And paradoxically, tension headaches may actually arise after the stress itself has subsided!

As for migraine headaches, one-quarter of everyone you know will experience one sometime in their lives. Some sufferers have a family history of migraines, usually beginning in the teenage years, peaking in the thirties and forties, and ending in the fifties, except in cases where hormonal imbalance due to menopause is the cause. Migraine pain seems to stem from abrupt fluctuations in blood vessel dilation, and the pain can be debilitating. Similar to classic migraines are cluster headaches—several headaches will occur at close intervals, perhaps three in one week, then will not recur for months. Physicians also report a new condition, called "mixed headache syndrome," combining components of both migraines and tension headaches. Whatever the type or tenacity of the headache, these treatments may help ease the pain.

relief at your fingertips

At a 1995 conference of neurosurgeons in Phoenix, Arizona, it was revealed that a tense neck can adversely affect the nerves in the head, causing headache. To that end, it was suggested that a relaxing massage or an ice pack is a more effective treatment for a headache than over-the-counter pain relievers that don't really stop the muscle tension that's causing the pain. For an easy way to massage your own neck, stuff two tennis balls into a large sock and tie a knot in the open end so that the tennis balls don't slip around. Lying on your back on the floor, set the sock under your neck so that a ball is on either side of the spine. Using your heels, push your body up and back so that your neck rolls over the balls for a soothing, headache-relieving massage.

If tennis balls aren't handy, an ice pack or cold wet face cloth held at the base of the skull for 10 minutes may help to ease the tension in your head by helping to dilate constricted blood vessels. For a migraine, some people report that at the first sign of an attack, alternating hot and cold packs on the forehead and temples at 3-minute intervals helps lessen the symptoms.

potent pose

A German massage therapist taught me to banish a tension headache by lying on my back with fists under my neck and knuckles touching it. With knees bent, I lift my rear up and down, and as I do, my neck is automatically massaged by my knuckles.

The higher I lift, the more intense and soothing the massage. On a practical level, the pose is so nutty-looking that it usually gets my mind off whatever it is that's causing me stress.

try a tea

Although it's best to assuage head pain by eliminating the cause, it may not always be practical to have a massage, self-performed or otherwise. An alternative is to sip a cup of rosemary tea, which contains a compound called rosmaricin that soothes a headache like aspirin but is easy on the stomach. To make the tea, steep 1 teaspoon of dried rosemary or 2 teaspoons of fresh rosemary in 1 cup of just-boiled water, covered, for 5 minutes. Strain and sip. For extra stress reduction, add 1 teaspoon of relaxing dried valerian root (available at herb shops and natural food stores) to the rosemary and increase the steeping time to 10 minutes. Alternatively, if the headache has just begun, mix 1 eyedropper of tincture of black cohosh (available at herb shops and natural food stores) in $1/4$ cup of water and drink. The root of black cohosh, a North American remedy for pain, contains salicylic acid, the pain-relieving ingredient in aspirin. (Black cohosh comes in tea form, but the taste is awful, so stick with the tincture and knock it back quickly.)

best foods

Some experts maintain that headaches come from a deficiency of the mineral magnesium, attesting that nearly 90 percent of Americans are magnesium-deficient. People used to get magnesium from drinking water, they say, but modern water softeners negate the mineral. Leafy greens, such as mustard, dandelion, arugula, kale, and collards are rich in magnesium. Half a cup, steamed, should be eaten daily by those who suffer from headaches.

To avoid headache pain, don't chew ice or other hard foods. Cold foods such as iced beverages and ice cream can also cause headaches. The food additive monosodium glutamate (MSG) may cause headaches as well, but since the reaction is sometimes delayed by up to 10 hours, it's difficult to trace the headache to MSG in a specific food, making avoidance the best choice. Eat foods that are as fresh as possible, avoiding junk foods and packaged foods.

PURSUE A PRO

Regular massages by a professional therapist can prevent and cure common tension headaches. To find a massage therapist, ask friends, ask your doctor, or consult the sources at the end of this section, deciding before you make an appointment whether you would be more comfortable with a male or female therapist. Chiropractic treatments may help too by increasing blood flow to the brain and eliminating neck and shoulder tension.

GET MOVING

Regular exercise, such as walking, biking, or yoga, oxygenates the tissues and thus may lessen the occurrence of tension headaches.

RESOURCES FOR A PAIN-FREE HEAD

- American Massage Therapy Association (referrals to therapists): 1-800-986-4636
- National Headache Foundation (information, newsletter, and support groups): 1-800-843-2256
- Headache Information Hotline (sends printed information on causes and treatment): 1-800-352-9424
- New England Headache Treatment Program (general information): 1-800-245-0088 (in Conn., 203-968-1799)
- American Chronic Pain Association (support for sufferers): 916-632-0922
- American Council for Health Education (brochures on headache types): 1-800-255-ACHE
- National Chronic Pain Outreach Assoc. (provides kit to develop local support group): 301-652-4948

SEE ALSO

- Easing an EARACHE (page 336)
- Healing HAY FEVER (page 342)
- Taming NECK AND SHOULDER TENSION (page 374)
- Releasing SINUS PRESSURE (page 392)
- Managing STRESS (page 406)

halting
hot flashes

halting
hot flashes

when symptoms may occur:

| During the night | In hot weather

*J*ust after being shampooed at a hair salon, I had a hot flash so intense that I glanced in the mirror to see if steam was rising from my head. Although the feeling was rather interesting, I decided to prevent further incidents as best I could.

Hot flashes are primarily caused by fluctuating hormonal production as the ovaries cease ovulating and estrogen levels drop. Stress, however, especially in headache-prone menopausal women, can also cause flashes. This happens because the hypothalamus, the part of the brain that controls heat production in the body, can stimulate a flash to warm the body when blood vessels in the brain dilate from a headache. Unmanaged stress also can lead to chronically low hormone levels, since stress prevents the adrenals from producing estrogen, a job they adopt as the ovaries slow their production of this hormone. This underproduction can result in moodiness, irritability, depression, fatigue, weight gain, insomnia, aged skin, headaches, and, of course, hot flashes. To prevent these symptoms, I have successfully adopted the remedies offered here.

relief at your fingertips

To help balance and increase hormone levels in the body, one option is a daily application of wild yam deep-tissue cream or gel to such soft tissue as the abdomen and below the armpits near the breasts. Wild yam contains phytohormone precursors, or plant forms of female hormones, which naturally support the body's own hormone production. There are a number of wild yam cream brands from which to choose, available at natural food stores and some pharmacies. For the best absorption, avoid brands containing mineral oil and petroleum products, opting for a brand containing ingredients such as aloe vera, jojoba oil, sunflower oil, safflower oil, vitamin E oil, wheat germ oil, or apricot kernel oil. Women report a feeling of rejuvenation free of side effects from applying wild yam cream on a regular basis.

TAKE ACTION

Exercise in the form of swimming, walking, yoga, tai chi, or light aerobics can help balance hormone production by stimulating the endocrine system. In addition, exercise helps to oxygenate and thus energize your body.

try a tea

Herbs such as wild yam and dong quai (the root of Chinese angelica), available at herb shops and natural food stores, contain plant forms of female hormones that can help to balance hormone production in the body. To make a tea of wild yam, combine 2 teaspoons of the dried herb in 1¼ cups of water and bring to a boil. Continue to boil until the liquid has been reduced to about ¾ cup, about 10 minutes. Discard the wild yam and sip. Dong quai can be prepared the same way, and if headaches or dizziness accompany the hot flashes, add a slice of soothing fresh ginger to the brew while boiling.

Although it is always prudent to check with a health professional before introducing a new substance into your body, especially if you are taking other medication, note that the suggested dose of both wild yam and dong quai tea is three ¾ cups a day. Alternatively, wild yam and dong quai, as well as other hormone-normalizing herbs such as black cohosh, Chinese licorice, and raspberry leaf, are available in capsule form, which should be taken according to manufacturer's instructions. Note that women with uterine fibroids should not take dong quai, as it may cause uterine bleeding.

To cool the skin, lessening the severity of hot flashes, drink peppermint or sage tea. To brew a cup of either, steep 1 teaspoon of the dried herb of choice in 1 cup of just-boiled water, covered, for 4 minutes, then sip. Peppermint works faster than sage, which begins its cooling action about 2 hours after ingestion. For that reason, if you suffer from night sweats, you may wish to sip sage tea before retiring. To infuse the peppermint and sage together, Egyptian style, combine a handful (about 1 cup) of each fresh herb with 4 cups of room-temperature water. Cover to keep out dust and let the tea steep overnight. In the morning, discard the herbs and sip the revitalizing beverage throughout the day.

If you're prone to hot flashes, buy a pretty hand fan to keep in your purse for emergencies. It is especially handy in crowded elevators.

Since stress may increase the frequency and intensity of hot flashes, it pays to manage it through meditation (see pages 6 and 136). Try a relaxation tape, available at music stores and natural food stores, featuring the soothing sound of ocean surf or tension-relieving tonal bells. You can also learn a meditation technique from an expert, in which case you should poll friends, contact Buddhist centers or centers for Transcendental Meditation, or enroll in classes to learn other meditation techniques.

making scents

Aromatherapists, who study the science of natural plant essences and how they affect our health, hold that the volatile oils in certain flowers and herbs contain phytohormones that can help balance hormones in the body. One such essence is from the tropical flower ylang-ylang. This essence has a deep, rich, floral aroma. To employ it, combine 25 drops of essential oil of ylang-ylang (available at herb shops and natural food stores) with 1/2 cup of distilled water. Pour the combination into a spray bottle and mist around your face and head when you feel overheated or hot-flashy. Take the bottle with you in the car, to work, on airplanes, or anywhere you go. Essential oil of rose geranium, which smells like a slightly lemony rose, can be enjoyed in the same way. For an astounding restorative, combine 12 drops of each essence in one spray bottle.

You may also wish to take an aromatherapy bath by adding 10 drops of either essence (or 5 of each) to warm bath water. Soak for about 15 minutes, relaxing, meditating, and inhaling the nourishing aroma.

best foods

Some experts feel that lack of magnesium may promote hot flashes. Therefore, eating such high-magnesium foods as mustard greens, dandelion, collards, kale, arugula, and prepared mustard is a good idea. Including 1/2 cup of the cooked greens or 1 cup of the raw salad greens in your diet each day may diminish hot flashes. Soybeans, avocado, black-eyed peas, and kidney beans are also good sources of magnesium. For the best results in avoiding hot flashes, refrain from ingesting dairy products, meat, refined sugar, caffeine, and alcohol, as these foods may cause hormonal swings.

smart supplements

Researchers report that 1,500 mg a day of evening primrose oil (especially when accompanied by the herb dong quai) may completely abate hot flashes. (Women with uterine fibroids should avoid dong quai, as it may aggravate the condition.) Vitamin C, taken in the form of 1 teaspoon of chavanprash (available at natural food stores and Indian markets) twice daily, may also help reduce the frequency of flashes. And to aid adrenal function, take 100 mg a day of B complex vitamins.

COOL RESOURCES
- The Monroe Institute (catalog of meditation tapes): 1-800-541-2488
- National Menopause Foundation (phone support; help in starting a local group): 1-800-MENOASK
- Bajamar Women's Health Care Pharmacy (provides alternatives to hormone replacement therapy): 1-800-255-8025

SEE ALSO
- Curing a HEADACHE (page 346)
- Eradicating IRRITABILITY (page 354)
- Managing STRESS (page 406)

cooling peppermint-mango mousse

MAKES 4 SERVINGS
102 calories per serving; no added fat

The mangoes and banana in this refreshing repast provide nondairy creaminess. And peppermint, when taken internally, cools the skin. The most decadent and flash-free way to enjoy this treat is while sharing a ylang-ylang bath (see page 352) with someone very close to you. For the quickest results, make the peppermint tea ice cubes ahead of time.

2 ripe mangoes

1/2 cup low-fat vanilla soy yogurt

1 small banana, peeled

3 ice cubes made from peppermint tea

fresh peppermint sprigs for garnish

PEEL THE MANGOES and slice right into a blender to catch all the juices. Add the soy yogurt, banana, and ice and process until smooth.

SCOOP THE MOUSSE into chilled dessert dishes and garnish with the mint.

IF THE WEATHER IS HOT AND/OR DRY:
Add 2 teaspoons of fresh lemon juice to the mixture before processing.

IF THE WEATHER IS COLD AND/OR DAMP:
Add 1 teaspoon of pure vanilla extract to the mixture before processing.

MORE RECIPES
FOR FLASHES

*Roasted Soy Nuts
(page 118)*

*Spinach Salad with
Tempeh Croutons
(page 190)*

*Lentil Salad with Red
Wine Vinaigrette
(page 192)*

eradicating irritability

eradicating irritability

when symptoms may occur:

| In very hot weather | At the change of seasons

*i*n Kuala Lumpur, Malaysia, I met a Buddhist monk who explained that since life is constantly changing, it's best to be an adaptable person. When we are at odds with the fluctuating rhythms of the world, we become frustrated and irritable. He then talked about a small sect of monks in India, called Avadhupta, who consult with nature to stay flexible and prevent irritability, advising that Westerners can easily adopt the practice. For instance, if your day is not going smoothly, instead of becoming irritated, take a lesson from a flowing stream that keeps on its course in spite of curves, rocks, and tight, narrow places. Or during a confrontation, grasp the wisdom of a bird in flight, who lands and waits for rough, windy weather to subside rather than flying against it.

Similarly, Chinese philosophy teaches us that a balanced attitude is a good way to achieve peace and harmony, since being locked into one way of thinking can cause irritability as life changes around us.

For example, during menopause some women become irritable, a symptom of changing hormone levels. But by adapting to menopause, finding out how best to work with our hormonal fluctuations, irritability can be prevented. Constipation is often a result of irritability, occurring when a person can't cope with change, literally becoming "stuck." Since even the most well-adjusted person gets off balance from time to time, here are some recommendations to help you work through irritable moments.

potent pose

One symptom of frustration and irritability is neck tension. To help relieve it, sit in a comfortable chair and get control of your breath, focusing on breathing from your diaphragm, deeply and slowly. When you're ready, inhale, scrunching your shoulders up around your neck. Hold the pose as long as you hold your breath, noting a warmth in the shoulders and lower neck. Exhale as if you were blowing out a candle, dropping your shoulders and releasing irritability and tension with your breath. You may repeat the pose as needed.

try a tea

In Chinese healing philosophy, in which conditions and their cures are categorized by energetics, irritability is considered a "warm" condition, comparable to the Western phrase "hot under the collar." To soothe such a warm condition, Chinese herbalists recommend cooling teas such as hibiscus and peppermint. Technically, these herbs are refrigerants, or substances that when taken internally actually refresh the body by cooling the skin. Hibiscus gives brewed teas a lovely magenta hue; consequently, it's one of the most common ingredients in commercial herbal tea blends. Look for it on labels at supermarkets or natural food stores, along with other supporting herbs such as lemongrass and rosehips. Drink such teas at room temperature or slightly chilled. You can make your own peppermint tea by steeping 4 teaspoons of the dried herb in 4 cups of just-boiled water, covered, for 4 minutes. Strain and allow to cool to room temperature, or enjoy slightly chilled.

making scents

Aromatherapists, who study how natural scents affect our moods, recommend essential oil of lavender to ease irritability. For emergencies, use the essence (available at herb shops and natural food stores) by dotting 2 drops on a tissue and inhaling deeply for 1 full minute. You can also inhale the essence while meditating, either by

VOCABULARY LESSON

The next time you're faced with a new concept, to stay flexible and avoid irritability, replace such phrases as "I can't," "I don't know how," and "I won't" with the words "I'll try."

CHANGE YOUR MIND

Regular meditation (see pages 6 or 136) can help you to become more flexible, since it gently shifts your view of the world to allow for more open thinking. The next time you feel irritated, instead of doing what you usually do, try quietly sitting in a chair, eyes closed, breathing fully, while you feel/think the word "cool" for 5 minutes.

employing the tissue method or by filling an essential oil diffuser (available at herb shops and natural food stores) with the lavender to create a peaceful atmosphere throughout the room. For an aromatherapy combination, essential oils of bergamot (orangy) and ylang-ylang (richly floral) may be balancing when you're hot, tired, and cranky. Use them in the same ways as the lavender, or combine 5 drops of each with 2 tablespoons of unscented body lotion and rub your arms and hands with the pleasing mixture.

best foods

FAST FIX

For a quick anti-irritant, pop a cooling, rejuvenating peppermint candy into your mouth.

According to Western experts, a diet deficient in magnesium and calcium may aggravate irritability-based conditions. Foods high in calcium include broccoli, kale, collards, turnip greens, mustard greens, and soybeans. Soybeans are also a good source of magnesium, as are black-eyed peas, avocado, kidney beans, lima beans, prepared mustard, and banana. To soothe irritability Chinese style, eat such "heat-clearing," cooling foods as cucumber or restorative sweet fruits like mango, papaya, plum, peach, or nectarine.

Both Eastern and Western schools of thought agree that caffeine, alcohol, and highly salty prepared foods and junk foods may trigger an irritable mood.

HARMONIOUS RESOURCES
· The Monroe Institute (catalog of meditation tapes): 1-800-541-2488
· The Aromatherapy Catalog (essential oils): 1-800-898-PURE

SEE ALSO
· Adjusting ANXIETY (page 296)
· Calming CAFFEINE TREMORS (page 308)
· Correcting CONSTIPATION (page 317)
· Curing a HEADACHE (page 346)
· Halting HOT FLASHES (page 350)
· Taming NECK AND SHOULDER TENSION (page 374)
· Securing SOUND SLEEP (page 402)
· Managing STRESS (page 406)

rasayana for irritability

MAKES ABOUT 20 (1-TABLESPOON) SERVINGS

25 calories per serving: no added fat

A *rasayana* is an Ayurvedic rejuvenating tonic made from foods and herbs, prepared specifically for a particular condition. In this rasayana, cooling fruits and spices combine to restore inner harmony.

2 oranges, peeled, seeded, and chopped
(including juice)

2 plums, pitted and chopped

4 dried figs, finely chopped

1 tablespoon pure maple syrup

1/4 cup lemon juice

seeds of 2 cardamom pods, crushed

pinch of saffron threads

COMBINE ALL OF the ingredients in a saucepan and bring to a boil. Reduce the heat and simmer, stirring frequently, until the rasayana is fragrant and the consistency of a fruit preserve, about 15 minutes. Let the rasayana cool, then store in a covered jar in the refrigerator, where it will keep for about 3 weeks. To use it, spread 1 tablespoon of the mixture on toast or a muffin or enjoy the tonic right off the spoon.

IF THE WEATHER IS HOT AND/OR DRY:
Use chopped fresh figs instead of dried.

IF THE WEATHER IS COLD AND/OR DAMP:
Swirl 1 tablespoon of the rasayana into cooked oatmeal before enjoying.

MORE RECIPES
FOR ERADICATING
IRRITABILITY

Broccoli with Black Bean Sauce (page 163)

Plum and Pear Compote (page 269)

Cool Melon Ice (page 274)

overcoming jet lag

overcoming
jet lag

when symptoms may occur:

| Morning (grogginess and dizziness) | Mid-afternoon (sleepiness) | Night (inappropriate body temperature and wakefulness) |

*t*he worst case of jet lag I ever had was during a one-week trip to Hong Kong. Between the 16-hour flight, the 12-hour time change, and the short duration of my stay, my body never had a chance to adjust to Hong Kong time before I hauled it onto another plane to fly back home, halfway around the world. I was groggy, irritable, achy, awoke during the night, and experienced digestive distress and hot and cold flashes. I then resolved to devise a plan that conquered jet lag, a task that took me 12 years.

Early discoveries taught me that keeping hydrated while flying averted digestive distress, dry skin, and grogginess upon arrival, so I drink one 8-ounce glass of water for each hour I fly. I bring my own six-pack or two for long flights, avoiding airplane water. My other time-tested jet lag preventatives are offered here, but the most important finding was one I learned on a recent flight from Los Angeles to

Philadelphia. Seated next to a therapist, I listened while she told me that her doctor recommended she take a homeopathic formula called radium bromatum, one pill dissolved under the tongue, four times a day the day before travel, the day of travel, and the day after travel. In addition, she was instructed to take a warm Epsom salt bath before retiring on her first and second nights, adding about 1/2 cup of salts to the tub. Epsom salts, her doctor maintains, help to eliminate any toxins that may prevent the homeopathic remedy from working. Excited to explore these new possibilities, I supplied my husband with the radium bromatum and Epsom salts for a one-week trip he took to the Philippines. Following the instructions, he slept straight through the night he arrived (and subsequent nights), despite the 13-hour time change, was alert in the mornings, experienced no dizziness, and had normal body temperatures throughout the trip. He did report, however, that he fell asleep by nine o'clock each night, a small price to pay for such pleasing results. If you wish to try this method yourself, note that homeopathic medications work best without interference from peppermint (including peppermint-flavored toothpaste and mouthwash) and caffeine, which may block absorption.

potent poses

Stretching your body during an airplane flight oxygenates tissues and stimulates circulation, thus helping to prevent achy joints and muscles, constipation, headaches, and fatigue. Try this easy and invigorating stretch while seated: lacing your hands together in front of your body, straighten your arms, palms up, stretching them overhead, and breathe for three full, deep breaths. To intensify the pose, while your arms are overhead, flex and point your feet and keep your abdominal muscles tight. As you resume a normal position, note the energizing feeling gently streaming through you. Perform this stretch at least once an hour or as needed.

To keep your back limber, try to fly in business class or first class because the seats in those sections are orthopedically designed for good support and have comfortable foot rests. If you are flying in coach, where the seats are less thoughtfully designed, ask for a pillow to prop between your lower back and the seat for lumbar support. Then, once an hour, stand up and stretch side to side from your waist. Inhaling, bend forward from the waist, letting your arms drop loosely and stretching out your lower back. Tightening your abdominal muscles as you are stretching will magnify the stretch. Straighten up as you exhale.

Some airlines offer in-flight stretching videos prior to landing, and following along helps increase alertness upon arrival. Also be sure to check the in-flight entertainment guide, as many airlines now offer an audio channel entirely dedicated to meditation. Recently, on a trip to England, I enjoyed two hours of gently bubbling streams and tingling chimes, arriving at Heathrow airport for a most mellow passage through immigration and London's morning rush hour.

IT'S ALL TIMING

On long flights, such as those to Europe, Asia, or Africa, I always try to arrive in the morning. Having slept on the flight, upon landing I am revived and ready to start the day.

try a tea

Chinese licorice root contains compounds that make it a hydration tonic for the entire body. Buy thin slices of the dried root at Chinese markets or herb shops and add 1 slice to 8 ounces of room-temperature water. Before take-off, I drop a slice into each of my 8-ounce water bottles, making cold tea infusions as the trip continues. Because licorice can be hypertensive, those with high blood pressure should avoid it, opting for plain water instead.

If you tend to retain water, dehydration is not your problem and you should avoid licorice. Instead, take along a quart of parsley tea, which contains compounds that make it a natural diuretic. To make it, steep 4 teaspoons of dried parsley in 4 cups of just-boiled water, covered, for 4 minutes. Then strain, let cool, and bottle. Some people who normally don't retain water may find their hands and feet swelling on a long flight, sometimes from eating an overly salty meal. In that case, ask the cabin attendant for a couple of sprigs of fresh parsley to eat, and drink plenty of fresh water to flush the salt from your system.

making scents

To avoid catching colds, coughs, and other viruses while flying, I make an anti-infective, antiviral spray by combining 25 drops of essential oil of lavender (available at herb shops and natural food stores) and ½ cup of distilled water in a spray bottle. I spray my seat before I sit down and mist my face and head throughout the trip. As well as keeping me healthy, the lavender spray has a hydrating and softening effect on my complexion.

best foods

I avoid unnecessary dehydration by eliminating alcohol, coffee, tea, colas, salty peanuts and other snack foods, and salty cheeses and meats. I usually pack my own freshly peeled grapefruit and orange sections, since I find citrus to be extremely hydrating. In addition, I order a vegetarian meal when I purchase my tickets because the low-fat water-rich veggies are a hedge against fatigue, dry skin, and constipation. Since my requested meals do not always appear, however, I try to bring along such steamed vegetables as asparagus, broccoli, snow peas, and carrots packed in tightly sealed plastic bags. Green salads with light dressings are also a good food choice for flying, but avoid iceberg lettuce, which can give you gas.

RESOURCES FOR FLYERS

- · International Travelers Health Institute (investigates health problems): 212-737-7380
- · The Monroe Institute (catalog of meditation tapes): 1-800-541-2488
- · Arrowroot Natural Pharmacy (homeopathic preparations): 1-800-234-8879
- · International Foundation of Homeopathy (answers questions): 206-324-8230
- · The Aromatherapy Catalog (essential oils): 1-800-898-PURE

SEE ALSO

- · Lulling LOW BACK PAIN (page 362)
- · Taming NECK AND SHOULDER TENSION (page 374)
- · Negotiating the NIGHT SHIFT (page 377)
- · Surmounting SORE MUSCLES (page 399)
- · Securing SOUND SLEEP (page 402)
- · Managing STRESS (page 406)
- · Alleviating WATER RETENTION (page 418)

lulling low back pain

*a*t a recent lecture, a man in his early twenties asked me what to do about his chronic lower back pain. When I explained the importance of drinking eight 8-ounce glasses of water a day to lubricate the spinal column; sitting in straight-backed chairs with knees bent above hip level; wearing sturdy shoes; and partaking in such exercises as walking swimming, biking, yoga and tai chi (avoiding twisting exercises such as golf and strenuous weight lifting), the man responded in amazement, saying that he previously had heard only of drugs and surgery as options for his complaint.

The fact that Americans spend $80 billion a year on drugs and surgery to treat back complaints, and that one in four people still suffer, has led some physicians to look to forms of therapy such as the ones I mentioned to the aforementioned young man. They also recommend sleeping on a firm mattress and sleeping on your back (with a pillow under your knees) or on your side with bent knees, since sleeping on the stomach may aggravate an already sore back. Although other suggestions follow, if your back pain is accompanied by digestive distress, numbness, or muscle weakness, or moves into the legs, consult a health professional.

relief at your fingertips

The flowers of the herb Saint-John's-wort contain hypericin, a natural topical muscle relaxant that can temporarily soothe pain in the lower back. Buy Saint-John's-wort oil or balm at natural food stores or herb shops, and rub it on as needed. Heat, in the form of a heating pad or towel dipped in hot water and wrung out before applying, helps relax tight lower back muscles and also intensifies the healing properties of Saint-John's-wort. Many people rub on Saint-John's-wort prior to exercise or take it to a massage therapist to apply during treatment.

To make your own low back reviver, grate 2 tablespoons of fresh ginger and squeeze the gratings into a small bowl to get about 1 teaspoon of ginger juice. Stir in an equal amount of olive oil or canola oil and rub the mixture on your sore back. The ginger increases circulation to the area, helping to temporarily relieve the pain.

SEEK A PRO

Chiropractors work by adjusting the spine into proper alignment, which can prevent and cure many kinds of lower back pain. To find a chiropractor, ask friends or see the resources.

potent pose

Gently stretching the lower back helps to relax tight muscles. To try it, lie on the floor on your back, legs straight and arms extended to each side. Bend and lift your left knee and slowly move it toward your right elbow, twisting your lower back as far as you can *comfortably* go. The movement originates from your lower back, which may pop and crack a bit, but that's okay. Once you've gone as far as you can go, close your eyes and breathe into the stretch for about one minute. Some people report a clearing and openness in the lungs during this time. When you've finished, very slowly return your leg to its original position and repeat the move with the right knee. Perform this pose at least three times a day or as needed. If sharp pain or discomfort occurs, discontinue the stretch and consult a health professional.

BAN THE BELLY

A pot belly puts strain on the lower back, causing unnecessary pain. To avoid it, first of all, don't overeat. Secondly, tighten the muscles in your gut by doing abdominal crunches. These are similar to sit-ups, but the knees are bent to put less strain on the lower back. And saying you don't have time for a tighter tummy is no excuse. Tightening your abdominal muscles as hard as you can for 10 seconds is equal to one crunch and can be done on the subway, waiting in line at the supermarket, while driving, or while watching television.

try a tea

German herbalists recommend burdock, echinacea, chamomile, and nettle for pain in the lower back, as each contains compounds that soothe inflammation. Burdock, available in dried root form from natural food stores and herb shops, is best during hot weather, since it can be cooling to the body. Three times a day make a cup by combining 1 teaspoon of chopped dried root with 1¼ cups of water and boiling to reduce to 1 cup for 10 minutes. Then strain and sip. Echinacea, which can be drunk in any season, is brewed the same way. For chamomile or nettle, steep 1 teaspoon of the dried herb in 1 cup of just-boiled water, covered, for 4 minutes. The nettle is slightly stimulating and is best taken in the morning. But since it is hypertensive, if you have high blood pressure, opt for the more relaxing chamomile tea.

homeopathic healers

Some doctors recommend the following homeopathic medications, taken orally, to soothe sore backs. Homeopathic medicines, which are minute doses of plant and other natural substances, are available at natural food stores and pharmacies, or consult the sources at the end of this section.

·   For muscular spasms and stabbing pains: Bryonia
·   For rainy weather pains: Rhododendron
·   For rheumatic pain and pain at night: Colchicum

RECIPES FOR A
HEALTHY LOWER
BACK

*Spinach Gazpacho with
Fresh Basil (page 212)*

*Millet Croquettes with
Warm Onion Relish
(page 224)*

*Barley with Sun-dried
Tomatoes, Mushrooms,
and Pine Nuts
(page 226)*

best foods

Since both calcium and the B vitamins are needed to relieve tension in muscles, adding them to your diet can help soothe your sore lower back. For calcium, eat broccoli, kale, collards, turnip greens, sardines, and soybeans. B vitamins are present in whole grains such as brown rice, barley, millet, and whole wheat, as well as in salmon, chickpeas, soybeans, black-eyed peas, and spinach. Spices such as cayenne pepper may also help ease back pain by increasing circulation. Some experts recommend avoiding such nightshade vegetables as tomatoes, peppers, white potatoes, and eggplant because the solanine they contain may aggravate a sore lower back. Meat, which contains uric acid, may do the same.

RESOURCES TO EASE LOW BACK PAIN
- · Arrowroot Natural Pharmacy (homeopathic preparations): 1-800-234-8879
- · The American Chiropractic Association (referrals): 703-276-8800
- · The American Massage Therapy Association (referrals): 708-864-0123
- · Gaia Herbs (catalog of botanical preparations): 508-772-5400
- · Back Pain Hotline (advice): 1-800-247-BACK

SEE ALSO

mending menstrual cramps

mending menstrual cramps

when symptoms may occur:

| In the afternoon or night, especially if accompanied by a headache | At the change of seasons |

a Brazilian woman I interviewed said she liked getting her menstrual period, found the changes interesting and womanly, and anticipated missing it when menopause began. She was therefore shocked to learn that half of the women with whom I spoke on the subject spend a day or two in bed each month, medicated, because of menstrual cramps.

One cause of cramps may be the release of hormone-like prostaglandins, which stimulate contractions in the uterus, combined with dilation of the cervix. Other factors, such as unmanaged stress, pelvic tension, lack of exercise, depression, and anxiety about menstruation in the first place, may intensify the condition. Cramps may be accompanied by insomnia, water retention, and skin breakouts. The ideas that follow can help prevent and cure such symptoms, especially if they are employed as part of a comprehensive plan. In other words, a preventative diet, exercise, self-massage, and appropriate teas support the body as a group, making a more potent treatment. Note, however, that if painful cramps and increased bleeding begin after years of normal menstruation, you should see a health professional.

relief at your fingertips

At the very onset of cramps, Chinese doctors recommend pressing this pair of pain-soothing points, called Crossroads of the Three Yins. Briskly rub your hands together for about 10 seconds. Then, placing a thumb on each inner ankle bone, run the thumbs up the sides of your shin bones about 4 or 5 inches, until you come to a notch in the bone. It will feel sensitive, and that's okay. Press firmly in small circular motions for about 2 minutes, eyes closed and breathing deeply. One way these points may work is by releasing tension in what the Chinese believe are the nerve channels to and from the uterus. To intensify the treatment, put a hot-water bag on your abdomen and repeat the massage at 5-minute intervals until the cramps have subsided.

A massage therapist in England taught me to use another set of anticramp points by placing the tip of each index finger between each big and second toe, pressing up and back firmly. Breathing deeply helps negate sensitivity in the area. Hold the points for 2 minutes, noting a more open feeling in the lower back and pelvis as you release the points. The toe points may be repeated as needed.

A different way to manage menstrual cramps is to rub on a wild yam cream twice a day. Wild yam, which contains a plant form of female hormone, helps to regulate hormone levels in the body when rubbed into soft areas such as the belly and under the arms at the edge of the breasts. The cream is available at natural food stores and some pharmacies and comes in different forms. The best ones contain nut or seed oils, aloe vera, vitamin E, and no mineral oil or petroleum products.

try a tea

Dong quai, the root of the Chinese angelica plant, contains volatile oils that act as natural pain relievers. To make an anticramp tea, steep 1 teaspoon of finely chopped dried root (available at natural food stores, herb shops, and Chinese markets) in 1 cup of just-boiled water, covered, for 4 minutes. Then strain and sip up to three times a day as needed. If dizziness accompanies the cramps, add a thin slice of fresh ginger to the tea while steeping. Note that women with uterine fibroids should avoid dong quai, as it may aggravate the condition.

COMBATING CRAMPS

The root of the black cohosh plant has been used for centuries by many North American Indian tribes to soothe menstrual cramps. It contains aspirin-like compounds that prevent pain, as well as plant forms of hormones that help balance the body. Buy it in capsule or liquid tincture form at natural food stores, herb shops, and some pharmacies and take as directed. Black cohosh comes in tea form, but the taste is awful, so avoid it.

making scents

Essential oil of clary sage (*Salvia sclarea*, not common sage) is often prescribed by German herbalists to treat menstrual cramps and related female complaints. Available at herb shops and natural food stores, clary smells like a slightly tobacco-ish common sage. It is used by combining 5 drops of essential oil with 1 teaspoon of canola oil and rubbing the mixture into the abdomen once a day in the morning. One reason clary sage may work to soothe menstrual cramps is that it contains plant forms of hormones, which may help balance hormonal levels in the body. Another plus is that clary's warm, balancing aroma helps lift the moodiness that some women experience.

MONTHLY HARMONY

Some women report success in alleviating menstrual cramps by taking the appropriate homeopathic medications (minute doses of healing plants and other material in tiny pellet form). For menstrual cramps associated with headaches, for instance, a health professional might recommend a homeopathic preparation of magnesia phosphorica, available at natural food stores, herb shops, and some supermarkets, or see the resources below. Note that homeopathic medications work best when you eliminate peppermint (including mint-flavored toothpaste and mouthwash) and caffeine from your life, as these substances may block absorption.

best foods

To help prevent and soothe cramps, about 10 days before menstruation, eat foods that contain the minerals calcium and magnesium. Good food sources of calcium include sardines, canned salmon with bones, broccoli, okra, and scallops. A tablespoon of dillseed contains about 100 mg of calcium, so add it to salad dressings and soups. Dried nettle, which contains about 175 mg of calcium per tablespoon, is a parsley-like addition to stews and sauces. To obtain magnesium, eat soybeans, avocado, black-eyed peas, kidney beans, and lentils. Dark leafy greens such as collards, bok choy, kale, and mustard greens contain both calcium and magnesium. As a bonus, magnesium in these forms may help keep you slim, since some experts believe that the chocolate cravings associated with PMS are caused by lack of the mineral. Avoiding high-sodium junk foods, caffeine, alcohol, meat, and dairy products may also help banish menstrual cramps.

smart supplement

For the best absorption, take combined calcium-magnesium supplements with your evening meal. Look for calcium from a "citrate" source, which is less likely to cause digestive distress. If you are off dairy products, buy a supplement that contains no milk or whey. Natural food stores and some pharmacies offer such supplements.

RESOURCES FOR CRAMP-FREE DAYS AND NIGHTS
- *The Complete Guide to Exercise Videos* (over 250 workout tapes): 1-800-433-6769
- Arrowroot Natural Pharmacy (homeopathic preparations): 1-800-234-8879
- Bajamar Women's Health Care Pharmacy (homeopathic preparations): 1-800-255-8025
- PMS Access (information and support groups): 1-800-222-4767
- American College of Obstetricians and Gynecologists Resource Center (answers questions): 1-800-673-8444
- National Women's Health Resource Center (information and self-help group referral): 202-293-6045

SEE ALSO
- Banishing BREAKOUTS AND RASHES (page 304)
- Disarming DEPRESSION (page 324)
- Curing a HEADACHE (page 346)
- Eradicating IRRITABILITY (page 354)
- Securing SOUND SLEEP (page 402)
- Managing STRESS (page 406)
- Alleviating WATER RETENTION (page 418)

MORE RECIPES TO
COMBAT CRAMPS

*Roasted Soy Nuts
(page 118)*

*Collards with Black
Pepper and Red Wine
(page 169)*

*Soft Tacos with Spicy
Summer Vegetables
(page 244)*

roasted vidalia onions with collard puree

MAKES 4 SERVINGS

233 calories per serving: 1 gram fat: 4% calories from fat

Each serving of this dish contains about 500 mg of calcium, helpful in preventing menstrual cramps as well as soothing the nerves.

4 large Vidalia onions, peeled

1/2 cup vegetable stock

2 10-ounce packages frozen collard greens, thawed and drained

1 tablespoon minced fresh thyme or 1 1/2 teaspoons dried

1 tablespoon dried nettle (see The Savory Pantry, page 424)

1 clove garlic, finely minced

4 ounces nonfat soy mozzarella, grated

2 tablespoons bread crumbs

about 1 teaspoon olive oil

PREHEAT THE OVEN to 450°F.

CUT A SLICE off the bottom of the onions so they can sit without rolling. Using a melon baller, scoop out the insides of each onion, leaving about a 1/4-inch-thick shell.

CHOP THE SCOOPED-OUT parts and place in a large sauté pan with the stock. Simmer for about 5 minutes, or until the onion has wilted.

SCOOP THE MIXTURE into a processor, whizzing until pureed, adding the collards, thyme, nettle, garlic, cheese, and bread crumbs halfway through. Using a teaspoon, pack the puree into the onion shells. (If there is leftover puree, place it in a small baking dish.) Lightly rub each onion shell with olive oil and set in a lightly oiled baking dish. Bake both dishes, uncovered, until the onions are fragrant and roasted, 20 to 25 minutes. Serve warm.

IF THE WEATHER IS HOT AND/OR DRY:
Before serving, top each onion with minced fresh tomatoes.

IF THE WEATHER IS COLD AND/OR DAMP:
Increase the garlic to 2 cloves and sprinkle the puree with freshly ground black pepper before packing into the onion shells.

negating nausea and morning sickness

when symptoms may occur:

In the morning

On a choppy flight from Amman, Jordan, to the Gulf of Aqaba, the cabin attendant gave me a teaspoon of pale green fennel seeds to chew to deter nausea. The bright licorice taste was refreshing, and the cure was successful. In Aqaba I discovered that fennel is an ancient Unani, or Middle Eastern, herbal remedy for nausea and indigestion; the seeds contain volatile oils that have an antispasmodic, soothing effect on digestion and equilibrium.

Besides motion sickness, nausea, which is an extreme feeling of imbalance and disharmony, can come from a virus, narcotics, inner ear trouble, alcohol abuse, antibiotics, chemotherapy, sinus pressure, arthritis medications, migraine headaches, indigestion, diabetes, pregnancy, and unmanaged stress. If nausea lasts for more than a few days or is accompanied by diarrhea, headache, or severe digestive distress, see a health professional. But for light cases, try these comforting cures.

relief at your fingertips

To avert motion-induced nausea, before you travel, put on a pair of accupressure wrist bands, available at pharmacies. Inside each band is a round bead that stimulates a point on each wrist, preventing motion sickness, air sickness, sea sickness, and even morning sickness. I now carry a pair with me at all times, and they keep me on an even keel during airplane flights, boat trips, and long car trips.

potent pose

Some experts say that nausea can occasionally be a conditioned response. For instance, chemotherapy patients may become nauseated before they even get to the hospital, merely from recalling how the treatment made them sick in the past. In such cases, a technique called Progressive Muscle Relaxation Therapy seems to help. Those with any type of nausea, including morning sickness, can try it.

Sitting in a comfortable chair, close your eyes, breathing deeply and fully. Continuing to breathe, flex and tighten your abdominal muscles for 10 seconds. Upon release of the muscles, look for a clear, balanced feeling starting in the abdomen and easing up to the crown of the head. Repeat the exercise until the nausea is gone. Along with Progressive Muscle Relaxation, guided imagery may be helpful in breaking the nausea pattern, particularly for chemotherapy patients. For a simple example, picture yourself in the hospital without the chemotherapy and nausea, having a pleasant time.

try a tea

Ginger tea is an effective remedy for the nausea caused by motion sickness, morning sickness, and flu. In one motion sickness study, 90 percent of the people who used ginger were free from nausea when they took 2 to 4 capsules of the dried herb before traveling in a car, boat, plane, or train. Ginger capsules (each containing 125 mg of ginger), which are available at natural food stores and herb shops, can be broken open and swirled into a cup of hot water to make tea. For morning sickness, it's best to take the tea before getting out of bed, mixing 3 capsules into 1 cup of hot water. Four to 6 capsules are often recommended to avert nausea from stomach flu, but since doses vary with the individual, check with a health professional about what's right for you.

A peppermint-chamomile combo tea can also banish nausea. The herbs contain volatile oil compounds that have what herbalists call "smooth muscle activity," or in this case, a relaxing effect on the stomach and abdominal muscles. To make the tea, steep 1 teaspoon each of dried peppermint and chamomile in 1 cup of just-boiled water, covered, for 4 minutes. Then sip.

GO FOR GINKGO

Studies from England, France, and Germany show that extract of the herb ginkgo can help reduce dizziness by increasing blood flow to the brain. Ginkgo, available at natural food stores and herb shops, should indicate on the label that it is "standardized to contain 24% ginkgo flavoglycosides," and the standard dosage is 40 mg three times a day. Since ginkgo may increase blood pressure levels, those with hypertension should check with a health professional before taking the herb.

making scents

Essential oil of basil, available at herb shops and natural food stores, contains antispasmodic properties that can help soothe nausea. For the quickest cure, dot 2 drops of the essence on a tissue and inhale until you feel stable. Ayurvedic Indian herbalists say that basil gives us *sattva*, or harmony, precisely what we need when imbalanced by nausea.

best foods

Warm, clear liquids, such as tea or vegetable stock, accompanied by plain crackers, are tonifying without being taxing to a nauseated system. Avoid chocolate, greasy foods, dairy products, and alcohol, which can aggravate the condition.

RECIPES TO NEGATE NAUSEA

Spring Vegetable Stock (page 202)

Winter Vegetable Stock (page 203)

RESOURCES FOR PREVENTING NAUSEA

- Be Healthy, Inc.: Positive Pregnancy and Parenting Fitness (catalog with informational materials): 1-800-433-5523 (in Conn., 203-822-8573)
- American Cancer Society (information for cancer patients going through chemotherapy): 404-320-3333
- Gaia Herbs (catalog of botanical products): 508-772-5400

SEE ALSO

- Easing an EARACHE (page 336)
- Curing a HEADACHE (page 346)
- Mending MENSTRUAL CRAMPS (page 366)
- Releasing SINUS PRESSURE (page 392)
- Managing STRESS (page 406)
- Settling an UPSET STOMACH (page 415)

taming neck and shoulder tension

S ome time ago, I consulted a doctor about loss of range of motion in my neck, as well as neck and shoulder tension. He told me that my head was like a bowling ball supported by a broomstick neck, a seemingly unwieldy structure. My broomstick was slightly curved in the wrong direction, the result of what at the time had seemed an inconsequential automobile accident. As a result, the doctor said, I had the neck of a 90-year-old arthritic woman.

My plan for healing began with chiropractic sessions three times a week for four weeks to realign my head, neck, and shoulders. These adjustments did not correct the curve but served to prevent further degeneration. After the four-week intensive, however, I had regained complete range of motion in my neck. In addition, I began to hold one-pound hand weights while doing my usual light aerobics, to help tone the muscles in my neck and shoulders. I also tried a special bone-shaped neck pillow to take stress off my neck while sleeping. (Although this pillow soothed my neck, I did not continue using it, since sleeping with my head in such a tipped manner tends to make me awaken with bags under my eyes.) I now use a firm regular pillow and sleep on my back, resting my shoulders, neck, and head on the pillow for support. Massage therapy sessions once a week (with a doctor's note, my insurance company helps with payments) relieve tension in my neck and shoulder area, as do these palliative pointers.

relief at your fingertips

To reduce pain and tension temporarily in the neck and shoulders, apply a penetrating rub that works by stimulating circulation and increasing blood supply, thereby soothing inflammation. Buy a menthol- or camphor-based potion at a pharmacy or natural food store. Or try a boswellia cream, made from a relative of the herb frankincense; menthol, from mint; and capsaicin, from hot peppers. To apply these creams and lotions, use your right hand to rub the left side of your neck and left shoulder, then use your left hand to treat the right side. In an emergency, simply use your hands to rub the areas, and the warmth will be soothing.

potent pose

A chiropractor taught me to do a daily exercise that, over the years, has helped strengthen and tonify my neck and shoulders. To try it, lie on the bed on your back, neck and head hanging down and off the bed. Firmly press your shoulder blades into the bed. Inhaling, lift your head, chin aiming for your chest, as far as you can go. Exhaling, slowly release your head to the hanging position. Repeat the exercise four times, for a total of five. Pause briefly and repeat five more times. Then lie on your stomach and perform a "counterpose" by raising your head up and down. If the exercise is difficult in the beginning, just do as many repetitions as you feel comfortable with, building up gradually. For extra support, engage your abdominal muscles while lifting your head.

In an emergency, for temporary relief of acute neck and shoulder tension, stuff a sock with two tennis balls, tying a knot so the balls don't roll around. Lying on your back on the floor, position the sock so that a ball is on either side of your center neck bone. Lifting your knees, feet on the floor, rock your rear up and back, rolling the balls as you go so that they automatically massage the neck and shoulder area. Repeat this appeasing pose as needed. Take the sock to work and you can soothe a tense neck and shoulders any time of the day.

try a tea

Advocated by some French herbalists, chamomile and linden flower (lime flower or tilia) each contain compounds that act as mild nervines, helping to calm a tense neck and shoulders. (The herbs are available at natural food stores and herb shops.) To make a tea, steep 1 teaspoon of dried linden flower in 1 cup of just-boiled water, covered, for 5 minutes; then add 1 teaspoon of dried chamomile flower and continue to steep for an additional 4 minutes. Drink the tea warm as needed.

PILLOW TALK

For neck and shoulder support, it's best to sleep on your back, using a firm pillow. But if you're a side sleeper, a medium pillow is for you. If you sleep on your stomach, a soft pillow will put the least strain on your neck and shoulders.

LOOKING UP

If you work at a computer, position the screen so that your chin is slightly elevated. Looking down at the screen places stress on the neck and shoulders.

For temporary pain relief, Navajo, Pima, Papago, and Hopi herbalists recommend the root of the black cohosh plant, available at herb shops and natural food stores. Classified as a nonsteroidal anti-inflammatory, black cohosh is best taken in tincture form, one eyedropper (about 28 drops) in ¼ cup of any kind of tea, and swallowed quickly. Black cohosh tea is available to brew but the taste is awful, so stick with the tincture.

As a tonic, Ayurvedic herbalists advise taking ginkgo biloba, available at natural food stores and herb shops. Buy ginkgo capsules or tincture, making sure the label says "standardized to contain 24% ginkgo flavoglycosides." Add the product as directed on the label to a cup of warm tea. (Standard dosage of ginkgo is 40 mg three times a day.) Though not an anti-inflammatory, ginkgo increases circulation, which may help to ease your pain. Note, however, that since ginkgo may be hypertensive, those with high blood pressure should check with a health professional before imbibing.

best foods

Foods containing anti-inflammatory compounds, such as alfalfa sprouts, dark leafy greens, and turmeric (the spice that makes curries yellow) may help to soothe neck and shoulder discomfort temporarily.

RECIPES FOR A
RELAXED NECK AND
SHOULDERS

*Broccoli with Black Bean
Sauce (page 163)*

*Grilled Tofu with Indian
Curry Paste and Mixed
Greens (page 233)*

In addition, foods high in calcium and magnesium may help to relax your neck and shoulders, since studies show that people with this condition tend to be deficient in these particular nutrients. For calcium, add broccoli, collards, turnip greens, mustard greens, and sardines to your daily diet, and to increase magnesium, eat soybeans, avocado, black-eyed peas, lima beans, and lentils. A "clean" diet consisting of fresh fruits and vegetables is important, because it helps ensure that your body will absorb these essential nutrients. Coffee, alcohol, fatty meats, excessive white flour, refined sugar, and fried foods may block absorption. In addition, ingesting these foods can deplete B vitamins, leading to stress and tension. Meditating or relaxing before you eat may also help with nutrient absorption, since stress weakens the body's ability to assimilate vitamins and minerals. For meditation tips, see pages 6 and 136, buy a relaxation tape at a music store, or check the sources. Regular meditation can also help you manage stress, thus taking the load off of tense neck and shoulders.

RESOURCES FOR A RELAXED NECK AND SHOULDERS
  · *The Complete Guide to Exercise Videos* (over 250 selections): 1-800-433-6769
  · The American Chiropractic Association (referrals): 703-276-8800
  · The American Massage Therapy Association (referrals): 708-864-0123
  · The Monroe Institute (catalog of meditation tapes): 1-800-541-2488

SEE ALSO
  · Easing ARTHRITIS PAIN (page 289)
  · Curing a HEADACHE (page 346)
  · Lulling LOW BACK PAIN (page 362)
  · Managing STRESS (page 406)

negotiating the night shift

a cardiologist recalled to me his resident years, working nights, sometimes on duty for 36 hours straight. It's like having constant jet lag, he said, not imagining anything else that could bring such discord to a person's natural rhythms.

Despite the disharmony, more than 20 million Americans are on the night shift, including new moms, factory workers, truck drivers, nurses, and cops. And though night shift work can cause irritability and other emotional problems, as well as poor work performance (the accidents at Chernobyl and Three Mile Island both occurred on the night shift), much effort is being made to make shift workers more comfortable. For example, one study of police officers showed that clockwise shift rotation was easier than counterclockwise, and law enforcement agencies as well as factories have taken the cue. Some factories have gone a step further, illuminating the workplace at night with full-spectrum lights to increase on-the-job alertness and decrease worker depression. If your job requires you to be at peak performance when most of the neighborhood is asleep, and if you must sleep while others are wide awake, try these tips.

try a tea

To be clear-headed at work, you may wish to drink Chinese (Panax) ginseng tea before you go. Ginseng, available at herb shops, natural food stores, and Asian markets, contains saponin compounds that work at a deep internal level to conserve and generate energy. You can buy teabags or packets of dried ginseng and brew them according to the instructions on the package. Make extra tea to pour into a thermos and take to work to sip on the job. Note that since ginseng can be hypertensive, those with high blood pressure should avoid it. Alternatively, drink an energizing peppermint-thyme tea by steeping 1 teaspoon of each dried herb in 2 cups of just-boiled water, covered, for 4 minutes. Then strain and sip a cup, putting the rest in a thermos to take to work.

If sleeping while the rest of the family is awake is a problem, steep 1 teaspoon each of valerian root, skullcap, and passionflower (available at herb shops and natural food stores) in 2 cups of just-boiled water, covered, for six minutes, strain, and drink both cups. The herbs contain volatile oil compounds that sedate and soothe stress. For extra relaxation while sipping your tea, listen to such soothing music as flute, tonal bells, or ocean surf. The effects of music therapy to promote relaxation are currently being studied, and a gentle tune may indeed help lull you to sleep.

stress-free sleep

If you have trouble falling asleep, avoid sleeping pills, since they can interfere with normal sleep patterns and in the end may result in insomnia. Instead, try meditating before you go to bed. One way is to use a meditation tape, available at music stores and natural food stores. Or lie in bed, eyes closed, and feel-think SO as you inhale and HAHM as you exhale, gently disconnecting your mind from the outside world, continuing until you fall asleep. (SO and HAHM, some therapists say, mimic the natural sound the breath makes.) If you are only able to disconnect your thoughts for several seconds at a time, that's okay. The good results will show up later. For added encouragement, keeping the room cold may help promote sleep, since the body temperature normally drops at more natural sleeping times.

making scents

Essential oil of the herb rosemary, available at herb shops and natural food stores, contains volatile oils that stimulate the central nervous system, promoting alertness and clarity. To use it, before you go to work, dot 2 drops on a cotton pad and tuck it into a shirt pocket or bra, where you will be able to smell the energizing aroma throughout your work time. You can also add 15 drops of essential oil of rosemary to 1/4 cup of unscented body lotion and rub the mixture on your body before you dress.

As for promoting sleep, 1 drop each of essential oils of marjoram and lavender, available at herb shops and natural food stores, can be dotted between your pillow and pillowcase. The essences contain volatile oils that act as mild sedatives. They can also be added to a warm bath, 4 drops of each, to relax and ready you for slumber.

best foods

For energy, before work it's best to eat lean protein-containing foods, such as grilled fish, chicken, or tofu. Protein foods help to stimulate potent antifatigue chemicals in the brain, making you more alert on your shift. To promote calm and sleep, choose such complex carbohydrates as brown rice, barley, oats, or whole wheat, which stimulate stress-relieving serotonin. In either case, avoid fatty foods, alcohol, and caffeine, since they can block the release of the appropriate brain chemicals, leaving you edgy, fatigued, and even constipated. For night shift workers, a "clean" diet high in fresh fruits and vegetables is critical, since your rhythms are off in the first place. Make extra food at home and pack a nutritious meal to eat on break at work. Or stop at a Chinese restaurant and order steamed fish and vegetables before work or steamed noodles (or brown rice) and vegetables after work, omitting the salt, fat, and MSG.

RESOURCES FOR NIGHT SHIFTERS
- Institute for Labor and Mental Health (answers questions): 510-653-6166
- The Aromatherapy Catalog (essential oils by mail): 1-800-898-PURE
- *The Complete Guide to Exercise Videos* (over 250 selections): 1-800-433-6769
- The Monroe Institute (catalog of meditation tapes): 1-800-541-2488

SEE ALSO
- Fighting FATIGUE (page 339)
- Eradicating IRRITABILITY (page 354)
- Overcoming JET LAG (page 358)
- Securing SOUND SLEEP (page 402)
- Managing STRESS (page 406)

prepping
for
presentations

| In the morning, for jitters | In the mid-afternoon and evening, for lack of energy and poor mental acuity |

Moments before my appearance on the Susan Powter show, the stage manager instructed me in breathing long and fully three times. "It's more for me than you," he insisted, but I appreciated it all the same.

The stage manager knew a secret about preparing for presentations: some adrenaline rush is good, but to prevent going over that edge and getting serious jitters, headaches, dizziness, sweating, diarrhea, and shortness of breath, you need to take some calming precautions, like deep breathing. Another helpful activity is attending other people's presentations and lectures, regardless of the subject matter. (Check at local colleges or community groups or rent a presentation-type video.) You'll pick up some techniques, and even if you don't like the style of the presenter, at least you'll know what you want to avoid in your own presentation. Knowing your material and feeling excited about it is also critical for a great presentation, as are these tried and true tips.

potent pose

While preparing for a multi-city media tour, I learned this easy tip for corralling nervous energy. Sitting in a comfortable chair, close your eyes and breathe deeply, imagining your nervous energy as tiny balls bouncing around in your body. As you visualize the balls, inhale very deeply, and as you exhale, whoosh all of the balls into one pinky finger, locking an imaginary door behind them. Inhaling, slowly open your eyes, knowing that you can release a ball or two back into your body any time you need some energy.

EQUIP YOUR EMOTIONS

If you often appear in public, you may wish to consider meditating regularly, the long-term effect of which is well-balanced emotional energy. Start with a relaxing meditation tape of woodland sounds or tonal bells from a music store or natural foods store; look in the phone book for meditation centers; see pages 6 and 136; or consult the resources in this section.

try a tea

Radio announcers like to sip a warm beverage before a show because it soothes throat tissues, producing a more velvety voice. To employ this technique for your own presentation, make a tea by steeping ½ teaspoon each of dried chamomile and peppermint in 1 cup of just-boiled water, covered, for 4 minutes and strain. As a bonus, the brew can help balance you emotionally, since chamomile contains compounds that soothe the nerves, and peppermint's volatile oils help gently lift energy levels and settle a fluttery stomach.

making scents

Aromatherapy, or the therapeutic use of pure plant essences, can have beneficial effects on both you and your audience. The essences, called essential oils, stimulate specific neuropeptides in the brain, which in turn produce various emotional states, such as calm, attentiveness, or euphoria. For my presentations I like to use a combination of calming lavender and uplifting rose geranium essences, creating a receptive, sharp, and happy mood. To try it, combine 10 or 15 drops each of essential oil of lavender and rose geranium (available at herb shops and natural food stores) and ½ cup of distilled water in a spray bottle and mist the presentation room. (I even mist television and radio studios before shows.) If misting the room is impossible, mist yourself in

WHAT THEY SEE IS WHAT THEY GET

Brilliant and prepared though you may be, people will judge what you say by how you look, and the best way to look is relaxed and comfortable with yourself. Wear clothes that you feel good in and shoes that are comfortable on your feet, especially if you will be standing. And if you're thinking of a drastic new hairdo, save it for another time.

the restroom prior to the presentation. For a personal aromatherapy treatment, dot 2 drops of each essence onto a cotton ball and tuck it into a bra or pocket, where body heat will emit the aroma as needed.

To really set the tone, you may want to dispense the lavender and geranium essences from an aromatherapy diffuser. These devices gently vibrate, emitting aromas throughout the room. Available at herb shops and natural food stores, aromatherapy diffusers come in a wide array of styles and prices.

essences to the rescue

The Bach Flower Remedies (available at herb shops and natural food stores) is a system of 38 plant essences, each of which, when taken internally, help correct a specific state of emotional disharmony. A popular potion for pre-presentation jitters is a blend of five of the Bach flowers called Rescue Remedy. To try it, drip 4 drops of Rescue Remedy into $1/4$ cup of water or tea and sip. In a pinch you can just drip the drops right under your tongue. The process can safely be repeated at 10-minute intervals until you feel more balanced.

best foods

For think-on-your-feet energy, it's best to eat lightly the night before a presentation, opting for such easy-to-digest meals as broiled fish and a salad or steamed vegetables tossed with whole wheat pasta or brown rice. Similarly, eat a light breakfast the morning of the presentation, including such foods as fresh fruit, or tea and toast. Your energy levels will be the highest if you go into a presentation being very slightly hungry. To tell how hungry you are, think of hunger levels on a scale from 0 to 10 with 0 being starving and 10 being full. Unless you're a 1 or 0, don't eat. And if you are a 1 or a 0, make it a light snack, such as a molasses-sweetened licorice candy (available at natural food stores), which acts as an adrenal tonic to generate and conserve energy on a deep, internal level.

As for beverages, be sure to drink enough water (eight 8-ounce glasses a day) the day before the presentation, as dehydration can deplete mental capabilities. Dehydration can also be caused by a diet high in such salty foods as bacon, ham, aged cheeses, smoked fish, smoked meats, and junk food. Additionally, avoid caffeine jitters by avoiding coffee or limiting your coffee intake to two cups a day, and remember that icy beverages constrict throat and voice capabilities, so drink room-temperature water and warm or hot herb teas.

RESOURCES FOR SUCCESSFUL PRESENTATIONS
·   Gavel Clubs (promote the study and practice of public speaking): 714-858-1207
·   International Platform Association (seeks to improve the quality of American lecturing):
     708-446-4321
·   International Training in Communication (courses): 714-995-3660
·   National Speakers Association (communications vehicle to speakers): 602-968-2552
·   Toastmasters International (programs: home study): 714-858-8255
·   The Monroe Institute (catalog of meditation tapes): 1-800-541-2488

SEE ALSO
·   Adjusting ANXIETY (page 296)
·   Relieving DIARRHEA (page 328)
·   Managing STRESS (page 406)

grilled salmon with fennel

MAKES 4 SERVINGS
195 calories per serving: 6 grams fat: 29% calories from fat

In addition to being the perfect light entrée to enjoy the evening before a presentation, the salmon contains essential fatty acids (EFAs), which may give your complexion an extra glow. The fennel is useful too, helping to prevent nerve-induced digestive distress.

1 pound salmon fillet (see Note)	3 cloves garlic. peeled and halved
1 tablespoon prepared mustard	$3/4$ teaspoon fennel seed
$1/4$ cup vegetable stock	pinch of sea salt
2 tablespoons dry white wine or nonalcoholic wine	minced fresh chives for garnish

PREPARE THE GRILL or preheat the broiler. Brush the salmon with the mustard and grill or broil about 4 inches from the heat source until just cooked through, about 4 minutes on each side for 1-inch-thick fillet.

MEANWHILE. IN A small saucepan, combine the stock, wine, garlic, fennel seed, and salt and bring to a boil. Continue to boil until the liquid has been reduced to about $1/4$ cup and the garlic has softened slightly, about 2 minutes. Let the mixture cool slightly, then place in an electric spice grinder or mortar and puree into a paste. Drizzle the paste over the salmon, then garnish with chives and serve.

Note: For the lowest fat, when buying the salmon ask for a fillet from the tail end.

IF THE WEATHER IS HOT AND/OR DRY:	IF THE WEATHER IS COLD AND/OR DAMP:
Serve the salmon slightly chilled with an accompaniment of chopped fresh tomatoes and cucumbers.	*Sprinkle the salmon with freshly ground pepper before grilling or broiling.*

pacifying the prostate

a friend from California called to say that after two years of being troubled by frequent insomnia-causing night urination, his prostate problems were over. After enduring embarrassment, worry, and unpleasant side effects from various prescription drugs, he worked with his doctor to devise a plan centered around the herb saw palmetto, a berry containing gently astringent volatile oil compounds that tone and strengthen the prostate.

The reason my friend and many other men have prostate problems is that as the gland attains adulthood, it wraps itself around the urethra to conveniently supply the fluid that accompanies sperm during ejaculation. Due to this arrangement, any swelling of the prostate may block the flow of urine. This is a problem in an estimated one-third of men over 50, since normally fluctuating hormone levels can cause the prostate to swell. As with my friend, this can generate frequent night urination as well as interrupted urine flow, bacterial infections, and burning during urination. Although it's always wise to consult with a health professional for prostate problems—and mandatory if there is blood in the urine or if you have pain—my friend's plan may provide comfort and relief.

try a tea

GOOD MOVES

Medical experts advise exercise to help diminish prostate problems, since it stimulates circulation and helps move fluids through the body. Walking, aerobics, tennis, golf, yoga, and tai chi are good choices, but bicycling, they say, may cause further irritation.

Saw palmetto (*Serenoa serrulata*) is prescribed by German doctors to help shrink swollen prostate glands, and studies show that it has eliminated the need for prostate surgery in numerous cases. To brew a cup of saw palmetto berry tea, available at natural food stores and herb shops, combine 1 teaspoon of the dried berries and 1¼ cups of water in a small saucepan and bring to a boil. Continue to boil for 5 minutes, then strain and drink, repeating twice more on the same day for a total of 3 cups a day. If your saw palmetto is in a teabag, steep it in 1 cup of just-boiled water, covered, for 5 minutes. For convenience, saw palmetto berry is available in tincture and capsule form, available at herb shops and natural food stores. These products sometimes also contain the herb damiana, which aids the prostate by offering a plant form of testosterone, helping to balance fluctuating hormone levels in the body.

In addition to the saw palmetto, to help prevent infection and stimulate urine flow, it's critical to drink eight 8-ounce glasses of fresh water a day.

best foods

RECIPE FOR A HEALTHY PROSTATE

Roasted Pumpkin Seeds with Garlic and Dill (page 119)

Since lack of zinc in the diet has been linked to prostate problems, eating such high-zinc foods as oysters, black-eyed peas, crab, shrimp, lima beans, and peanuts can be a hedge against trouble. For a daily high-zinc snack, eat 1 or 2 tablespoons of unsalted green pumpkin seeds (pepitas). You can even wrap them up in a small plastic bag and take them to work, enjoying them as an energizing, zinc-rich, mid-afternoon snack. Since essential fatty acids (EFAs) are vital to a healthy prostate, add 1 teaspoon of EFA-packed flaxseed oil to your morning oats or drizzle it on a muffin.

RESOURCES FOR A HEALTHY PROSTATE
- Gaia Herbs (catalog of botanicals): 508-772-5400
- *The Complete Guide to Exercise Videos* (over 250 choices): 1-800-433-6769
- Prostate Health Council (education): 1-800-242-2383
- PAACT (support for cancer patients): 616-453-1477
- Us Too (support, referrals): 1-800-US-TOO
- National Kidney and Urologic Diseases Information Clearinghouse (resources, referrals, education): 301-654-4415
- American Prostate Society (education): 410-895-3735

SEE ALSO
- Securing SOUND SLEEP (page 402)
- Managing STRESS (page 406)
- Settling an UPSET STOMACH (page 415)

reviving romance

*Mid-afternoon through
evening, for fatigue and
decreased interest*

*h*aving written about diet and health for over 20 years, I don't find it unusual to be asked the same questions time after time. And the query I receive most often—be it on national television or at the local supermarket—is "What about aphrodisiacs?"

What indeed. Most people don't really expect me to answer, especially not with specifics, but I do, because most of the world's health systems offer well-documented information on increasing sexual desire. Doctors of traditional Chinese medicine and Indian Ayurveda, for instance, believe that sexual activity is directly related to a person's general energy level. If it's low, perhaps due to a diet high in fatty foods, excessive alcohol consumption, or lack of exercise, more time may be spent dozing in front of the television than at amorous pursuits. What's more, they believe that by strengthening sexual vitality, you can enjoy good health and prevent premature aging. To that end, exhaustion and low sexual appetite are treated together with such suggestions as those that follow. Note, though, that while I heartily agree that hot romance is quite a health tonic in itself, that very same romance can cause illness and even death as a result of the devastating diseases that can be contracted from engaging in casual sex. And since monogamy is not always an available mode, please be smart and careful.

relief at your fingertips

For a sensuous and relaxing rub, massage your partner with a clean feather duster by gently tickling the feathers across the skin. Although ancient Chinese sexologists used a peacock feather for this technique, modern sexologists advise employing such methods as part of precoital love play or even noncoital love play. The latter skill is foreplay without penetration, used to treat temporary impotence in men. The idea is to caress and kiss daily over a prescribed period of time, and without the pressure of intercourse, until the man eventually becomes relaxed enough to proceed with coitus.

If no feathers are available, you may wish to massage your partner using your hands and a massage oil, many varieties of which are available at natural food stores and herb shops. Or make your own using a formula in "Making Scents" (page 389). Use the palms of your hands for such large muscular spaces as the back and legs, and the pads of your fingertips for more sensitive areas. Be sure to spend time on the big toes, especially the area just below the nail, in the center, as some Chinese accupressurists say that it activates a nerve, or energy channel, that leads directly to the groin.

Although you may not have considered performing a massage with your tongue, Tantric (ancient Indian) texts state that during an impassioned kiss, you should flick and massage the little tendon in your partner's mouth (attached between the upper lip and front upper gum). Aficionados of the practice say it is quite titillating.

SEXUAL SALVATION

Throughout history, various societies have decreed that sexual union was a ticket to heaven. During China's Tang Dynasty (A.D. 618–907), the Taoists decided that immortality could be achieved through regular sexual intercourse, prompting them to devise a sex schedule for their emperors based on the rhythmic phases of the moon. Shortly thereafter, Tantraism began in India, holding that sex would bring nirvana. New schools of sexual intercourse, Vajrayana and Saiva Sakta, to name two, raised sex from the lowly bedchamber to a high and lofty pedestal. Today temples ensconced with erotic statues of couples engaged in such heavenly pursuits remain a testimony to these ancient Indian beliefs.

potent pose

Chinese Taoists were the first to inscribe that regular exercise of the pelvic muscles enhances sexual enjoyment. Throughout the centuries lovers have adopted the custom, but it became very famous and fashionable in the West beginning in the 1940s, when a

THE HORMONES HAVE IT

Alcohol, cigarette smoking, tranquilizers, high blood pressure medication, and high blood cholesterol levels can reduce the body's ability to produce testosterone, a hormone that can stimulate sexual desire in both sexes.

physician, Arnold Kegel, devised a pelvic exercise for his incontinent women patients. The exercise was successful at stopping slow-leaking urine, but as a bonus, as the women developed previously neglected muscles, they became more adept at lovemaking. To do Kegels, as they are now called, sit, stand, or lie down and contract your pubic muscles quickly 10 times, three to five times a day. For women that means engaging your vaginal and rectal muscles at the same time; for men, engage the muscles surrounding your scrotum and your rectum simultaneously. Kegels can be done anywhere, including while sitting in your office chair, waiting for the subway, or even dining, but note that Taoists hold that the best time to exercise pubic area muscles is between five and seven in the morning, a time when testosterone levels are usually at their peak for the day.

For a change of pace, as a variation on the 10 fast Kegels, inhale deeply while contracting your pubic and abdominal muscles and hold your breath for about 10 seconds. Exhale as you release your muscles, repeating the process four times (for a total of five), three to five times a day. Some people report a flow of energy from the groin upward after performing this pose, as well as more intense orgasms from doing fast or slow Kegels regularly. Others spice up intercourse with a Kegel or two during the act.

TAKE A POSITION

Ancient love texts, such as the Indian Kama Sutra, boast literally hundreds of positions for lovemaking. The Classic of the Arcane Maid, *a Chinese treatise on the subject, offers such positions as Wrestling Tigers, Soaring Phoenix, and Mounting Tortoises. If all this thought on positioning makes you feel uncreative, note that most of the positions are variations on two: penetration from behind and the missionary position with the bottom person's legs on the upper person's shoulders. The ancients felt that these two positions, including variations, provided for the deepest and most exquisite penetration.*

try a tea

Some herbs, such as Chinese (Panax) ginseng, Siberian (Eleuthero) ginseng, astragalus, schizandra berry, and ginkgo, are considered aphrodisiacs because they contain compounds that help increase overall body vitality on a deep, internal level. All are available at herb shops, natural food stores, and Asian markets; ask for dried tea blends to brew at home or liquid tinctures to add to black or green tea and follow the instructions on the label. If the label is in a foreign tongue, ask for instructions from the shop's purveyor. And if you don't want to say you're looking for an aphrodisiac, ask for a "vitality tonic." For acute low sexual vitality, these herbs are generally prescribed to be taken daily, two or three times a day, for two weeks. For chronic cases, the herbs may be prescribed for three or four months, but check with a health professional before imbibing, especially if you are on any type of medication.

Another classification of aphrodisiacs actually contains plant forms of testosterone, the romance hormone. The most widely used is the herb yohimbe, the inner bark of an African tree containing the testosterone-like hormone yohimbine. You'll find yohimbe at natural food stores and herb shops, sometimes blended with other testosterone-containing herbs such as damiana. To make a cup of tea, combine about 1 teaspoon of chopped yohimbe bark or tea blend with 1¼ cups of water in a small saucepan and bring the mixture to a boil. Continue to boil gently for about 8 minutes, or until there's about ¾ cup of tea. Then strain and sip. General dosage is two cups a day until symptoms subside, which may be in three or four days, followed by two maintenance cups a day once a week. Note that yohimbe and other aphrodisiacs work best when alcohol, caffeine, tobacco, and fatty foods are eliminated, as these substances may block the absorption of testosterone.

In a class by themselves are the aphrodisiac-relaxants that help to eliminate the stress that often dampens romance. Linden flower (lime flower or tilia) is the classic choice of French herbalists: 1 teaspoon of the dried herb steeped in 1 cup of just-boiled water, covered, for 10 minutes. General dose is a cup taken each evening. You can also check herb shops, natural food stores, and some supermarkets for special relaxing or antistress tea blends containing such natural nervines as chamomile, catnip, skullcap, and valerian root and enjoy a brewed cup anytime you wish to enhance romance.

making scents

Scientists studying the scents that make us sensual find that vanilla and lavender score high with both men and women. So do pumpkin pie and Coca-Cola, which makes me think that cinnamon may aid sexual desire, since both products contain the sassy spice. To employ this knowledge in an intimate manner, browse herb shops and natural food stores for massage oils containing pure essential oils of vanilla and lavender. Or make your own using about 12 drops each of essential oil of vanilla and lavender combined with ¼ cup of canola oil. (Cinnamon rubbed on the skin, especially in sensitive places, may cause irritation, so bake cinnamon-scented items or try the recipe on page 391.) The erotic scent of choice among many aromatherapists is essential oil of ylang-ylang, a tropical flower with a voluptuous, flowery fragrance. Make your own massage oil using 25 drops of essential oil of ylang-ylang (available at herb shops and natural food stores) with ¼ cup of canola oil. Ylang-ylang comes in five grades, five being the lowest and extra-special being the best. Buy grade three or above, and if the people at the store don't know what grade they have, buy your ylang-ylang elsewhere.

For a different twist, try a Victorian love trick by strewing fresh leaves of the rose geranium plant over the bedsheets. As you and your lover lie on the soft, velvety leaves, body heat causes them to emit an invigorating lemony-rose fragrance.

best foods

When the son of a Chinese carp farmer mistakenly fed the fish oats instead of their usual feed, the farmer subsequently noticed lots of extra little carps. Believing that the oats increased the sexual vitality of the fish, people began paying more attention to their morning porridge. And when curious scientists investigated oats, they discovered that the plant contained not only compounds that treat sensual-stopping nervous debility and fatigue but romance-reviving testosterone as well. To reap the benefits of this homely tonic, buy whole oats, sometimes called Irish oats (available at natural food stores and some supermarkets) and eat a bowl for breakfast five or so days a week. Since whole oats take about 30 minutes to prepare, cook them all night in a crock pot on low, or make a large batch and reheat daily portions in the microwave. Second best are the readily available rolled oats, which take less than 5 minutes to cook. For an extra boost, add ¼ teaspoon of dried ginseng root per portion to the cooking oats. You may also wish to garnish your bowl of oats with 1 tablespoon of green pumpkin seeds (pepitas, available at natural food stores and some supermarkets), since they contain the mineral zinc, which is important to the healthy functioning of the sex organs. Zinc may also have led researchers to say that oysters are aphrodisiacs, since they are another good source of the mineral.

Not without their own secrets, Ayurvedic Indian physicians, who believe that sexual energy is linked to general vivacity, call aphrodisiacs *vijakaranas*, from the Sanskrit meaning "vitality of a horse." Asparagus is especially prescribed to women because it contains compounds that nourish the female reproductive system. Those foods that are believed to contain substances that increase the functional activity of the sex organs in both men and women include raw garlic, saffron, and raw onions. Similarly, some Filipinos believe raw onions to be a sex tonic, combining them, chopped, with ginger and honey. But regardless of which foods you choose to say "I love you," note that alcohol consumption, cigarette smoking, caffeine, fatty foods, and junk foods may block the release of testosterone, thus inhibiting sexual desire.

smart supplement

Essential fatty acids (EFAs) encourage the healthy production of sex hormones in both men and women, but since the body does not produce EFAs, many experts recommend supplementation. Although it is always prudent to check with a health professional before introducing a new substance into the body, one EFA choice is evening primrose oil, 1,500 mg taken daily.

raisin-oat breakfast bars

MAKES 8 BARS
125 calories per bar; 4 grams fat; 28% calories from fat

For a robust dose of hormone-enhancing oats, make these bars ahead so they'll be ready in the morning. They also make a handy portable finger food for commuters.

2 tablespoons canola oil	2 cups rolled oats
1/4 cup frozen orange juice concentrate	1/4 cup raisins, chopped
1/4 cup pure maple syrup	1/2 teaspoon ground cinnamon

PREHEAT THE OVEN to 350°F.

IN A SMALL saucepan, combine the oil, orange juice concentrate, and maple syrup and bring to a boil. Remove the pan from the heat.

IN A MEDIUM bowl, combine the cereal, raisins, and cinnamon. Pour on the warm syrup and combine well.

LINE AN 8 × 8-inch glass baking dish with parchment paper and spray with nonstick cooking spray. Press in the oat mixture firmly and bake in the middle of the oven until firm and lightly browned, about 15 minutes.

LET THE DISH cool in the refrigerator for about 25 minutes. Then lift the bars from the dish, peel off the parchment, and use kitchen shears to cut into 8 bars. Store in a tightly sealed container for up to 5 days.

IF THE WEATHER IS HOT AND/OR DRY:	IF THE WEATHER IS COLD AND/OR DAMP:
Serve the bars with slightly chilled peppermint tea.	*Increase the cinnamon to 1 teaspoon and serve with a warm spicy tea.*

releasing sinus pressure

Night and morning. because lying down can aggravate the condition

At the change of seasons, especially in cold or damp weather

One March in Hong Kong, I accompanied a sinus-suffering friend to an acupuncturist. There I learned that in Chinese medicine, good health hinges on the balanced flow of energy, or chi, throughout the body. Illness, such as my friend's clogged and painful face, is seen as an imbalance of chi. I watched as the doctor painlessly inserted thread-thin sterile needles into specific points around my friend's face and head, dispersing and balancing chi, thus releasing sinus pressure and improving his overall stamina.

In my friend's case, sinus pressure was caused by pollution and irritating pollen, but other causes of sinus pressure include injury, small growths in the nose, and pressure changes from air travel and scuba diving. Half of all sinus trouble, however, is caused by bacterial infections and, besides facial pain, can cause headaches, earaches, and reduced sense of smell. These sinus soothers can help release the pressure, but if the problem persists for more than five days, or if green or dark mucus comes from your nose, see a health professional.

relief at your fingertips

This series of three accupressure massage points can help relieve sinus pressure and clear the head. Begin by briskly rubbing your hands together for about 10 seconds. Using the insides of your thumbs, press up firmly on the ledges just under the inside corner of each eyebrow. The areas will feel sensitive, so breathe deeply and slowly while pressing for 1 or 2 minutes. Remove your thumbs and observe a lightness and clarity in your forehead.

STAY CLEAR

Some experts say that avoiding carpeting, house plants, basements, and other mold-prone scenes can avert sinus pressure.

Next, use the tips of your index fingers to press down firmly on the mid-bottom of each eye socket bone for 1 or 2 minutes. Release your fingers, noting a clear feeling under your eyes and in your cheeks and upper jaw area.

Finally, use your index fingers again to press the areas just next to each nostril. Continue to press for 1 or 2 minutes, releasing to a clearer nose and lower cheek area. For the best results, perform this trio of points three times a day.

You can also treat your face to a hot compress by wetting a face cloth with hot water and wringing it out before applying the soothing heat for 5 minutes. A blue face mask, available at pharmacies, can be heated for 30 seconds on medium power in the microwave and applied the same way.

potent pose

Since horizontal positions can aggravate sinus pressure buildup, it's best to sleep propped up a bit until the condition improves. Use pillows or a comfy study cushion with back support and arms.

THE WASH OUT

Ayurvedic Indian physicians recommend using a water-filled neti pot to prevent and cure sinus pressure. The pot, shaped like a magic wish lamp, is available at natural food stores and Indian markets. Water is poured into the nose, and with the head correctly positioned, it travels around to flush the sinuses. For a more automated approach, some people gently use their water pick appliances to do the same. Two long squirts in each nostril with a commercial saline spray (available at pharmacies) is also helpful.

try a tea

Echinacea, used by Native Americans for centuries, contains compounds that act on a cellular level to help prevent and cure sinus infection. Buy the tea at natural food stores and herb shops and combine 1 teaspoon (or bag) in $1\frac{1}{4}$ cups of water in a small saucepan and simmer gently for about 12 minutes. Strain and sip, repeating twice more each day, for a total of 3 cups daily. Continue drinking echinacea tea until your sinus pressure subsides or for as long as 14 days. To lend a Unani (Middle Eastern herbalism) touch to the brew, add 1 teaspoon of anise seed to the simmering echinacea. The fragrant seeds are a gentle decongestant and lend a sweet taste to the brew. Be sure to drink the tea hot to help mucus flow, further reducing pressure.

Though not a hot tea, you may wish to explore kombucha, a fermented mushroom brew, to relieve sinus pressure. One woman I interviewed said she was addicted to Afrin sinus medication for more years than she could remember, and to Seldane sinus medication for an additional two years. After three weeks of drinking 8 ounces of kombucha tea a day, she no longer needed her sinus pills and also stopped the pills she took for anxiety and depression. Kombucha, which is available in extract, capsule, or bottled form at natural food stores, contains glucuronic acid and other compounds that may work to relieve sinus pressure by enhancing the body's immune system.

making scents

Essential oil of tea tree, available at herb shops and natural food stores, has a spicy-medicinal odor and is strongly antibacterial and antiviral. To use it to soothe sinus pressure, dot 2 drops between your pillow and pillowcase before sleep. Or add 15 drops to the bottom of your shower before turning on the water to make a penetrating steam. You may also wish to carry the bottle of tea tree oil with you to work or when traveling, dotting 2 drops on a tissue and inhaling as needed.

best foods

Spicy, sinus-opening foods such as garlic, ginger, and hot peppers are good for relieving sinus pressure. So are steaming soups and stews if they don't contain dairy products, which may cause mucus buildup.

smart supplements

Some sinus experts advise aiding the body with the following complements:

· To deter mucus production, 50,000 IUs of beta carotene a day

· To fight infection and boost immunities, 10 mg of zinc three times a day

· For immune function, 100 mg of vitamin B complex a day

· Also for immune function, vitamin C in the form of the Ayurvedic gooseberry jam, chavanprash, 2 teaspoons a day (available at natural food stores and Indian markets)

RESOURCES TO RELIEVE SINUS PRESSURE

· Arrowroot Natural Pharmacy (homeopathic preparations by mail): 1-800-234-8879

· Gaia Herbs (botanical extracts): 508-772-5400

· The National Accreditation Commission for Schools and Colleges of Acupuncture and Oriental Medicine (referrals): 202-265-2287

· Acupuncture Research Institute (seminars, referrals): 213-722-7353

· American Academy of Medical Acupuncture (referrals): 213-937-5514

SEE ALSO

· Abating ASTHMA (page 300)

· Comforting a COLD (page 310)

· Easing an EARACHE (page 336)

· Healing HAY FEVER (page 342)

· Curing a HEADACHE (page 346)

· Overcoming JET LAG (page 358)

soothing sore gums

| In the morning, when
nerves in the area are the
most sensitive

a dental hygienist in Vermont told me of a middle-aged woman she had had as a client for 15 years who suddenly began to exhibit radiant oral health, including tight, pink gums with reduced incidence of loose areas around the teeth. The patient disclosed that she had been using an herb-based toothpaste containing such astringent and antibacterial ingredients as myrrh, fennel, ginger, and tea tree. To try it for yourself to prevent and cure such problems as gingivitis and periodontal disease, you can buy the toothpaste at natural food stores and some pharmacies.

Inflamed and sore gums can be caused by bacteria buildup, mucus, or plaque, resulting in infection, swelling, and bleeding. When gums swell, pockets or loose areas form and more plaque lodges there, worsening the condition. That's where the herb-based toothpaste comes in handy. Sore gums can also be caused by ill-fitting dental fillings, mouth breathing, smoking, immune disorders, and diabetes, so check with a health professional as well as trying the herb-based toothpaste and these suggestions.

relief at your fingertips

Although one of the best preventatives against sore gums is daily flossing and brushing the gums as well as the teeth, for relief of an occasional sore gum, rub the area with a fresh sage leaf. Sage contains antibacterial compounds that will soothe the area and help prevent infection. After rubbing a few times, wad the leaf up into a ball and place it against the area for about 15 minutes, repeating two more times a day for a total of three times daily.

If sage is not at hand, pop open a capsule of vitamin E oil and apply it to the area. Or in a pinch, tuck a small piece of ice on the area to help relieve inflammation.

try a tea

For extra gum protection, make a strong infusion by steeping 1 tablespoon each of dried thyme and sage in 1 cup of just-boiled water, covered, until cool, at least 20 minutes. Use the tea as an anti-infective mouth rinse or dip your floss into it before using. The infusion will not harm you, but the taste is too strong to drink enjoyably.

Alternatively, buy powdered goldenseal tea at an herb shop or natural food store and sprinkle a pinch on your toothpaste before brushing. Goldenseal contains compounds that are astringent and highly anti-infective to gums, but since it may cause uterine contractions, pregnant women should avoid it.

Green tea, made by steeping 1 teaspoon of dried leaves in 1 cup of just-boiled water, covered, for 2 minutes, can be sipped as a gum-soothing beverage. In fact, if you're going to lunch and can't brush afterward, order green tea, and its astringent properties will do the job for you.

THERAPEUTIC RINSE

At natural food stores and pharmacies, look for homeopathic gum rinses containing minute doses of such soothing herbs as calendula, arnica, and plantain (Plantago). Used first thing each morning (no food or water for 15 minutes before or after), these rinses can cure inflammation and prevent further bouts.

best foods

To prevent sore gums, eat an apple. While you're chewing, the flesh of the fruit will massage and soothe your gums. Since vitamin C deficiency may cause sore gums, eat such high-C foods as fresh broccoli, red bell peppers, collard greens, turnip greens, mus-

To help prevent sore gums, change your toothbrush monthly, buying one with soft bristles. When brushing your teeth, hold the brush at an angle to clean between the teeth and gums. Some experts also suggest brushing the tongue to remove bacteria.

tard greens, cauliflower, Brussels sprouts, kale, oranges, strawberries, papaya, mango, and grapefruit. If your gums are currently sore, avoid crunchy foods, as well as salty and acidic foods. Smoking, alcohol consumption, and excessive amounts of refined white sugar may exacerbate the condition.

smart supplement

Japanese gum experts advise taking a daily dose of vitamin E-like CO Q 10, an enzyme that helps oxygenate gum tissue. Available at natural food stores and some pharmacies, buy CO Q 10 in 30-mg capsules, and take one each day.

RESOURCES FOR HEALTHY GUMS
- National Institutes of Health (information on periodontal disease): 301-496-2563
- Holistic Dental Association (referrals): 614-366-3309
- International Dental Health Foundation (information and referrals): 703-471-8324

surmounting sore muscles

when symptoms may occur:

| In the evening | At the change of seasons

Pat, a municipal cop, was answering a domestic disturbance call when he was shot twice in the chest with a .357 Magnum. A bulletproof vest saved his life, but the blunt impact seriously bruised his heart, changing his life forever. Although a doctor's order of restricted activity required Pat to retire from law enforcement, he kept up his study of rku kyu, an ancient Japanese form of martial arts, an activity that, especially since the shooting, caused him sore muscles. Through rku kyu, however, Pat learned about dong quai, an Asian herb (available in capsule form from natural food stores and herb shops) containing anti-inflammatory compounds that soothe sore muscles faster than anything else he had tried.

After thinking about my own experience with dong quai, taken (in capsule form, 520 mg a day) to abate female complaints, I had to admit that ever since dong quai became part of my routine, I, too, have experienced fewer bouts with sore muscles. Now, doubly glad for dong quai, I offer some accompanying suggestions.

relief at your fingertips

To prevent sore muscles, apply a penetrating topical rub before exercise or other strenuous activity. At natural food stores and pharmacies, look for a product containing menthol, from mint; camphor, from an Asian tree; capsaicin, from hot peppers; or odorless arnica, from a daisy-like mountain flower. (Minute homeopathic doses of arnica, in pill form, can be taken orally to accompany the topical treatment.)

The rubs will also soothe sore muscles after exertion, especially when massaged on with firm strokes. After massaging, to further soothe the area, apply heat for 10 minutes in the form of a heating pad or a towel soaked in hot water and wrung out.

KEEP MOVING

Most sore muscles occur as lactic acid builds up during movement and the tissues can't disperse it quickly enough. Maintaining a regular exercise program improves dispersal of lactic acid and prevents sore muscles.

potent pose

In combination with a pain-relieving rub, stretching muscles can also palliate sore areas. For calf muscles, for instance, stand on tiptoes for one full breath, then stand on your heels with toes off the floor while breathing again. Repeat four times, for a total of five stretches, three to five times a day.

For an overworked lower back, curve forward from the waist while inhaling, arms hanging down. While bent, breathe fully three times and tighten your abdominal muscles; repeat the stretch three to five times a day.

To stretch a sore neck, sit or stand, right arm at your side, left hand atop your head. Inhaling, gently stretch the right side of your neck by pulling your head toward your left shoulder. Hold the pose for two full breaths, then repeat on the other side; perform the pose three to five times daily.

RX FOR PAIN

Physicians sometimes treat sore muscles, especially leg cramps, with drugs made from quinine (cinchona), but some patients report getting headaches from the medication. The solution is a new drug that adds vitamin E to the quinine. Patients using it report they are virtually headache-free.

try a tea

Experts recommend that to prevent and treat sore muscles, especially leg cramps, drink eight 8-ounce glasses of water a day, as dehydration may exacerbate the condition. But instead of drinking plain water, make a sun tea with rosemary, using two 2-inch sprigs of the fresh herb for each 8 ounces of room-temperature water, soaking for at least 1 hour. Longer soaking is fine and won't alter the taste. Rosemary contains compounds that can help increase circulation, thus reducing muscle inflammation.

making scents

To augment the rosemary tea treatment, take a soothing rosemary bath. To try it, run a tub, adding 1½ cups of pain-diminishing Epsom salts, available at pharmacies. When the tub is filled, add 7 drops of warming essential oil of rosemary, available at natural food stores and herb shops. Essential oil of pine is a helpful alternative. After the bath, lightly massage sore muscles with a lotion you make yourself by combining ¼ cup of unscented body lotion with 10 drops of essential oil of rosemary or pine. Or use 5 drops of each essence for a deeply penetrating combination. Then put on a warm robe, or socks if your feet are sore, and relax.

best foods

To prevent sore muscles, experts advise eating lots of potassium-rich fresh fruits and vegetables such as bananas or broccoli, since lack of the mineral may aggravate the condition. Lack of calcium and magnesium in the body may also lead to sore muscles, so some people may wish to supplement their diets with 1,000 mg of calcium and 500 mg of magnesium a day. Many people who suffer digestive distress from calcium supplements have good luck with calcium citrate, which sometimes includes magnesium in the formula. Check the label. Additionally, at least 400 IUs of vitamin E daily may also help to keep muscles tuned.

RECIPES FOR PAIN-FREE MUSCLES

Chopped Vegetable Salad with Oregano and Lemon (page 88)

Apricot-Banana Mousse (page 264)

RESOURCES FOR PAIN-FREE MUSCLES
- Arrowroot Natural Pharmacy (homeopathic preparations by mail): 1-800-234-8879
- *The Complete Guide to Exercise Videos* (over 250 titles): 1-800-433-6769
- National Arthritis and Musculoskeletal Clearinghouse (sends information): 301-495-4484
- Aerobics and Fitness Association of America (publishes exercise magazine): 1-800-446-AFAA (in Cal., 1-800-255-2584)

SEE ALSO
- Easing ARTHRITIS PAIN (page 289)
- Lulling LOW BACK PAIN (page 362)
- Taming NECK AND SHOULDER TENSION (page 374)
- Managing STRESS (page 406)
- Coddling TIRED FEET (page 413)

securing
sound
sleep

when symptoms may occur:

| At night (sleeplessness) | In the morning (grogginess) | In the mid-afternoon (fatigue) |

*J*oni bakes a mean cake at 11 P.M., but her husband doesn't enjoy it until the next day because he's out like a light by 10. In the morning he's up and chatting at 6, while Joni's in a fog.

Joni is what sleep researchers call an owl, or a person who is lively at night. Her husband is a lark, or one whose activity level is highest in the morning. Both owls and larks are healthy, experts say, and both get the sleep they need. The point is that the sleep habits that are right for one person aren't necessarily right for another. You may need only four hours of sleep, for instance, while your friend needs seven, yet both of you are healthy.

Problems arise, however, when sleeplessness or interrupted sleep prevents a person from functioning alertly during the day. In fact, sleeplessness is one of the three most frequently heard complaints by primary care doctors, who cite situational and emotional problems as the biggest blocks to sound sleep. Job worries, financial woes, family hassles, health problems, anxiety, and depression can interfere with healthy sleep patterns. So can diet pills, hormone replacement therapy, chemotherapy, high blood pressure medication, thyroid medication, alcohol, recreational drugs, diabetes, hypoglycemia, ulcer pain, asthma, arthritis, itching, prostate problems, sleep apnea, obesity, jet lag, and night shift work. If your sleep-wake cycles are abnormal for you for more than one week, see a health professional. But for the odd bout of sleeplessness, these suggestions can help.

SNORE SOLUTION

Sleep experts say that snoring can impede sound sleep, for both snorer and bedmate. One device to try that reduces and sometimes eliminates snoring is called a septum stimulator, which works by encouraging air flow through the nose. Looking like slender nose plugs, the unobtrusive gadget fits inside the nose, where little balls stimulate the septum nerves for what users report as easy, quiet breathing. Seek septum stimulators at pharmacies and natural food stores.

relief at your fingertips

To help release tension from your head, thus encouraging sound sleep, press a pair of Chinese accupressure points called Tai Yang. To find them, use your index fingers to trace your eyebrows from your nose to the outside edges. Go a bit farther until you reach the hollows just before the temples. Press in medium-firmly and breathe deeply and fully five times, noticing a tension-draining feeling in your head afterward. You may repeat the Tai Yang points every 2 minutes as needed.

SHEDDING LIGHT

When it's dark, your brain releases the sleep-inducing hormone melatonin, lulling you to slumber. Light, even a small night light, can inhibit the release of melatonin, so those who have trouble sleeping may want to wear an eye mask to ensure sound sleep. Some people have good luck taking melatonin orally in 3-mg tablets, available at natural food stores and pharmacies. One woman, aged 70, hadn't slept more than four hours a night for 15 years and felt like a zombie. After one month on melatonin, she was sleeping soundly six to seven hours a night. In those who don't need extra amounts of the hormone, melatonin may actually cause sleep disorders, so check with a health professional before taking it. Additionally, since melatonin may cause fatigue, it should not be taken by those with immune disorders.

try a tea

Natural nervine herbs such as valerian root, skullcap, linden flower (tilia), passionflower, hops, chamomile, and catnip may help you sleep. Start by trying a slumber-inducing blended combination, available at natural food stores and some supermarkets. Brew and sip a cup or two about an hour before bed. In the stronger, sedative category is the herb motherwort, available in liquid tincture form from natural food stores and herb shops. Adding 15 to 30 drops to a brewed tea puts most people in dreamland.

CLEAN WITH GREEN

Chemicals such as formaldehydes, glues, and resins may cause insomnia, so check your bedroom for possible sources. Carpeting, plywood, foam insulation, particle board, facial tissues, room deodorizers, and permanent-press bedsheets can be culprits. Eliminating the source is best, but if that's not possible, let such plants as aloe vera, Boston fern, ivy, fig trees, philodendron, and spider plants clean the air for you by neutralizing pollutants with the microbes around their roots. For every 100 square feet, use at least three 10-inch plants.

making scents

Essential oils of lavender and marjoram, available at herb shops and natural food stores, contain volatile oil compounds that signal the brain that it's time to sleep. Sprinkle 1 drop of each on your pillow before you lay your head down. Or run a warm bath, adding drops of each essence to the water before you get in to soak for 15 minutes. You may also wish to add the essences to an aromatherapy diffuser, which emits cool puffs of sleep-encouraging essence into the room.

best foods

For sound and uninterrupted sleep, it's best not to eat, especially heavily, before bed. But a good midnight snack should consist of one of the foods containing the sleep-inducing amino acid tryptophan. Try a banana, a slice of lean turkey, or half a grapefruit. Avoid caffeine, alcohol, and refined sugar, which may keep you awake. Abstain from foods like eggplant, spinach, potatoes, and tomatoes, which contain a compound called tyramine that encourages the release of the stimulant brain chemical norepinephrine.

smart supplements

Lack of these nutrients may cause insomnia and interrupted sleep, so some experts advise taking the following:

· Calcium, 1,000 mg, taken at night
· Magnesium, 500 mg, taken with the calcium
· B complex vitamins, 100 mg, taken anytime

RESOURCES FOR SOUND SLEEP
· The Monroe Institute (catalog of meditation and relaxation tapes): 1-800-541-2488
· National Sleep Foundation (promotes development of support groups): 310-288-0466
· Better Sleep Council (information on sleep and bedding): 703-683-8371
· American Sleep Disorders Association (listing of sleep disorder centers): 507-287-6006
· Shut-Eye Hotline (literature and tips): 1-800-SHUT-EYE

SEE ALSO
· Easing ARTHRITIS PAIN (page 289)
· Adjusting ANXIETY (page 296)
· Abating ASTHMA (page 300)
· Disarming DEPRESSION (page 324)
· Smoothing DRY SKIN (page 332)
· Overcoming JET LAG (page 358)
· Night (page 279)
· Negotiating the NIGHT SHIFT (page 377)
· Pacifying the PROSTATE (page 384)
· Managing STRESS (page 406)

sleepytime shake

MAKES 2 SNACK-SIZED SERVINGS
192 calories per serving; no added fat

The banana, grapefruit, and chamomile in this shake all contain compounds that can help you sleep. For convenience, make the chamomile ice cubes ahead by freezing brewed and cooled chamomile tea.

1 large banana, peeled and chunked

1 pink grapefruit, peeled, seeded, and sectioned

1 cup nonfat vanilla soy yogurt or regular yogurt

2 chamomile ice cubes

COMBINE ALL OF the ingredients in a blender or processor and whiz until smooth.

IF THE WEATHER IS HOT AND/OR DRY:
Add 1/2 teaspoon of rose water to the ingredients before blending.

IF THE WEATHER IS COLD AND/OR DAMP:
Add a pinch of freshly grated nutmeg to the ingredients before blending.

managing
stress

managing

when symptoms may occur:

| At night, causing | In the afternoon, causing | In the morning, causing |
| sleeplessness | fatigue | sluggishness and headache |

stress

*i*mmediately after beginning a lecture on health to women with AIDS, I realized I was on the wrong course. Most of the women were on disability and had HIV positive children, so discussing supplements, herbs, and foods to buy made no sense; purchasing a seven-dollar bottle of echinacea tincture was an unaffordable luxury.

Changing my tack, I showed the women how to make their own echinacea tincture; how to identify, pick, and use three local plants that contained immune-boosting vitamin C and beta carotene; and how to manage stress.

Stress, the women discovered, causes the release of too much of the brain chemical ACTH into the bloodstream, resulting in a weakened immune system and susceptibility to disease. In addition, stress makes nerve-related body systems go haywire, causing such ills as colitis and diarrhea, as well as irritability, headaches, and tight neck and shoulders. Unmanaged stress due to health woes, money problems, and worrying about their children could actually make these women more ill than ever. Relaxation, they came to know, is critical.

To shift their perceptions and reactions to stressors, I taught the women a simple meditation technique that I saw for the first time in Germany. To begin, a group of people gather and sit comfortably on the floor, eyes closed and breathing deeply. A specially designated person then plays one clear, resonant note on a musical instrument for about one minute—in Germany that was a 4-foot Tibetan flute, but a gong or Western flute will work. The musical note then becomes each person's mantra, or the sound she feels/hears during meditation while emptying the mind of current stressors. They leave the group and practice meditation every morning and evening for 15 minutes, sitting quietly, eyes closed, internally feeling and hearing their mantra. The group meets weekly or monthly to replay and freshen the musical mantra and meditate together. The following antistressors help also.

relief at your fingertips

A medicine man from Kenya taught me a calming point to press the minute stress begins. Turn one hand palm up. Using the thumb of your opposite hand, feel for the round bone at the base of your palm, on the pinky side. Press firmly above the bone. While pressing, drop and relax your shoulders. You may notice a feeling of energy moving in your chest area, which the Kenyan medicine man explains is stress dissipating. In addition, as you're pressing, you may feel some crunchy areas around the wrist bone, another signal that you are stressed and should keep pressing until the areas feel smooth. If you're at a tense meeting or are stressed on the subway, just press this point and, as the man from Kenya says, it will bring you down to earth. You need only to press one hand for results, and you may press this point as often as you like.

MECHANIZED MEDITATION

Some cities have brain machine centers where you don light-emitting goggles and sound-emitting earphones that are programmed to help ease you into a deep, meditative state for 45 to 60 minutes. (One such group of centers is called Synchro-Energize.) Users report a feeling of extreme stress relief after a session, likening it to Buddhist or Transcendental Meditation. Home brain machines are also available from catalogs and some specialty shops.

KEEP MOVING

Any type of exercise undertaken for at least 20 minutes three times a week can help reduce stress by working off physical tensions before they have time to manifest into disease. Try walking, yoga, bicycling, gardening, tai chi, or swimming.

*Stressors are not going to
go away. But by manag-
ing stressors, we disarm
their negative effects.*

try a tea

Mild nervines such as lemon balm (*Melissa*), chamomile, and catnip help reduce stress by calming the nerves. Buy a blended tea at an herb shop, natural food store, or super-market and sip a cup as needed. Brew extra to take to work in a thermos and be sure to drink a cup or two about an hour before bed, since sound sleep is critical to stress management.

making scents

Essential oil combinations such as lavender, lemon balm, and tangerine can be restora-tive and highly relaxing. Buy a blend at an herb shop or natural food store and dot 2 drops on a tissue to inhale. You can also tuck the aromatic tissue into a bra or shirt pocket as a calming, personal scent. Before sleep, dot 2 drops on your pillow or run a warm bath, adding 10 drops of the essential oil combo to a full tub before soaking. For stress relief anywhere, combine 10 drops of the calming combination with $\frac{1}{4}$ cup of unscented body lotion and rub it on your hands and arms as needed while enjoying the rejuvenating aroma. Or use the lotion for massaging yourself or another person. Mas-sage helps manage stress by soothing tense muscles, thus calming mind and body. Make up your own massage routine, enroll in a massage class, or consult a library for books or videos on massage techniques.

best foods

Eating complex carbohydrates such as whole wheat, barley, buckwheat, brown rice, and other whole grains causes the brain to release serotonin, the calming hormone. In addi-tion, be sure to use calming herbs in cooking, such as lemon balm, chamomile, and lavender. Add fresh leaves and flowers to green and fruit salads to taste or sprinkle dried versions into simmering soups and stews, 1 tablespoon for each four servings. Or make a calming syrup by combining 2 tablespoons each of dried lemon balm, chamomile, and lavender (or 6 tablespoons of one) and 1 cup of pure honey in a small saucepan, heating gently until the honey is warm and liquid; don't boil. Let the syrup cool, then store in a jar and use 1 teaspoon of the elixir to sweeten a cup of relaxing herbal tea.

ANTISTRESS RECIPE

*Morning Immune-Boost
Spread (page 32)*

smart supplements

Unmanaged stress can prevent the body from absorbing nutrients, resulting in vitamin and mineral deficiencies and fatigue-causing depleted adrenal function. If you have just begun to manage your stress, you may wish to supplement with the following nutrients:

- B vitamin complex, 100 mg a day
- Calcium, 1,000 mg a day, taken at night with magnesium
- Magnesium, 500 mg a day, taken at night with calcium
- Vitamin C in the form of the Ayurvedic Indian gooseberry jam called chavanprash (available at Indian markets and natural food stores)

RELAXING RESOURCES

- The Monroe Institute (catalog of meditation and relaxation tapes): 1-800-541-2488
- *The Complete Guide to Exercise Videos* (over 250 selections): 1-800-433-6769
- The Aromatherapy Catalog (essential oils by mail): 1-800-898-PURE
- Myotherapy Institute of Utah (home study school of massage): 1-800-338-8950
- International Association for Clear Thinking (teaches coping skills): 414-739-8311
- American Institute of Stress (sends information coping with stress): 1-800-24-RELAX
- International Stress Management Association (sends information on coping with stress): 619-693-4698

SEE ALSO

- Adjusting ANXIETY (page 296)
- Correcting CONFUSION AND MEMORY LOSS (page 314)
- Disarming DEPRESSION (page 324)
- Relieving DIARRHEA (page 328)
- Fighting FATIGUE (page 339)
- Eradicating IRRITABILITY (page 354)
- Taming NECK AND SHOULDER TENSION (page 374)
- Securing SOUND SLEEP (page 402)

relieving tired eyes

*i*n San Francisco I learned about Japanese eye pillows: silk envelope-shaped pouches filled with aromatic herbs and raw seeds or small beans. The herbs, usually chamomile and lavender, provide a faint aroma that promotes relaxation, and the seeds or beans add a firm but gentle weight to the eyes and surrounding area. To use an eye pillow (available at Japanese markets, herb shops, and specialty stores), lie down and place the pillow over your eyes. It's especially soothing mid-afternoon when tired eyes are common, perhaps from working on a computer. Try to use the pillow for 15 minutes, but even a 5-minute session will help to relax the muscles around the eye area. In addition, the eye pillow blocks out light, and with that external sensation quelled, you can use the time to meditate, relax, and rejuvenate.

Although eyes tire most often from overuse, drugs such as steroids, aspirin, and antihistamines can also be culprits, and these suggestions can help revitalize. However, if you see spots or flashes, or if you have blurred or double vision, see a health professional.

relief at your fingertips

For immediate refreshment, try a cold compress by wetting a face cloth with cold water, wringing it out, and arranging it on the eye area for 10 minutes. Or use a cold eye mask (available at pharmacies) that you keep on hand in the refrigerator.

Those who study foot reflexology hold that certain points or areas on our feet connect, by nerves, to particular organs and body parts. The points in the feet that correspond to the eyes are the fleshy middle parts of the big toes. To try it, soak your feet for 10 minutes in a basin of warm water to which you've added a handful of Epsom salts. Using your thumbs, massage the aforementioned area in circular or back and forth motions for about 5 minutes. If soaking is not convenient, rub your hands together briskly for about 10 seconds before massaging as described. Finish by drinking 8 ounces of water with a slice of fresh lemon, noticing a slight alertness in your eye area.

try a tea

German studies show that bilberry, a relative of blueberry, contains compounds that help to improve eyesight, especially night vision. Buy bilberry teabags, available at natural food stores and herb shops, and brew a cup according to the directions on the box for an afternoon break. For convenience, bilberry is also available in capsule form.

Cherokee healers have used the herb eyebright (available at natural food stores and herb shops) for centuries to soothe tired eyes and have added it to compounds that help soothe inflammation. Brew an afternoon tea by steeping $1\frac{1}{2}$ teaspoons each of dried eyebright and dried peppermint in 1 cup of just-boiled water, covered, for 4 minutes. Strain and drink. You can also make an overnight infusion by combining a handful of each fresh herb in 1 quart of room-temperature water, leaving the brew to steep at room temperature overnight. In the morning, discard the plant material and sip the eye-opening tea, which is especially helpful to allergy-affected tired morning eyes. (If you can't find fresh eyebright, use two handfuls of peppermint.)

To make soothing tea-based eye packs, steep 1 tablespoon of dried chamomile in 1 cup of just-boiled water, covered, until cool, at least 20 minutes. Discard the

HERBAL EYE DROPS

To refresh your eyes naturally, try homeopathic eyedrops (available at pharmacies, natural food stores, and herb shops) made from distilled water and a tincture of the herb eyebright. Take the bottle along on long car trips or keep it near your computer at work.

chamomile, then soak two cotton pads in the tea and place one on each closed eyelid for about 10 minutes. Both the scent and the tea itself help soothe and renew the eye area. (Although drinking the tea will not harm you, the taste is too strong to be enjoyable.)

best foods

RECIPES FOR
HEALTHY EYES

*Warm Sweet Potato Chips
(page 129)*

*Strawberry-Mango
Frappé (page 134)*

Foods high in eye-healthy beta carotene, such as carrots, sweet potatoes, winter squash, dark leafy greens, mangoes, papayas, peaches, and apricots, may help to strengthen eyes when eaten daily. For example, cut two carrots into sticks, wrap in plastic, and take the pack to work for a snack. Experts also warn against the nutrient-robbing effects of tobacco, caffeine, and refined sugar, especially when these substances are ingested at the same time.

smart supplements

To promote good eye health, some scientists recommend the following supplements:
- Beta carotene, 25,000 IUs daily
- Vitamin E, 400 IUs daily
- Zinc, 10 mg three times daily
- Vitamin C in the form of the Ayurvedic Indian gooseberry jam, chavanprash (available at natural food stores and Indian markets), 2 teaspoons daily

RESOURCES FOR HEALTHY EYES
- Arrowroot Natural Pharmacy (homeopathic preparations by mail): 1-800-234-8879
- National Eye Research Foundation (answers questions): 1-800-621-2258
- The Lighthouse Center for Education (sends information about eye health): 1-800-334-5497

SEE ALSO
- Healing HAY FEVER (page 342)
- Curing a HEADACHE (page 346)
- Releasing SINUS PRESSURE (page 392)

coddling
tired feet

An Italian herbalist told me that to prevent and cure tired feet, I should wear a pair of exercise sandals twice a day for 10 to 15 minutes. Originally created in Germany and now available at natural food stores and some shoe stores, exercise sandals are contoured to complement the feet and have little foot-stimulating nubs that massage and stimulate as you walk. I have followed the herbalist's advice for years and even take the sandals along when traveling so I can have energized feet throughout the world. In emergencies, however, I follow the advice below.

relief at your fingertips

To give yourself a revitalizing foot massage, rub your hands together briskly for about 10 seconds. Lightly coat the palms with a refreshingly scented lotion (see "Making Scents" later in this section). Sandwiching a foot between your palms so that the bottom touches one palm and the top touches the other, briskly move your hands toe to heel and back for several minutes. Then massage each toe individually. Next, rest your thumbs atop a foot for support while "walking" the four remaining fingers of each hand

*Always wear the most
comfortable, supportive
shoes you can. High heels
look great but can eventually hurt your feet, hips,
and back, so save them for
evenings when you'll be
getting out of the car and
going straight into the
restaurant—not walking
distances or standing for
hours.*

down the sole of your entire foot, repeating 10 times. Massage your other foot in the same way. You can also buy a foot reflexology chart at natural food stores and massage centers, which will guide you through a detailed and invigorating foot massage.

potent pose

For a stimulating stretch you can do anywhere, barefoot or not, alternate standing on your toes and heels for 5 seconds each, performing at least three repetitions. The stretch helps tone foot muscles as well as the supporting calf muscles. As a seated variation, simply alternately flex and point your feet, holding each position for 5 seconds.

making scents

To make your own stimulating foot massage lotion, combine 15 drops of essential oil of rosemary, available at herb shops and natural food stores, and 2 tablespoons of aloe vera gel and rub your feet with the mixture (or see "Relief at Your Fingertips" for a foot self-massage technique). The rosemary helps energize your feet by increasing circulation, and the aroma keeps feet fresh for hours.

Essential oil of rosemary can also be used in a vitalizing foot bath by combining 10 drops in a basin of warm water along with $\frac{1}{2}$ cup of Epsom salts. Dip your feet in, cover the basin with a towel to keep the heat in, and soak for 20 minutes. Towel-dry your feet, and for an extra lift, apply a light coating of rosemary foot lotion. For an extra refresher, thyme-scented body powder, available at pharmacies, can be sprinkled into shoes or rubbed onto feet to keep them dry and energized.

best foods

A diet high in light, low-fat foods such as fresh vegetables and fruits, lean protein like grilled fish, and such whole grains as brown rice and barley is best for your feet, since it will help to keep you from being overweight—a condition that puts stress on your feet.

RESOURCES FOR HAPPY FEET
· Footcare Information Center (answers questions): 1-800-366-8227
· American Podiatric Medical Association (sends pamphlets): 301-571-9200

SEE ALSO
· Easing ARTHRITIS PAIN (page 289)
· Surmounting SORE MUSCLES (page 399)

settling
an upset
stomach

settling
an upset
stomach

when symptoms may occur:

| *At night, for indigestion*

One winter, several days of indigestion in Kuala Lumpur, Malaysia, sent me seeking the advice of a Jamu man—a Malaysian herb doctor. Stop eating for a while and drink only water was the first thing he recommended, deducing from my complaints that I had ingested something disagreeable. Then he told me to take a capsule of acidophilus each morning 20 minutes before eating, supplying my digestive system with the "friendly" bacteria it needs to stay healthy. I've continued to take the acidophilus because, like the other digestion suggestions I've gleaned from around the globe, it works!

I have also learned that alcohol, aspirin, some prescription medications, stress, overeating, viruses, bacteria, not chewing food well, and food allergies can cause indigestion, with symptoms including abdominal pain, nausea, bloating, burping, gas, diarrhea, and heartburn. And while these suggestions can help, if you have rectal bleeding, black stools, or are vomiting blood, see a health professional.

potent pose

After eating, or at the first twinge of upset stomach, lie down on your left side. The pose encourages the flow of digestive secretions that can help avert discomfort.

try a tea

In Germany, where people go straight to the pharmacy with health complaints—and much of what they complain about is indigestion—the prescription is often for tea. Black tea contains compounds that can soothe an upset stomach. I like a combination I learned from an Italian friend: $1/2$ teaspoon each of orangy Earl Grey and smoky lapsang souchong, steeped in just-boiled water, covered, for about 3 minutes, then strain and sip as needed.

For a caffeine-free tea, try yarrow (available at herb shops and natural food stores), as recommended by German herbalists. Steep 1 teaspoon of the dried herb in 1 cup of just-boiled water, covered, for 4 minutes, then strain and sip as needed. Dried peppermint is also soothing and can be brewed the same way, but since peppermint aggravates heartburn, it should be avoided if that condition exists. Both yarrow and peppermint are what herbalists call carminatives, or substances that relieve digestive distress.

To make a stimulating tea to relieve an upset stomach, combine 3 slices each of fresh ginger and lemon in $1 1/4$ cups of water in a small saucepan and bring to a boil. Continue to boil until the water has been reduced to 1 cup, about 5 or 6 minutes, then strain and sip a cup as needed.

HERBAL RELIEF

For a quick nostrum to soothe an upset stomach, chew a teaspoon of toasted fennel seed, available at supermarkets, natural food stores, and herb shops. To toast the seeds, place $1/4$ cup in a dry small sauté pan and heat on high, stirring constantly, until fragrant and lightly browned, about 2 minutes. Let the seeds cool, then store them in a small jar so you can take them to work or keep them in the car.

making scents

Essential oils of lemongrass and peppermint (available at herb shops and natural food stores) contain volatile oil compounds that, when inhaled, can help soothe an upset stomach. (Peppermint may aggravate heartburn, and those who suffer from it should stick with lemongrass.) For a simple approach, dot 1 drop of each (or 2 drops of either single essence) on a tissue and inhale for a few moments as needed. Take the essential oil with you to work to negate a stress-induced upset stomach, dotting 1 drop on a cool light bulb just before lighting it. As the bulb warms, it will emit a stomach-calming aroma.

Although essential oils of lemongrass and peppermint may irritate the skin and should not be used in a bath, essential oil of lemon balm (*Melissa*) offers nerve-soothing volatile oils that can calm an upset stomach. To try it, run a warm bath, adding in 10 drops of essence before you climb in to soak for 15 minutes. You can also buy a ready-made melissa herb bath at natural food stores and herb shops and use it as directed on the package.

best foods

If you have an upset stomach, tea and dry toast will keep you from becoming dizzy from lack of food while not upsetting you further. To prevent an upset stomach, avoid foods containing refined sugar, as well as junk foods, fatty foods, fried foods, spicy foods, caffeine, orange juice, and red meat. If dairy products or wheat make your stomach upset, don't eat them in any form (read food labels). You may be one of the many people who are allergic to those foods and should seek the advice of a health professional to help you make a healthy food plan.

RESOURCES FOR GOOD DIGESTION
- National Digestive Diseases Information Clearinghouse (sends pamphlets): 301-654-3810
- Digestive Disease National Coalition (provides information): 202-544-7497
- American Cancer Society (information for cancer patients who are undergoing chemotherapy): 404-320-3333

SEE ALSO
- Adjusting ANXIETY (page 296)
- Relieving DIARRHEA (page 328)
- Overcoming JET LAG (page 358)
- Negating NAUSEA AND MORNING SICKNESS (page 371)
- Managing STRESS (page 406)

alleviating water retention

One of the interesting things about being a woman is the changes that accompany the gender. For example, as a very young woman I realized that I retained water before menstruation—sometimes up to 5 pounds of water weight, an alarmingly large amount for a small person. I quickly learned that drinking eight 8-ounce glasses of water a day helped to flush out the excess water in my system. In addition, over the years I have adopted gently diuretic herbs and foods that I have discovered around the world.

Aside from hormones, water retention can be caused by some medications and medical conditions (such as heart, bladder, kidney, and liver problems). If you retain water and are unsure of the cause, see a health professional.

try a tea

Parsley tea is a natural flush for the system and can be made by steeping 2 teaspoons of dried or 4 teaspoons of the fresh herb in 1 cup of just-boiled water, covered, for 5 minutes, then strain; sip 1 cup three times a day. In a pinch, eat about 2 tablespoons of fresh parsley three times a day. As a bonus, fresh parsley is a good source of the nutrients beta carotene, vitamin C, and iron, in addition to potassium, a mineral that is depleted by most prescription diuretics.

In France I learned to drink a cup of linden flower (tilia or lime flower) tea each evening as a mild diuretic and gentle nervine. To make a cup, steep 1 teaspoon of dried linden flower tea (available at herb shops and natural food stores) in 1 cup of just-boiled water, covered, for 10 minutes, then strain. If I've eaten an unusually salty food, I notice that the linden flower tea flushes the excess sodium from my system, so I do not waken the next morning with swollen fingers or puffy under-eye areas.

best foods

A diet high in low-sodium fresh fruits and vegetables can help prevent water retention. Try nutrient-rich leafy greens such as arugula and kale. Add fresh dandelion leaves, a natural diuretic that's high in potassium, to green salads. But the single most important thing you can do to prevent water retention is to avoid salty junk foods, canned foods, processed foods, salty cheeses, pickles, olives, soy sauce, dried meats, and smoked and cured fish and meats.

KEEP MOVING

Exercising for 20 minutes at least three times a week with such activities as walking, yoga, bicycling, tai chi, and swimming can help prevent water retention.

RESOURCES TO PREVENT WATER RETENTION
- National Kidney Foundation (conducts seminars): 1-800-622-9010
- American College of Cardiology (answers questions): 1-800-253-4636
- Arizona Heart Institute & Foundation (answers questions): 1-800-345-HART

SEE ALSO
- Mending MENSTRUAL CRAMPS (page 366)
- Pacifying the PROSTATE (page 384)

the savory pantry

i have always dreamed of writing a food book with no recipes. With it, the reader would be inspired to fling open pantry and refrigerator, creating delicious and vitalizing dishes from what is immediately at hand. Alas, most people prefer measurements and specific ingredients in their food books, but by suggesting how to stock a pantry, I can in a small way encourage you to invent your own meals, as well as to have on hand what you need to cook the recipes in this book.

Whole grains, such as brown rice, barley, millet, whole wheat, oats, and buckwheat, appear frequently in *Savoring the Day*. Buy whole grains that have been grown without chemicals and pesticides, available at natural food stores and many supermarkets. The labels usually read "organically grown." Grains should be evenly sized, dust-free, and smell fresh and nutty. Since whole grains are attractive to insects, store them for up to 12 months in the refrigerator or freezer to protect your supply.

Buy and store organically grown dried beans the same way, noting that they should be bright and uniform in color (fading indicates improper or overly long storage).

For the tastiest and most nutritious vegetables and fruits, buy organically grown produce, in season, as close to the time of preparation as possible. Most vegetables and fruits need to be stored in the refrigerator, but if you're unsure about a particular specimen, call your county extension office or the produce department of a nearby supermarket to ask. If you can't buy organically grown produce, peel off the skin or outer layers. Keep your menus interesting by buying a variety of shapes, sizes, textures, and colors of vegetables and fruits.

As for flavor, stock up on fresh garlic, shallots, and organically grown fresh herbs. Buy organically grown, nonirradiated dried herbs at natural food stores and some supermarkets, purchasing small amounts at a time. Store them in tightly closed glass jars, away from sunlight and heat, for up to 6 months. Prepared mustards, hot pepper sauces, salsas, and herbed vinegars are good to keep on hand as salt-free, fat-free flavor enhancers.

The following are particulars on selected foods used in *Savoring the Day* recipes that you may find unfamiliar.

ADUKI BEANS Sometimes labeled "adzuki," these are smallish, kidney bean–colored legumes that Ayurvedic Indian cooks often call red mung beans. They are available at natural food stores, Asian markets, and some supermarkets. Buy organically grown, dried aduki beans that are evenly sized, uniformly colored, and a bright, not faded, brownish-red. Store them in the refrigerator for up to a year. Aduki beans taste like creamy-sweet kidney beans, cook comparatively quickly, may cause less intestinal gas than some other bean varieties, and are said by Japanese and Chinese doctors to promote good kidney health and overall body vitality. For convenience, store a cooked batch of aduki beans in the fridge for up to a week, swirling 2 tablespoons into 1 cup of cooked herbed brown rice for a quick lunch or dinner entrée.

ARAME Pronounced ARE-uh-may, this briny-tasting sea herb is available dried from natural food stores, Asian markets, and some supermarkets. It's usually packed in see-through plastic and should look like very black, wavy, thin ribbons, not faded or dusty in appearance. Arame is prized in coastal Asian cooking for the small amounts of trace minerals it contains—particularly calcium, phosphorus, and iron. In addition, studies have indicated that eating arame and other sea herbs such as dulse and nori may neutralize the effects of environmental radiation. To try it, rinse $1/4$ cup of arame under running water, then add it to a vegetable soup to serve four, simmering for at least 10 minutes. For a change of pace, substitute the similar but more beany-tasting sea herb hijiki.

BURDOCK This foot-long brown-skinned root can measure up to an inch in width and has a savory-green flavor and the texture of a carrot. Buy fresh burdock roots in the refrigerated sections of natural food stores, Asian markets, and some supermarkets. To check for freshness, gently try to bend the roots, which should be stiff, not flaccid. Fresh burdock will keep, refrigerated, for up to 3 weeks. You may also wish to check with a garden center about easily growing your own burdock. Sliced dried burdock, for use in tea blends or in long-cooking soups is available packaged at natural food stores and herb shops and will keep at room temperature for about a year. Japanese herbalists recommend burdock, fresh or dried, to gently cleanse the intestines while treating breakouts and rashy skin, and to squelch craving for sweets. Since burdock can be cooling to the body, it is commonly prescribed in warmer seasons. To try fresh burdock, make a recipe for carrot soup or stew, substituting sliced burdock for half of the carrots.

CHINESE FERMENTED BLACK BEANS These are black soybeans that have been preserved in salt. Buy a small package off the shelf at Asian markets and some supermarkets, storing the beans tightly covered at room temperature, where they will last indefinitely. Since Chinese fermented black beans are extremely salty, they are used in very small amounts—1 teaspoon in a recipe to serve four—to richly flavor sautés, stir-fries, soups, and stews. To prepare them, rinse well under running water to remove excess salt, then mince and add to the dish before cooking. Some Chinese herbalists prescribe adding fermented black beans to the diet to treat reproductive disorders in both men and women.

DAIKON RADISH. FRESH Popular in Japanese, Vietnamese, and Chinese cuisines, this long white radish is crunchy and sweet when more than 2 inches thick, and hot and spicy when thinner. Buy it at natural food stores, Asian markets, and most supermarkets, choosing specimens that are bright white and have edible greens attached. Daikon radish roots will keep for up to 1 month when refrigerated, but the greens should be used at once. To prepare daikon root Japanese style, coarsely grate about 1 tablespoon for each diner, dotting 1 or 2 drops of tamari soy sauce or reduced-sodium soy sauce atop each serving. This condiment, a sort of Japanese salsa, accompanies fatty foods because its taste is refreshing and it aids in the digestion of fats. Daikon root can also be sliced and added to vegetable soups and stews and to miso soup. Daikon greens can be mixed and enjoyed with other salad greens or steamed like spinach.

DAIKON RADISH. DRIED This is made by thinly slicing fresh daikon root into ribbons and drying it in the sun. Buy it off the shelf in cellophane packages at natural food stores, Asian markets, and some supermarkets. The color should be creamy to pale yellow, not deep brown. The texture should be pliable, not stiff, which indicates too-long storage. Once at home, store dried daikon in a covered glass jar on a shelf, where it will keep for 3 months before becoming too hard. Some Japanese herbalists hold that adding dried daikon to the diet twice a week may help to lower high blood pressure levels. To use dried daikon, rinse a handful well under cool running water, then add it to taste to a soup (such as onion soup) or stew before cooking. Dried daikon is prized by Japanese cooks for its rich, sweet taste, and for its ability to enhance flavors without adding salt, fat, or sugar.

GARAM MASALA A lively spice combination from India, garam masala is composed of at least 6 ingredients and can contain up to 20, depending on the blender. Aromatics such as cumin seed, coriander seed, fennel seed, turmeric, garlic, and hot peppers are common additions to garam masala. Two ready-made versions are available at Indian markets, natural food stores, and some supermarkets. Garam masala paste comes in glass jars and contains oil, which contributes to its texture. Swirl 1 teaspoon into 2 cups of steamed vegetables, soup, or hot rice for an effervescent flavor. Store garam masala paste in the refrigerator for up to 4 months. The powdered form, comprising ground spices and no oil, can be used the same way, but since oil carries flavor, a bit more of the powder is required to reach the same pungency. Ayurvedic Indian healers hold that regular consumption of garam masala promotes good digestion.

MISO A rich and hearty flavoring paste, miso is made from soybeans and sea salt. Often such grains as rice and barley are added. Japanese, Chinese, and Vietnamese cooks use miso to flavor soups, stews, sautés, stir-fries, sauces, and rice and noodle dishes, using ¼ to 1 teaspoon of miso paste for each serving. Buy miso from the refrigerated case at natural food stores, Asian markets, and some supermarkets, noting of the several varieties that the lighter the miso, the less salty it will be. Keep miso in the refrigerator at home, where it will last indefinitely. Miso is a fermented food, thus containing the "friendly" bacteria needed for healthy digestion. For that reason, a recipe should not be boiled after miso has been added, since the heat will destroy miso's beneficial organisms.

MUSHROOMS, SHIITAKE When fresh, these flat-topped fungi are golden brown; when dried, they are dark brown and wrinkly. Buy meaty-tasting shiitakes at natural food stores, Asian markets, and many supermarkets. The fresh version will keep, refrigerated, for up to 2 weeks, and the dried ones will keep, tightly covered, at room temperature indefinitely. Shiitakes are celebrated in the cuisines of Japan and China for their strong, appealing flavor, as well as for purporting to prevent hardening of the arteries and high blood pressure. In addition, research indicates that shiitakes contain polysaccharide compounds that may repel viruses. To prepare fresh shiitakes, discard the stems, adding the caps, whole or sliced, to vegetable sautés, stir-fries, soups, stews, and rice and noodle dishes to taste. To prepare dried shiitakes, discard the stems and soak the caps in hot water or stock for 5 minutes before adding to the recipe. Be sure also to use the flavorful soaking water in the recipe.

NETTLE This parsley-flavored herb is used frequently in *Savoring the Day* because it contains small amounts of such important nutrients as calcium and iron. In addition, it is supportive to the adrenals, helping to generate and conserve energy. Buy organically grown dried nettle at herb shops and natural food stores, looking for a bright green-blue color and uncrushed leaves. Stored in a tightly closed glass jar, dried nettle will keep for about 6 months. To use nettle, add 1 teaspoon for each serving to soups and stews, where it adds a sprightly fragrance and taste. Note that ingestion of nettle may aggravate high blood pressure conditions, so those with hypertension may wish to avoid it.

NOODLES, JAPANESE Those who are interested in adding more whole foods to their diets may wish to stock up on nutritious, easily digested Japanese noodles. Soba is made from buckwheat and looks like tan angel-hair pasta. The buckwheat—and sometimes the addition of mountain yam or herbs—gives soba a nutty, hearty flavor. Buy it at natural food stores, Asian markets, and some supermarkets, substituting whole wheat angel-hair pasta if soba is unavailable. Since soba cooks in about 5 minutes, it's a quick yet nutritious food to keep on hand. So are udon noodles (available in the same places as soba), made from whole wheat flour and looking like light tan linguini. Somen are similar to udon but slightly thinner. Whole wheat linguine can be substituted for both somen and udon.

REDUCED-FAT TOFU Although tofu, to many, means "health food," investigation shows that a whopping half of its calories come from fat. Reduced-fat tofu, available in the refrigerated sections (or vacuum packed on shelves) of natural food stores and many supermarkets, is 30% fat—not a lowfat food, but certainly lower in fat than the original. To try low-fat tofu, slice it into slabs, pressing out the excess liquid. Marinate the slabs in a spicy mustard sauce, then grill or broil until burnished, about 4 to 5 minutes on each side.

REDUCED-SODIUM SOY SAUCE Spoonful for spoonful, regular soy sauce and tamari soy sauce contain about a sixth as much sodium as table salt. But at 1,029 mg of sodium per tablespoonful, that can still be a lot of sodium, especially for those who are hypertensive or tend to retain water. In those cases, reduced-sodium soy sauce, with 500 to 660 mg of sodium per tablespoonful, is a better choice. Buy it at natural food stores and some supermarkets, looking for brands that contain no preservatives, coloring agents, additives, or MSG. Depending on how the soybeans are manufactured (soy sauce is made from soybeans and water), reduced-sodium varieties can be as flavorful as regular soy sauce and can be used in exactly the same quantity.

SEITAN For those attempting to reduce the meat in their diets, seitan is a vibrant option. Also called wheat meat or wheat gluten, seitan is made from wheat flour and water, with the occasional addition of soy sauce, kombu seaweed, chickpea flour, and herbs such as garlic. Buy it refrigerated, frozen, or canned off the shelf at natural food stores, Asian markets, and some supermarkets. Store seitan accordingly, abiding by the "use by" date. Marinate and grill seitan, grind it and make vegetarian burgers, slice it to use on sandwiches, or add it to soups, stews, stir-fries, and sautés before cooking.

SOY CHEESE Those who are allergic to dairy or who are trying to eliminate it to help prevent asthma, sinus congestion, and other respiratory complaints should keep this soy milk–based alternative on hand. Soy cheese comes in mozzarella, jack, cream cheese, and Cheddar varieties, with jalapeño, low-fat, and nonfat options available. Soy cheese tastes cheesy and melts nicely when gently heated on pizzas or in sandwiches and casseroles. Find soy cheese at natural food stores and some supermarkets in the refrigerated sections. For home storage, keep soy cheese refrigerated, abiding by the "use by" date. Do, however, check for mold before that date, as some soy cheeses spoil before the indicated date.

TAHINI This rich, tan-colored paste, also called sesame paste or butter, is made when sesame seeds are ground to a paste. It's like peanut butter, with sesame seeds instead of peanuts. Two types are available, roasted and nonroasted, the former being made from roasted sesame seeds. As the roasting tends to encourage rancidity and spoilage, buy the nonroasted kind. Also note that tahini comes salted and salt-free, so those who are hypertensive or tend to retain water have a low-sodium option. Tahini is available at natural food stores, many supermarkets, Indian markets, and Middle Eastern markets. Store tahini in the refrigerator, where it will last for up to a year. Tahini is favored in small amounts by Ayurvedic Indian herbalists for its ability to help soothe anxiety, perhaps due to the small amount of calcium it contains. Use tahini in small amounts to add body and richness to sauces, soups, stews, and dips, or instead of peanut butter on sandwiches, crackers, and apple slices.

TEMPEH Invented in Indonesia for Buddhist vegetarians, this meaty-textured soybean patty has an interesting, slightly winy flavor, as if it has been marinated. Buy it in the refrigerated or frozen sections at natural food stores, some Asian markets, and some supermarkets. Keep it in the refrigerator for up to 2 weeks or in the freezer for up to 6 months. Sauté, bake, or broil tempeh, adding it to stir-fries, soups, stews, or casseroles. Proponents of tempeh claim it promotes vitality.

UMEBOSHI PLUM These small, deep rose-colored fruits are preserved in sea salt and sometimes in the herb perilla (also called chiso leaves). Their salty sourness helps neutralize stomach acid and abates dizziness due to travel sickness and the flu. Sometimes called *ume* plum, they are available at natural food stores. Asian markets, and some supermarkets. Look for whole plums or plum paste, 1/2 teaspoon of which is equal to one plum. Store ume plums in the refrigerator or in a cool pantry for up to a year. To promote good digestion, use ume plums in cooking, adding 1/2 mashed plum to a salad dressing, casserole, or soup to serve four (omit the salt) or mashed atop a steaming bowl of brown rice. Be sure to pack some ume plums in a little jar for traveling, for cases of jet lag and digestive distress. If these situations occur, pop a whole plum in your mouth and let it slowly dissolve. Then continue to suck on the pit for about an hour.

bibliography

Balch, James F., and Balch, Phyllis A. *Prescription for Nutritional Healing*. Garden City Park, New York: Avery Publishing Group, Inc., 1990.

Beinfield, Harriet, and Efrem Korngold. *Between Heaven and Earth: A Guide to Chinese Medicine*. New York: Ballantine Books, Random House, 1991.

Feit, Richard, and Paul Zmiewski. *Acumoxa Therapy: Reference and Study Guide*. Brookline, Mass.: Paradigm Publications, 1989.

Gach, Michael Reed. *Acu-Yoga*. Tokyo and New York: Japan Publications, 1981.

Gagne, Steve. *Energetics of Food*. Santa Fe, N.M.: Spiral Sciences, 1990.

Hurley, Judith Benn. *The Good Herb: Remedies and Recipes from Nature*. New York: William Morrow and Company, Inc., 1995.

Kaptchuk, Ted J. *The Web That Has No Weaver: Understanding Chinese Medicine*. Chicago: Congdon and Weed, Inc., 1983.

Kelder, Peter. *Ancient Secret of the Fountain of Youth*. Gig Harbor, Wash.: Harbor Press, Inc., 1985.

Lamberg, Lynne. *Bodyrhythms*. New York: William Morrow and Company, Inc., 1994.

Orlock, Carol. *Inner Time*. New York: Birch Lane Press, Carol Publishing Group, 1993.

Turner, Kristina. *The Self-Healing Cookbook*. Grass Valley, Cal.: Earthtones Press, 1987.

recipes index

general index

Page numbers in **boldface** refer to recipes.

burgers:
　　garbanzo, **74**
　　pinto-buckwheat, **72**
burritos with quinoa and jalapeño, **243**
butter:
　　apple, with blueberries, **51**
　　banana-date, **49**
　　pumpkin-cranberry, **50**
butternut squash:
　　black bean stew with, **205**
　　with leeks, **184**
　　soup with scallions, spicy, **313**
B vitamins, 63, 69, 165, 298, 316, 327, 340, 344, 364, 395, 405, 409

cabbage:
　　coleslaw with roasted peppers, **182**
　　red, with balsamic vinegar, braised, **186**
　　red, pickled, soba with tahini-mustard sauce and, **111**
　　savoy, soup with Chinese licorice root and white miso, **215**
caffeine, 11, 39, 171, 340, 359
　　tremors, 308–309
cakes, red lentil, with garlic and sage, **154**
calendula:
　　gum rinse, **397**
　　tea, 333
calming evening churna, **140**
calming recipes:
　　aduki bean salad with lemon-ginger dressing, **97**
　　asparagus with lemon-garlic paste, **91**
　　black bean–veggie burgers, **75**
　　buckwheat with roasted peppers and fresh sage, **100**
　　carrot soup with light miso and ginger, **62**
　　chilled noodles with miso-basil pesto, **106**
　　chopped vegetable salad with oregano and lemon, **88**
　　cracked wheat with fresh herbs, **99**
　　creamy cucumber and cracked wheat salad, **105**
　　cucumber spears with citrus and soy, **95**
　　dilled potato pie, **78**
　　elbows with dandelion greens, **107**
　　fresh tuna salad with tomato and capers, **96**
　　grilled chicken sandwiches with sesame and chives, **69**
　　herbed tostadas with zucchini, carrot and red onion, **70**
　　lemony rice with saffron and fresh peas, **104**
　　lentils with fragrant spice paste, **98**
　　mashed potatoes with garlic and scallion, **90**
　　mixed greens with orange, radish and whole wheat croutons, **87**
　　mixed greens with sea herbs and sesame-lime dressing, **92**
　　mochi soup with green beans and corn, **63**

one-hour whole wheat sage and garlic bread, **83**
pinto-buckwheat burgers, **72**
pizza with fresh basil, **79**
potato salad with tomatoes and fresh basil, **94**
seitan with sugar snaps, **102**
sesame-scented couscous, **108**
sesame squash soup, **61**
shiitake stock, **68**
soba with tahini-mustard sauce and pickled red cabbage, **111**
spicy potato salad, **89**
spring greens with pea shoots, **93**
white bean and eggplant stew, **66**
white bean hummus with tomato and fresh basil, **81**
whole wheat spaghetti with fresh spinach sauce, **110**
wild rice salad with lavender, **86**
ziti with asparagus and fresh thyme, **109**
camphor, 375, 400
candles, ear, 336–337
canola oil, 284, 334, 338
cantaloupe ice, cool, **274**
caper(s):
　　fresh tuna salad with tomato and, **96**
　　grilled tofu with lemon and, **231**
　　-tomato salsa, red lentil chili with, **217**
caramel-maple corn with raisins, **130**
cardamom essence, **41**
carrot(s):
　　-aduki soup with sage, **221**
　　and burdock, Kinpira style, **170**
　　-ginger breakfast cookies, **17**
　　-ginger marinade, **162**
　　herbed tostadas with zucchini, red onion and, **70**
　　jet lag and, **360**
　　-raisin muffins, **45**
　　soup with light miso and ginger, **62**
catnip, 282, 389, 404, 408
　　-chamomile tea, 138, 298
cauliflower pâté, savory, **201**
cayenne pepper tea, **39**
cedarwood incense, 139
celery, in ten-vegetable stew, **323**
celery seed, 293
Center of Power, 138
cereal, *see specific grains*
chamomile, 389, 404, 408, 410
　　-catnip combo tea, **138**
　　-catnip tea, 298
　　for hay fever, 343
　　-peppermint tea, 38–39, 372, 381
　　tea, 58, 282, 329, 334, 364, 375, 411
chavanprash, 32, 39, 310, 321, 353, 395, 409
cheese, soy, 425–426
cheesecake, pumpkin, **261**
cherry jam with walnuts, **28**
cherry-vanilla granola, **25**
chervil, for hay fever, 343

chi candy, 340
chicken sandwiches with sesame and chives, grilled, **69**
chickpea(s) (garbanzo beans):
　　burgers, **74**
　　filling, spicy, whole wheat crepes with, **151**
children, asthma and, 301
chili:
　　red lentil, with tomato-caper salsa, **217**
　　spicy lentil, **208**
chilled soups:
　　avocado soup with lemon, orange and lime, **218**
　　potato, with leek and fennel, **219**
　　spinach gazpacho with fresh basil, **212**
　　zucchini puree with roasted pepper and marjoram, **216**
Chinese angelica, *see dong quai*
Chinese date tea, 292–293
Chinese fermented black beans, 423
Chinese (Panax) ginseng tea, 378, 388
Chinese licorice root:
　　savoy cabbage soup with white miso and, **215**
　　for serenity tea, 58
　　tea, 115–116, 333, 351, 360
Chinese recipes:
　　miso-vegetable soup, **34**
　　rice cereal, 21
　　tofu salad with honey-ginger dressing, **76**
Chinese theory, xii, xiii, 36, 37, 50, 66, 84, 103, 155, 181, 191, 204, 239, 242, 322, 386, 392
　　see also accupressure; acupuncture
Chinese vinaigrette, "un-chicken" salad with, **197**
chips:
　　pita, **128**
　　warm sweet potato, **129**
chirazushi (cucumbers with sushi rice), **196**
chiropractors, 292, 363
chiso leaves, 426
chives:
　　corn crepes with fresh, **152**
　　grilled chicken sandwiches with sesame and, **69**
chlorophyll, 306, 334
　　constipation and, 318
cholesterol, 194
chowder, fragrant corn, with fresh herbs, **327**
chromium, 275, 307
chutney, plum, **155**
cider:
　　-citrus dressing, blanched asparagus with, **176**
　　cranberry, **52**
　　pears in, with rosemary, **272**
　　tea, 10
cinnamon:
　　-blueberry muffins, **44**
　　bread pudding with apricots and, **266**

poses (*continued*)
    for sore muscles, 400
    for upset stomach, 416
posole (dried corn stew), **209**
potassium, 107, 165, 269, 401
    deficiency of, 223
potato(es):
    -leek cobbler, savory, **223**
    mashed, with garlic and scallion, **90**
    pie, dilled, **78**
    red, curried, **168**
    red, in fragrant corn chowder with fresh
        herbs, **327**
    salad, spicy, **89**
    salad with tomatoes and fresh basil, **94**
    salad with watercress and smoked trout, **85**
    soup with leek and fennel, chilled, **219**
    warm red, with tomato and scallion, **178**
pot belly, 363
presentations, prepping for, 380–383
Progressive Muscle Relaxation, 136, 372
prostaglandins, 366
prostate gland, 384–385
pudding:
    apple-scented rice, with dates, **267**
    bread, with cinnamon and apricots, **266**
    creamy date, with cinnamon and
        coconut, **268**
pumpkin:
    cheesecake, **261**
    -cinnamon yogurt, frozen, **278**
    -cranberry butter, **50**
    pie scent, 389
    polenta with black bean salsa, **245**
pumpkin seeds, 334
    with garlic and dill, roasted, **119**
punch, peppermint, **53**
puree, collard, roasted Vidalia onions with,
    370

quinoa, burritos with jalapeño and, **243**

radish(es), 84
    mixed greens with orange, whole wheat
        croutons and, **87**
    in spring greens with pea shoots, **93**
    see also daikon radish
raisin(s):
    -carrot muffins, **45**
    and date granola, **26**
    maple-caramel corn with, **130**
    no-cook oats and, **23**
    -oat breakfast bars, **391**
rashes and breakouts, 304–307
raspberry(ies):
    and apricot jam, **30**
    filling for a tart or pie, **262**
    sauce, giant pancake with, **14**
raspberry leaf tea, 351
ravioli:
    with basil sauce, **257**
    with mushroom sauce, **258**

relaxation tapes, 352
relaxing herbs, vegetable soup with, **206**
relish:
    warm onion, millet croquettes with, **224**
    warm tomato, with basil and pine nuts,
        157
Rescue Remedy, 297–298, 382
rheumatoid arthritis, 28, 289–295
rhododendron, 364
rhubarb-strawberry crisp, **262**
riboflavin, 234
rice:
    brown, *see* brown rice
    cereal, Chinese style, **21**
    chirazushi, **196**
    cream, **22**
    green, with shallots and parsley, **195**
    Italian, with black beans and mushrooms,
        239
    Italian with zucchini and fresh sage, **238**
    lemony, with saffron and fresh peas, **104**
    pudding, apple-scented, with dates, **267**
    rolls, **101**
    saffron-scented beans and, **236**
    wild, salad with lavender, **86**
ricotta:
    crust, spicy tofu pie with, **229**
    faux, **127**
rolls, rice, **101**
romaine with lime-anchovy dressing, **191**
romance, reviving of, 386–391
rose essence, 35, 41
rose geranium essence, 59, 116, 139,
    325–326, 334, 381, 389
rosemary, 294
    in braised vegetables with couscous, **260**
    dry hair massage with, 331
    and lavender tea, **325**
    onion gravy with, **158**
    onion soup with miso and, **213**
    pears in cider with, **272**
    sweet potato bread with orange and, **48**
    tea, 315, 348, 400–401
    tempeh with roasted peppers and, **251**
    -tomato dressing, grilled vegetable salad
        with, **173**
rosemary essence, 41, 379, 414
    for early morning, 11
    to prevent pain, 6
rose water:
    hydrating, 333
    oatmeal scones with, **43**
rotini with cumin-tomato sauce, **255**
Royal Bee jelly, 335
rubs:
    for asthma, 301
    for neck and shoulder tension, 375
    see also accupressure; massages

SAD (seasonal affective disorder), 324
saffron:
    enchiladas with barley, squash and, **225**

    lemony rice with fresh peas and, **104**
    -scented beans and rice, **236**
sage, 397
    aduki-carrot soup with, **221**
    buckwheat with roasted peppers and
        fresh, **100**
    dressing, grilled tofu salad with fresh, **230**
    fusilli with fresh mushrooms and, **253**
    Italian rice with zucchini and fresh, **238**
    kibbe with sweet potato and, **147**
    red lentil cakes with garlic and, **154**
    tea, 39, 351
    whole wheat and garlic bread, one-hour,
        83
sage essence, 304
Saint-John's-wort, 363
salicylic acid, 293, 348
saline nose sprays, 312
salmon:
    with fennel, grilled, **383**
    soup with garlic and ginger, **67**
    spread, herbed, **71**
salsa:
    basil-sesame, baked tofu with, **232**
    black bean, pumpkin polenta with, **245**
    fresh, **73**
    fresh peach, **124**
    habanero, **125**
    spicy orange, **123**
    tomato-caper, red lentil chili with, **217**
sandals, exercise, 413
sandalwood essence, 139, 284, 334
sandalwood incense, 139
sandwich spread, energizing, **80**
satay, seitan, with garlicky peanut sauce,
    241
savory cauliflower pâté, **201**
savory pantry, 421–426
savory potato-leek cobbler, **223**
savoy cabbage soup with Chinese licorice
    root and white miso, **215**
saw palmetto (*Serenoa serrulata*), 384, 385
scallion(s):
    mashed potatoes with garlic and, **90**
    spicy squash soup with, **313**
    warm red potatoes with tomato and, **178**
schizandra berry, 388
scones:
    oatmeal, with rose water, **43**
    three-grain, **18**
sea herbs, *see* arame
seasonal affective disorder (SAD), 324
seasonal rhinitis (hay fever), 342–345
seitan, 425
    with green beans, garlic and ginger, **242**
    with portobello mushrooms and fresh
        basil, **240**
    satay with garlicky peanut sauce, **241**
    with sugar snaps, **102**
    "un-chicken" salad with Chinese vinai-
        grette, **197**
    "un-chicken" salad with watercress, **198**

Seldane, 394
septum stimulator, 403
serenity, tea for, 58
Serenoa serrulata (saw palmetto), 384, 385
sesame:
 -basil salsa, baked tofu with, **232**
 dressing, couscous salad with, **259**
 grilled chicken sandwiches with chives and, **69**
 -lime dressing, mixed greens with sea herbs and, **92**
 sauce, chilled somen noodles with snow peas and, **188**
 -scented couscous, **108**
 seeds, warm onion salad with toasted, **183**
 squash soup, **61**
sesame oil, 294
 to prevent pain, 6
seven-step limbering for fingers, hands, arms and neck, 290
Severent, 301, 302
sexuality, enhancement of, 386–391
shake:
 pineapple wake-up, **33**
 sleepytime, **405**
shallots:
 Brussels sprouts with shiitakes and, **174**
 green rice with parsley and, **195**
shampoos, 331
shiitake mushroom(s), 424
 basmati pilaf with asparagus and, **235**
 Brussels sprouts with shallots and, **174**
 fusilli with sage and fresh, **253**
 Italian rice with black beans and, **239**
 sauce, ravioli with, **258**
 -spinach spread, **144**
 stock, **68**
Siberian (Eleuthero) ginseng, 9–10, 114, 340, 388
sinus pressure, 392–395
 clearing of, 37
skewers, spicy grilled tempeh on, **249**
skin, 332–335
 recipes for smooth, 307, 335
 see also breakouts and rashes
skullcap, 282, 378, 389, 404
sleep, 279–281, 362–363, 402–405
 accupressure for, 403
 aromatherapy for, 404
 best foods for, 404
 night shift and, 378
 promotion of, 379
 sinus pressure and, 393
 supplements for, 405
 teas for, 404
 television and, 280
 windows and, 302
sleeping pills, 281
sleepytime shake, **405**
smoking, winter squash and, 184

snoring, 403
snow peas:
 chilled somen noodles with sesame sauce and, **188**
 jet lag and, 360
soba (Japanese noodles), 425
 with tahini-mustard sauce and pickled red cabbage, **111**
sodas, 38
soft tacos with spicy summer vegetables, **244**
somen noodles with snow peas and sesame sauce, chilled, **188**
soybean(s), 423
 cucumber spears with citrus and, **95**
 see also tempeh; tofu
soy cheese, 425–426
soy nuts, roasted, 118
soy sauce:
 -mustard vinaigrette, bulgur with asparagus, green beans and, **247**
 reduced-sodium, 425
spaghetti, whole wheat, with fresh spinach sauce, **110**
spearmint, in grilled eggplant in lettuce petals, **146**
spice paste, fragrant, lentils with, **98**
spinach:
 gazpacho with fresh basil, **212**
 -mushroom spread, **144**
 salad with tempeh croutons, **190**
 sauce, fresh, with whole wheat spaghetti, **110**
 spicy white bean salad with, **193**
spread:
 creamy basil, **126**
 eggplant, with Greek olives and garlic, **142**
 energizing sandwich, **80**
 herbed salmon, **71**
 morning immune-boost, **32**
 mushroom-spinach, **144**
spring greens with pea shoots, **93**
spring vegetable stock, **202**
squash:
 baby, with garam masala, braised, **179**
 butternut, black bean stew with, **205**
 butternut, with leeks, **184**
 enchiladas with barley, saffron and, **225**
 sesame soup, **61**
 soup with scallions, spicy, **313**
 and sugar snaps with black bean sauce, **177**
 summer, in grilled vegetable salad with tomato-rosemary dressing, **173**
 yellow summer, in Italian rice with zucchini and fresh sage, **238**
stock:
 shiitake, **68**
 spring vegetable, **202**
 winter vegetable, **203**
stomach upset, 88, 149, 415–417
strawberry(ies):
 -mango frappé, **134**

-rhubarb crisp, **262**
 syrup, orange-scented, **31**
stress management, 406–409
stretches, *see* poses
sugar, white, 117, 294
sugar snap peas:
 seitan with, **102**
 and squash with black bean sauce, **177**
sulfites, 268, 309
summer fruits with maple-cinnamon topping, baked, **270**
summer squash, in grilled vegetable salad with tomato-rosemary dressing, **173**
summer vegetables, spicy, soft tacos with, **244**
summer vegetable soup with miso and fresh herbs, **211**
sun-dried tomatoes:
 barley with mushrooms, pine nuts and, **226**
sunflower seed oil, 283
sunflower seeds with miso, toasted, **117**
supplements:
 for breakouts and rashes, 307
 for constipation, 318
 for depression, 326
 for dry skin, 335
 for hay fever, 344
 for hot flashes, 353
 for menstrual cramps, 369
 for sinus pressure, 395
 for sleep, 405
 for stress management, 409
 for tired eyes, 412
sushi rice, cucumbers with, **196**
Swedish bitters, 138–139
Swedish massage, 292, 340
sweet potato(es):
 bread with orange and rosemary, **48**
 chips, warm, **129**
 cutlets, **153**
 kibbe with sage and, **147**
 -tempeh stew, **103**
syrup, orange-scented strawberry, **31**

tacos with spicy summer vegetables, soft, **244**
tahini, 426
 -mustard sauce, soba with pickled red cabbage and, **111**
 sauce, lemony, grilled falafel with, **228**
tamari:
 almonds with fresh basil, **120**
 soy sauce, 38
 soy sauce, with Swedish bitters, 139
tangerine essence, 139, 283, 408
tarts, raspberry filling for, **262**
tea tree oil, 11, 343–344, 394, 396
tempeh, 426
 croutons, spinach salad with, **190**
 cutlets with ginger and lemongrass, baked, **252**
 with lemon, garlic and parsley, **250**
 lemony dipping sauce for, **159**